More Important Than Good Generals

CIVIL WAR SOLDIERS & STRATEGIES
Brian S. Wills, Series Editor

Richmond Must Fall: The Richmond-Petersburg Campaign, October 1864
HAMPTON NEWSOME

Work for Giants: The Campaign and Battle of Tupelo/Harrisburg, Mississippi, June–July 1864
THOMAS E. PARSON

"My Greatest Quarrel with Fortune": Major General Lew Wallace in the West, 1861–1862
CHARLES G. BEEMER

Phantoms of the South Fork: Captain McNeill and His Rangers
STEVE FRENCH

At the Forefront of Lee's Invasion: Retribution, Plunder, and Clashing Cultures on Richard S. Ewell's Road to Gettysburg
ROBERT J. WYNSTRA

Meade: The Price of Command, 1863–1865
JOHN G. SELBY

James Riley Weaver's Civil War: The Diary of a Union Cavalry Officer and Prisoner of War, 1863–1865
EDITED BY JOHN T. SCHLOTTERBECK, WESLEY W. WILSON, MIDORI KAWAUE, AND HAROLD A. KLINGENSMITH

Blue-Blooded Cavalryman: Captain William Brooke Rawle in the Army of the Potomac, May 1863–August 1865
EDITED BY J. GREGORY ACKEN

No Place for Glory: Major General Robert E. Rodes and the Confederate Defeat at Gettysburg
ROBERT J. WYNSTRA

From the Wilderness to Appomattox: The Fifteenth New York Heavy Artillery in the Civil War
EDWARD A. ALTEMOS

Adelbert Ames, the Civil War, and the Creation of Modern America
MICHAEL J. MEGELSH

The Forgotten Battles of the Chancellorsville Campaign: Fredericksburg, Salem Church, and Banks' Ford in Spring 1863
ERIK F. NELSON

More Important Than Good Generals: Junior Officers in the Army of the Tennessee
JONATHAN ENGEL

More Important Than Good Generals

Junior Officers in the Army of the Tennessee

JONATHAN ENGEL

THE KENT STATE UNIVERSITY PRESS
Kent, Ohio

© 2025 by The Kent State University Press, Kent, Ohio 44242
All rights reserved
ISBN 978-1-60635-489-6
Published in the United States of America

No part of this book may be used or reproduced, in any manner whatsoever, without written permission from the Publisher, except in the case of short quotations in critical reviews or articles.

Cataloging information for this title is available at the Library of Congress.

29 28 27 26 25   5 4 3 2 1

To the glory of my Lord Jesus Christ

Contents

Acknowledgments   ix

Introduction   1

1 Doing All Things Well   9

2 Wives and Children Dear   20

3 Prayer and Providence   41

4 A Great Big Heart   53

5 The Daily Grind   65

6 Red Tape and Triplicate Forms   91

7 More Important Than Good Generals   102

8 For the Cause   114

9 Suffering   129

10 A Dawning Day of Liberty   143

11 The Very Life of the Country   167

12 That Class of Generals Who Think That War Means Fighting   184

13 Nothing but Victory   206

Conclusion   222

Notes   225

Bibliography   279

Index   284

Acknowledgments

A veritable army of people has helped make this book possible. First and foremost, my mentor Dr. Steven Woodworth, in addition to his inspiring example as a scholar, gave me indispensable guidance throughout this project. His favorable response to a random idea helped me realize I had stumbled into a worthy research topic. He also helped me take my first steps into the world of archival research, and he provided advice and feedback down to the last nitty-gritty details of finishing this project. Many other professors at Florida College, Florida State University, and Texas Christian University also contributed to my academic growth. I would especially like to thank Dr. Todd Kerstetter, Dr. Kenneth Stevens, Dr. Gene Smith, Dr. Sally Hadden, and Dr. Brian Crispell.

The curators and librarians at each of the archives I visited provided patient assistance to a new researcher who did not know what he was doing. At the Abraham Lincoln Presidential Library, the Wisconsin Historical Society, the Indiana Historical Society, and the Ohio History Connection, the archivists enabled me to peruse countless boxes and folders whose contents now form this study's foundation.

This project faced some big nonacademic hurdles, and I'm grateful to the various medical professionals who have helped me along the way, particularly the doctors and nurses at Baylor Scott & White All Saints Medical Center who took care of me when I showed up at the emergency room with a headache that turned out to be a brain tumor. I'm also particularly grateful to Dr. Geoff Weckel, who helped me manage the emotional challenges throughout this rough season in my life.

Numerous other individuals contributed, directly and indirectly, to the completion of this book. Dana Summers and Stacy Theisen, in the TCU History Department, did much to make my time at TCU easier. Michael

Bridgford generously shared with me the letters of his ancestor, a private collection I would otherwise have missed. My friend Caroline Craig gave me immense assistance with proofreading and stylistic improvements to the manuscript. Dr. Jonathan Steplyk is dear friend and partner in crime who served as a valuable sounding board and pointed me to several useful sources. Numerous people at Centerville Road Church of Christ in Tallahassee and Northwest Church of Christ in Arlington, Texas, showed me much kindness. Many more family members, friends, peers, and acquaintances provided encouragement and support, or even just a laugh and a smile, as I ran the marathon that is writing a dissertation and then converting it to a book. I thank them all.

Finally, I want to express gratitude to my mom, Colleen Engel. She was my first teacher, and I have never stopped learning from her. There is no one I respect more highly. This book would not exist without her unflagging support. She listened patiently as I thought aloud about puzzling questions, proofread the entire document, and encouraged me to keep going so many times when I felt like giving up. I cannot thank her enough.

Introduction

"We have good corporals and sergeants, and some good lieutenants and captains, and those are far more important than good generals," Gen. William T. Sherman declared to Gen. Henry W. Halleck shortly after capturing Atlanta, Georgia, in September 1864.[1] Despite Sherman's lofty opinion, scholars have devoted little attention to the American Civil War's company and field grade officers—that is, to its lieutenants, captains, majors, lieutenant colonels, and colonels. Generals have headlined countless books and more continue to appear. The application of social history methods to the study of military topics lead to many insightful studies on the common soldier, but typically these works either fail to distinguish between officers and privates and treat them all as one category, or they explicitly excluded officers from consideration. The work and experience of Civil War armies' middle management has been largely ignored.

Officers held a substantially different array of duties than the soldiers they commanded and had a meaningfully different wartime experience than either the soldiers below them or the generals above them. It is not only Civil War officers who have been ignored but also the army Sherman commanded when he penned the preceding quote. Among the major armies of the Civil War, the Army of the Tennessee has received by far the least scholarly examination, despite the fact that it was arguably the single most victorious army of the war. This study of the Army of the Tennessee's junior officers thus lies at the confluence of two neglected subjects in Civil War research: company and regimental officers and the Army of the Tennessee.[2]

The scholarly study of the common soldier in the Civil War effectively began with Bell Wiley and *The Life of Johnny Reb: The Common Soldier of the Confederacy*. Wiley followed up with *The Life of Billy Yank: The Common Soldier of the Union*, the first substantive contribution to the study of the ordinary Union soldier. Wiley's study examined non-generals, soldier and officer alike, but included some comments specifically regarding officers. Among his comments, Wiley offered a theory of what motivated Union volunteers. He argued that Union soldiers lacked any motivation or cause for fighting comparable to the emotional intensity of Confederates' desire to defend their homes. Wiley claimed that many Union volunteers exhibited a limited sense of patriotism and that whatever patriotic motivations they maintained were "indistinguishably blended with practical urges."[3] For such men, moral or political ideals were "vaguely comprehended if at all."[4] Wiley conceded that a paltry few spoke of fighting for ideals like liberty, justice, or the rule of law but considered such men unrepresentative outliers. Wiley's works are foundational to the study of the Civil War soldier, but his depiction of nonideological Civil War participants has come under critique from later scholars.[5]

In *Embattled Courage: The Experience of Combat in the American Civil War*, Gerald F. Linderman asserted that Civil War soldiers may have begun the war idealistically, but "the experience of combat frustrated their attempts to fight the war as an expression of their values and generated in them a harsh disillusionment."[6] He defined this disillusionment as "the deeply depressive condition arising from the demolition of soldiers' conceptions of themselves and their performance in war" and conceded that this phenomenon "is not an easy state of mind to detect or to verify in large groups."[7] According to Linderman, soldiers felt victimized by the war and hopeless about the outcome, while the horrors of battle dramatically altered their values, coarsening men to the point that many lost their religious faith and developed a "gratuitous malevolence."[8] As part of this posited coarsening process, officers purportedly drifted apart from their men, grew less cordial in their interactions, and increasingly prized the approval of superiors over the respect of their subordinates. Linderman's study is undeniably influential and provocative, but many of his claims have faltered under later scrutiny. More recently, Andrew S. Bledsoe produced the first published, in-depth scholarly analysis of Civil War officers. Among his findings in *Citizen-Officers: The Union and Confederate Volunteer Junior Officer Corps in the American Civil War*, Bledsoe concurred with Linderman's theory of morally coarsened soldiers.[9]

A couple of studies have raised the role of competency examinations and screening boards in flushing inept officers from the army. In *Training, Tac-*

tics and Leadership in the Confederate Army of Tennessee: Seeds of Failure, Andrew Haughton emphasized flawed training and inadequate tactics as keys to the Confederate Army of Tennessee's defeats. Although the Confederacy implemented boards of examination to evaluate newly elected or promoted officers, the standards were vague, optional, and often ignored. Haughton believed that the Union put into place a much more effective system of officer examinations. James I. Robertson Jr., in *Soldiers Blue and Gray,* also emphasized the role of screening boards on both sides and claimed that many unqualified officers resigned rather than face examination. Robertson also contended that Civil War soldiers largely did not understand the cause of the war, a finding similar to that of his mentor Bell Wiley.[10]

Other studies have disputed both Wiley's portrayal of Civil War soldiers as nonideological and Linderman's disillusionment narrative. In *For Cause and Comrades: Why Men Fought in the Civil War,* James McPherson argued that soldiers on both sides fought primarily because of their ideals and that these ideals remained operative all the way to the end of the war. *The Union Soldier in Battle: Enduring the Ordeal of Combat* by Earl J. Hess likewise argued that Union soldiers retained their ideals throughout the war's trials rather than becoming coarsened or disillusioned. Hess contended that most Union soldiers retained their ideological views or moral values, whether political or religious, throughout the war. Like McPherson, Hess offered a substantive challenge to earlier depictions of Civil War soldiers as either nonideological or prone to giving up their prewar beliefs. Gary W. Gallagher has also argued that Union soldiers had thoroughly ideological motivations for serving. In *The Union War,* Gallagher explored in depth what the Union meant to Northerners: the embodiment of political freedom, economic opportunity, and democratic hope for the world. When aristocratic slaveholders threatened to destroy this benevolent institution, Northerners rose up to preserve it, and they continued fighting for those values throughout the war.[11]

As noted above, the Army of the Tennessee has received surprisingly little academic attention, being the subject of only one scholarly monograph: *Nothing but Victory: The Army of the Tennessee, 1861–1865,* by Steven E. Woodworth. Woodworth's most distinctive contention about the army is the role Ulysses S. Grant played in shaping its character. Woodworth compared the process to the way Gen. George B. McClellan came to define the Army of the Potomac (the Union's primary eastern-theater army), arguing that Grant built his army in his image, imparting to its men his own "matter-of-fact steadiness and his hard-driving aggressiveness."[12] By the time Grant left the army for higher command, his men had internalized a sense of calm confidence from their commander's example and leadership, and they retained this spirit long after Grant's departure. The Army of the Tennessee's soldiers began the war with an unproven sense of confidence, and Grant shepherded that confidence into a defining characteristic of the army.[13]

Within the foregoing studies, the leading point of contention centers on ideology. Wiley argued that Union soldiers were largely nonideological; Robertson later echoed this perception. In contrast, Linderman presented soldiers as very much guided by a set of beliefs and values and argued that the war caused them to reject or substantially alter those ideas. Bledsoe has advocated a similar, although narrower and more nuanced, thesis about wartime changes to officers' ideology, confining his argument to the topic of leadership and the American citizen-soldier tradition. Scholars such as McPherson, Hess, and Gallagher have also emphasized that Union combatants were highly ideological. However, instead of finding trauma-driven changes in belief caused by the war, they highlighted continuity and argued that Union soldiers' values endured the stresses of war. In the context of this historiographic conversation, this study aligns more closely with the conclusions put forward by such scholars as McPherson, Hess, and Gallagher.

More Important Than Good Generals concludes that the Army of the Tennessee's company and field grade officers endured the war's trials with their moral and political worldview intact. The war did not disillusion them because little of the perspective on life they brought into the army was illusory. It is true that they were somewhat naive about warfare and that their expectations regarding the war's duration were greatly mistaken. However, in numerous key areas, such as belief in the Union's value, trust in divine providence, commitment to egalitarianism between officers and soldiers, and confidence in their ability to win, officers' attitudes proved sufficiently well formed and substantive to resist the stresses the war imposed. In only one area did officers reveal signs of major change in their outlook—namely, the matter of slavery and race. Officers who started off heavily racist and uninterested in slavery became staunch advocates of emancipation. However, they changed their stance on slavery precisely because of their unchanging commitment to values such as compassion or their devotion to the Union cause, such that even their one major point of change reflects consistency in their underlying political and moral values. The Army of the Tennessee's officers maintained the attitudes and ideals with which they began their service, even while enduring all manner of difficulties.

This study examines the relationships and values that helped define the Army of the Tennessee's junior officers, considers the work they did as officers, and explores their attitudes on a number of major issues connected to the war. Marriage and family were a defining part of officers' identities, and how their commitment to their families remained strong throughout the war. Likewise, religion—Christianity specifically—remained a fundamental part of officers' lives for the duration of the war. Officers cared for their men throughout the war, both in the sense of meeting their needs and in the sense of feeling concern for them. Officers' routine activities included drill, guard duty, discipline, and bookkeeping, but they performed numerous other tasks as well. Ultimately, officers were leaders, and their comments indicate that their views on good leadership remained largely unchanged. Through all these challenges, officers displayed resistance to letting the war change their way of life.

Establishing who the Army of the Tennessee's junior officers were and what they did provides the context for the latter part of this study, which explores what officers thought about major issues pertaining to the war. They remained firmly committed to the Union cause, regarding themselves as defending a genuinely good government against a wicked rebellion, and they proved the resilience of their commitment to this cause by risking the perils of capture, illness, wounds, and death. Although a few men started out the war opposed to slavery, many more showed clear signs of changing their stance to become staunch advocates of emancipation. However, officers' comments on slavery, emancipation, and the idea of Black US soldiers reveal continuity amid change: the two driving forces behind officers' evolving attitudes on slavery were their devotion to the Union and their compassion for other human beings. Officers remained politically engaged all through the war, and the political concerns on which they focused often reflected their dedication to the Union. Officers consistently preferred aggressive, tenacious generals to ones they judged overcautious and too timid to get anything done. This study concludes by surveying officers' enduring sense of self-confidence, which, though it faltered briefly in the winter of 1862–63, never turned to despair and disillusionment but rather surged back stronger than ever and grew more certain as the war continued. Through countless hardships, instead of becoming coarsened by the war, the Army of the Tennessee's company and regimental officers held firm to their morals, ideals, and attitudes.

After identifying junior and mid-level officers as an under-studied subject with rich potential, I focused this study on the officers of just one army in order to keep the scope of this project small enough that it could actually be finished. Early in the research process, two important questions appeared. It was necessary to delineate, for the purpose of this study, what the "Army of the Tennessee" was, and what an "officer" was. For the first point, there is no official list to which one can go to determine which regiments count as part of this particular army. Identifying which men to consider as officers for the purposes of this study raised similarly thorny issues.

To categorize units as part of the Army of the Tennessee, I consulted the Union order of battle for several major campaigns: Shiloh, Vicksburg, Chattanooga, Atlanta, and Savannah. From these, one could piece together a list of units associated with the Army of the Tennessee. But this was only a starting point. Not every regiment that happened to get included in an order of battle actually spent any appreciable time with the Army of the Tennessee or shared in its collective experience to a meaningful degree. For example, a number of units came under U. S. Grant's command solely during the siege of Vicksburg (a period of about six weeks) and never otherwise operated with the army. However, once in a while one comes across a case where a unit's record unquestionably showed that it served with the Army of the Tennessee, yet for whatever reason it did not appear on any of the extant orders of battle. Ultimately, the orders of battle provided a useful foundation, but there was no clean, easy rule for categorizing units as part of the Army of the Tennessee, and this study does not claim to offer an authoritative list. This issue is the chief reason this book makes no attempt to collect a scientific sample of officers that would represent states proportionally. Doing so would have required establishing definitively which regiments should be considered as members of the Army of the Tennessee, so that one could then count how many there were from each state.

Another issue to consider was when and for how long a regiment served with the Army of the Tennessee. Some fought under Grant at Fort Donelson and Shiloh but transferred away afterward, others missed the early campaigns but joined up during the struggle for Vicksburg and stayed with the army for the rest of the war, and so on. This study generally opted to pass over source material that pertained to an officer after his regiment transferred away from the Army of the Tennessee. At that point, the unit was no longer sharing in the common experiences that made the Army of the Tennessee a distinct entity about which one could make meaningful generalizations. For source material produced before an officer joined the Army of the Tennessee, it is necessary to distinguish between attitudes and experiences. If, for example, a man outspokenly condemned slavery while serving in a three-month regiment in spring 1861, it is probable that he retained those beliefs when he enlisted in a three-year regiment later that fall and joined the Army of the Tennessee. Consequently, this study regarded expressions of ideology and values as relevant even when penned before a man was serving in the Army of the Tennessee or before he became an officer. However, this work generally left out military anecdotes that predated a regiment's association with the Army of the Tennessee. Such stories have value, but they do not shed light on the characteristic or common experiences men of this particular army would have shared.

That leaves the question of who counted as an officer. Again, there was no simple answer to how long a man should serve as an officer before one regards his account as relevant. For example, in the summer of 1865, numerous men received what were essentially honorary promotions, but the fact that a man held a commission for a couple months after the war ended does not actually contribute to an understanding of officers' wartime experiences. This study generally sought to find men who served at least one full campaign as a company or regimental officer, but of course even defining *when* a man became an officer could be hard to nail down. The date a man's commission became effective, the occasion he received the commission, the time he mustered in at the rank on the commission, and the point at which he actually started serving in the role of an officer were not always congruent nor even possible to identify from the available sources. This study also limited itself to what are sometimes called line officers, those who actively commanded companies and regiments. Staff officers such as quartermasters, chaplains, and surgeons performed distinctly different duties from their counterparts and warrant separate study. However, it is worth noting that the staff officer versus line officer distinction is not absolute. One man might begin his service as regimental adjutant and go on to become colonel. Another might start as a lieutenant, rise to regimental quartermaster, then return to his company to serve as its captain. In the end, it was necessary to judge men and their stories on a case-by-case basis to determine their relevance to a study of the Army of the Tennessee's company and field grade officers. It simply is not possible to offer the scientific precision of a neat and tidy rule for these issues; the best one can do is point out some of the important questions and suggest the factors worth taking into account.

On a few occasions, this study cites fractions or percentages of officers who did or experienced such and such. The research process for this book involved creating a record every time primary sources mentioned the name of an officer. In the end, the record file contained 518 names. Of those, it was possible to piece together semi-complete service records for 481 of them. For each of those 481, it proved feasible to determine when a man joined the army, at what rank, in what units he served, what promotions he received and approximately when he attained them, and when and under what circumstances he left the army. When this study estimates what share of officers enlisted in 1862, or how many died during their service, it is based on this sample of 481. For example, 368 of them (about 77 percent) began their service as officers, while 113 (approximately 23 percent) served some time as enlisted men before receiving a commission. These are the men who served as the middle management of the American Civil War's most successful army.

CHAPTER 1

Doing All Things Well

The duties of Civil War–era army officers were expansive, encompassing the roles of caretaker, battlefield leader, bureaucrat, and more. In addition to the routine leadership functions officers performed and the administrative duties that dogged them throughout the war, they had a wide variety of other responsibilities that they discharged with varying levels of frequency and competence. Officers served as managers or overseers for all manner of tasks the army needed done, filled in for superiors when their commander was absent or incapacitated, recruited new volunteers for their regiments, and persuaded current soldiers to reenlist. Amid all these other duties that filled the days of their military service, they also led their men in combat.

The regimental historians of the Fifty-Fifth Illinois attempted to summarize the scope of military duties: "For war purposes, the volunteer became on the march a pack-mule, a fighting machine, and at intervals an intelligent thinker and talker upon the strategy of campaigns, prospects of foreign intervention, and the policy of the government. When occasion demanded he built bridges, repaired railroads, ran engines or steamboats, printed newspapers, cut cordwood, killed men, or stole chickens; and did all these things well."[1] These authors (two of whom were themselves officers) were speaking of volunteer Union soldiers generally, but their descriptions apply to the officers who shared in and presided over all these activities.

Officers functioned as managers for all sorts of work outside of what one might think of as a soldier's usual duties. When the Union army foraged from southern fields, it was officers who led their men in shucking corn, threshing grain, and operating gristmills. One ran a printing press, another supervised a steam-powered cotton gin, and yet another captained a ferryboat. Officers oversaw many construction projects, including not just field

9

fortifications but the building or repairing of roads and bridges. Once in a while, officers seem to have been involved with scouting or spying. A soldier of the Twelfth Wisconsin told of how Col. James K. Proudfit sent an alleged southern civilian out through their lines. Upon the man's return, soldiers of the regiment realized this "civilian" was a Union spy. Activities like these were not daily routines that all officers performed, but they are illustrative of the many different tasks that officers intermittently supervised.[2]

One essential function officers performed was filling in for their superiors. Someone always had to be in charge of the company, the regiment, or the brigade. When a captain, colonel, or even brigadier general was sick, wounded, captured, killed, arrested, detailed to special duty, away on leave, or had resigned from the service, command responsibility devolved onto a junior officer. Depending on the nature of the superior officer's incapacity or unavailability, a junior officer might fill in for a few days, or the absent superior might never return or be officially replaced and the subordinate would effectively take over his role (albeit without any promotion commensurate to the duty). Moreover, this phenomenon had a cascading effect. Captain Alphonso Barto found himself serving as acting major of the Fifty-Second Illinois late in April 1862, because the major had taken command of the regiment, because the colonel was busy substituting for a brigadier general as brigade commander, and the lieutenant colonel was absent sick. Filling in for a superior inevitably kept officers busy and forced them to neglect regular duties—much to their frustration. This system of junior officers filling in for superiors could even be exploited at times, with a more senior officer claiming to be indisposed in order to foist some particularly annoying task onto a hapless subordinate. Normally officers from within a unit stepped up to fill gaps, but on rare occasions instead an officer from some other unit was brought in to command temporarily.[3]

At two major points in the war, officers served as recruiters, and they conducted sporadic additional recruiting activity throughout their service. First, many of the men who became officers canvassed their hometowns and the surrounding municipalities or counties to recruit their companies or regiments at the start of their service. If they could not quite get their units to full strength before the regiment was sworn into service, officers did a little more recruiting after mustering into the army. After the initial major recruiting efforts, a small number of officers were temporarily detailed for additional recruiting duties at other times during the war, trying to replace losses their regiment had suffered. Officers particularly appreciated this assignment if it meant spending a few weeks near their families. Recruiting could involve opening an office, running newspaper ads, and holding public rallies featuring patriotic exhortations from officers and other public figures. The second major point at which officers functioned like recruiters came in late fall 1863 and early spring 1864, when many helped encourage their men to reenlist as veterans to see the war to its conclusion.[4]

Recruiting, and the managing of those new recruits, posed a variety of special challenges. Oscar Lawrence Jackson secured a permit to raise a company and on his twenty-first birthday printed some handbills and started recruiting. After six weeks, he had only about forty men of the hundred needed for a company. He scrounged up a few more in the following weeks but was far short of his quota and nearly gave up the project before a friend convinced him to keep trying. Jackson found that by November 1861 "the first excitement of enlisting" had faded, saying, "It was after long, hard work, and overcoming many discouragements, as well as receiving much friendly help, that I succeeded in completing my company."[5]

Edward Gee Miller, a student at the University of Wisconsin, had recruiting troubles of a different sort. Miller went to the state government in May 1862 and obtained an appointment for himself and two fellow students to raise a company for which they would become the officers. Unfortunately, one of his comrades took the recruits he collected and turned them over to another company, so Miller and his other friend "were left in the lurch," without enough men.[6] Fortunately, another man jumped in to help with the recruiting, receiving a second lieutenancy for his trouble.

By April 1864, Jake Ritner had yet another kind of recruiting problem. Shepherding "a detachment of 55 recruits, 10 stragglers, and one deserter, belonging to 12 different regiments" from Iowa to the front sorely tested his patience.[7] "I suppose the worst misfortune that could possibly befall an *officer* is to be placed in charge of a lot of raw recruits on the way south. They have no sense and can't learn any—and think the officer can do anything," he grumbled from a Nashville hotel room.[8] On the whole, recruiting new soldiers was not a large part of officers' work, but it was a significant task in which many participated, especially the initial crop of officers at the start of the war.[9]

"It is, I think, the grandest thing of the war. These old soldiers so enthusiastically and unanimously 'going-inimously,'" wrote Charles Wills in January 1864 regarding the recent reenlistment of several regiments.[10] By late 1863, the government and army began thinking about how to retain the veteran soldiers who had joined in 1861 when their three-year enlistments ran out in 1864. There was a major effort to convince soldiers to commit to serve for the rest of war, with promises of special veteran status and a month of furlough if three-fourths of a regiment reenlisted. Officers helped persuade their men to keep fighting, and they kept busy filling out reenlistment documents. Henry Ankeny was very proud of his men in the Fourth Iowa who reenlisted and wrote home to ensure they received a properly grand welcome during their furlough. Their families and friends "should be very proud of them and the people cannot do too much for them while at home . . . for *they are every one of them heroes, all*."[11] The furlough itself became another opportunity for recruiting, as officers tried to replenish their depleted ranks before their regiments returned to the front. After the entire reenlistment-and-furlough process was over, Capt. Oscar Lawrence Jackson noted that the furlough had been pleasant, "but the unusual labor which I had to do as an officer made me conclude that it was like the pleasure of opium smoking. I would not want to repeat the dose of having a veteran furlough."[12] By encouraging and facilitating veteran reenlistment, junior officers played a key role in keeping the army's ranks full.[13]

Edward Jesup Wood, commanding the Forty-Eighth Indiana, noted in December 1863 that many in his regiment were thinking about reenlisting, motivated by the promise of the thirty-day furlough. "If I can be assured that they can have it soon, I shall feel like advising them to it," Wood mused.[14] Wood mentioned that Gov. Oliver Morton of Indiana had been writing to him, encouraging him to get the Forty-Eighth to reenlist so the men could be counted toward Indiana's draft quota. Once the men made their decision, actually reenlisting the veterans proved a tremendous bureaucratic hassle, involving "duplicate enlistment papers & a discharge for each man, 3 muster-out rolls, 3 muster & pay-rolls, 5 muster-in rolls for each Company . . . 8 consolidated receipt rolls—only 19 rolls to the company & 3 papers to each man."[15] At least in the government's eyes, all this was necessary for soldiers to reenlist, and officers like Lieutenant Colonel Wood made it happen.[16]

Army life encompassed a far richer and more complex array of experiences than just an endless string of battles, but combat was fundamental to the work of Civil War officers. The Army of the Tennessee's officers benefited from serving in the war's most victorious army, but that did not mean combat was easy for them. On the battlefield, officers' role mainly involved directing their men from place to place and keeping them together, not unlike a shepherd herding sheep, and they seemed to have only rarely taken direct part in the shooting and killing. There are relatively few accounts of officers taking up arms or killing rebels, and most of the examples this study did find took place during the unusually chaotic Battle of Shiloh. After some initial enthusiasm to see what battle was like, officers' feelings toward combat settled into a mixture of anxiety, acceptance of it as a necessary evil, and confidence that their side would win. Writing in fall 1863, Jake Ritner described prebattle tension: "Indeed it is enough to make anyone feel sober to see an army prepare for battle. Every man is brought into the ranks and ordered to load his gun. The doctors get out their knives and saws and bandages, and you see a squad of men with a white rag tied to their arm in the rear of each regiment carrying stretchers."[17] Of course, fighting did not always come with advance warning that allowed such preparations. Officers made many efforts to describe combat itself, though they commonly indicated that they lacked the words or ability to capture what it was like to be on a battlefield. It was loud and chaotic, unpleasant and overwhelming, but never something of which to be ashamed. Notwithstanding officers' protests to the contrary, their descriptions of combat enable us to form some sense of what it was like.[18]

"If we see a battle you will never be ashamed of the way I behave in it—I intend to fight and to kill at least one secesh, God being my helper," Luther Cowan boasted mere hours before embarking on the Army of the Tennessee's first campaign.[19] Cowan's bloodthirsty enthusiasm subsequently waned, as did the ardor for combat of many other new soldiers, replaced by a mix of apprehension plus willingness to fight because it was necessary. A week and half before the Battle of Shiloh, James Balfour wrote from Pittsburg Landing to discuss the prospects of battle with his wife Louisa. He could fight if needed, but "the terrible sight of the wounded" at Fort Donelson was "too disagreeable to make a repetition very acceptable. I like the honors of war but I hate to see so much human suffering without being able to do anything for the poor men."[20] DeWitt Clinton Loudon was pleasantly surprised to realize during the May 1862 Corinth Campaign that he did not feel "half as nervous & timid as I used to when I had to speak at a college exhibition" and found he was able to relax even with the enemy relatively near.[21] Later in the campaign, he humorously told his wife Hannah that if he were to be shot, he would want it to be in a major battle and "not a trifling skirmish."[22] Loudon realized the rebels shared his aversion to dying, noting, "After all their bragging they don't like to see the point of a bayonet coming at them any better than other people."[23]

Around the same time, Captain Cowan expressed similar thoughts on adjusting to danger: "By degrees we become careless of danger, and look upon it as sport, such acts at home would look like perfect madness."[24] He quickly added that he was not eager for danger or getting himself killed, just that he could face it when called upon. Cowan also attempted to portray for his daughter Molly how officers felt on the verge of battle: "You could see, in the countenances of the officers on whom rest the responsibilities of the plans of the battle, all the anxiety and care that it is possible to conceive of. While they sit as firm as iron on their impatient horses watching every movement of the enemy, encouraging and advising the subordinate officers on whom lies the more inordinate responsibility of executing the orders."[25] John Quincy Adams Campbell likewise wrote of being "not *anxious*, but *ready* for a fight."[26] Whatever eagerness for combat officers may have possessed at the start of the war, the prevailing feeling became one of anxiety tempered by acceptance of the need to fight.[27]

Lieutenant Campbell expounded on the topic of prebattle anxiety in a revealing November 1863 letter to his hometown newspaper. He was not impatient to fight, he said, but when a battle loomed there was such an intense feeling of suspense that he desperately wished to get it over with. He felt determination to perform his duty mixed with the awareness that many (including, perhaps, himself) would soon be dead. Campbell saw gamblers throw away their cards, profane men cease their cursing, jokesters lose their sense of humor, "and they all march together in silence to the field, thinking, fearing, and hoping but remembering it is necessary and right, they should thus take their lives in their hands and stand in the breach of death."[28] Addressing his hometown audience, he continued, "You may think you can imagine the feelings of a soldier on the eve of a conflict, but no, you cannot. Not even the soldier himself can, 24 hours after the battle is over."[29] In another letter, Campbell described his prebattle feelings as "a fear of consequences and an anxiety as to results," though not one that interfered at all with his focus on performing his duties.[30] After seeing several of his men killed or wounded right in front of him, Campbell marveled that in the heat of battle, "I felt no emotion—not the least at these sights and stood over these dead men as if life had never existed in their bodies, instead of having been my daily companions."[31] Only after the battle did normal emotions return and he began to mourn the dead.

During battle, officers seem to have done very little shooting or fighting themselves, likely because trying to manage dozens or hundreds of soldiers amid the battlefield's chaos required their full attention. Sometimes orders from above never arrived. Sometimes they did arrive but were misinterpreted. And thanks to the constantly changing conditions, many orders were no longer applicable by the time they traveled from generals to junior officers. Indeed, in some ways junior officers could be said to face greater difficulties than the generals did. Generals mostly came to the front as spectators, to get a better view of events, not to personally lead soldiers. Company and regimental officers actually had to lead on the front lines. After the failed 22 May 1863 assault on Vicksburg, Col. Manning F. Force pondered the nature of combat leadership:

> What a transformation it was for these men, full of individuality and self-reliance, accustomed always to act upon their own will, to so completely subordinate their wills to the wills of other men, many of them their neighbors and friends at home. But their practical sense had told them that an army differs from a mob only in discipline, and discipline was necessary for their self-preservation. They had also soon perceived that military obedience is a duty enjoined by law; and, besides, their enthusiasm and fire came from the feeling that, like the crusaders of old, they were engaged in a sacred cause.[32]

Officers cheered on their men and praised courageous behavior, while also striving to clamp down on cowardice and skulking. Some officers reported forgetting the danger around them as they focused on getting their men to do their duty. During the Atlanta Campaign, a soldier in Capt. Charles Dana Miller's company boasted that Miller could not make him fight. Prior to a charge in one battle, Miller approached the man and informed him "that if he stepped back one foot I would empty my revolver into his head. I also charged the sergeant to watch him and if he fell back to promptly shoot him on the spot."[33] The man stayed with the company during the charge, but that night he went skulking back to the rear, forcing Miller to have him dragged back.[34]

Unrelenting force was one way to manage skulkers, but Capt. Albert Arndt illustrated another approach when recalling a fight during the Savannah Campaign. Arndt's battery of the First Michigan Light Artillery came under heavy enemy fire, and one of his artillerymen grew so anxious and frenzied that he became a hindrance to aiming the gun. Captain Arndt told the man to pull himself together or else Arndt would have him tied to a nearby tree that had been riven by enemy shells. The soldier calmed down and made it through the rest of the fight. Afterward, the soldier began to apologize for his conduct, to which Arndt answered that no apology was necessary: "I had always known him to be a brave and faithful soldier, and that I felt sorry for him at the time, and would have much preferred sending him to the rear, than to talk to him the way I did, but that he could easily see it was the only thing that I could do, under the circumstances, for had I sent him to the rear, every one of my men might have left their post, as all were exposed as much as he was, and feared death as much as he did."[35] Arndt's story reflects an understanding that loss of nerve was not simply a character defect to be solved by punishing cowards, but it was a problem that even reliable soldiers could face, one which required active management by officers.

A battlefield could be a horrific place, officers testified, both during the fight and afterward. Luther Cowan wrote just after the Battle of Fort Donelson, attempting to capture his first combat experience. "I have seen one of those scenes which, long ago in my boyish imaginations, I so much wished to see—a battle. It is an awful thing. I cannot describe it," he wrote.[36] He offered a list of adjectives—"awful, horrid, unnatural and fiendish"—as he tried to capture the aftermath of the battleground.[37] On 28 December 1862, at Chickasaw Bayou, Warren Gray witnessed a cannonball kill a nearby soldier: "He was sitting by a log smoking when the ball passing downward struck him on top of the head scattering his brains all around. It was an awful sight but such as I suppose a soldier must often see."[38] Such scenes surrounded officers as they endeavored to carry out their duties amid combat and following it.

Second Lieutenant Friedrich Martens made a rare admission of uncouth behavior during battle. He wrote to his family in Germany, "You people over there in civilized Europe can't possibly have any idea of the dreadful atrocities this war has produced."[39] He went on to tell how a supply train and its escorts were wiped out by the rebels. Martens's Seventeenth Missouri arrived too late to stop the massacre: "We saw our comrades lying there *slaughtered,* and shouting out *'to hell with them rascals'* we closed in on them. Our colonel ordered some good maneuvers, and this time the enemy was surrounded, and so well that none of them could escape. But I don't want to write more about it, you don't know how sweet revenge can be, and so you wouldn't understand how I can justify retaliation that was so appalling."[40] Referencing the poem "Das Lied von der Glocke" by Friedrich

Schiller, Martens declared, "The most fearsome of the fearsome, that is man! and this is very true. If you provoke a man to the limit, he becomes a tiger."[41] This instance of a man suggesting that the folks back home might find his conduct immoral was almost unparalleled among the Army of the Tennessee's officers, suggesting it was very much a minority sentiment.

Much of the fighting in the Civil War took place not in famous battles where entire armies clashed but in relatively inconsequential skirmishes involving limited numbers on both sides. Jake Ritner described skirmishing through northern Alabama as the army moved toward Chattanooga in late October 1863. They started marching at about 3 A.M. on 26 October and by dawn had encountered rebel pickets and begun driving them back. Soon artillery joined in the fight. The shooting lasted a few hours, until the US troops outflanked the rebels and they fell back. When the rebels made another stand, the federal troops charged and drove them off again. After breaking for the night, the skirmishing resumed on the second day, driving the rebels still farther. On the third day, Ritner's regiment marched eighteen miles back to the camp it started from on 26 October, feeling "that we had driven them away so far that they would not annoy us soon again, and thought we could get one night's good sleep without being called up at midnight to drive them away."[42] In this Ritner was disappointed: "But don't you think the nasty devils attacked us the next morning before we had our breakfast? Yes, they did—they followed us right back."[43] When the Twenty-Fifth Iowa set out that morning after breakfast, they found the rebels on the same ground they fought over the first day. The enemy started advancing but halted just out of reach of the US artillery, "and then both sides maneuvered around all day in sight of each other, without coming into a fight."[44] Since the rebel forces were mounted, the Iowans knew there was little point in chasing after them. "We tried all day to get them into a *trap*, but they wouldn't 'bite,'" Ritner concluded.[45] The war was peppered with days and even weeks like these, occupied with persistent, low-intensity fighting that accomplished relatively little.[46]

Benjamin Grierson described a somewhat different kind of fighting, participating as he did in cavalry skirmishes. He proudly reported that in one fight, "Both officers & men behaved with the utmost Coolness & bravery and gallantly charged upon what they deemed a larger force."[47] At one point, a rebel aimed his carbine directly at Grierson, "but I was charging at full speed at the time with my revolver Cocked and in the position of raise pistol I was to quick for him for I fired upon him twice and he droped his Carbine at his side and whirled his horse and '*skedaddled*.'"[48] Another fight began when some rebel cavalry struck while Grierson and about forty of his men were eating breakfast. At first the Union cavalrymen fell back about twenty or thirty feet, but with the help of his subordinate officers Grierson got them to make a stand, and after about twenty minutes the rebels began to withdraw. Grierson led some of his men in mounting up and charging, driving the enemy back half a mile to where the rebels had a reserve force. He summoned reinforcements, but before they arrived, he had to pull back to avoid being surrounded by the Confederates. Seeing that the rebels seemed to be in a state of confusion, though, he called his men to halt the retreat and again advanced on the rebels. Around this time, he began to hear the firing of his summoned reinforcements, and Grierson immediately ordered a charge, achieving "a complete rout of the enemy."[49]

Oscar Jackson participated in an expedition that set out from Athens, Alabama, to cross the Tennessee River and capture Decatur, to the south. That night was misty and drizzly. Almost every boat (one to a company) leaked, complicating the crossing, which moved out about 1 A.M. on 8 March 1864. A man at the stern of each boat held a rope connected to the bow of the following boat, keeping the flotilla together and in line. They descended from Limestone Creek down into the Tennessee River, using muffled oars to row when necessary but mostly relying on the current to carry them forward. The night remained "still as the grave" until the flotilla entered the river, where they disturbed a huge flock of wild ducks, some of which cacophonously took flight, while others swam ahead of or alongside the boats, quacking loudly in protest.[50] A rebel picket post, illuminated by a campfire, stood on the south shore opposite the mouth of the creek, and Jackson feared the guards would be alerted by the ducks' pandemonium. The pickets, however, did not investigate the cause of the raucous waterfowl. The long line of boats hugged the right (north) bank, riding the current for six or seven miles, striving to remain as quiet as possible. As dawn and their destination neared, the boats formed up to land each regiment and its respective companies in proper battle order and crossed over to the south shore. This required rowing, and rowing meant noise. As they closed on the south shore of the river, there were still no signs of the enemy. Less than a hundred yards from land, a Confederate sentinel hailed them, and receiving no answer, he fired. The time for stealth ended and the boats rowed hastily for shore. Rebel pickets got off a few more shots, but the guards were too few in number to make a difference. The expedition did not land exactly where intended, but in short order the regiments had debarked and formed up. The rebel guards gave way with little resistance. By now it was full daylight, but heavy fog still limited visibility. The rebels tried to escape in the mists, and the Union forces struggled to avoid firing on each other. The rebels got away because a second Union force that was to cross below Decatur and cut off the rebels' escape did not move quickly enough. The failure to capture the enemy garrison was disappointing, but the Union expedition did capture Decatur with minimal losses.[51]

The role of an officer embraced multifarious activities carried out on an irregular basis. They fought in countless small engagements where neither side accomplished any grand strategic aims or suffered substantial loss. Large-scale battles pitting field army against field army had both strategic and personal significance to officers, but minor skirmishes are more representative of their typical combat experience. Officers also supervised construction work and other odd jobs that soldiers performed. They filled in for superiors when those superiors were absent or incapacitated. Many early officers played leading roles in recruiting their companies or regiments. Some returned home at various times to glean a few more recruits. In 1863 and 1864, officers played a significant role in facilitating the reenlistment of veteran soldiers whose three-year terms would soon expire. Despite intermittent battles livening things up, leadership for junior officers was typically more mundane than exciting.

CHAPTER 2

Wives and Children Dear

No doubt you are now at home. What a world of thought, and meaning there is in that good old-fashioned word, and Tina, how often I think of it, for there dwells all that is most dear to me on this green earth. . . . True our little Jessie is gone, was taken from us when least expected, but she is with the Angels in heaven where we must strive to join her. Then through the goodness of God, we have another to fill her place in our love and affections—a guide for our future happiness and contentment. Although, Tina, our happiness has been equal to most others during our wedded existence, the experience of the last twenty months of ours will draw us still closer together in our daily walk, love and reverence. We have additional motives to live a life on earth that in the end will lead us to join our own dear children in heaven. Oh, my dear wife, you will never know how much I love you, and you only.[1]

Henry Giesey Ankeny wrote this to his wife Tina (her full name was actually Horatia Fostina, but she understandably went by Tina) in March 1863, and while the sentiments are deeply personal, they capture the significance of "home" not just for Captain Ankeny but for many who served as army officers. Much of what we know about the Civil War comes from the countless letters that soldiers wrote to parents, siblings, wives, and children. Thus, our very knowledge of the war is in some measure a testimony to the central place of family for Civil War soldiers.

More than anything else, they expressed love and concern for their wives and children. Concerns ranged from their loved ones' health to their children's educational progress and business and financial issues. They wrote to keep their families from worrying about them and to express confidence in their wives' judgment and abilities. Their letters were filled with wishes that they could visit their families or laments after returning from furloughs over how much they already missed their loved ones. If a regiment stayed in a safe place long enough, officers occasionally brought their wives to visit them. They dispensed advice and shared news of relatives and friends in the army with the folks back home. They dreamed of their families. Not all officers were married, of course, but even the unmarried had families, and they carried on lively correspondence with parents and siblings. They wrote of the desire to see them again, inquired about their health and material well-being, and remembered their mothers' birthdays. The exact dynamics of each family or relationship were unique, but the crucial importance of family was universal. A defining element of the Army of the Tennessee's officers' wartime experience is their relationships to their families.[2]

Officers retained a strong sense of connection to home and family throughout the war. They never tired of hearing news from home, always looked forward to the next chance to visit home, and eagerly awaited the end of the war because then they could go home. Oscar L. Jackson observed that desire for home was so strong it could manifest even in attachment to campsites. When Jackson's Sixty-Third Illinois returned to a campsite it had previously occupied, he noted, "So strongly is the love of home implanted in the breast of man that veterans of three years campaigning talk of returning to a temporary camp where they rested but a few hours, and only expect to remain a few hours again, like going home. I felt the sensation very plainly myself."[3] As the regiment marched north after the war ended, he wrote, "Homeward bound. Can it be true? All hands in great glee and fine spirits. We have such feelings as men do not often have more than once in a life time; such a feeling of relief that the war is over and peaceful home is near."[4] Henry F. Hole, answering a letter from his sister Minerva, mused, "How dear that one word 'Home.' I long to be beneath the sheltering care of my Paternal roof again; to be admonished by Ma for my many shortcomings—and perhaps for numerous *out* goings."[5] Like many officers, Hole often dwelled on happy memories of home and these only strengthened his wish to get back: "To be reunited with those I love is the dearest wish of my life."[6] Benjamin H. Grierson believed that "the great motive power of that great machine of destruction of the army was really generated at home."[7] Grierson seized every possible opportunity to spend time with his family during his military service, including obtaining leave to go visit them and also bringing them to see him when his cavalry regiment looked to be staying in one place for a while and he had money available for their fare.[8]

"I wish this unholy rebellion was at a close so that we could be together once more," Col. John Nelson Cromwell declared when reporting intense homesickness to his wife Sallie.[9] Unsurprisingly, married officers greatly missed their wives. Most officers' correspondence—with all its expressions of love, loneliness, and wishes to be home—was to their wives. As with thoughts of home more generally, their wives in particular were sources of strength as officers endured the challenges of war. The innumerable professions of love reveal that the coarseness of army life did not diminish their ability to show tenderness and affection. Officers' comments to their wives shared broad themes, but they also showed variations unique to each relationship or the circumstances that officer faced. Statements looking forward to the end of the war as a time of family reunion were common, as were declarations of unfailing loyalty. Officers supplied updates on their prospects of getting a leave of absence any time one seemed possible. Worry was another common topic; officers recognized the strain their absence placed on their families and did their best to acknowledge their wives' hardships and to provide encouragement. When Zachariah Dean's wife Emily apologized for worrying him by talking about some troubles she had recently faced, Dean assured her that he wanted to hear all about her struggles: "Of course it troubles me, but how can I help it when I see the one I love above all others in trouble, and the character of the wife of my house assailed. I must sheare her troubles. Why Em, if I had no love for you I would have no trouble about you. I married you to share your joy and sorrows and when I see you unhappy I am Unhappy and when you are happy I am happy too. It is our duty to share each others joy and sorrows for if we cannot who can?"[10] Dean's own ability to support Emily in her troubles soon came to an end, for he died of illness less than two months after penning those words. Still, such sentiments were representative of the feelings officers expressed.[11]

It is impossible to convey the distinctive tenor of every married officer's correspondence, but surveying the way several communicated to their wives illustrates both the common themes of such letters and the unique character of those relationships. Edward Jesup Wood's desire to be with his family leapt off the page in letter after letter. He regularly inquired about affairs at home and how life was going. He deeply missed his wife Jane (nicknamed Jeanie) and daughter Mary and felt keenly the loss of not being around to watch his little girl grow. He described his impatience when waiting for a leave of absence and lamented when such opportunities fell through. When rumors arose that the Forty-Eighth might be consolidated with another regiment, which would make many officers superfluous and lead to their discharge, he promised Jeanie he would seek to be among that number. "I don't feel as if I could live away from you & I know it is even more of a sacrifice for you to live so unsatisfactorily," he wrote.[12] Absence from his family grew increasingly difficult for Wood to tolerate: "It will require a fresh installment of patriotism to keep me away from them every month longer."[13] While looking forward to the Forty-Eighth's veteran furlough in 1864, he wrote: "God knows it has been the hardest trial of my life, to give up for so long the sweet society of my wife and child, and to lose forever the delight of watching that dear God-given pledge of our mutual love as she expanded from promising but little bud of infancy to the sweet flower of childhood."[14] Wood did not reenlist, but he accompanied the Forty-Eighth on veteran furlough. He returned to the front in March 1864 and by April wrote wistfully, "Papa wishes he could play hide-and-seek and have a real frolic with his little girl tonight."[15] The next month, he asked his wife to tell their daughter that "Papa don't love the naughty rebels, either, but he is getting most tired of fighting them & wants to come home to his little girl."[16] Wood continued to protest his firm belief in the Union cause, but he was no doubt quite happy to muster out in January 1865.[17]

Wood did what he could to encourage his wife and assure her of his love. When she was despondent in fall 1862, he sympathized: "I can't blame you at time for feeling *blue*. I know I am sometimes 'deeply, darkly, beautifully blue,' when I am a little unwell especially" (a reference to either Robert Southey or Lord Byron).[18] Wood also kept track of his wedding anniversary. "I had forgotten to mention that this is the anniversary of our wedding day, not because I had not thought of it, for it was my earliest thought this morning," he wrote to Jeanie on 25 October 1863. He continued, "Four years! & half the time separated! Not much such a wedded life I fancy as we looked forward to four years ago. Let us pray God that the next four years may be spent together, in a peaceful land."[19] When Jeanie expressed discouragement, he answered with comfort and attempted to praise her and build her up. Though Colonel Wood found it trying to be away from home, he did not lose sight of the fact that the separation was hard on his wife as well, and perpetually sought to encourage her.[20]

24 MORE IMPORTANT THAN GOOD GENERALS

DeWitt Clinton Loudon's letters to his wife Hannah contained direct statements of his care, prayers for her well-being, inquiries about her welfare, and even apologies that he could not do more to cheer her. He painted hopeful visions of days to come. His and Hannah's tenth wedding anniversary moved him to an especially lengthy expression of his love for her:

> God bless you, Hannah, for your kindness & patience, for your industry & your watchfulness for my comfort & welfare. I am afraid I have not always repaid you as you deserved; but if I have not, I know that you have forgiven me. You have grown dearer & dearer to me the longer you have been my wife. Now, the mother of my children in full womanhood, I love you more deeply & earnestly than when a blushing girl you stood by my side, as we took upon us the solemn vows whose obligations were to bind us so long as "you both shall live."[21]

Loudon prayed that he would live to see the evil rebellion suppressed and peace and order restored so he could enjoy more years with Hannah and their children. He appreciated the significance of the Union cause yet earnestly desired to be done with it as soon as possible. "Embrace our children for me. How I long, my duty faithfully done, to fly to you. Good bye, my love, my gentle & loving wife," he concluded.[22] Their anniversary moved Loudon to exceptional eloquence, but the tone was representative of his communications to Hannah.[23]

Benjamin H. Grierson's correspondence with his wife Alice included many typical representations of his love but also some truly unique expressions. "God knows I wish you all a merry Christmas," he wrote on 19 December 1861, wishing he could spend the holiday with them.[24] Late one night a few days later, he wrapped up another letter to Alice with the conclusion that he would "try to dream *of you and Home sweet Home. This has been a bitter cold day. I'd like to cuddle up to you* to-night and get warm."[25] A few days later, he wrote of his hope to return home after the war and share with his wife in raising their children, as well as any additional children they might have, playfully hinting in a parenthetical comment "*such things sometimes happen in the best of families you know.*"[26] Grierson also produced multipage letters consisting entirely of rhyming poetry. He seemed especially inspired in January 1862, churning out a succession of such letter-poems. He wrote Alice four pages of this poetry on 2 January 1862, following up that holiday missive with another four-page letter-poem a few days later, and penned yet another the following week. Grierson's poetry sometimes reflected a sense of humor and other times turned in a more romantic direction, as seen in a letter from late January 1862. He wrote to Alice:

My love of days by-gone,
I loved thee, long ago,
Yet as fleeting time glides swiftly on,
My love for thee doth grow,
Though the fire of youthful passion may,
Be modified some-what,
Still you're more dear to me to-day,
Than when in joy I sought,
To gain your heart & hand in youth[27]

Grierson also supplied non-rhyming declarations of love and exhortations to hope in the future. After a particularly long gap without letters from Alice, Grierson reported that the lack of correspondence "has caused me to feel so lonely, that it is almost equal to the *Blues*."[28] He flirtatiously continued, "I would like to see you and be with you always, never to leave you again, it would most surely do me a great deal of good to *love kiss* and *hug* you now, although this would be a very warm day to be so near a woman."[29] Many officers wrote lovingly to their wives, but none matched Grierson's creative style, and few were as blatantly romantic.[30]

Jacob B. Ritner of the Twenty-Fifth Iowa spent a lot of time thinking about his wife Emeline, musing on everything from missing her cooking to wishing they could travel the south together after the war. He wrote often of his love and devotion for her. Once, he noted that while he enjoyed writing to her (a claim verified by his vast correspondence), "what I want all the time, is just to take you in my arms and tell you 'something'—I do love you dear, and if I am spared to see you again, am determined to treat you more kindly, and show you that I love and appreciate you better than I ever done before."[31] A few days before their twelfth wedding anniversary, at the end of March 1863, Ritner wrote, "Remember the 3rd of April, won't you, Dear. Tell me whether you thought about it or not. I am going to celebrate it some way. I hope we may never be separated again when the dear anniversary comes round."[32] The day itself passed occupied by army activities, but the morning of 4 April 1863, Ritner had the leisure to go out for a morning stroll: "The sun was just rising clear and beautiful, the air fine and invigorating. The trees are all out in full foliage and full of birds, the grass is green, the white clover is in blossom. At the farthest place I saw the most splendid flower garden I ever saw. I gathered a few which I will send to you in remembrance of the *third* day of April. When you look at them you will think of me and *that* time, won't you?"[33] As the war dragged on, Ritner framed his desire for Union victory in terms of how it would allow him to reunite with his family. Following a visit home late in the summer of 1863, he wrote, "I don't believe I will ever be so well satisfied with the army as I was before. I do wish the war was over so I could be at home with dear, sweet wife."[34] On his thirty-sixth birthday, 16 September 1864, Ritner wished that he could spend the rest of his years at home with his family, "and for that reason I want the rebels completely subdued now."[35] A few weeks later, remarking on the irony that he could feel so lonely while surrounded by thousands of people, he declared, "There is a place in my heart for you, dear, and no one, or anything else, can fill it. I do wish the nasty rebels would behave themselves so we could go home, if it was only for a few days."[36] Such sentiments were typical for Ritner.[37]

Jake and Emeline's marriage appears to have been a mutually strengthening relationship. On Ritner's side, he wrote of the moral strength he gained from thinking about his wife. On the steamboat ride back toward the army after his leave of absence in summer 1863, Ritner reported there were many other officers who like him had just parted from their families but who showed a disturbing lack of respect and restraint in their behavior. "What disgusted me more than anything else," he explained, "was the slightly disrespectful way they talked about women. A lot of them tried to get me to join them in a spree one night. What do you think I did? I just took out my 'picture' and showed it to them. They had sense enough to be ashamed of themselves and let me alone after that."[38] Ritner claimed his desire to be worthy of Emeline's love and respect helped motivate him to avoid behavior he deemed disreputable, such as drinking, swearing, and playing cards. In another letter from fall 1864, he wrote, "There is one thought that cheers and strengthens me more than anything else, and that is that I have a dear, sweet wife at home who loves me and is true to me. What more could a man want?"[39] Missing his family was at times a source of distress, but love for his family could also be a source of strength to carry on with the business of the war. As his wife was a source of strength for him, so also Ritner strove to keep up her spirits. In summer 1864, amid fears that rebel guerrillas rampaging through Missouri might cross into Iowa, Ritner advised his wife, "If they should get there, do you stay at home, and let on you are not afraid of them. That is the safest way."[40] Ritner also counseled Emeline to face more prosaic fears, such as being more sociable and attending parties and other community events. To bolster her confidence for one such occasion, he assured her she was "just as good as any of them, and better too. You are smarter and better looking than any of them, and you need not be afraid to go."[41] Whatever fears or challenges his wife faced, Ritner tried to encourage her.[42]

Compared to many husbands' letters to their wives, Ritner was exceptionally playful and flirty. One Saturday evening in November 1862, he addressed her thus: "Come and sit down on my lap and let us have talk—come right along now. I want to tell you something. There now, ain't you sweet? If I had you in my arms again I would kiss you a thousand times. I have just been looking at your picture and I just know it is the prettiest thing that ever was. Be still now!! You ain't going to get away yet. If you wasn't such good stuff I believe I would scold you a little. But you are my own sweet dear and I can't."[43] He showed a similar jocular intimacy in April 1864; Ritner had gone home in December 1863 to recover from a wound and spent a few months there convalescing. Now on his way to rejoin the Twenty-Fifth Iowa, he wrote, "I kept a sharp lookout all through Indiana to see if there were any more Hoosier girls as good-looking as the one I boarded with last winter, but I couldn't see her."[44] (The jest alluded to the fact that Emeline herself was from Indiana.) Later that summer, in reference to the news that Emeline's brother, Alvah Bereman, and his wife had a baby girl, Ritner asked her, "We will have to show them how to have boys. When the war is over, we can do it, can't we?"[45] A few weeks later, discussing the faint hope that he might obtain a brief leave, he queried, "What time of the moon had I better come?" an obvious reference to his desire for more children.[46] Reflecting Victorian strictures on sexuality, this is about as sexually explicit as private letters from a husband to his wife seem to have ever got.[47] This hope of a furlough did not pan out, prompting Ritner to joke, "General Sherman thinks he can't get along without me."[48]

Some officers married during the war. Z. Payson Shumway joined the Fourteenth Illinois in May 1861, and after obtaining a long-sought furlough, he went home to marry Hattie Pray in February 1862. He jotted down the following diary entry for 12 February 1862: "Strange things happen in ones life but none *more* strange than the motive which prompts a man to unite his destiny with one of the fairer sex but thus it is & to night I find myself united to one whose life God grant I may never render less pleasant than now."[49] A mournful note for 17 February described Hattie's tears as he left to return to the army and Shumway's own misery at leaving his new wife. Being away did not stop Shumway from pondering marriage, and several weeks later he wrote at length on the nature of their relationship:

> Now Hattie I want you to write me oftener, please do, if it is only a few lines just to let me know that you are well though I would rather you write me *long* letters & tell me all your thoughts, for you know that it is by an expression of them that we become better acquainted with each other. Indeed I was reflecting today, that, even now while we are married & consequently each bound in some measure to respect the wishes & to bear with the failings of the other yet even now I am hardly acquainted with you, fondly as I love you. At first the thought startled me as I thought that I should hardly be able to anticipate your wishes & wants for Hattie I have learned by observation that it is this carefull attention to the wants & wishes of each other that makes the whole sum of happiness not only in married life but also between man & man everywhere. So when you write me, state your thoughts & reflections upon anything you may write about.[50]

Newlywed though he was, Shumway seems to have had some profound insights into marriage. He concluded his discourse by asking Hattie not to mistake the foregoing discussion as having any critical intent toward her. Shumway followed his own advice by keeping up a steady stream of letters. He also encouraged Hattie to connect with her new in-laws and write to his family. When she expressed doubts in her letter-writing ability, he answered, "Now Hattie you must be aware that no one can write a good letter and at the same time make it interesting without *practice* so that all you have to do is to *try it.*"[51] His letters to her were full of longing to see her again.[52]

Officers' letters to their wives generally display a warm, congenial tone, but occasionally they reveal hints of marital conflict. Captain Harley Wayne of the Fifteenth Illinois was irked to discover that his wife Ellen made inquiries through mutual acquaintances whether her husband swore or got drunk while away in the army. Upon learning of this, he wrote to declare "how childish to imagine and thus to betray a want of confidence in me by admitting Such possibilities."[53] Wayne had little time for such misbehavior, for he was killed at Shiloh three months later. Another clash appears in the letters of Maj. Thomas Thomson Taylor. Following a "strangely enigmatical, wonderfully obscure" letter from his wife Margaret (nicknamed Netta), Taylor answered with a gruff demand for specificity.[54] Margaret had written to him hinting at troubles and at being insulted by someone, without supplying details. He rebuked her, saying, "I don't like letters written in riddles, if the news is disagreeable give it me in full if not I want it plain and simple so that I may rejoice with you, but for heavens sake don't indulge me in such unsatisfactory missives any more."[55] Although not perceptible in the majority of exchanges between officers and their wives, moments of obvious strain like this do appear in a few of these relationships. In the broader context, though, they do not detract from the overwhelmingly positive way officers wrote about their wives. The marriages described in the foregoing examples provide a glimpse into the countless such relationships that defined the lives of so many of the Army of the Tennessee's officers.

"We have a great many big guns to kill Rebels with," Robert Steele informed his son Wesley, one of a number of attempts by fathers to explain the nature of the war—and their long absences—to their children.[56] Unquestionably, officers' most important relationship, as seen through their wartime writings, was to their wives, but their next great preoccupation with home centered on their children. Many officers were fathers, and the extended separation from their children weighed heavily on them. They frequently inquired about their children's health, growth, learning, and behavior, and they attempted to advise their wives in raising them. Some left pregnant wives behind when they went to war and only got to see their new babies months later on some brief furlough. They fretted over whether young children would still remember them when they returned. Sometimes they wrote letters to older, literate children, but more commonly, they simply included some comments addressed to their children within letters to their wives. These usually emphasized their love for their children and dwelt on how much they wished to hug and kiss and play with them. Robert B. Latham, colonel of the 106th Illinois, charmingly drew strings of asterisks in his letters to represent kisses bestowed upon his family. They exhorted their children to obey their mothers and promised to bring gifts when they returned. For older children, officers inquired about how their schooling was progressing and talked of the importance of learning. Such were typical comments as officers sought to stay informed and involved in their children's lives while away at war.[57]

The breadth of parental comments officers wrote is somewhat narrower than what they wrote to their wives. A couple of extended examples are valuable for illustrating the place of children in the lives of the Army of the Tennessee's officers. Jake Ritner's letters abounded with questions about his children (three daughters and one son). A typical volley of questions to his wife Emeline is in one letter: "I want you to tell me all about our babies, the next time you write. I think of them a great deal. I want to know if they ever talk about Pa, and what they do. Did you get the little sled for Tommy? How are Lulie's eyes? Have you got good warm clothes for them all?"[58] He also peppered his letters with encouragement for the children to behave and obey their mother and teachers. The two eldest daughters, Lulie and Nellie, apparently started school during the war, prompting frequent declarations of his hopes for their education. While he rejoiced in their progress at learning to read, he also exhorted them to "learn to wash the dishes and sweep the floor, and to sew and knit, and sing,"[59] and to "walk light and like ladies, over the floor—and not romp so much in the street."[60] He believed they needed "to learn to act like young ladies" because they were "getting old enough to think about something besides playing and romping."[61] Regarding the two younger children, he asked, "What do they do and say? Do they ever talk about me? I cannot bear to think of their forgetting me. You won't let them, will you?"[62] Thinking about his son, Ritner wrote, "I hope he will never have to be a soldier."[63] Lulie, the eldest, occasionally wrote letters to her father, which he always praised for how informative they were. Ritner sometimes addressed letters specifically to the girls. To Nellie, he ruefully observed, "I never tried to write a letter to such a little girl before and I am afraid you won't think it very interesting. I suppose you don't care anything about 'War News.'"[64] Christmas in particular brought his children to mind. Prior to his first Christmas away from home, he instructed Emeline, "You must be certain to make 'Santa Claus' fill all stockings clear full at Christmas."[65] Ritner did his best to stay involved in his children's lives, within the limited medium of letters.[66]

Luther Howard Cowan also had a great deal to say to and about his three children (two daughters and one son). He made a point of noting that although a letter of his might be addressed to just one member of the family, he still meant for all of them to share it. Cowan wrote quite a few letters to his eldest, Mary (nicknamed Molly), who was about thirteen when the war began. Once, Cowan had an extremely disconcerting dream that his young son George drowned in a well; so greatly did it perturb him that he wrote to his wife Harriet to hire a carpenter to seal off a well on their property. Beyond the usual fears about how much the younger children would remember him and the usual inquires about their growth, Cowan, more than many officers, directed comments to his children, urging them at various times to be kind, honest, diligent about their schoolwork and to trust God and obey their mother. Following one such exhortation to be industrious and good, he waxed philosophical to his children, describing how "the human character, like time itself, never stands still, it is on the advance or retrograde all the while."[67] He also looked forward to the future, promising to tell them in more detail of his adventures after the war when he could return home for good.[68]

Cowan strongly desired that his children acquire a good education and wrote of it often, such as when he suggested Harriet begin teaching little George the alphabet and numbers. However, Cowan directed his most extensive comments about education to Molly. He encouraged her to study Latin, French, German, algebra, and geometry. "Nothing so balances the mind and trains it for close and correct *thinking* as the study of mathematics," he advised her in one letter.[69] He wrote to Molly of his hopes that he could afford good schooling for her and her siblings. He explained that "education depends in a great measure on your own exertions; going to school merely don't make an education, it is only had by *long* and *hard devoted study;* but it pays, it is the only thing that does pay for young people."[70] At one point, he sent Molly some books, and after she conveyed her appreciation, Cowan responded: "You know I think that young folks now a days read too much light or fashionable reading and too little historical and scientific; though I think a little fashionable literature is not objectionable but highly necessary to qualify a person for good appearance in company!! though you will always find that knowledge of science and history is of far greater use than all the novelty that can be procured."[71] After another letter from Molly, Cowan praised her writing, declaring, "Writing a nice letter is one of the greatest accomplishments that a person can possess, and every young lady and gentleman should strive to improve in that kind of writing."[72] He also counseled his daughter that when writing, if she was ever "at all uncertain about the orthography of a word, to lay down the pen, take the Dictionary, look it up and be sure."[73] He even wished that Molly could visit the army's camp and see what it was like, believing it would be a valuable educational experience for her. Finally, not only did Cowan encourage Molly's own academic pursuits, but he also asked that she share in teaching her younger sister and brother. Some of Cowan's educational aspirations for his children were exceptional, but his efforts to stay informed about and involved with his children's lives through letters mirrored those of many other officers.[74]

The Army of the Tennessee's officers had family beyond wives and children who also remained a meaningful part of their lives. After letters to wives, letters to parents were most common, then letters to siblings. The latter occurred more frequently if the officer was unmarried. William K. Barney once cautioned his brother, "Sam, be careful that you do not write in any of your letters to *any one* things or *words* you would not be willing to have anyone see in after years"—advice that seems remarkably foresighted considering who just read that quote.[75] Elder brothers dispensed a variety of life advice to younger siblings back home. However, not all familial connections engendered positive feelings. Popular culture often frames the American Civil War as a conflict of "brother against brother," and while this was rarely true of the Army of the Tennessee's officers, there were a few who had to navigate the problem of rebellious relatives. Edward Jesup Wood was raised by his paternal grandfather in Connecticut while his mother lived in Florida and Georgia. During the Savannah Campaign, the army passed close by a plantation where Wood's mother was living, though he did not have the opportunity to visit. Wood also had at least one half brother, Robert, who Wood once lamented was "a full blooded Southerner & determined to die in the last ditch"[76] Family conflict also occurred when an officer had rebel-sympathizing relatives in the North. Tom Taylor engaged in some kind of feud with his wife's brother, Chilton White, after White apparently denounced the war and accused soldiers of committing rapes, theft, and vandalism. In his typically verbose and melodramatic style, Taylor compared his brother-in-law to Benedict Arnold and fretted that a similar enduring reputation of dishonor would attach to Taylor's wife and children, as blood relatives of the miscreant. He also declared the quotation "Whome the Gods wish to destroy they first make mad" appropriate for White.[77] A further dramatic turn came when soldiers of Taylor's Forty-Seventh Ohio, home on leave, pelted White with eggs (Taylor disclaimed any involvement). The final outcome of this contretemps cannot be ascertained from Taylor's letters, but he revealed enough to provide an instructive example of the kind of familial conflict some officers faced.[78]

Some officers experienced the loss of a parent or other family member during their service. In January 1862, Henry Otis Dwight first learned of his father's unexpected death by reading a newspaper one morning and observing a note that a Dr. Dwight of Boston had been killed in a railway accident. The next day's paper expanded the story with a note that the late Dr. Dwight had been a clergyman. At first Dwight did not connect the story to himself. The third day, another officer asked Dwight if the unfortunate clergyman was his father: "I was shocked for I had not thought of it."[79] Later, Lt. Col. Manning Force summoned Dwight, confirmed that his father was dead, and offered a furlough so he could attend the funeral. Unsure when or if there would be a funeral, Dwight asked if he could visit his sister Susie in Delaware, and Force gave him a week. Dwight admired the way his sister was "very very sweet in her resignation to the will of God."[80] After only three days, a telegram called Dwight to return immediately, cutting short his time to mourn.[81]

Jake Ritner faced an exceptional string of family deaths during the war. His father Henry was struck by a train in late February 1863, and he was unable to get home for the funeral. Ritner sought comfort from musing on the good example his father left: "I hope we will all be able to say The Lord's will be done, and that we may be as well prepared for our final end as I have no doubt he was."[82] The next to die was Jake's younger brother, Judson. A soldier in Ritner's company, Judson died suddenly of a seemingly minor illness in April 1863. "Poor boy, his soldiering in this world is over, and he has gone where there are no more wars or fighting. I never felt so bad hardly, about anything in my life," Ritner lamented.[83] Writing to inform their mother was nearly as dreadful as burying his brother. He prayed, "May God who tempers the wind to the shorn lamb, enable us all to bear this new affliction with fortitude and resignation to his will who doeth all things well."[84] Ritner's third family death in four months occurred during the 22 May assault on Vicksburg. James Freeman, his first sergeant and his wife's brother-in-law (being married to Emeline's sister Caroline), was killed in the attack. Ritner could not bear informing Caroline himself and begged his wife to break the news to her sister personally. He wrote repeatedly of his sadness at Sergeant Freeman's death and urged Emeline to take good care of her widowed sister. "I hope God will give her strength to bear her great affliction. I believe she is a true Christian and knows where to go for help," he concluded.[85] Ritner got a break from family deaths for just over a year, until July 1864, when his father-in-law, Samuel Bereman, died. He wrote to Emeline of how much he respected her father, acknowledged the suffering of her widowed mother, and enjoined Emeline to do whatever was necessary to see to her mother's needs. Ritner also wrote to his mother-in-law, Eleanor Bereman, admitting that he was not skilled at comforting but offering his sympathy and promising to do anything he could to help her. Ritner related how the night before, sleepless, he arose at midnight "and sat on the breastwork in the moonlight and thought of the difference in our family since the war began. How we were all at home—safe—contented—prosperous—happy—Now we are scattered everywhere and no one knows how many of us will ever meet at the old homestead again."[86] Ritner faced an unusual number of family deaths, but whether from the war itself or from other circumstances, plenty of officers had to cope with family loss during their service.[87]

Among the many family-related topics officers covered in their letters, two stand out as areas where officers showed special concern: health and money. Officers waited apprehensively for news of every toothache, cold, and sore throat. News that family members were ill was a great source of worry and stress for men stationed far from home. A lack of letters from someone, or the absence of references to one family member by another, often provoked anxiety and fear that the silent or unmentioned loved one might be deathly ill. Real or imagined illness prompted desperate pleas for news. To make matters worse, though officers could try to obtain leave, typically they were stuck in the field knowing a loved one faced a potentially fatal illness back home. They often exhorted their families to take good care of themselves and counseled preventative measures, such as getting small-pox vaccinations, avoiding infected people or locales, and taking care not to overexert themselves. Family health problems became even more stressful if the folks back home needed money for medical care and an officer had nothing to send because he had not been paid in six months. News that a family member recovered brought tremendous relief. However much they wished otherwise, officers could do little but worry and pray about their loved ones' health and hope for better times in the future.[88]

Alongside health, officers' other omnipresent concern when writing to their families was money. The war kept these men away from the financial and business matters to which they normally would have attended. Since they could not be there themselves, they relied on their wives (and sometimes parents, siblings, or other relatives) to attend to their affairs. Officers went out of their way to express trust in their wives' judgment to handle these decisions yet also frequently dispensed business directions or advice through their letters. They were constantly concerned for the material well-being of their families. There were crops to plant, harvest, and sell; pigs to keep out of the garden; cows to acquire; real estate deals to work out; debts to pay; creditors to fend off; property improvements to implement; investment options to explore; wood and hay to collect for the winter; goods to buy (everything from food and clothing to sewing machines and wallpaper); and postwar plans to consider. Some officers gave thought to saving for their children's futures. Officers sent home as much money as possible and otherwise did all they could to look after their families' interests. They commonly expressed distress at their inability to see more directly to their loved ones' needs while away in the field.[89]

A common element of officers' letters was requests for more letters and notes of gratitude for recently received letters. With infrequent exceptions, letters were officers' sole means of communicating with their families, and they treasured the ability to send and receive mail. Letters allowed officers to maintain the family relationships they prized even while far away. The reception of a letter could tremendously bolster an officer's morale and trigger effusive thanks. A long gap in letters led to a frantic spiral of discouragement, anxiety, and even anger, expressed in desperate pleas, statements of loneliness, and accusations of neglect. The arrival of a new epistle brought forth elation and prompt apologies for previous complaints or accusations. Officers desired not only frequent letters but long ones. Some officers also recognized that their interlocutors could suffer similarly and would apologize for long gaps in their own writing. Where some men seemed to place all blame for a shortage of mail on their loved ones, others acknowledged how the forces of war could make mail miscarry and realized that neither they nor their family received all the letters the other sent. Since family relationships, especially marriage, were a foundational part of officers' identities—and mail was the leading expression of those relationships during the war—their feelings toward mail itself warrant exploration.[90]

"Write, write, write! Even if it is the worst," Henry A. Kircher exhorted his mother in September 1862, in a typical instance of officers' ubiquitous pleas for more and longer letters.[91] Letters from home provided peace of mind that helped soldiers endure the separation caused by military service. As Luther H. Cowan put it, soldiers were "all anxious to hear from homes and friends every day, and at the same time to stay in the field as long as their duty prompts them and to fight whenever it is necessary for the constitution and laws which they enlisted to sustain."[92] As time elapsed since the last news from home, officers' emotional state progressed from mere disappointment at the lack of mail to acute anxiety. They would start making gloomy comments about feeling forgotten by the rest of the world and fearing that their loved ones no longer cared about them. If too much time passed, men were prone to assume something was wrong and grow frantic for confirmation of their loved ones' well-being. Some men even grew angry or jealous when other soldiers received more mail than they did. One officer claimed a letter from family was valued more highly than a month's pay. Another said he skipped meals to read newly arrived mail. Many officers insisted that if their loved ones just understood how profoundly encouraging a letter from home could be, they would write more often. The content of the letters did not need to be elaborate. "Just sit down and write any nonsense or anything like I do. Everything you say and do is interesting to me," wrote Jake Ritner in a representative request.[93] Nothing about their families and homes was too trivial for homesick officers to appreciate.[94]

Officers followed up their petitions with profuse gratitude when letters arrived, again testifying to the role of family letters in sustaining morale and emotional health. In the absence of new letters, officers resorted to rereading old ones. Many officers claimed the folks back home could never fully grasp how much letters lifted their spirits, but they still made the attempt to convey their appreciation. Z. Payson Shumway reported to his wife Hattie how receiving two letters from her completely turned his mood around after he had just marched fifty miles in two days on little food. "Certainly no tired hungry footsore man felt sooner at ease with mankind generally or was sooner fast asleep than I & let me assure you that at such a time no one appreciates the fact that he is 'remembered at home' more fully than the soldier," he told her.[95] Alphonso Barto shared a similar thought with his sister during the Atlanta Campaign: "Perhaps you think it don't do a soldier any good to get a letter when he is lying in the face of an enemy and expecting to have a fight every moment but I tell you sister if there is any thing in the world that will cheer a soldiers heart it is his mail."[96] One officer told his sister the refreshing quality of letters surpassed that of a cool autumn breeze, while another pronounced his wife's letters more valuable than jewels. Sentiments of this sort typify the sense of satisfaction officers ascribed to letters from home.[97]

The mail was subject to numerous disruptive factors, and many officers acknowledged how external forces interfered with the mail. They made a point of saying they did not blame their loved ones for the lack of letters (a contrast with officers who suggested a dearth of letters signified deliberate neglect). Whether letters that officers wrote ever reached home was equally a matter of suspense. Rebel forces commonly attempted to disrupt Union lines of communication, a fact of which many officers were keenly aware. The unreliability of the mail could lead to confusion, as a later letter might include a seemingly cryptic reference to something explained fully in an earlier letter that had never reached its destination. Just getting a letter written could be a challenge. Rebel attacks, or the threat thereof, could preempt any time for letter writing. In winter weather, officers sometimes grew so cold that numb fingers made good handwriting a trial. A lack of shelter during rain made writing impossible. Other days, the need to complete government reports filled an officer's time. Injuries and illnesses could also prevent writing. The sheer busyness of camp life, with numerous soldiers clamoring for an officer's attention, could be so noisy and distracting as to make writing a thoughtful and intimate letter nearly impossible. Being on the march, or newly arrived at a destination and setting up camp, likewise left officers with little free time. When an officer did have time to write, he needed writing materials, which were not always easily available and sometimes had to be scrounged from captured rebel supplies. Considering how difficult letter writing could be, the number that officers penned is a testimony to their dedication.[98]

Officers and their families exchanged packages as well as letters throughout the war. The folks back home could supply all manner of material comforts unavailable in an army camp, such as clothing, food, stamps, paper, and even luxuries like books, candy, flowers, and gold pens. Stamps were by far the most requested item; as Henry A. Kircher observed to his mother, "The letters don't go for free."[99] William K. Barney told his brother Sam that "P. O. stamps are an article we cannot get for love or money out this way."[100] Officers requested packages far less often than letters, but their requests still reveal fascinating things about their interests and activities. Kircher requested reading material on such topics as mechanics, geometry, physics, algebra, astronomy, and physiology; at one point he decided books were too heavy and that old magazines "would be quite pleasant to kill the time dead with," only to subsequently reverse himself and ask for more books, so long as they were not expensive ones.[101] Kircher also asked for such items as shirt collars, shoe polish, and tobacco. DeWitt Clinton Loudon's wish list included saddlebags, a protractor, a book on geometry, mittens, a wool hood, a silk handkerchief, and a Bible. Hannah Loudon supplied her husband with these goods as well others, such as recent newspapers. Clint Loudon described these packages as emblems of her love and care for him, investing books and mittens with tremendous emotional significance. Other officers agreed that parcels from home possessed emotional meanings well beyond their basic usefulness. "Two letters and *the* box all the same day! You may be sure I am a happy boy—so many reminders of my dear kind, thoughtful wifey, and so many things of real comfort and use," wrote Edward Jesup Wood, his gratitude blending the emotional and practical meanings of a package.[102] Packages from home were an important way families strengthened officers.[103]

Like with letters, officers sent packages home as well as receiving them. Sometimes these were simple gifts for their children, but many officers showed an awareness that they were engaged in a matter of historic importance and consciously desired to provide their families with relics of the events. When George Lee Thurston's sword was struck by a bullet and damaged during the Battle of Shiloh, he sent it home to his wife with a note: "If you ever get it, give it to Willie; and tell him his father fought at Shiloh, and that he would rather lie with his face to the moon than that a son of his should ever fear to give his life for his country's honor."[104] The Cowan children received several souvenirs from their father Luther. In January 1862, he sent home brass buttons for little George (who was about three years old) and later added one of his army blankets, so that his son could sleep in it and pretend to be a soldier. Around mid-April, Cowan "sent Phine and Molly [the nicknames for Josephine and Mary, who were around 8 and 13, respectively] each a secesh book I took out of a Secesh Church. I hope they will keep them as long as they live, just for reminiscences of the war etc."[105] He later obtained more buttons for George, these removed from the overcoat of a dead rebel. He wrote in May 1862 that he sent other items (including a broom taken from Fort Donelson) "not for their worth but as Reminiscences."[106] Jake Ritner wrote from Beaufort, South Carolina, "I have also mailed to Tommy a Confederate spelling book that I confiscated on the march. You will find it a great curiosity; don't let them destroy it. I want to preserve it as an evidence of Southern civilization and intelligence!"[107] Parcels were by far secondary to letters as a means of communication, but still represented another way for officers and their families to display care for each other.[108]

The relatively new phenomenon of photography provided another method for officers to maintain connections and relationships. Numerous officers in the Army of the Tennessee displayed a fascination with obtaining and sharing photographs that is strikingly similar to the twenty-first century's fondness for Facebook, Instagram, and other social media. Many officers found opportunity to get their picture taken and mailed home. Most often, they requested photographs of their wives and children (and always poured out their gratitude upon receiving new photos). However, officers also liked to exchange photographs with each other. They collected pictures of fellow officers, friends in other regiments, and even generals. Upon receiving a photo of his son, Harley Wayne wrote to his wife that it brought "pleasure and pain" to be able to see his son "but could not hear his voice nor could I grasp him in fond embraces as my whole Soul yearned to do—and I was sad."[109] In common with many people today, officers expressed annoyance or even embarrassment if they felt their own pictures did not look good. If they had multiple pictures taken of themselves, they would make an effort to distribute only the ones they thought made themselves look best.[110]

Jake Ritner's fond references to pictures highlight the emotional function pictures of family could perform. He wrote frequently of the joy he derived from having a photograph of his wife Emeline, mentioned admiring it daily, requested more pictures of her and their children, and expressed his distress when he lost her photo. Late in 1862, when Emeline asked her husband what the women were like in the south, he answered that her picture was prettier than any woman in the country, not just the south. In May 1864, Ritner declared that receiving a new picture of Emeline in the mail left him feeling like "the biggest man in the regiment."[111] He thanked Emeline for sending it and concluded, "I think it is a very good picture. Your mouth is all right this time. I have nearly spoiled it already, kissing it. I am going to keep it."[112] But it was on the last day of July 1864 that Ritner most fully captured the way photographs could give officers a sense of connection to home, even in the middle of a brutal, grinding campaign: "I have just been looking at your picture, and I think I see you now. . . . I often think about you, and wonder almost if it is really so, that a beautiful and pure-minded woman loves me and thinks of me—yes, I know it is so. How I wish I was there with you. I would have a kiss first, and go with you to meeting?"[113] Ritner was exceptionally voluble on the joys of family photos, but the underlying sentiments were common to many officers. Through photographs, they could be a little more connected to their loved ones back home.[114]

Marriage and family were a defining part of officers' identities. Understanding their concerns and motivations in the war is impossible without appreciating what a significant place family relationships held in their lives.

The Army of the Tennessee's officers displayed and maintained their connections to home and family chiefly through letters but also through secondary means such as packages and photographs. The many thousands of letters that supply so much of our knowledge about the war testify to their intense desire to carry on their relationships with their wives, children, parents, and siblings despite the war. They accepted their military service as a necessity, but they always looked forward to both the next chance at a furlough and even more to the end of the war when they could return home for good. They did their best to remain involved in family life, from the education of their children to caring for ill loved ones and managing family finances. They sought to encourage and comfort their loved ones at the same time that they found inspiration to persevere in their duties from thinking about their families. Thoughts of home were never far from the minds of the Army of the Tennessee's officers.[115]

CHAPTER 3

Prayer and Providence

The Army of the Tennessee's officers existed in a theological milieu dominated by Christianity and left behind numerous indications of this faith, especially in the form of prayers and statements of trust in divine providence. Many officers described their circumstances and feelings in language taken from the Bible or from Christian hymns (as when Ephraim Brown applied the stanza "Hail land of rest for thee I Sigh when Shall the moment come when I can lay my armor by and dwell in peace at home" to capture his desire to see his family).[1] Appreciating officers' religious expressions provides insight into their worldviews and how they coped with the stresses of war.

They rarely self-identified by denominational affiliations, nor did they discuss theological intricacies, so it is impossible categorize them by denomination or specific doctrinal beliefs. In their religious expressions, they most frequently discussed God's providence, stating their trust in it, giving thanks for how God had cared for them, and praying for His continued favor. They also showed the practical side of their religious belief by attending church, seeking religious instruction for their children, relying on their faith when dealing with death, and seeking to understand the war in theological terms. Throughout the war, religious officers found in their faith strength to cope with difficulties, guidance for conduct, and hope for the future. Religiously expressive officers remained consistent in their beliefs throughout their service, leaving no indication that wartime trials inflicted disillusionment or loss of faith. It is difficult to quantify the number of "Christian" (using that term broadly) officers and impossible to judge the quality of their piety in any meaningful way. Some clearly seem to have possessed a much deeper trust in God than others did. But even acknowledging the limitations of the sources, enough officers wrote of religious

41

matters to make clear that Christianity held widespread influence among the Army of the Tennessee's officers.[2]

Trust that God actively superintends the world in a wise and benevolent way is a basic tenet of Christianity, one clearly accepted by the numerous officers who made reference to this trust as a source of hope and encouragement. "Providence" in this context refers to the idea of God acting in the world by subtle, rather than overtly supernatural (i.e., miraculous), means. Officers spoke of finding peace by relying on providence, and they likewise encouraged their loved ones to cope with wartime fears by trusting God. Accompanying these sentiments came an emphasis on accepting God's will, particularly regarding turns of events they found undesirable (chiefly, the possibility of their own deaths). They did not presume they possessed some divine invincibility but did think they had reason to hope an all-powerful and benevolent God would protect them. Early in December 1862, Robert Steele encouraged his wife Rhoda to trust that God would protect him and bring him back to her, reminding her that "there is one who watches over us whose eye never slumbers nor sleeps and all things shall work for good to them that love God" (quoting from Romans 8:28).[3] Seeking to encourage his wife Jeanie, Edward Wood observed, "I don't wonder, my dear girl, that you should sometimes feel *blue,* but I know you have too much native strength of mind, assisted by true Christian faith to give way to feelings of despondency. God rules over all, and however hard and dark His ways may seem, He means that we should walk in them for His purposes and for our own good."[4] Addressing his daughter Alice, Troy Moore lauded God's care: "It fills my heart full to hear of the goodness of him who watches over us all and not a Sparrow falls to the ground without his notice" (an allusion to Matthew 10:29).[5] Officers found comfort in the belief that God was orchestrating events for wise and good ends, which they hoped included their survival but accepted might not.[6]

The benevolent intervention of divine providence was not merely a hypothetical possibility for many officers, but it was also something they believed had affected them personally. Numerous officers penned expressions of thanksgiving, crediting God with some good they had experienced, especially survival in battle. They also credited prayer, particularly the prayers of their loved ones back home, as playing a role in their survival. They thanked God for other positive developments, but deliverance in battle was the chief topic for which officers expressed gratitude to God. From Shiloh to the war's end, officers believed God providentially spared their lives. Officers did not merely credit God with their survival in the immediate aftermath of a narrow scrape; more than one stopped to reflect months or years later at what they still regarded as providential escapes. After the conclusion of hostilities, Oscar Lawrence Jackson reflected over the whole war in his diary entry of 29 April 1865: "My heart is filled with gratitude to Almighty God who has granted such great success to our arms, and has so mercifully preserved my life through the dangers I have passed during the last four years in camp and field."[7] Officers' belief that providence had spared their lives did not fade or collapse but persisted even as they looked back on past battles. Their trust in God had not been disappointed but had endured the war intact.[8]

Logically, given officers' belief in a God who benevolently acts in the world, they prayed for God's continued care in addition to crediting His past deeds. Topics they commonly reported praying about included protection for themselves or for their families, requests for victory, and comfort for those who had suffered loss. Amid rumors of an impending rebel attack in October 1862, Z. Payson Shumway jotted in his diary, "No one may tell what the morrow may bring forth but 'Sufficient unto the day is the evil thereof' & if *fight* we *must* then may the Great God give us courage to fight as becomes *men*" (quoting Matthew 6:34).[9] While at Beaufort, South Carolina, Lieutenant Colonel Stuart pondered his "lonely prayers down here in this Swampy Country," then observed, "after all I trust they are not so lonely for I feel as if *God* is all the time with me when I try to serve *Him*."[10] DeWitt Clinton Loudon produced the most thoughtful commentary on prayer in my research, combining belief in the efficacy of prayer with acceptance that even a good God's will might not grant his requests. Loudon wrote to his wife Hannah:

> I earnestly pray that when this wicked war is over & peace & order established it may be my good fortune to return to you & pass the years yet allotted to me with you & our dear children; & if my home shall continue to be as pleasant as you have made it since you have been my wife, I will be satisfied with whatever may [illegible] come ill or well. But this may not happen. God may require as the price of the reestablishment of our noble government that yet more lives be sacrificed & still other hearthstones be made desolate. We may be called on to bear our share of the awful burden as thousands of others have already done. The price whatever it may be must not be withheld.[11]

This ability to reconcile the reality of unfulfilled requests with continued belief in the value of prayer goes back to the fundamental issue of the trust in God that these officers expressed.[12]

"I attended and participated in the communion services at the Presbyterian Church this forenoon—the first opportunity I have had to partake of the 'Lord's Supper' since I have been in the service," John Quincy Adams Campbell recorded one Sunday in September 1863.[13] By far the most common way officers reported acting on their religious beliefs was attending some kind of religious service, including prayer meetings, sermons by the chaplain, and worship at local churches where the officer was stationed. Worship-starved officers appreciated any chance to attend church and were not picky about the denomination of the group. They scrutinized ministers more for pro-Union or pro-rebel sentiments than for their theology, and openly pro-Confederate ministers provoked strident commentary from visiting officers. The sermon was consistently the chief element of a church service that officers mentioned, though occasionally one wrote of the singing or prayers as well. Campbell's mention of the Lord's Supper, while representative of the many times officers visit southern churches, is also unique as the only time in my research that an officer claimed to partake of the Eucharist.[14]

When attending a local church was impracticable (which was often) but the army was not otherwise engaged (e.g., inspections, marching, or combat), soldiers conducted their own religious services. As Oliver Bridgford wrote to his wife Eliza shortly after joining the army, "they are Great many christian People here among the Rougher Class. They Have meeting here every night (prayer meeting) and Preaching Sundays & Thursday Evening."[15] Officers appreciated having a good chaplain in their regiment to lead such services. Troy Moore wrote glowingly of the impact the Thirty-Second Illinois's chaplain had on the men: "A good many of the boys have become Religiously Serious we have the best Chaplain I expect that's in the United States Service."[16] Other officers praised chaplains they respected and mourned the death or retirement of effective chaplains. Officers not only appreciated chaplains for their effect on the soldiers, but they themselves took chaplains' messages to heart. Z. Payson Shumway once heard a sermon so good that it completely changed his opinion of the chaplain (a man he had previously viewed with contempt) and moved him to ponder the importance of religious practice as well as theory in his own life. Shumway concluded, "that a *living* religion is much better than a *dead* one, no matter in what society one moves."[17] Attending worship organized by chaplains or soldiers was one element of how officers recorded practicing their religion. Occasionally, officers even led these services, sharing with chaplains in the work of spiritual leadership. Officers also revealed the premium they placed on church attendance by lamenting when they were unable to go.[18]

The group worship efforts of men in the 124th Illinois resulted in a truly exceptional source of insight into the content of some officers' religious beliefs. The regiment's initial contingent of officers was exceptionally devout, containing five ministers (besides the chaplain). They led prayer meetings and, after the chaplain preached on Sunday mornings, often preached additional lessons on Sunday afternoons. When the regiment's first chaplain resigned in the summer of 1863, a petition unanimously signed by the regiment's officers led to Lt. Richard Howard (a minister before the war) being appointed as the new chaplain. In addition to teaching singing, this now former officer led the organization of a regimental church, and two other officers, Capt. Henry Field and Lt. Abraham Newland, worked with him to draft formal articles of association for the congregation, among which were the following:

> We do solemnly covenant and promise with each other and before God, that we will live lives devoted to the service of our Lord Jesus Christ, following His example while here upon earth, walking as far as in us lies in all the ordinances of God's house blameless. That we will love and carefully watch over each other, reprove, rebuke and exhort, with all long-suffering and prayer, maintaining gospel discipline in our midst.
>
> That we will sustain the means of grace to the best of our ability, and labor by precept and example to bring sinners to a knowledge of the truth, by pointing them to the Lamb of God, who taketh away the sin of the world. That among special sins we will discourage and prayerfully counsel against profanity, intemperance, card-playing and all games of chance, and other kindred vices. And in general we will endeavor, by well ordered lives, to honor and glorify God, assist each other in the way to heaven, and do good among our associates.[19]

Essentially a creed, this text stands without peer as a summary of the beliefs of the officers who produced or subscribed to it (and quite a few of the 124th's officers did join the regimental church). Such statements are so rare because officers writing to wives or parents had little reason to describe beliefs their readers would already have known. Beyond revealing doctrinal views and illustrating how officers could act as religious leaders, this statement also overlaps with another way religion manifested in officers' lives: as a basis for moral behavior.[20]

Officers associated religion with moral behavior, and their efforts to live according to those standards were one of the ways they acted on their religious beliefs. In the writings of morally conscientious officers, three chief sins stood out: drinking, swearing, and playing cards. These are not the only misdeeds they ever referenced, but they are the three most commonly condemned in others or that officers made a point of saying they themselves avoided. John Quincy Adams Campbell produced several diatribes against the evils of whiskey, as well as recording an occasion where he ostentatiously dumped his whiskey ration on the ground, offending some men fond of the drink. He couched his rejection of drinking in religious terms, and when railing against the dehumanizing effects of drunkenness, he declared, "He alone who puts his trust in God, is certain that he will be able to avoid the vices of this world and live, *a man*."[21] Insofar as the values expressed in writing are concerned, officers showed little sign that war or army life led to major changes in their moral outlook. Whatever beliefs and values they voiced in the earlier phases of the war were the same ones they kept on expressing later.[22]

"Try and bring up our little ones to love and fear the Lord," Robert Steele beseeched his wife Rhoda.[23] Another way that officers evinced practical application of their beliefs was the concern they expressed for the religious and moral instruction of their children. Sylvester Gridley Beckwith discoursed at exceptional length about his children's moral instruction, writing in late March 1863 to his wife about how he hoped she would teach them "to walk in the paths of virtue & honesty & tell them of me if providence never permits me to return again. teach them to climb up the ladder of Science & above all not to disdain to labor & also to keep clear from bulls, & wild scenes, & bad company."[24] He also insisted, "that it is against my wishes that any of my babes should ever go to dances or drink liquors, or use tobacco, or to gamble."[25] Beckwith explained to his wife that he wrote this exhortation only to help her in case he should not survive to share in teaching their children himself. He also promised to write up "some requests and advices & precepts for those little lambs to follow when grown to years of accountability & understanding," which could be framed and preserved for them to read in the event he never made it home.[26] He must have followed through on this plan, for in early April he declared, "I have written some advice that I wish the children to follow if I never return & I wish you to have it put in a frame & a glass over it, but not unless I should fall & never live to get home & also teach their little minds the spirit of all of them and as many more good rules as you can & fall not into temptations yourself."[27] Beckwith's precautions for his children's posthumous moral instruction proved warranted; he was wounded at the Battle of Big Black River Bridge, 17 May 1863, and died that July without ever seeing his family again.[28]

Officers also turned to their faith when confronting death. Most obviously, they had to wrestle with the looming prospect of their own death. Beyond that, many had to live with the deaths of loved ones back home or friends in the army. Officers turned to the hope of heaven and trust in God's wise providence for comfort in these situations. Friedrich Martens remarked that the Union war effort in the winter of 1862 reminded him of Napoleon Bonaparte's infamous 1812 Russian expedition, and he looked to God for comfort as he considered the prospective casualties. He wrote that many soldiers "will not be returning home to their loved ones, instead they'll be crossing over to the great army where the Lord God will assign them good quarters; for He also loves a true soldier."[29] Zachariah Dean (a minister before the war) wrote to his wife Emily after the death of their baby: "The Lord giveth and the Lord taketh away. Blessed be the name of the Lord. I feel resigned to his will for I know that he will do all things well."[30] In his loss, Dean quoted from Job 1:21, the words of the eponymous Job reacting to the deaths of his own children. When discussing the possibility that he could die in the war, Robert Steele concluded that as comforting as it would be spend one's last moments among friends and family, "it would afford us much more satisfaction to know all is well beyond the grave. This hope I have both sure and steadfast reaching to that within the veil."[31] This hope of heaven was a source of comfort to many officers, whether living with the prospect of their own demise or facing the deaths of others.[32]

Religious faith did not make it easy to cope with death when it actually happened, however. Writing to his siblings about the sudden death by disease of his orderly, Lyman Updyke, Charles C. Ammack wrestled with his grief not just regarding Sergeant Updyke's death but at all the casualties the war brought. He lamented the loss to Updyke's wife and children, then continued, "and when I remember that thousands of just such instances are occurring every day & and the wail of the widows & orphans are heard broadcast all over our once peaceful & happy country my feelings sometimes almost rebels."[33] Ammack confessed that at times he "would be willing to have this accursed crusade against human life stopped at almost any price or any terms however dishonorable."[34] He looked to God for some meaning to all the death: "In the language of scripture The ways of God truly are misterious & past finding out."[35] As an example of God's mysterious ways, Ammack wrestled with a sense of unfairness that some of the most useless and worthless men in his company survived while good men like Updyke perished. At the close of the discussion, Ammack entrusted his orderly's death "to the justice and mercy of God."[36] A couple weeks after this sad event, three more men from his hometown died. Ammack again looked to God to make sense of their deaths. "I feel that we are in the hands of an all wise being who shapes our destiny," he wrote, "& although it may look dark to our short sighted vision yet he is able to heal all our griefs and sorrows. And though we cannot see the end of all this mystery yet I feel that our cause is right & just & it must prevail."[37] Trusting God and hoping in heaven, as so many officers did, did not in itself make the war's many losses easy to stomach.

When Henry Ankeny enlisted in the Fourth Iowa in July 1861, he left at home his pregnant wife Tina and their young daughter Jessie. Jessie died suddenly on 15 September 1861 after a brief illness. Tina wrote two days later informing Henry of their daughter's death. He revealed "the great fountain of grief that I was overpowered with" in a letter to Tina shortly after the news first reached him.[38] He insisted that God must have ultimately good purposes for this tragedy, "and if we will be faithful to our trusts in the future, he will bless us ten-fold."[39] Ankeny believed, "Jessie, my dear dear child, waits for us and in a short time we will be with her in heaven, to part no more, no more."[40] He also inquired about Jessie's burial, requesting a proper tombstone and fence around it, and he offered to resign if his wife wished it: "I will leave that for you to decide, for I will sacrifice everything for you, my own dear Tina. . . . Write to me what you would prefer to do, as I will be guided entirely by your decision."[41] The day after this letter, Ankeny produced a second grief-filled letter to his wife, and on the third day, a third such letter. Despite his confusion and heartache over his daughter's death, he continued to express trust in God's providence and hope for the future: "Oh God, I ask, why is this? But why do I ask? Thy will be done and we must respond, so mote it be,[42] to the power which is superior to our will."[43] He again looked for comfort to the prospect of reuniting with his daughter in heaven. In his assurance of future blessing, Ankeny seems to have been preaching to himself as much as trying to comfort his wife. He also begged Tina's forgiveness for having joined the army and leaving her to face Jessie's death alone. "My head feels so heavy with pain, that I can scarcely see," Ankeny wrote.[44] In his third and last meditation on Jessie's death, Ankeny persisted in the same themes of trust and hope as his previous letters, but his overall tone seemed more at peace. He mused to Tina: "Let us forever remember the past, in love that liveth for all time and look to the future, for that peace of mind and body that God alone can bestow."[45] These three letters, written over three consecutive days, provide a candid look at how Ankeny's religious beliefs strengthened him as he responded to tragedy and helped him cope with his grief. His trust in a good and superintending God and his belief in heaven were central to the way he dealt with the loss of his child.

Battlegrounds and long marches did not always facilitate theological musings, but officers occasionally found opportunity to record ruminations regarding weighty topics such as God's nature or His purpose for the war. A week after the Battle of Shiloh, when the area around Pittsburg Landing was a horrific battleground strewn with the dead, Z. Payson Shumway wrote to his wife Hattie of sitting up late and enjoying a particularly beautiful night. "Surely the Character of God must be very lovely, shining as it does through all his works, the twinkling stars & the blue sky & the clear calm light of the moon, all are like Him," Shumway declared.[46] Edward Jesup Wood suggested there must be a providential purpose behind the war: "This war is for the purification and sanctification of the nation and the iron must enter the soul of the North as it has entered the South before its wise purposes can be accomplished."[47] Wood theorized that the Northern people as a whole had not been sufficiently self-sacrificial yet and suggested that they needed to be more willing to give up material prosperity for the cause of liberty before God would grant victory. Clint Loudon likewise contemplated God's purpose for the war, observing in July 1862 that "sooner or later, Providence in the end will beat all the politicians. God's work is never left undone."[48] He thought the war might be prolonged because the Northern people deserved to suffer for their sins, but the Union cause was just and God would eventually grant it victory. At the intersection of faith and war, these men applied their religious beliefs to make sense of the events around them.[49]

John Quincy Adams Campbell incorporated religion into two reflections on the nature and course of the war, penned in his diary about a year apart. In the fall of 1862, alluding to the preliminary Emancipation Proclamation that President Lincoln had issued a month prior, Campbell declared, "I trust (now, that we are fighting for *Liberty* and Union and not Union and *Slavery*) that the God of battles will be with us. I feel confident that I am fighting for a righteous case, from true motives and whether successful or not, I will fight on and leave the result to God."[50] Just over a year later, as he anticipated victory in the impending fight near Chattanooga, Campbell posited that success on the battlefield would mean little to the course of the war. "Every day my conviction becomes firmer that the hand of *God* is in this," he explained, "and that in spite of victories and advantages he will deny us Peace unless we grant to others the liberties we ask for ourselves—'break every yoke and let the oppressed go free.'"[51] He prayed for God's mercy on the nation and predicted the Union would not triumph until it "has been purged with fire."[52] Victory for the Union was in God's hands, Campbell believed, and depended on embracing a righteous cause—namely, ending the sin of slavery.

A trio of epistles from Jake Ritner, penned in the summer of 1864 amid the Atlanta Campaign, reveal one believer's struggle to reconcile biblical teaching with his own feelings about his wartime enemies. In June, Ritner scoffed to his wife Emeline at how the rebels could be such "hypocritical rascals" as to fight in the day and then hold prayer meetings at night, the sound of their songs and prayers sometimes carrying across the battlefield.[53] The affronted Ritner continued: "The rascals! I wonder what kind of deity they must fix up for themselves who will hear the prayers of liars and drunkards and slave holders and *traitors*."[54] The rebel cause was so obviously wicked in Ritner's eyes that he puzzled over how Southerners could possibly deceive themselves into thinking God would sanction it.

Ritner fell ill late in late June and was sent by train back to an officers' hospital atop Lookout Mountain. The train just ahead of Ritner's carried rebel prisoners, and at each stop, Ritner found "a great deal of satisfaction" to see crowds of grief-stricken women turn out to greet the prisoners.[55] Some found their loved ones among the captives, and others learned for the first time that their family members or friends had been killed or wounded. "And the way they cried and slung their snot around, was a sight," Ritner gloated, adding, "I enjoyed it hugely; it made me feel good all over. I felt like taunting them and adding to their misery if I could."[56] Following this schadenfreude, Ritner addressed his wife Emeline:

> Now I expect you think these were not very Christian like feelings. I don't know about that. But they came very natural to me. And when I thought how I had to leave my own dear wife and family and spend years of the best part of my life, undergoing dangers and hardships of all kinds on account of their accursed treason, I could not help it. And then when I thought how I have shortened my own days and seen my best friends and nearest relatives lose their lives in endeavoring to sustain the government which these rebels were trying to destroy, I felt that I could see the direst calamity befall them with the utmost complacency. Indeed if Christianity requires love such enemies I acknowledge myself woefully deficient. I can't and I won't.[57]

Ritner clearly implies awareness of such Bible passages as Jesus' exhortation to "Love your enemies" (Matthew 5:44) but found his own feelings clashing with the biblical command.

If Ritner seemed at least slightly uncertain about the propriety of hating the rebels in July, by August he had quelled his doubts. Based on Ritner's comments, it appears Emeline's mother Eleanor Bereman had asked her son-in-law about this very issue, to which he responded: "When I think what this war has cost our family in blood and suffering, I detest more than ever the wicked traitors and their more inhuman abettors in the North. I do not think your feelings on the subject are unchristian. I think they are very right and natural. We are not required to love and pray for Public enemies and traitors. David and all the old prophets expressed their hatred and detestation of such men and prayed for their speedy destruction."[58] Ritner's conclusion that hatred is permissible if one's enemy is awful enough is less than orthodox, but the tension he acknowledged between war and moral teachings like "Love your neighbor as yourself" (Leviticus 19:18) is one with which Christians throughout the centuries have grappled. Ritner's struggle on this point reflects another of the ways officers attempted to make practical application of religion to their lives.

Numerous officers proclaimed their trust in God and expressed themselves in the vocabulary of Christianity. Wartime letters were not a place for creedal statements; there is no way to administer a test of orthodoxy and quantify how many of the Army of the Tennessee's officers were, by some broad definition, "Christian." Nonetheless, their faith appears in the way officers wrote of prayer and providence, quoted scripture and hymns, and gave thanks for success and safety. They sometimes wrestled with how to apply and practice their beliefs amid the challenges that the war imposed. Their religious faith served as a source of fortitude and of guidance in difficult circumstances, as well as providing hope of survival and a better postwar future—or hope of heaven if they did not survive. Their faith appears to have remained strong throughout the war. Religious officers stayed religious throughout their terms of service, continued expressing themselves in religious terms, and kept drawing strength from their faith down to the war's victorious conclusion.

CHAPTER 4

A Great Big Heart

"Men may have great respect for dignity in a superior, but dignity alone does not draw to itself much of love and affection," a soldier of the Twelfth Wisconsin wrote when remembering his colonel.[1] What did garner soldiers' affections was for their officers to practice genuine care for them. Many of the Army of the Tennessee's officers did care for their men, both in the sense that they felt concern and regard for their soldiers and in the sense that they provided for their needs and looked after their best interests. Officers were responsible for making sure their men had food to eat, clothes without holes, shoes on their feet, blankets at night, and weapons that functioned. (The lack of shoes seems to have been a particular problem for an army that marched as far as the Army of the Tennessee did over the course of the war.)

Officers were, in a sense, advocates for their men. They personally worked to supply their soldiers' needs and also endeavored to placate the men when various necessities were unavailable. They took pains to pace their units on long marches and give them rest during times of intense heat. They worked to have deserving subordinates promoted. When officers resigned or were transferred, they attempted to ensure that their successors were trustworthy and responsible. They provided reading material for their men. They dispensed advice (as seen when one young soldier reported to his sister that he was taking up drinking tea and giving up coffee because his captain advised that tea was better for him than coffee). They made sure their men bathed somewhat regularly. Officers oversaw burial details, which could include procuring coffins, selecting burial sites, and conducting the actual burial services. Rarely, they might even attempt to ship a man's mortal remains home. They grumbled (at least partially) on behalf of their soldiers when newspapers failed to give due credit for successes. When the army did not get paid, they lent money to subordinates facing financial need. They helped soldiers get their pay sent back home to their families. Officers let tired men ride their horses and lent their coats to cold men. They tried to give men exercise, set up healthy campsites, and secure furloughs for the sick. Officers who earned the regard of their men were sometimes recognized through gifts; swords seem to have been the default present. There were exceptions. Officers who did not treat their men kindly (like the colonel who insisted on drilling his men in the worst of the afternoon sun) earned ill will. While not all officers were paragons of benevolence, many displayed compassion for their men and diligently performed the caretaker function inherent in their role as officers.[2]

Caring for one's subordinates was a tremendously complex task fundamental to the role of being an officer. Captain Charles Dana Miller of the Seventy-Sixth Ohio expounded on the role of company commander in his memoir. "I would like to record here my opinion," he wrote, "based upon observation and experience, that a captain commanding a company has the hardest task, the most dangerous position and, I may add, the greatest responsibility of any officer below the rank of colonel."[3] He proceeded to summarize the myriad ways a company commander cared for his soldiers, adding that a captain must take care not only of men but of all government property in his company's possession. Every lost rifle, spade, and tent was charged to him personally. Miller claimed to have faced moments where he had to choose between taking care of a soldier or preserving some piece of government equipment, choosing the soldier, and then literally paying the price for lost or damaged gear. Other officers shared similar thoughts about how all-consuming it was to take care of dozens or hundreds of men. Setting up a campsite properly had ramifications for safety; without due care, for example, a campfire might spread out of control and menace not only the men who started it but every other nearby regiment. Edward Jesup Wood once explained to his wife Jane that he had been unable to write because his "time was so completely taken up getting located in our new camp and the thousand things that you know occur to beset and worry a Regimental commander."[4] Luther Cowan likewise mentioned that it was difficult to write home while "having forty things to do at once, and so many men to talk to at the same time. More importunities to listen to than an old woman with sixteen young ones."[5] Providing this attention was a round-the-clock job.[6]

"It is not the Battle that kills the men, I think there is five dies of disease when there is one killed by the Enemy," Robert Steele wrote to his parents.[7] He correctly captured the massive problem that disease posed to Civil War armies. Consequently, one of the areas in which officers took care of their men involved ill health. Officers knew morale and combat effectiveness were directly related to health and wrote frequently about how healthy their companies or regiments were. They pondered the causes of ill health and what they could do about them. They showed concern for sick and wounded soldiers and lamented those who died. Everything from smallpox to scurvy to getting shot could disable soldiers, and their officers took great interest in seeing they got proper treatment. Officers worried over those they thought would die and fumed at their powerlessness to do anything about it. In February 1863, the thirty-six healthy men in 1st Lt. Robert Steele's company made it one of the largest companies in his entire regiment; more than half of the Twenty-Third Wisconsin was laid low by illness and about fifty had died. Colonel Robert B. Latham noted in May 1863 that about two hundred men in his 106th Illinois were sick. Henry Miller Culbertson mentioned in mid-July 1863 that the Sixteenth Wisconsin had only sixty-four men in the entire regiment fit for duty, "and every day lessens the number."[8] That August, Capt. Robert Whittleton reported he had only ten men fit for duty in his entire company, stating, "Men who never have been sick before since they started out are now coming down with disease."[9] When writing about illnesses in his Thirty-First Indiana, Capt. George Harvey would distinguish the severity of the sickness by whether a man was merely unfit for duty, "*seriously*" ill, or, worst of all, "*dangerously*" ill.[10] Harley Wayne attempted to comfort his wife Ellen, who was fretting that her husband would be killed in battle, by pointing out that sickness would kill far more men than combat. Wayne was entirely correct about this, although one questions the wisdom of pointing out that fact while his wife was worrying about him dying.[11]

Officers were often frustrated by their inability to do more to care for ill soldiers. They sought proper medical care but frequently complained that the army's medical services were deficient. "The treatment the sick get on the boats would kill a well man in a short time," Lieutenant Steele declared.[12] Henry Ankeny found it incongruous to see "a great deal of sickness in the army and very little medicine. There is a great fault committed somewhere."[13] Oscar Jackson recorded early in the Atlanta Campaign: "I have much cause of complaint on account of the manner in which sick and exhausted men are cared for. In fact frequently no care whatever. No ambulances with the regiment on march and men who should be sent to hospital are forced to trudge along with the column. The Medical Department of the Army is most shamefully managed."[14]

Outside of dispensing an extra whiskey ration, officers could do little except show sympathy for their suffering men. As Joseph Stockton wrote in September 1862, "I pitied the poor sick soldiers but could do nothing for them but let them see I was willing if I had the power."[15] Soldiers too ill to move got left behind, causing officers even more stress as they worried their men would be neglected without their personal oversight. Theoretically, officers could try to get deathly ill soldiers discharged, but in practice officers often found this avenue closed. Captain Charles C. Ammack vented his frustration in a February 1863 letter to his siblings. Six men of Ammack's company, including one relative and four men from his hometown, had recently died of disease. The relative, Lyman Updike, had perished despite Ammack's best efforts to get him sent home, and Ammack reported that many other sick men likewise died before the government could process discharge paperwork for them. Many people, he wrote, supposed "that if a person gets to be Commander of a company he can do almost anything he pleases but nothing is farther from the fact."[16] If he could have his way, he would have discharged a number of his men the next day. The situation was enough to make him ponder resigning, "but there is my pledge to the boys that if they would go I would stay with them and I am not quite ready to violate that pledge."[17] Numerous officers shared this sort of frustration at their inability to do more for their sick soldiers.[18]

Many officers gave thought to the causes of ill health among their men and explored potential means of averting sickness. Writing to his wife Harriet, Luther Cowan blamed soldiers' sickness on "carelessness and gluttony," adding, "If a great many had not India rubber stomachs they would surely burst."[19] Z. Payson Shumway would have agreed, blaming too much food and too little exercise for sickness. Others likewise linked activity with health. DeWitt Clinton Loudon observed that soldiers "are always healthier on the march then when lying in camp."[20] Edward Jesup Wood reached the same conclusion. (It is probable that sanitary issues, such as contamination of water supplies by seepage from latrines, better explain the correlation between camp and illness that these officers observed.) Another time, Lieutenant Colonel Loudon wrote that "ten days of dry sunshiny weather will cure most of the sick," although he mentioned new recruits required a time of seasoning to adjust.[21] Other officers also recognized that new recruits were especially vulnerable to disease. Perhaps the most entertaining of all theories to explain sickness was Henry A. Kircher's view that regiments of Germans were healthier than those composed of Americans or Irishmen. However medically dubious such ideas were, they stand as part of officers' efforts to care for their men and ensure their good health.[22]

Tending to dying soldiers could especially bring out officers' sense of compassion for their men. "I heartily wish the war was over although I will not flinch from my duty yet many families lose their relatives in this rebellion," James Balfour wrote to his son (Balfour himself died not long afterward).[23] Captain Charles Wills pitied James Colton, a soldier in his company and "a real good young man and has a wife," as Colton appeared to be dying in early February 1863.[24] He wrote to his sister: "You don't know how much I love these men under me. Not as individuals many of them, but as soldiers, of my company, for whose actions, and in a measure, health, I am responsible. Something, I suppose, like the love of a parent for his children. I never thought I could feel half the interest in the welfare of my brother man as I do now for these men."[25] Colton, it turned out, would survive, but Wills's feelings for dying soldiers remained relevant because he lost his first soldier soon after, George Trader, to a combination of typhus and measles. Wills lost his second man in early March, Pvt. James Convers, and he continued to chronicle the ill health and deaths of his men throughout the war. Thinking on the many men of the 103rd Illinois who died of disease, he remarked in September 1863, "The consolation is that these folks would all have to die sometime, and they ought to be glad to get rid of their sickly lives, and get credit as patriots for the sacrifice."[26] In ten months' time, disease had reduced his own Company G from seventy-two men to thirty-one (though not all died; some were discharged or left behind).[27]

Henry Ankeny vividly revealed the pain of losing soldiers. On 27 November 1863, the Fourth Iowa charged up Taylor Ridge in northern Georgia to drive off some rebels, "but in doing so we met with severe and irreparable loss."[28] Ankeny described to his wife Tina how his Company H had two men killed. Ankeny felt quite distressed for late Sgt. Rufus Campbell's mother, "who is again called in old age to mourn for her second martyr, who have so nobly dedicated their lives to their country."[29] The prospect of writing to tell her of the death of her son so demoralized Captain Ankeny that he asked Tina to pass on the news personally and spare him from having to break it himself. He had no address for Corporal Moore's mother and asked Tina to investigate how the sad news could be transmitted. Ankeny next listed the wounded by name and noted the nature of each wound; happily, he expected all of them to recover. Then he returned to the dead: "Yesterday was as hard a fight as we were ever in. I hope never again to be called on to report another loss, but God's will be done."[30] He wrote again four days later to ask Tina to share the news that he had arranged a proper burial for Campbell and Moore:

> We placed them side by side in one coffin, with a headboard to mark their last resting place on earth. Beside them are fourteen men of the 76 Ohio and Duncan, of the 4th Iowa. All of these men fell in a perfect line, as though they were on a dress parade, and their faces to the foe. I hope to God I may never see the like again, and then again some of our very best appear to be the victims. The d—d cowards, of which we have some, escape. Where they are buried is secluded, and their bodies will never be molested until the Great Day.[31]

Ankeny also collected whatever money each man possessed or was owed and whatever possessions they had so he could send them to the dead men's families. Another of his soldiers, George Wolf, perished during the Atlanta Campaign. The nonveterans of the regiment had been due to muster out of the service relatively soon, leaving Ankeny to reflect glumly, "Poor George expected to go home in November, but he went sooner, and I hope to a better one."[32]

Other officers likewise acknowledged the weight of having their men die. David F. Vail strove "that no one of old Company K found himself in a place of needless danger through my advice or command."[33] John Quincy Adams Campbell was sitting near a man who was struck in the head by the accidental discharge of a revolver; the soldier died within a couple hours, and Campbell declared, "Nothing, not even the horrors of the battlefield— ever gave me such a shock as this."[34] Alexander K. Ewing wrestled with the death of a man from his company during the Yazoo Pass Expedition. From aboard a steamboat on the Tallahatchie River, Ewing wrote to his parents that Cpl. Wright L. Nield had died: "In loosing Corporal Nield Co 'D' loosed one of her best soldiers and one we all regret to loose from among us, but we must abide by the fortunes of War as we well know some have to fall. His friends and relatives can have the consolation that he gave up his life in a glorious and noble cause, and that too, while in an engagement with the enemy and in a place where shot & shell fell thick and fast arround him never flinching but standing to his post untill his right arm was carried away by a cannot shot."[35] One day during the Siege of Vicksburg, amid a bombardment, Col. Manning F. Force was told a soldier wanted to talk to him. Force went and found a young man lying on the ground, "pale and speechless—there was a crimson hole in his breast. As I knelt by his side, he looked wistfully at me."[36] Force attempted to offer comfort, saying, "'We must all die some time, and the man is happy who meets death in the discharge of duty. You have done your whole duty well.' It was all he wanted. His eyes brightened, a smile flickered on his lips," and within moments the young man was dead.[37] Jake Ritner revealed his own sense of loss in a June 1863 missive to his wife: "All the best friends I had here have been killed or died."[38] Death in war troubled Ritner, though he accepted it as necessary. "It is really sad," he wrote in November 1863, "to think how fast the war uses up men, and what a fearful destruction of human life, and what sorrow and misery follow in its track. But the end justifies the means; I feel that no sacrifice is too great to be made, and no loss can equal that of our country and government."[39] Throughout the war, these officers' responses to the deaths of their soldiers revealed an unwavering sense of concern.

Officers displayed concern and sympathy toward their fellow soldiers in numerous other situations. Soon after the Fifteenth Illinois assembled in May 1861, Harley Wayne found one of his soldiers "crying this morning but he says he will get over that I tried to comfort him but had hard work to keep from joining him."[40] Marching dozens or hundreds of miles across enemy territory, as the Army of the Tennessee frequently did, wore out shoes and made it hard to obtain replacements. Officers sometimes mentioned a lack of clothing, but much more frequently they lamented how their men had to go barefoot. Captain Henry S. Nourse remembered in late September 1864 meeting some US soldiers who had been held at the Confederate prison camp at Andersonville, Georgia, before being exchanged. The encounter moved him so deeply that he floundered for words: "any pen must ever utterly fail to adequately convey such conception of the horrors of that prison-pen as those received who, gazing into the wan faces of the emaciated victims, listened to the unvarnished stories that fell from their quivering lips, when just relieved from its tortures."[41] Neither harsh wartime experience nor their positions of authority deprived these officers of their ability to care for their subordinates.[42]

When Charles Dana Miller was offered a position as a staff officer, he struggled with the reality that this would mean leaving his company, the men with whom he had enlisted and whose captain he had become. He went to his soldiers and explained that this new position as a brigade inspector would be much easier for him in light of poor health he had been facing but would take him away from Company C. He asked the men whether they thought he should accept the job. "They looked at my emaciated form and replied that for my good I had better accept: but they made me promise to use my influence to have a good officer placed in command," Miller recorded.[43] He effectively handpicked his replacement, going to his colonel and asking that Lt. Zebulon P. Evans of the Seventy-Sixth Ohio's Company A be transferred to lead Company C. The colonel granted his request, and Miller's men appreciated his effort to give them a good commander. Ironically, the most unhappy person in this story was Lieutenant Evans, who did not wish to leave his own company to lead Miller's.[44]

Benjamin Grierson endured great difficulties to get weapons for his cavalrymen. Having unsuccessfully tried various means to arm his men, he jested in late March 1862 that his soldiers "had no *arms* except which God had given us naturally and sabres."[45] He tried to obtain captured rebel weapons. He also sought assistance from Illinois governor Richard Yates. At first Grierson was just trying to acquire arms for his battalion. Then Col. Thomas Cavanaugh left the service, and in April 1862 Grierson succeeded him as colonel, becoming responsible for trying to get weapons for the entire Sixth Illinois Cavalry. Finally, later in April, the newly minted colonel heard that a shipment of carbines had arrived at Cairo, Illinois, and he approached General Sherman himself for an order to the quartermaster:

> The general quickly answered: "No use, Grierson, no use at all. There are no arms there." But I persisted, and the general . . . wrote the desired order. Upon handing it to me, he said "there, there you won't get any." Proceeding at once to Cairo, I presented the order to the quartermaster, who said, "no carbines here, issued the last yesterday." But assuring him that my information made it clear to my mind that the desired arms were there, I prevailed upon him to go with me. Upon search, we found 150 new Sharps carbines that had in some manner been shoved aside and overlooked in the issue made the day before.[46]

The quartermaster was still reluctant, but Grierson talked him into handing over the rifles. It was not enough to equip the whole regiment, but it was a good start and a refreshing change from months of service without receiving any weapons.[47]

Colonel George E. Bryant's warm relationship with the men of his Twelfth Wisconsin became the subject of many stories and exemplified the kind of positive relationship officers and soldiers could enjoy. Bryant's men nicknamed him "the Little Corporal," and though he was loud and gruff and sometimes rather peculiar, they nonetheless grew quite fond of him.[48] The men soon learned "that under his rough exterior there beat a great big heart that was so full of human sympathy with his men that he would grant us any favor he could consistently with the military discipline necessary in the regiment."[49] On one occasion, Colonel Bryant returned to camp to find a man bucked and gagged in the guardhouse. (Bucking was a form punishment in which a man was bound with his knees against his chest and his arms wrapped about them, with a rod running under his knees and over his arms, inflicting intense discomfort.) After learning from the officer of the day that the man had been wildly, uncontrollably drunk, the colonel took a knife and cut the man free. The surprised soldier jumped to his feet in relief as the colonel "looked him in the eye and merely said, 'Go to your tent now, and behave yourself.'"[50] The man caused no further commotion.

While the Twelfth was stationed in Kansas in early 1862, one rainy night Bryant mysteriously ordered the whole regiment to assemble in front of his tent: "We could not think what he could want of us out in the pitchy, rainy darkness, at that time of night."[51] Just inside his tent, the colonel stood holding a newspaper. He broke the news that there had been a major battle at Pittsburg Landing, Tennessee, and knowing that many in his regiment had friends in the Wisconsin regiments that participated, he called the Twelfth together to read the newspaper report to them: "When he came to the long list of the killed and wounded, his voice more than once trembled with emotion, and the tears rolled down his cheeks into his yellow whiskers as here and there he came across the name of one of his friends. For the same reason, we boys stood, unmindful of the falling rain, dropping tears of grief when he read names that had been familiar and dear to us back in Wisconsin. . . . A regiment and its Colonel silently wept together."[52] Colonel Bryant also regularly played cricket with his soldiers, proving himself quite skilled at the game. In an incident from late 1862, Bryant once ordered that no man should be allowed out of the camp without a pass, and he strictly charged the camp guard to enforce this rule. One night, just after dark, the colonel started to go for a walk and upon reaching the boundary of camp was forcefully commanded to halt. The guard explained he was just trying to follow orders, at which Bryant smiled "and then, turning his face toward the camp, shouted so that all in the regiment could hear him, '*Adjutant! adjutant! bring me a pass! this darned guard won't let me out*,'" evoking roars of laughter from the entire camp.[53] Such were representative tales of how Bryant endeared himself to his regiment.[54]

The author of the foregoing stories, a soldier of the Twelfth Wisconsin, had one more personal memory of Colonel Bryant to share. In July 1864 during the Atlanta Campaign, Hosea Rood had been grazed in the arm by a bullet, leaving him in a good deal of pain from the swelling, in addition to the normal exhaustion of campaigning. Rood was on guard at the front one night, watching for rebel attacks and struggling mightily to stay awake. He dozed off: "Just then someone shook me, and said, 'Wake up, Bub, wake up!' I was, indeed, startled, and got upon my feet. A man was walking rapidly away from on top of the works, but I did not see who it was."[55] The next guard down the line informed Rood that the man who awakened him was none other than the colonel. Rood became quite anxious—his commanding officer had caught him asleep while on guard at the front line. "I supposed Colonel Bryant might have had me shot—had he been like some other officers."[56] The colonel never spoke a word about the incident. Bryant, Rood gratefully declared, "knew how to sympathize with one of his boys who was sick and wounded."[57]

Officers' words matched their actions, displaying their regard for their soldiers through praise and statements of affection. They wrote home to boast of how courageous, patriotic, or disciplined their men were or simply to state how fond they were of their soldiers. The way soldiers endured harsh conditions and went without the comforts of ordinary life consistently evoked expressions of respect from officers. "I didn't know that I could take as much interest in any strange humans as I feel in these men of my company," wrote Charles Wills in September 1863.[58] Jake Ritner boasted in October 1864 that the men of his company were "just the bravest, best, and noblest set of men in this army. They will do their whole duty all the time, and I am proud to be the leader of such a company."[59] Observing that many soldiers who looked forward to victory and going home would not survive to do so, or would only make it back maimed or crippled, Capt. Luther Cowan wrote: "It makes me feel very sad to look over the fields, covered with brave and generous men, devoting their lives to their country. Most people think that the army is made up of course [*sic*], hard hearted, thoughtless men who never saw or thought of anything nice, or refined but those who think this are badly mistaken. There are bad and thoughtless men in the army to be sure, but in proportion to their number a braver, nobler, more refined and generous set of men are not in the world."[60] He acknowledged soldiers' vices, such as drinking and playing cards. However, he suggested sympathetically that men often turned to such pursuits only to keep themselves from dwelling too much on "things that would corrode their minds and be even worse for them than their indulgence in these things."[61] Z. Payson Shumway offered a similar perspective on how men dealt with the war, musing in his diary, "The better part of a soldiers life is *dreamed* away. He dreams of home & the loved ones there until he half imagines himself there all the while forgetting the stern realities of his situation which at any moment are liable to break in upon him."[62] Through such direct statements of respect, affection, and empathy, officers revealed their care for the men they commanded.[63]

Many officers similarly commended the character of the men they led. Popular opinion held that being a soldier "hardens the heart and dulls the sympathies," Luther Cowan explained to his daughter Molly, but "no opinion can be further from a correct one."[64] Cowan claimed to have seen more and greater displays of kindness among the army than he had witnessed in all his life before enlisting. Not even the crucible of combat could strip away this underlying sense of compassion. Contrariwise, when soldiers prepared for battle, Cowan averred they did not feel "savage or barbarous."[65] The pause before battle was the time the soldier "feels the most generous and kindly impulses of which his nature is capable."[66] On a related note, Henry Culbertson held that the army was "no place for a man to get wild,"[67] and Charles Ammack observed that "seven months today have now passed since I became a soldier but I don't know as I feel anymore savage than I did when I enlisted."[68] Of course, this rosy picture of righteous soldiers was not universal. Dissenting from such views, Henry Hole claimed there was "no place I ever saw where the bad passions of men are drawn out like they are in camp life."[69] Officers' concern with the moral well-being of their men was another manifestation of the care so many of them practiced for their soldiers.

Throughout their service, officers took care of, and felt care toward, the men under their command. Positive relations between officers and men appear to have been the norm in the Army of the Tennessee, though that did not mean the men were above mischief. Charles Wills reported how soldiers discovered that putting green wood in a fire could create a sound like a rifle shot, as the heated sap expanded and burst. Soldiers also could generate artificial artillery sounds by putting half-filled canteens, tightly sealed, into a fire and waiting for steam to explode the canteen. The army had firm orders against unauthorized firing, a rule for which the officers were held accountable. In light of these supposed weapons discharges, one night in September 1863, many officers were assigned to patrol the camp in order to clamp down on the gunfire. "This, of course, tickles the men hugely, and from their beds in their tents they have been talking over the duties of a sentry for the benefit of their officer's ears. The devilment that soldiers cannot contrive must be unearthly," Wills concluded.[70] Notwithstanding such pranks, the Army of the Tennessee's officers remained cordial and socially close to their men throughout their service. I saw few signs of class consciousness or other types of elitism among Army of the Tennessee officers; indeed, they actively condemned putting on airs of superiority and never ceased to value their relationships with their men. War was horrible, and officers never lost sight of the suffering it entailed, expressing compassion for many suffering people (such as Black or white civilians) but most especially for their own soldiers.

CHAPTER 5

The Daily Grind

"As each day passes, it brings with it each time the same dull monotonous routine of daily duty & besides *that* no news & no nothing," Z. Payson Shumway wrote to his wife Hattie during an especially uneventful period of railroad guarding in February 1863.[1] Active campaigns could involve almost daily movement and combat, but the rest of the time, officers reported periods of routine, monotony, and boredom, in which the only day-to-day variations involved the weather. Common activities between campaigns included drilling, inspections, and reviews. At all times, there were guards to supervise. Officers also had a perennial responsibility to maintain discipline, keeping their men well behaved and punishing troublemakers. Officers sometimes became eager for the start of active campaigning just for the change of pace. No one had enlisted to protect train tracks in an unknown southern hamlet, and while they accepted pauses as necessary, officers chafed at long stretches of inaction that did not seem to advance final Union victory.

They also recognized that the army tended to be healthier on the move than when resting in camp for long periods of time, giving them another reason to favor action. Charles Wills sarcastically described going into long-term camp as entering a "headquarters of red-tapeism" and "the Elysium of the enlisted men, and purgatory of company commanders."[2] While stationed at Jackson, Tennessee, Wills wrote to his sister, "You certainly should not complain of my neglect, in writing no more than once in ten days while we are quartered at such an intolerably stupid place as this, for there really have not been two incidents occurred worthy of notice, since we pitched our tents on this ground."[3] Officers wanted to spend their military service doing things that would help win the war. Unsatisfying though they were, routine duties such as drill, guard duty, and enforcing discipline occupied much of officers' wartime experience.[4]

Officers' daily routines were largely similar, though while the army was in camp it could adhere more strictly to a schedule than while facing the enemy on a campaign. With remarkable detail, Henry Otis Dwight recalled his Twentieth Ohio's regularly scheduled activities, which he noted the regiment adopted soon after enlistment and then "continued throughout the war except when actually on the march."[5] At six o'clock each morning the drums played reveille and everyone scrambled awake for a roll call, "buttoning our last buttons en route, like college students on the way to prayers."[6] At 6:30 A.M., they practiced squad drill, in which each company broke into groups of five or six men. After an hour of that, they got half an hour to eat breakfast. About 8:00 A.M. was sick call, when unwell soldiers could present themselves to the regimental surgeon for treatment or to be excused from further duty. Men assigned to serve as guards that day hustled off to the parade ground by 8:30 to join other units from the brigade with the same responsibility. Anyone not detailed to guard duty for the day spent the hour cleaning their quarters and sweeping the streets of their company's camp. They spent the balance of the morning engaged in company drill, before another roll call at noon and eating "dinner."[7] They resumed drilling at 1:00 P.M., spending a couple hours in regimental drill. Late in the afternoon, around 4:30 or 5:00 P.M., they held dress parade and yet another roll call. That marked the end of the day's work; after that they ate supper. Tattoo and the day's final roll call took place at 9:00 P.M., after which everyone was to go to bed, with a drum signaling lights out at 9:30. Other men reported following a substantially similar schedule while their regiments were in camp. (One officer reported that officers were exempt from the lights-out rule.)[8]

The daily camp schedule of each regiment would have varied, but a focus on drill was very much the norm. In the mid-nineteenth century, the limitations of both weapons and command and control technology made massed formations of soldiers a logical, practical way to fight. Close formations concentrated firepower and kept groups of soldiers near enough that officers had at least some chance of effectively directing their men during combat and averting total chaos. Soldiers and officers alike required a great deal of practice to respond to commands and perform maneuvers correctly and quickly under pressure. Officers were responsible for ensuring their men received proper instruction in these matters. Company drill was just that, individual companies (theoretically units of a hundred men but in practice routinely below that for most of the war). Battalion drill involved a plurality of companies, and of course regimental drill brought all ten companies of a regiment together for practice. Less frequently, larger organizations such as brigades (two or more regiments) or even divisions (two or more brigades) held drill together.

Drill could last for several hours at a time; officers often drilled men in the morning, gave a rest in the hot afternoon, and drilled again in the evening before nightfall. Drill consisted of practice at giving and following commands and moving soldiers in massed formations; it did not include practice using weapons. This study turned up exactly three references to the holding of target practice, implying that efforts to cultivate marksmanship were rare. The frequency of drills would drop off dramatically once active campaigning began but would resume when the army stayed in the same place for an extended time. Bad weather was another factor that could prevent drilling. Benjamin H. Grierson explained in doggerel:

"No drilling has been done, since Wednesday last,
Had we tried, in the mud we'd still be fast,
To be drilling out in the pouring rain,
Would be a *trick* neither pleasant nor Sane,
When the weather permits, tis certain I,
To drill my men, will certainly try."[9]

Not even holidays distracted Grierson from drilling; he drilled his regiment on Christmas Day 1861 before going into town to enjoy a turkey dinner. When a regiment resided in barracks (a rare event after the army left the Northern states), officers sometimes tried to drill inside the barracks when weather was bad.[10]

Most officers began their service ignorant of military tactics. Some had served in three-month regiments right after war began, a few of the older men were veterans of the Mexican War, and a miniscule handful had attended West Point, but the vast majority of the Army of the Tennessee's officers had much to learn before they were capable of conducting drill and instructing their men. Grierson served as unofficial aide-de-camp to Gen. Benjamin Prentiss for several months, and he devoted his spare time to studying "the tactics of the various arms of the service, army regulations, military science, law, strategy, and especially the topography of the country southward."[11] This study served Grierson well when he ended up becoming major of the Sixth Illinois Cavalry; indeed, he quickly discovered he was the most knowledgeable officer in the regiment. Other officers similarly reported poring over tactical manuals and army regulations to give themselves the basic foundation needed to train their soldiers. Some regiments organized classes or drills to teach new officers about their job, but such practices were not universal. Early drilling was awkward and even comical, but successfully performing maneuvers built confidence in both officers and men. Officers who failed to master drill paid a price for their lack of diligence. Col. David Stuart relied entirely on Lt. Col. Oscar Malmborg to drill the Fifty-Fifth Illinois and never bothered to learn the commands himself (a Swedish immigrant, Malmborg had some military education in his native country and had served in the Mexican War). Stuart lost his men's respect as he fell far behind them in military knowledge. On the rare occasions that Stuart did attempt to issue commands, his mistakes were obvious to all and this "lack of technical training generated a species of contempt always fatal to the respect due a field officer."[12] Besides being relevant on the battlefield, drill was part of how officers and soldiers gained confidence in themselves and each other.[13]

Inspections, dress parades, and reviews tested the efficacy of soldiers' training. Inspections dealt with the condition of camps, uniforms, and gear. In dress parades or reviews, units put on a performance, showing off their prowess at following commands and maneuvering. These activities could involve anything from a regiment up to an entire army corps (an organization of two or more divisions). An officer of the 124th Illinois recalled his regiment's first attempt at dress parade thusly: "The awkwardness of that occasion will never be forgotten."[14] Success in inspections and reviews was a great source of satisfaction to both officers and men. When the Forty-Fifth Illinois received high praise in the report of an inspector general who was a regular army officer, Luther Cowan beamed at the validation of his long-held belief in the Forty-Fifth's superiority over other regiments. This report was doubly sweet because it came from an officer of the regular army: "Everybody knows that regular army officers won't say anything favorable of volunteer soldiers if they can avoid it."[15] Displays of martial proficiency sometimes took on a competitive edge as officers boasted of their respective units. When the Thirty-First and 124th Illinois staged a competition, the colonels of each regiment ordered paper collars to spruce up their men's appearance, but only the 124th's collars arrived, giving it a crucial advantage (or so the regimental historians of the Thirty-First believed). When Edward Jesup Wood's Forty-Eighth Indiana participated in a division review shortly before the Atlanta Campaign, Wood outfitted his regiment in white gloves to give them a stylish edge over the rest of their division. (One man reported that many officers dressed up only for parade, dispensing with their shoulder straps and other finery the rest of time and looking indistinguishable from privates.) The competitions fostered unit cohesion, generated excitement during downtime, and motivated both soldiers and officers to endure repetitive drilling.[16]

One puzzling issue related to officers' study of military tactics and procedure is the implementation of examination boards in the Army of the Tennessee. Early in the war, Congress passed a law that the army should convene boards "to examine the capacity, qualifications, propriety of conduct, and efficiency" of officers in volunteer regiments.[17] If a board found an officer unfit to serve, he would be discharged (if he did not first resign) and replaced. The army's adjutant general issued general orders pursuant to this law. In November 1861, Gen. Henry W. Halleck mentioned in a letter to a subordinate that he expected such a board of examination to be organized in his department relatively soon. A search of the official records turned up evidence of exam boards in other US armies and among the rebel armies but no definite evidence that any such board was ever organized in the administrative entity to which the Army of the Tennessee belonged (variously named the District of Cairo, Department of West Tennessee, Department of Tennessee, and Military Division of the Mississippi). Beyond the official records, one officer mentioned to his sister in October 1862 that no one in his regiment had faced examination but that he feared a vindictive lieutenant colonel might try to force officers he personally disliked to face examination in order to remove them. This officer clearly knew there were supposed to be boards, but his letter does not confirm whether any were implemented in the Army of the Tennessee. Another officer wrote to his wife that he and fellow officers had been studying tactics recently out of fear that they would face a board of examiners soon; again, he left no confirmation that such a board existed, only that it was a possibility. This study did find a singular instance of a sergeant writing about passing an exam to be promoted to second lieutenant, but that was a different matter than examinations to determine one's fitness for a presently held office.[18]

The two cases that come closest to showing an exam board in action seem to be the exceptions that prove the rule, implying either that no exam board was implemented for the Army of the Tennessee or that if it existed, it had little impact. Lt. Col. James Monroe Ruggles of the Third Illinois Cavalry produced a statement protesting the proceedings of a board that examined him as being "illegal and void" for not following statutory rules.[19] The statement was undated, but since he mentioned that his promotion to lieutenant colonel occurred relatively recently, and he was mustered at that rank in July 1862, we have a rough idea of when this incident might have occurred. Ruggles challenged the finding of the board of examination by arguing that it had not been called by proper authorities and that it was not composed of the proper number of officers of proper rank. Had the board Ruggles faced been established according to the terms of the 1861 law and general orders, these criticisms would have been patently absurd. Moreover, had the Army of the Tennessee established an exam board according to the law, there would have been no reason to convene an illicit one of the sort Ruggles described. Thus the very existence of the board Ruggles faced may imply that the Army of the Tennessee lacked any regular board of examination. Ruggles explained how when he joined the Third Illinois Cavalry as its major, he received a mere ten days' worth of instruction from the colonel, "whose duty it is to see that the officers in his command are properly instructed."[20] The colonel actively refused a request for more training, gave his officers no further instruction in drill, and never held regimental drill. Active field service—that is, "scouting, foraging, and picket and provost guard duty, guarding rebel property, etc., which services, though not most agreeable to the Soldiers or officers require no great proficiency in Cavalry tactics"—constrained Ruggles's opportunities for further training.[21] Ruggles argued that considering how recently he was promoted, he had not been in command long enough to be deemed responsible for the state of his regiment. He also protested the board's finding against him by quoting the law's mandate for boards to "examine the *capacity, qualifications, propriety* of *Conduct,* and *efficiency*" of officers, while the board he faced "confines its examination to *tactics* alone."[22] He contended that the law "seems to imply that tactics alone do not make an officer."[23] Ruggles's critique of the board of examination was apparently favorably received, since he retained his post.

The other story that almost reveals the operation of an examining board only to imply that the Army of the Tennessee had no such regular board comes from the 124th Illinois. The officers of that regiment collectively petitioned for their bitterly disliked commander, Col. Thomas J. Sloan, to face examination for his competence to lead the regiment. First lieutenant and later chaplain Richard Howard, author of the regimental history, prefaced the incident with a story that captured how the regiment felt about Colonel Sloan. The colonel had arrested some soldiers of Company G for attempting to seize a secessionist-owned pig. Shortly thereafter a grave appeared near the camp bearing this epitaph:

This sow has died without a moan,
Beneath the nose of Colonel Sloan,
Charged by men on murder bent,
She breathed her last close by his tent.
In digging her grave, we've done our best,
While we, the murderers, were under arrest,
Now Surgeon, let this poor corpse be,
So neatly buried by Company G,
For in this world her troubles are o'er,
She was a sow, but Sloan's a bore.
Reader, tread lightly on her head,
For if she gasps, by thunder, you're dead.[24]

According to Howard, "The feeling indicated by this poetry was pretty largely shared by the whole regiment."[25] During a regimental inspection, Sloan flung weapons back at the owners with such force as to bruise or cut the men's hands; this incident was the last straw that moved every officer of the regiment save one to sign a petition to their brigade commander asking that Colonel Sloan face an examination board. "If he blundered so in camp, what, we asked, would he do in the face of the enemy," Howard asked.[26] The petition was accepted, and Sloan received a summons to be examined on a particular date. Sloan called the officers together and begged them to withdraw the petition, which they refused to do. The colonel embarked on a frantic study of tactics and regulations, but it mattered little. According to the regimental history, the regiment moved before the exam date came and the matter was dropped, with Sloan never actually facing examination. This outcome implies that rather than there being a dedicated examination board in operation, some special group was going to convene explicitly for the purpose of evaluating Colonel Sloan, which would explain why the army's movements could scuttle the chance of it ever meeting.[27]

Had the Army of the Tennessee ever set up an exam board, one would have expected to find officers occasionally mention having passed exams or noting that a fellow officer had resigned or been dismissed as a result of flunking, but this study found no such thing. It is plausible to suggest, based on this striking lack of evidence, that perhaps the Army of the Tennessee never established an examination board to scrutinize volunteer officers. This supposition has interesting implications for the claims of other studies. One analysis of Civil War officers specifically mentioned the Army of the Potomac and the Army of the Cumberland as implementing officer examinations and credited the exam boards for improving officer performance. That study described such practices spreading to other armies (although it made no claims specifically about the Army of the Tennessee). A study of the Confederate Army of Tennessee mentioned that it adopted boards of examination but argued that the Union armies did so more effectively than the Confederacy's western army. If no such examination boards were implemented in the Army of the Tennessee, then they cannot explain the Army of the Tennessee's record as the war's most victorious army. Indeed, it would be intriguing if other major US and Confederate armies made a regular practice of examining volunteer officers and the Army of the Tennessee alone did not. Given the dearth of evidence that the Army of the Tennessee implemented examination boards for officer competence, it is plausible to suppose that it never did so.[28]

Even more than training, guard duty of one class or another was an omnipresent activity for officers. Generals needed bodyguards, foragers needed protection from rebel guerrillas, and wagon trains needed escorts. Someone had to watch for the approach of the enemy army, ward off raiders seeking to burn railroad tracks, prevent prisoners from escaping, and keep snipers from firing on passing steamboats. Common soldiers did all these things, but officers oversaw them every step of the way. The single most common sort of guard duty was being "on picket," in which soldiers were stationed near the rebel lines, well in advance of the army's main position, to serve as an early warning network for enemy activity. An "officer of the day" would be detailed to travel the picket line repeatedly throughout the night to check up on all the guards, making sure they were on post and awake. The size and positioning of the picket guard, the length of the picket line, and the number of trips an officer had to make along the line varied widely. The officer of the day also led first responses to minor disturbances, such as fires or disciplinary problems. Sometimes, an officer and body of troops got left behind to guard a town or supply dump while the rest of the army fought or ventured on an expedition. Some officers wrote of appreciating such easy assignments, but others chafed at missing out on the action. The subject they kept secure and the nature of the potential threat varied, but something always required keeping watch. Over and over through their letters and diaries, officers reported standing guard, often uneventfully aside from attacks by mosquitos and bombardments by rain.[29]

Making one's rounds as officer of the day commonly involved several hazards. Depending on the length of the line and the number of trips along it that an officer took, he might travel as much as ten or twenty miles in a single turn on the job. Luther Cowan described his journey the night of New Year's Day 1863, when he had charge of the picket guard for his entire division, covering a five-mile stretch. He made one trip just before nightfall and a second at 2:00 A.M., having to "ride through the thick brush, over logs, ditches, through mud and everything, and find every squad of four men placed on their posts to watch the approach of the enemy."[30] Jake Ritner described falling into a well and several ditches one night on picket duty as he struggled through heavy undergrowth up and down a two-mile line of guards amid pouring rain. Officers faced real danger of being shot by their own guards if they failed to stop quickly enough when called to halt. Jumpy and inexperienced soldiers sometimes mistook moles and cows for rebel raiders, to say nothing of uniformed humans. William Barney recalled one occasion when, as officer of the guard, he approached a jumpy soldier who would have shot him except that the man had been so scared he forgot to cock his gun. Besides one's own soldiers, rebel sharpshooters posed a danger to officers on picket, and occasionally the rebels would move beyond sniping to actually attacking the picket line. Another danger to officers came in the form of exhaustion. On his very first night assigned to the picket line, Henry Otis Dwight shared the duty with a captain and another lieutenant. Dwight received the first shift patrolling the line, then returned to a central guard post to rest while one of his colleagues took a turn. To Dwight's horror, he awoke in the middle of the night to find the other two officers both asleep beside him: "The picket line might all be killed or captured for all that we the officers in charge knew about it!"[31] Knowing they could be dismissed for neglect of duty, the trio agreed not to report what happened; clearly, this did not keep Dwight from recording the story in his reminiscences. Picket duty could have pleasant moments, such as serendipitous opportunities to forage, if, for example, the picket line happened to intersect a blackberry patch or field of ripe corn. Mostly, though, guard duty was sometimes boring, sometimes dangerous, and always hard work.[32]

74 MORE IMPORTANT THAN GOOD GENERALS

Oscar Jackson composed a detailed record of his adventure protecting a steamboat full of ordnance stores during the Siege of Vicksburg, one of countless times officers watched over the transport of supplies. Jackson had orders to take the *Luminary* from Memphis down to Vicksburg. He had permission to stop at Helena, Arkansas, and at Miliken's Bend and Young's Point in Louisiana, but he was not to let the vessel land anywhere else. The *Luminary*'s master seemed to dislike being subordinate to Captain Jackson and attempted to land at a small town to—as he claimed—deliver mail, but Jackson noted such was against his orders and forbade the stop. That night, one of Jackson's officers awoke him saying the steamboat crew was planning to put in to shore in Louisiana.

> I got up and saw how affairs were going and that they were collecting the steamboat men at the pilot house, where I had but one sentinel, determined to do as they pleased. I went into the pilot house soon and one fellow attempted to enter it. I asked him if he was a pilot and told him if he was not, he could not come in. He gave me a rough answer and I caught him by the collar and unceremoniously threw him down the stairs. I then placed a Lieutenant and a squad of men at the pilot house with orders to shoot the pilot if he attempted to land the vessel at Lake Providence . . . and they did not land.[33]

When the ship reached Chickasaw Bayou to deliver its cargo to the army at Vicksburg, the steamboat's captain complained to General Grant's staff about Jackson, but Jackson was fully vindicated for following orders and showing care to keep a vessel full of munitions away from chance encounters with rebel guerillas.[34]

Officers also served in command of the provost guard, a role in which soldiers acted more akin to police and often interacted with civilians. After a single night overseeing the provost guard in Helena, Arkansas, Alexander K. Ewing reported, "I was up all that night as disturbances was occurring almost every 1/2 hour. Men knocked down and robed, Negroes shot, Horses stole, Drunken soldiers Fighting, & every thing else that men can do was done that night."[35] Charles W. Wills recorded his activities commanding the provost guard while protecting a railroad bridge over the Tallahatchie River near Waterford, Mississippi: "My business is to attend to all prisoners, deal with citizens (administer oaths, take paroles, etc.), give all passes for citizens and soldiers leaving, have charge of all soldiers straggling from their regiments, issue permits to sutlers, etc., and overlook the cotton trade. Altogether, quite enough for any one man to attend to."[36] Wills did not care for the duty, adding, "Confound this railroad guarding; I'm down on it. 'Tis more dangerous than regular soldiering, harder work, and no shadow of a chance for glory."[37] Even when not serving on a formally identified provost guard, officers sometimes performed a similar law enforcement role. Oscar Jackson participated in the investigation of a Black US soldier found outside Memphis, Tennessee, "murdered by rebel citizens for enlisting in government service."[38] Guarding the roads near Memphis, soldiers interdicted rebel-sympathizing civilians smuggling goods, money, or information out of the city. Southern civilians routinely attempted to bribe their way through the lines, Jackson reported: "Male and female almost always asked the officer on duty to drink and if it so happened they had no whiskey they would almost always apologize for not being able to ask you."[39] The Fifty-Fifth Illinois's regimental historians recalled, "This duty oftentimes had its ludicrous features, not always being submitted to with equanimity by the victims. The stony stare and frigid deportment of the Tennessee dames was far more likely to produce laughter than the paralysis intended."[40] The provost guard also worked to protect the civilian populace from vandalizing soldiers and to restrain looting.[41]

Officers oversaw the handling of rebel prisoners. A critical first step in guarding prisoners was simply to disarm them. Harley Wayne helped process about five hundred of the prisoners captured at Fort Donelson in February 1862. His job was to examine each prisoner individually and take all weapons the man might have. He collected a large number of pistols, revolvers, knives, and bowie knives ("hideous looking weapons," he noted) from the captives.[42] One colonel denied being armed, but when Wayne frisked him, he found three revolvers hidden on the man. Another officer still had his sword, so Wayne asked him to hand it over. "He hesitated, Said it was worn by his father on the Battle field of New Orleans and he regarded it as he did his life I told him he had forfeited his right to the relic by his treason and that he must deliver it up," Wayne reported.[43] The man sighed deeply as he unbuckled it and turned it over. Wayne found he "could but pity the man when his affection and respect for his fathers name prompted him to resist the Surrender of sword which he claimed had never known dishonor before."[44]

76 MORE IMPORTANT THAN GOOD GENERALS

Once disarmed, prisoners needed to be kept under guard or escorted away from the front. In at least one case very early in the war, a colonel negotiated a small-scale prisoner exchange with nearby rebels. Once in a while, an officer personally took part in capturing rebels, such as by stumbling across convalescing Confederates during a country ride. Typically, though, officers merely secured captives or shepherded them northward. After the capture of Fort Donelson in February 1862, Henry Otis Dwight's Twentieth Ohio was charged with escorting some of the many prisoners down the river. Dwight's company, numbering about seventy men, had charge of a steamboat with three rebel regiments aboard. Dwight, soon to become an officer but just a sergeant at this time, recalled how his company commander, Capt. Charles H. McElroy, handled the voyage:

> The rebels formed a plot to take the boat and escape. The plan was for the men at a given signal to seize the guards stationed singly about the boat, and throw them overboard, while the officers would brake open the room where the arms were stored and force the boat to land them. The Captain of our Company saw that some thing was afoot, and ordered the guards to prevent communication between officers and men. This saved us. But we were all wore out when we reached Paducah, for we all had to be on guard all the time. The Captain and crew of the steamer like many of the river men were all rebel sympathizers and this gave rise to a very exciting incident. When we reached the town of Eddyville the pilot suddenly turned the boat toward the shore. The bank of the river was crowded with people cheering for Jeff. Davis and swearing at the Yankees, and the men of the 8th Kentucky who were mostly from that region began to shout to the people on shore. Capt. McElroy took in the situation at a glance and persuaded the pilot with his revolvers to keep on his course, while the shouts of the prisoners and their friends changed to a chorus of sad farewells.[45]

At other times, officers merely had to guard a group of prisoners until someone of higher authority could come along and take responsibility for them, a task irksome because it could force an officer to stay behind with his charges when his regiment moved out.[46]

Not all officers expressed compassion toward the prisoners in their care, but Joseph Stockton of the Seventy-Second Illinois illustrated the way some officers felt pity for their captives. In October 1862, Captain Stockton had a turn as officer of the day over a prison at Columbus, Kentucky. In his diary, he described a notable encounter:

A sickly looking woman with a baby in her arms, a little girl about five years old beside her, came to me and said she had walked thirty miles to see her husband, who had been confined for two months on charge of being a guerrilla. Her wan and dejected appearance confirmed her story and I escorted her to the sick ward where her husband was lying. The moment she saw him she rushed to his cot, threw her arms around him, the little thing climbed up on his bed, and such tears and exclamations of affection I have never heard before. At the same time another prisoner who was confined for the same offence and who was lying directly opposite, died. His friends crowded around his cot and they gave way to their tears and sobs. I could not but turn away and feel the hot tears trickling down my own cheek; there was not a dry eye in that room. I was the only Union soldier present and the wife turned on her knees toward me and begged that I would let her husband go home with her, that he was dying then, as he certainly was. He too, begged me for his life, but I, of course, was powerless to act in the matter. The friends of the dead man crowded around and begged that they might be permitted to send his body home, which was granted. I was only too glad to get away from such a scene.[47]

Such sympathetic feelings toward prisoners were consistent with the pity that many other officers showed people suffering from the war, whether soldier or civilian.[48]

On 24 July 1864, Charles Dana Miller and his company were detailed to escort eighty-two rebel prisoners to the rear. He marched with the captives in the middle of the road and his own men on either side. His men all carried loaded rifles with bayonets fixed, and, in earshot of the prisoners, Miller ordered his men to fire on any captive who started to run. Miller kept a cocked revolver in hand and walked with several rebel officers. "The Rebel men," he observed, "were very jolly and happy, laughing at my precautions, and said they were glad to be captured; but the officers were sullen and did not relish their situation."[49] Along with his company and the prisoners, a group of about fifty Black people also joined the party. They "gave me to understand that if there should be any attempt on the part of the Rebels to escape they would help me; and I felt that I could depend upon them."[50] The march passed without serious incident, and Miller and his men returned to the front that same day. Securing prisoners was not the most frequent form of guard duty that officers supervised, but it did occur throughout the war and furnished them with an array of intense experiences.

"It was often said that the western army could fight, but had no discipline," Manning F. Force recalled after the war. He then countered, "It had so much of discipline as is comprised in obedience to orders."[51] Officers were responsible for the good behavior of their men and for punishing those who caused trouble. Disciplining misbehavior was not a routine activity in the same sense that drill or picket duty were regularly scheduled occurrences, but it was a constant, ongoing part of officers' work. They had to keep their soldiers in line when marching and in camp when halted. They tried to prevent vandalism and made sure the men stayed on task when assigned work. Officers often had mixed feelings about discipline. While serving as a lieutenant in a three-month regiment (before going on to spend the war as a captain in the Twenty-Fifth Iowa), Jake Ritner expressed revulsion at the regular US Army's approach to discipline: "The regular army is the last place, as at present constituted, for any person to be who has any intelligence or self-respect. They are treated worse than the mules. I have seen many of them tied up and whipped like brutes for trifling offenses. I would sacrifice anything, even life itself for the good of country if it was absolutely necessary, but nothing else would ever induce me to join the regular army."[52] Rather than seeking to imitate the harsh discipline and aloof formality of regular army officers, the Army of the Tennessee's volunteer officers condemned pretentious behavior or putting on airs of superiority and developed their own perspectives on military discipline. They did employ standard punishments for such misdeeds as insubordination, desertion, theft, drunkenness, gambling, and dueling, but they also sought to persuade and inspire their men to behave, rather than just beat them into submission. While mentioned far less frequently than most other disciplinary issues, officers also had to address rape and prostitution. Besides carrying out military discipline, officers themselves sometimes faced punishment, which was dispensed by higher-ranked officers. Officers' disciplinary role applied to many different situations and was a continual part of their war experience.[53]

Officers had much to say of a philosophical nature about the need for and purpose of discipline in the army. Many people of the time held that the army was a place of immorality, corrosive to morals and good character.

Away from the good influence of civil society, men needed extra restraint. Some officers saw it as their duty to prevent corruption from taking hold or at least to keep wicked behavior in check. Captain Harley Wayne affirmed, "I cannot but feel that I can Save the boys from being ruined Morally."[54] Low views of soldiers were neither universal nor constant (as evidenced by officers' praise of their own men), but such attitudes did shape officers' outlook on the need for military discipline. How easily men accepted discipline varied greatly from one unit to another, with some officers emphasizing the resistance they faced. Alexander Ewing fumed to his parents in November 1862 that "one thing has become a self-evident fact to me that in the 46th there is no incentive for an officer commissioned or non-commissioned to do his duty. If a man talks to an officer disrespectfull and in direct violation of the Articles of War it is passed over and nothing more said about it."[55] Conversely, the regimental historians of the Fifty-Fifth Illinois noted that as the war went on, the regiment grew into a family that worked together and as such, officers suffered fewer and fewer occasions where punishing their men was necessary. The characteristics of soldiers played a part in how well behaved a unit was, but the differing approaches of officers themselves also shaped the quality of their units.[56]

Opinions varied among officers as to how severe or lenient discipline ought to be. In his memoir, Henry Otis Dwight declared that insubordination required harsh punishment because "the free born American has much ado to learn subordination to military discipline."[57] Dwight's feelings about military discipline were more complicated than the above quote might suggest, for elsewhere he cited a particular instance of punishing insubordination as "an occurrence that cast a shadow over all the rest of my military life."[58] As officer of the guard, he once ordered some men to get off a fence on which they were not supposed to climb. One sergeant initially refused, then complied after hurling several curses at Dwight. A relatively new lieutenant, Dwight asked his captain what to do: "He said that it was so grave a breach of discipline that unless I reported it he would report me for neglect of duty."[59] Dwight in turn reported the incident to the officer of the day. To Dwight's consternation, the offending sergeant was reduced in rank to a private. He recalled, "I was distressed that the man should be forced to serve as a common soldier as punishment for a sin against my dignity and none of the reasoning of my superiors that it was necessary to punish so bad an example relieved me from the feeling that I had been too sensitive and too hasty making known his fault."[60] The demoted sergeant was later promoted to lieutenant, but he never forgave Dwight and refused to speak to him to the end of the war. Dwight also recalled the frustration he and many other officers felt when, after unknown persons burned the gin house of a rebel sympathizer's plantation and no culprit could be identified, General Grant ordered the entire brigade fined to repay the owner, thus "punishing the innocent with the guilty."[61] Dwight may have appreciated strict military discipline in theory, but he found the practice of it less appealing.

Meanwhile, Col. George E. Bryant of the Twelfth Wisconsin was remembered fondly for his lenient handling of his soldiers. At end of the Twelfth Wisconsin's veteran furlough in April 1864, they embarked for the front by train. The officers rode in a passenger car at the back of train, ahead of which were a series of freight cars where the men rode. When the train stopped for water, "a coupling-pin in front of our officers' car got out of the proper place, by some means or other," one man remembered evasively.[62] When the train started up again, the privates went with it, sans officers, and greatly enjoyed themselves. At the next station, the train's engineer discovered something was missing and "was just a trifle mad."[63] He shunted the freight cars onto a side track and left them there while he returned to retrieve the errant passenger car, a task that took about an hour. The regimental historian judged it a mark of Colonel Bryant's wisdom that he let the matter slide when he had no means of ascertaining the culprit, rather than punishing the entire regiment. Such was apparently typical of Bryant's approach to discipline.[64]

At times, a commanding officer really did need firm measures to restore order. After Benjamin H. Grierson received his colonel's commission and assumed command of the Sixth Illinois Cavalry from his ineffective predecessor, he faced resistance when initially trying to assert control over the two battalions of the regiment that had not previously been under his command when he was a major. The two battalions had been scattered throughout town, rather than staying together in a regimental camp. Captain George W. Peck, a veteran of the Mexican War, set a good example by rounding up his men, inspiring the other company commanders to follow suit. Captain James B. Morray, however, vowed not to return to camp until he pleased. Grierson responded by preparing to dispatch Captain Peck with 150 men to bring in Morray and his company (a prospect Peck seemed to relish). Just then, Morray and his company turned up in foul temper. When Grierson told him where to make camp, Morray "blustered out that it wasn't a fit place, and his men wouldn't go there, and he would take them where he thought best."[65] Grierson snapped back "that he should camp there and nowhere else, and that at the first sign of mutiny in his company the captain would be the first man shot down in their presence."[66] Captain Morray presented no more trouble after that episode. In that situation, Grierson needed to act forcefully to establish his authority as regimental commander.

Some officers used persuasion to elicit good behavior from their men. The Twelfth Wisconsin's popular Colonel Bryant exemplified this approach when the regiment went home on leave in March 1864. He appealed to his men to remember how their actions would reflect on him—a request that only carried weight if the soldiers esteemed their commander, as Bryant's did. A more extended example of this practice came from Col. Stephen G. Hicks of the Fortieth Illinois soon after he rejoined his regiment after convalescing from a wound. Hicks took an occasion after the chaplain's sermon one Sunday to deliver his own exhortation. He commended the soldiers of the Fortieth for their record of good behavior and urged them to be more diligent in attending church. The government paid the chaplain to serve them in this way, Hicks explained, and the chaplain's responsibilities were just as serious as those of any other officer. The colonel moved on to urge the men of the Fortieth to keep in ranks on the march and refrain from any plundering or vandalism. Unnecessary destruction would only make national recovery harder after they won the war, Hicks told them. He also asked them to consider how people at home would view them: "You were all good citizens at home. . . . You have left your homes . . . to defend your country. You have nobly offered up your lives for sacrifice, if necessary; you are ready to give up your all for the preservation of our good Government, and, while you are thus striving to do your duty, do not dishonor yourselves. Conduct yourselves in such a manner, that it may be an honor to you after you get home—that you may tell your friends that you acted the part of good soldiers, and that you were good, moral men while in the glorious Union army."[67] He called on his soldiers to be good and moral so that they could return home with clear consciences and no regrets about what they had done: "Act, while in camp, as men having good moral principles; and, when you meet our enemies, fight like men; kill all you can; but, if you can take a man without killing him, make him your prisoner."[68] The efficacy of appeals of this sort very much depended on the tenor of a commander's relationship to his regiment. Respected colonels such as Bryant and Hicks were more likely to persuade their men to behave.[69]

The Army of the Tennessee does not seem to have struggled especially with desertion or with men going away without leave, but both deeds occurred, forcing its officers to charge men with desertion. If an officer believed one of his soldiers had deserted, he was obligated to file a statement to that effect, explaining the circumstances, which set in motion the wheels of the military justice system. Officers' feelings about charging their men varied. Charles W. Wills boasted in February 1863, "Mine is the only company that has no deserters yet, and I don't believe I will have any. Half of these desertions are the fault of officers."[70] This sense of smugness disappeared the first time a man did desert his company, as Wills denounced the individual as "the most worthless trifling pup in the army. I am accepting the disgrace of having one of my men desert, decidedly glad to be rid of him."[71] However, Henry Ankeny hoped that two of his men would turn up at a hospital somewhere so that he could avoid the duty of having to report them as deserters. When John Quincy Adams Campbell filed charges against two soldiers of his company for leaving without permission, he noted in his diary, "I expect no thanks and much ill will from my action, but discipline has become so lax that *something must be done.*"[72] In a subsequent entry, Campbell grimly confirmed that his action earned him the predicted hostility of the men he charged as well as of their associates. "It is desirable to have the good will of all with whom we may be called to associate, but it is more desirable to be *right*. As an officer, I have duties which must be performed 'come weal or woe,'" he concluded.[73] The relatively few references to desertion or men taking unauthorized leave suggest it was not an epidemic problem, though it was certainly part of the range of disciplinary issues the Army of the Tennessee's officers faced.[74]

Another major category of misdeed during the war was stealing. Separate from the practice of foraging (a legitimate action recognized by long-standing customs of war), soldiers did engage in acts of blatant thievery. Officers worked to restrain pilfering, though in many cases they had little chance of ever discovering thieves' identities. Several officers reported being the victim of theft. Henry Miller Culbertson, for example, wrote sadly in December 1862 about the theft of his knapsack, containing a Bible, photographs of family, clothing, letters, personal papers, a tent, and other useful articles. He concluded, "A soldier should never have anything with him that he thinks anything of, for if he has, it will be stolen from him."[75] While seemingly quite rare, officers could also commit theft, as Henry Otis Dwight learned in the fall of 1861. He reported:

One night I was ordered to go with a party under command of Col. Garfield of the 42d Ohio to arrest some men who had slipped out of camp to go to a grog shop not far away. I was put in a detachment sent around through the fields to cut off the retreat of the culprits and as we were starting Col. Garfield told us to leave our blankets with him as they would encumber our movement. He himself took my blanket—a nice English Railway rug that my father had given me, and tied it on his horse. We performed our duty, arrested the men and returned about midnight, but I could not find my blanket. I went to Col. Garfield who expressed annoyance at being troubled about such a matter. I then complained to Capt. McElroy and he applied to Col. Force who asked Col. Garfield about it with no satisfaction. The last that I saw of my blanket was when Garfield took it on his horse![76]

This story is intriguing for showing that officers could, at least on rare occasions, steal. One also wonders how this experience might have shaped then Sergeant Dwight's outlook on theft when he became a lieutenant a few months later. Chiefly, though, the fascinating aspect of this story is that the "Col. Garfield of the 42d Ohio" who allegedly victimized Dwight was James A. Garfield, future president of the United States.[77]

Officers could address theft in a variety of ways. Captain Alphonso Barto received an order to track down three horses stolen from his regiment, "so I buckled on the old sword and . . . before dark I had all three of the horses and had an officer of the 9th Ill cavalry under arrest."[78] Other officers participated in formal boards of inquiry to investigate reported thefts. The Fifty-Fifth Illinois's Col. David Stuart supplied a less constructive example of how a commander could handle theft among his men. In January 1862, the Fifty-Fifth moved to Paducah, Kentucky, and set up camp with several inches of snow on the ground. Some men raided a nearby barn for bundles of corn stalks to use for bedding. When the barn's owner complained to Colonel Stuart, he, "furiously enraged, rushed to the front of his tent, and at the top of his strong voice proclaimed that he would 'turn grape and canister' upon the men—that he 'would slaughter them' before it should be said that he 'commanded a regiment of thieves and vagabonds.' All this and much more was repeated over and over again, in the loudest possible tones, and garnished with an infinite variety of oaths."[79] Stuart's intemperate reaction to a relatively minor theft undermined his regiment's respect for him, in contrast to other officers' examples of realistic firmness or persuasive leniency.

Colonel Holden Putnam of the Ninety-Third Illinois responded to a slightly different case of stealing in a decidedly more constructive manner. Formed in the fall of 1862 and recruited with $40 bounties, the Ninety-Third soon found itself transferred to a brigade of older, veteran regiments from Iowa and Missouri. When the regiment reached the brigade in December 1862, they received from the veterans a derisive greeting: "How are you, forty dollar rats."[80] The Ninety-Third's new comrades added injury to insult, however; the night after they arrived in camp, almost every skillet, coffee pot, plate, cup, and piece of flatware disappeared from the regiment's camp. Not coincidentally, the Illinois soldiers observed that their neighbors in the Fifth Iowa had acquired a large supply of new dishes. The men complained to Colonel Putnam about the theft:

> "Well boys," said he, "I don't think you will gain much by complaint, or by asking for a court martial; but you are different men than I took you to be, if you can not get your own back with interest."—The Colonel was a banker.—The boys took the hint and through the day remained quiet. The next morning 90 per cent. of the missing articles with near as many more, that had not been missed by us, were in the possession of our men, a number of the Veterans of the 5th Iowa were not only short cooking utensils, but many of them were without those articles of clothing, which are necessary for a proper appearance in ladies society.[81]

Outraged, the Fifth Iowa complained to the brigade commander, giving Putnam the opportunity to broker peace between the regiments. Putnam's solution only worked because the identity of the thieves was so easily ascertained, but his placid, unorthodox response to the bullying behavior of the veterans certainly had a more positive impact on his men than Colonel Stuart's fierce wrath.[82]

"You might as well try to dam the Mississippi river as to keep men from getting liquor," Joseph Stockton concluded in January 1863.[83] Any time the army came near an outpost of civilization, there were likely to be sellers of alcohol eager to turn a profit off soldiers and (indirectly) make officers' lives difficult. Commanders at various levels attempted to impose prohibitions on selling liquor to soldiers and tried to use persuasion to keep their men away from strong drink, but soldiers persisted in obtaining it illicitly. In many cases, officers were not unconditionally opposed to drinking (as seen from other comments they might make about enjoying a drink sometimes), but they clearly opposed the effects of drinking on discipline and military readiness.[84]

Benjamin Grierson had a rough night in February 1862 when many of his troopers acquired whiskey just before they were supposed to set out on a steamboat. Grierson himself personally poured out a couple dozen canteens full of whiskey. He sent his company commanders to hunt down and dump out all the whiskey they could find, but they shrank back for fear of angering the drunken soldiers. Getting the cantankerous drunks aboard the boat proved difficult, so Grierson personally disposed of most of the whiskey while a squad of the most sober men he could find tried to herd the more inebriated ones toward the steamboat. Once the men got aboard, they promptly headed for the vessel's bar. Grierson had personally forbidden the barkeep from selling alcohol to his men, but the man attempted to carry on business covertly. Grierson "went to him and told him if I heard of him doing so again, I would throw him and the contents of his bar overboard."[85] Grierson was exhausted by the ordeal but later reflected that "by firmness and judicious management, the victory was won over them at last, and of course, they respected their commanding officer the more when their drunken spree was over."[86]

Another behavior officers worked to rein in was gambling. Beyond frowning on gambling as being immoral, officers worked to prohibit it for the good of their soldiers, some of whom would lose all their money in gambling. Despite the risks and the rules against it, soldiers carried on gambling in secret. Joseph Stockton explained that after the army got paid, gambling ran rampant, "till the sharpers have fleeced the green ones out of their last cent."[87] Soldiers proved both determined and sneaky, and try as officers might to prevent gambling, "It is about as hard to keep them from gambling as getting whisky, and where an officer could not get a drop men can get all they want."[88] Henry Hole pessimistically suggested that, as a way to curb gambling, soldiers be paid very little during the war and then provided large bounties at the end of their service. "The less money the majority of soldiers have during service the better it is for them," Hole declared.[89] During active campaigning, when soldiers had nowhere to spend their money, they seemed especially tempted to find alternative uses for it. Whenever an officer came upon men gathered for a game of chance, the erstwhile gamblers scattered wildly.[90]

Officers usually enforced or dispensed discipline, but they were also subject to it. One colonel found himself arrested in January 1862 for permitting his quartermaster to sell rations to his regiment's officers, something the new colonel did not know was forbidden; he spent a month under arrest before being allowed to rejoin his regiment. One officer mentioned an investigation into whether any officers had illicitly acquired and sold cotton. Another got arrested for failing to arrest one of his soldiers for looting. Under some generals, simply failing to keep their soldiers in order on the march could get an officer arrested. While marching toward Chattanooga on 7 November 1863, a soldier in John Quincy Adams Campbell's company fired his gun to clear a damp powder charge from it. The soldier "was arrested by the Colonel and I was arrested by the same *power* because I did not arrest the man who fired the gun."[91] Campbell found this unreasonable since he was neither in command of the company nor serving as officer of the day and thus not responsible for taking any action. Both those officers were present and did nothing, yet neither received censure. Campbell darkly suspected his brief arrest was an act of spite from Col. Jabez Banbury but concluded, "All I have to do is 'grin and bear it.'"[92] Three insights emerge from these stories: that many kinds of offenses could land an officer in trouble, that one of the roles of regimental commanders was to discipline their subordinate officers, and that getting arrested at some point throughout the war was not a wildly unusual experience for officers, nor one that necessarily boded ill for the rest of their military service.[93]

"As you are probily aware ere this that I am under arest for a very grave and serious ofence one of no less magnitude than going to Church on Sunday eavening," Erasmus D. Ward wrote to his sister Mary from Bolivar, Tennessee, in October 1862.[94] Ward and two fellow lieutenants of the Fourteenth Illinois, Adam Smith and Lauren Coe, decided to attend church in town one Sunday and duly requested permission of Lt. Col. William Cam, who had command of the regiment. Cam granted them permission, but to their surprise the three lieutenants returned from church "to find ourselves under arrest our Swords taken from us and we confind to our quarters."[95] Their crime was missing dress parade. Ward, Smith, and Coe pointed out to Cam that they had his permission to be absent. After leaving them to stew for a couple hours, Cam sent back their swords along with a note. In it, Cam apologized for hastily arresting the lieutenants but added, "I hope it will be a warning against any thing of the sort in the future."[96] When the three lieutenants received this note, "not fealing that we had comited any crim and fealing that there was a repramand in it we concludeid not to receive our Swords," they sent back a note of their own.[97]

It simply said, "Sir, we have received your not and decline to receive our Swords under the circumstances."[98] According to Ward, "This so enraged his Highness who by the way is an Englishman," that Cam immediately ordered them confined to quarters and promised to press charges."[99] Ward explained to his sister that confinement meant he was restricted to his company's camp and that he was using his time to read books, write letters, and rest. After jesting about the luxurious nature of his status, he concluded, "but Mary leying all Jokes aside it is not very pleasent to be so closely confined and especily for nothing only to Show his power."[100] Despite the possibility that he could be dismissed from the army, Ward suspected that when Col. Cyrus Hall returned to the regiment and resumed command, he would be released (as seems to have happened).

Officers also faced punishment for purported misconduct that plainly resulted from trying to care for their men. Major Rufus P. Pattison of the 124th Illinois got dismissed from the service in July 1862. Before his promotion to major, Pattison had served as captain of Company H. Between the time the company was formed and the time it started drawing government rations, the men had to buy their own food. Pattison submitted a claim to the government for the cost of the food, received reimbursement, and distributed the money to the men of his company. The government was not cheated and the major gained nothing, but the claim he filed indicated he had paid for the company's food. On this technicality, Pattison was dismissed, a decision that received strident condemnation and earned the major much sympathy. Pattison went to Washington and personally cleared his name with the War Department, which belatedly offered to reinstate him, but he declined.[101]

Captain Francis H. Shaw's service in the Fifty-Fifth Illinois came to an abrupt end with an act of insubordination during the Atlanta Campaign. As senior officer present, Shaw had command of the Fifty-Fifth, despite suffering from malaria. The regiment, numbering about 150 able men, was so exhausted from four days of duty on the front lines and night watches that the men were constantly dropping to sleep. The Fifty-Fifth was also running short on ammunition. Then, on the afternoon of 4 August 1864, orders arrived to advance to an exposed position nearer to the enemy. "Astonished at so insane an order, which could only mean useless murder," Captain Shaw asked that the details of his situation be relayed to the brigade and division commanders.[102] When they insisted Shaw give the order to go forward, he refused. The moment passed, and no one in the Fifty-Fifth thought more of it until three days later when Shaw was arrested for disobedience. He was summarily dismissed via general order, without even being tried by a court-martial in which he could make a defense. The remaining officers of the Fifty-Fifth drafted a petition outlining Shaw's service and the nature of the incident and sent it to the president, asking clemency for Shaw. All present officers of the Fifty-Fifth Illinois signed the letter, along with officers from several other regiments. Lacking any recourse, Shaw simply returned home to Illinois. The members of the Fifty-Fifth did not forget him, however, and twenty years later, in 1884 they banded together to petition Congress for redress. Finally, in 1887, a bill became law that granted Captain Shaw an honorable discharge.[103]

Major Thomas Thomson Taylor of the Forty-Seventh Ohio endured a frustrating experience with his brigade commander, Col. Edward Siber of the Thirty-Seventh Ohio. The colonel issued an order in August 1863 for the expulsion of all Black women working as servants in the brigade's camps. Some of these women took up refuge in an abandoned house about a mile from camp, continuing to come during the day to cook, until a group of soldiers "attempted to ravish them" and they fled to the Forty-Seventh's camp to hide.[104] Colonel Siber happened upon a group of these women while riding through camp and immediately had them driven from the camp at bayonet point. He also refused to send a patrol to the house to ensure the women's safety. According Taylor, this was the result: "Some time in the night a body of soldiers went out . . . they took possession of place at the point o the bayonet and then, Oh, God, horrible to relate, commenced the ravishment. Four men seized Capt. King's . . . servant held her while the fifth ravished her and then changed until each in turn had committed this most outrageous act. Other acts were committed too horrible to relate."[105] The day after this crime, Colonel Siber ordered Taylor to arrest four of the Forty-Seventh's officers for disobeying orders by sheltering the women the first night when they fled to camp. For Taylor's officers, at least, the story ended well. Taylor persuaded the arrested officers to seek an audience with Colonel Siber. One of the officers, Capt. Henry King, went to speak with Siber and after weathering some initial anger, found the colonel a good listener who accepted his explanation of events and admitted to wronging the four officers. Siber withdrew all charges and restored them to duty. None of this helped the women, of course.[106]

There were disciplinary concerns beyond rape regarding soldiers' sexual conduct. Oscar Lawrence Jackson claimed that in the summer of 1863,

Memphis was one of the leading scenes of prostitution in North America. "Virtue is scarcely known within the limits of the city proper and many a soldier boy contracted diseases here that will accompany him with their effects to the grave," he fretted.[107] DeWitt Clinton Loudon held similar concerns about Nashville, reporting to his wife Hannah that the city had "loose women plenty."[108] Major Jackson also asserted during the march through South Carolina in March 1865 that "the persons of women . . . have very seldom been molested and I have been in a position to know about this; but there were frequent examples of easy virtue."[109] Jackson supplied the sole reference my research turned up to pornographic material. In October 1864, one of Jackson's soldiers received "several packages of very filthy, obscene books, evidently to sell in the regiment."[110] Jackson delivered them to the man personally, then forced the man to burn them all in front of him, "advising him that if any more of that kind came by his order I would not only destroy them but would summarily and severely punish him."[111] Victorian squeamishness toward sexuality certainly affected how officers wrote about the topic (as seen in the vague circumlocutions men used even in private letters to their wives). Consequently, it is plausible that sexual misconduct was somewhat more common than officers' writings let on. However, even accounting for the impact of Victorian reticence upon reporting, it appears rape was a relatively infrequent (although quite serious) disciplinary issue for officers to address.

The Army of the Tennessee spent much time in routine pursuits, with officers leading their men on the parade ground, on guard duty, and through disciplinary measures. Officers were responsible for training their men, and though drilling fell off when the army was marching or fighting, it picked up again in quieter times. Officers stood watch on the picket line and oversaw countless other security details, including for foragers, supply shipments, transportation infrastructure, generals, southern civilians, and prisoners of war. Officers also maintained order among their soldiers and disciplined misdeeds. Keeping their men under control was a never-ending task. Soldiers (and their officers) could get in trouble anytime and anywhere. Officers tried to prevent or discourage harmful, destructive, or otherwise forbidden activities, and they punished perpetrators when they caught them. Though some feared army life would have a corrupting influence on men, Army of the Tennessee officers did not embrace the disciplinary orthodoxy of army regulations and formed their own views on how firm a hand soldiers needed to guide them. Officers led by enforcing discipline, in addition to issuing commands on parade or in battle. The tedious days of routine duties were far less satisfying to officers than occasions in which they felt their actions were bringing the war closer to final Union victory, but such activities were nonetheless a substantial part of officers' service.

CHAPTER 6

Red Tape and Triplicate Forms

"I have been working at my 'muster-out-and-in' rolls. . . . Then I have my quarterly returns of clothing, &c and ordnance return, &c. to make out yet, beside final statements, sick leaves, furloughs, descriptive lists, &c to make, and clothing to draw for the men. But it all won't take me many days to get ready if I am not tied up with red tape," Jacob B. Ritner wrote of the paperwork he faced.[1] Officers kept busy with a range of administrative duties. Chiefly, these fall into the two categories of bookkeeping and courts-martial. To keep the government happy, officers had to keep track of equipment and ill soldiers, prepare payrolls, file reports on their unit's activities, and fulfill various other documentary demands imposed by the War Department. Officers complained of the "administrative red tape" with which they had to wrangle.[2] Being detailed to a court-martial was an intersection of officers' more general disciplinary role with their administrative responsibilities. They commonly chafed at being stuck on a court because the task took them away from their units. Officers spent much time on the unpleasant tasks of courts-martial and bookkeeping throughout their wartime service.

"Signed pay Rolls to receive spondoolicks in the morning," Henry Adolph Kircher noted in his diary in February 1863 (using a nineteenth-century slang term for money).[3] It was one of a number of occasions when he mentioned administrative work. The government required officers to submit muster rolls (minute records of the status of the soldiers under their command) at regular intervals and demanded similar documentation any time the army got paid. The arcane process of filling out muster rolls and payrolls greatly challenged many officers. Richard L. Howard recalled the puzzlement he and other new officers felt as they started trying to maintain records according to government standards: "Muster-rolls soon became a vexation. They would not be correct. The names would not wheel into line alphabetically, with the privates reversed, while the officers were straight forward. And just where, if any where, might we 'dot under,' and could we erase a letter if we made a mistake, or scratch a little and not invalidate the whole?"[4] Without satisfactory documentation, units simply did not get paid, an unpleasant prospect for everyone. Henry Otis Dwight wrote of payday, "Like most joys it is accompanied with much pain, which in the case of the pay day, falls to the lot of the Company officers."[5] Active campaigning interfered with officers' ability to maintain muster rolls, though some managed it anyway. (Captain Charles Dana Miller recalled an occasion during the Atlanta Campaign when he "had to make out my four muster rolls on a cracker box while the Rebel bullets were whizzing over my head but I completed the job and had the rolls examined and signed the next day."[6]) The army only received pay on a highly irregular basis, so the frequency with which officers filled out records did not follow a consistent schedule. They could go months with little reference to such work, followed by several days with intense devotion to forms and records.[7]

Even before they could fill out the records, sometimes just obtaining the requisite government forms while out in the field was a challenge. Any time a man's status with the army changed (enlistment, promotion, reenlistment, discharge, etc.), the change had to be formally recognized and documented in a process called "mustering." When a man was promoted, he was technically mustered out of the army and then immediately mustered back in at the new rank. When the men of the Fourth Iowa decided to reenlist as veterans in the winter of 1864, the regiment could not go on the furlough promised to reenlisting soldiers due to a shortage of the government forms needed to muster the regiment as veterans. Capt. Henry Giesey Ankeny spoke with Gen. John A. Logan about getting his men furloughed but was told the shortage of blank forms meant the Fourth Iowa would have to wait to be officially reenlisted, thus postponing the furlough for several weeks. (Someone managed to scrounge up forms more quickly, for ten days after recounting this incident Ankeny reported the Fourth's officers were working on the muster rolls and four days later noted they were still busy with that task.) Other officers endured similar difficulties getting enough forms for their needs.[8]

Officers' bookkeeping duties covered not only their soldiers but government property as well. The government held company commanders liable for all clothing and gear issued to the company and required quarterly returns on their unit's war materiel. Officers had to painstakingly document the fate of coats, blankets, muskets, and other accoutrements to the War Department's satisfaction. A captain (or lieutenant if he was senior officer of the company) had to pay the government for any matériel for which he could not give an adequate account. Moreover, officers were not allowed to resign unless their accounts were in order. Captain Alphonso Barto described to his father the process of tracking his company's equipment: "I have to make returns to the government every 3 months of everything I have drawn from it with what I had on hand per last return and to each Department in triplicate I make returns to one office for Ordinance & Ordinance Stores to another for clothing & to Quarter Master gen[eral] for camp & Garrison Equipage and everything from Sybly [i.e., Sibley] tent to a shoe string or a blank cartridge has to be accounted for."[9] War Department circulars kept by Capt. Nathaniel Watson Foster reveal the kind of ongoing directives company-level officers received regarding bookkeeping. A circular from March 1863 announced that officers had authority to destroy condemned ordnance and stores but could not sell it without express War Department permission. This destruction could not occur without having the ordnance duly inspected, and officers first had to prepare inventories of the stores in triplicate. A notice from August 1864 gave officers detailed instructions for how to requisition specific parts to repair Springfield rifled muskets, including how to differentiate between the 1855, 1861, 1863, and 1864 models of the Springfield.[10]

The government even attempted to regulate the use of government forms. Lt. Col. Theodore Jones of the Thirtieth Ohio received a general order in February 1862 that complained that "the enormous waste, by the officers to whose care they are sent, of the blank forms issued from this office, calls for some prompt corrections."[11] Henceforth each company commander was to "keep a regular account of all books and blanks received and expended by him for the use of his Company."[12] Thus government paperwork begat still more paperwork. Captain Foster possessed a September 1863 circular from the War Department that mentioned "the immense number of blanks required for current use in the Army" and insisted that "the strictest care and economy in their use should be observed by all to whom they are supplied."[13]

Signs of officers' efforts to keep their accounts appear frequently in their papers. After a relatively small clash with rebel forces at Medon, Tennessee, in August 1862, 1st Lt. John O. Duer submitted to his lieutenant colonel a list of the gear lost by Company D of the Forty-Fifth Illinois. Duer meticulously counted out the Enfield rifles, bayonets, jackets, blankets, shirts, socks, canteens, kettles, knapsacks, and frying pans that had been lost in the fray. Sometimes, equipment was not lost but simply worn out. Charles Dana Miller dubbed the task of getting lost or worn-out equipment removed from an officer's account "an intricate 'red tape' process."[14] Only duly appointed inspectors had the authority to condemn worn-out equipment. Miller sometimes served as such an inspector himself, and in sympathy to fellow company officers he "considered it but an act of justice to be liberal in inspecting and condemning this property."[15] Whether lost in battle or worn out through extended use, the government expected satisfactory documentation for all equipment.[16]

All those ordnance records kept by company officers went to their immediate superiors. Colonels (and the lieutenant colonels and majors who assisted or filled in for them) received a deluge of papers as their company commanders transmitted requisitions for their respective companies. A colonel would see numerous requests for articles such as pairs of shoes, socks, drawers, pants, blankets, caps, knapsacks, canteens, haversacks, and rounds of ammunition. Colonels in turn had to fill out their own reports about the quantities of ordnance and other supplies their regiments possessed. At least some of the time, these requests were a weekly affair, with the colonel being responsible for consolidating the needs of all ten companies into one request for the whole regiment. Other paperwork that regimental commanders received from their subordinates included reports of company inspections and updates on how many sick and absent men each company had.[17]

In addition to keeping records for their men and their equipment, officers had quite a bit of other paperwork to do while in the field. They wrote up reports after major engagements, expeditions, and campaigns. In such reports, they described the movements of their units, commended subordinates who performed well, and occasionally censured those who neglected their duties. These reports were lengthy, handwritten affairs, which they not only wrote but also hand-copied to have one to keep and one to send up the chain of command. All sorts of things that might ordinarily have been simple became, in the army, complicated endeavors requiring reports, letters, and signed authorizations. Officers were obliged to document the status of men who got left behind due to illness when the army moved and draw up papers if the illness grew severe enough to require the man's discharge. They wrote passes authorizing men to leave camp or go on furlough. When one of their soldiers died, officers prepared inventories of the dead man's possessions. Along with being leaders, company and regimental officers were very much bookkeepers.[18]

Paperwork was not an everyday chore for officers, but their numerous comments about it make clear that it could be extremely time-consuming and that many of them disliked it. Some wrote of their efforts to keep the books in the middle of campaigns, carrying blank forms with them and seizing free moments to fill them out. Others described struggling to catch up on a backlog of paperwork once a campaign concluded. After describing to his sister how he was bogged down in bookkeeping, Capt. Alphonso Barto concluded: "I would like to have you see how a captain will make a man work night and day and then envy an officer if you will."[19] Henry Kircher told his father of spending a day "in quarterly, monthly, etc. returns up to my ears.[20] When 2nd Lt. John Quincy Adams Campbell became commander of a company, he characterized his new status as "not a desirable position" due to all the paperwork it gave him.[21] During the winter of 1862–63, Jake Ritner wrote to his wife Emeline, "I have more work to do than 4 men ought to do. There are more rolls and reports and returns to make than you ever heard of. I often work till midnight and then get up at 4 o'clock."[22] The frequent references to paperwork in officers' letters and diaries reveal what a significant part of their wartime experience their bookkeeping duties were.[23]

Captains often relied on the assistance of their lieutenants, noncommissioned officers, or even ordinary privates who happened to have some skill to maintain their records. They always found it frustrating when circumstances forced them to handle all the bookkeeping on their own, in part because filling out forms could take them away from other important responsibilities. Luther H. Cowan described his struggle to keep up with his paperwork in the absence of any helpers:

I have been writing all day, since I got up, and ate my breakfast; and must as soon as I finish go at my work again; I have to make out pay rolls for the company, also clothing account for the company for the present year, also descriptive rolls for all the men that are sick and wounded, and I have at the same time to attend company drills, inspection and all business of the kind and now, since Lt. [Nesbit] Baugher is wounded, I have every bit of the writing to do, and it is much, as in every company in the Regt. keeps a clerk busy all the time, but I cannot as yet get a clerk and have not a man in the company who is good enough penman to do it.[24]

Lieutenant Baugher, Cowan's subordinate, had been wounded at the Battle of Shiloh a few weeks earlier, and later died of those wounds.[25]

Lt. Col. Edward Jesup Wood reflected in January 1864 on his ignorance of army paperwork early in the war. Ordnance returns had been a point of special trouble. In the early days of the Forty-Eighth Indiana's service, its company commanders had completely (although inadvertently) ignored the regulations requiring them to account "for all guns, etc. even to cartridges & *caps,* issued to the Co."[26] As a result, more than a year after Wood received his promotion to major, he found himself called on to provide ordnance returns for his time as a company commander—records he could not possibly provide. Ever since the regiment started receiving blank ordnance forms and full instructions on how to keep records, the Forty-Eighth's company commanders had kept their accounts in-line, but Wood, Byrkit, and all the other original captains faced calls from the War Department to furnish returns for their first year of service. "I have frankly & fully written them that I can't do it—what the upshot of the matter will be I can't say," he declared.[27] Wood mentioned that he and Maj. Barnet Byrkit (another of the first wave of captains) regularly joked to each other about getting dismissed from the army for their "heinous" failure to submit their ordnance returns.[28] At a minimum, Wood feared, his chances of being allowed to resign would be scuttled by his inability to provide the returns.

When officers did keep records, they went to great lengths to secure those documents. An army on the march was not an ideal repository for important papers, so sometimes officers sent home records they thought they might need in the future. In February 1864, Lt. Col. George H. Hildt of the Thirtieth Ohio wrote to his parents asking them to find certain ordnance records he left with them and make copies to send him. He had turned over all his old company's equipment to his successor and needed proof of having done so. He described one particular receipt in minute detail, explaining "it is an important paper, and if lost will cause me to pay for the articles turned over; and the 79 guns at $13 a piece will alone amount to quite a sum."[29] Hildt added, "Mother will be perhaps most efficient as

Father will not be likely to have patience enough, as one paper must be examined at a time or it will be overlooked."[30] A follow-up letter at the end of the month revealed that both of Hildt's parents came through for him: "I am very thankful for the trouble Mother took in looking them up, as I know Father had nothing to do with that. They are in his handwriting and I am thankful for that."[31] Other officers similarly left behind vital papers for safekeeping and sometimes had difficulties accessing those documents later.[32]

The Fifty-Fifth Illinois furnished an amusing tale of a desperate adventure to obtain misplaced documentation. During the Army of the Tennessee's pursuit of John Bell Hood's Confederate army in October 1864, officers in the Fifty-Fifth Illinois discovered that "important and much needed company papers" had inadvertently been placed with superfluous baggage and shipped back to Chattanooga for storage.[33] Captain Francis H. Shaw, commanding the Fifty-Fifth, sought leave to go to Chattanooga and recover the papers. When he was refused, 1st Lt. Robert Oliver volunteered to venture back to Chattanooga to fetch the errant records, risking the possibility of court martial if detected away from his post. Captain Shaw consented. Oliver mingled among stragglers of other units who were moving north to get as far as Rome, Georgia, but the only people going north from Rome by train were from the hospital. Going to the hospital, Lieutenant Oliver managed to persuade one of the distracted, overworked doctors that he was seriously ill and snagged a ride aboard a train north. Southbound trains bearing supplies to Sherman's army constantly interrupted the trip, and it took four days before Oliver reached Chattanooga. He located the regiment's lost papers in storage, but he faced a new challenge. Just as orders prohibited soldiers at the front from going north without special dispensation, so also no one could get aboard the trains going south without special orders. To Oliver's good fortune, however, he chanced to meet a sergeant of the Fifty-Fifth who was bringing three new recruits to the regiment. Moreover, one of the sergeant's recruits had deserted back in Nashville, leaving the sergeant potentially in trouble for having lost a man. Thus, standing in as one of the recruits the sergeant was escorting, Lieutenant Oliver safely returned to the Fifty-Fifth Illinois six days after departing, papers in hand.[34]

Nathaniel W. Foster, the captain in the Seventieth Ohio who kept War Department bookkeeping circulars in his personal papers, apparently did so because he got in trouble over the matter. When an officer's records failed to live up to the War Department's exacting standards, a protracted exchange of letters ensued as the officer struggled to produce documentation, explain how he had complied with orders, and avoid literally paying the price for supposedly lost equipment. In February 1864, Captain Foster received a letter from the Ordnance Office demanding he produce returns for unaccounted ordnance. In March, the Ordnance Office judged his Return of Ordnance Stores unsatisfactory and informed Foster the government would confiscate his pay to make up for the purportedly missing supplies. Correspondence on the matter continued throughout the rest of 1864. Even when Foster was discharged for disability in December, the government still insisted that he had been derelict in caring for its property. Indeed, Foster's battle with the War Department dragged on long after the war ceased: not until April 1870 did he get a certificate of non-indebtedness that marked a resolution of the dispute. Few officers became embroiled in years-long fights with the government the way Foster did, but his case shows that when officers expressed anxiety over satisfying the government's bookkeeping demands, they had legitimate reason to fear.[35]

Colonel James W. Judy of the 114th Illinois fell victim to the War Department's bookkeeping enforcement, much to the disappointment of his men. Judy had once submitted to the government a claim for the costs of quartering a company of the 114th shortly after recruiting it. The War Department rejected the claim and accused Judy of trying to commit fraud. The government began withholding his pay and continued to do so for months. Feeling ill used, by April 1863 the colonel submitted his resignation, which was finally accepted in August. The men of the 114th drafted a resolution in support of their commander, which they sent to him as well as to several newspapers back home. They praised his loyal service and expressed full support for his decision to resign in the face of the government's mistreatment. They blamed the War Department for negligent handling of the situation. Even Judy's brigade commander wrote to the governor of Illinois criticizing how the colonel had been treated. Nevertheless, the resignation stood.[36]

A somewhat humorous anecdote resulted from Capt. Jacob B. Ritner's concerns about accounting for government property. By May 1864, Ritner and his wife Emeline were thinking about selling a house they owned and buying another. He expressed his trust in her ability to make the decisions regarding the transactions but cautioned her, "If you buy another house, have the deed made out to *yourself.* Although I have tried to keep my accounts correct with the government, and have been careful and honest in all my dealings, yet the regulations are such that I shall be afraid to own anything for years after this war is over."[37] Emeline responded with puzzlement and assumed her husband must have gotten himself into some sort of trouble and asked what the problem was. Ritner ruefully explained his fear of "red tape" and his responsibility for keeping track of his company's "tents, knapsacks, haversacks, canteens, camp kettles, mess pans, cups, pans, knives, forks, spoons, axes, spades, shovels, drums, fifes, &c."[38] Officers including Ritner had kept notes when equipment became worn out or broken but without getting proper approval from an inspector general, since none had visited the Twenty-Fifth Iowa. Since the government would come after him for the value of anything it considered was missing, Ritner felt that the less he had to his name, the better.[39]

One unusual administrative duty apparently fell uniquely to officers of Ohio regiments. The state legislature passed a law authorizing its volunteer officers to serve as notaries public for Ohio residents serving in the army. Officers had to swear to faithfully perform this duty, whose responsibilities included, according to one such oath, "to administer oaths and take depositions and affidavits and acknowledgements of deeds, mortgages, leases and other conveyances of lands, and all powers of attorney relating thereto."[40] All of the oaths to serve as notary that this study found belong to field officers. It is difficult say how frequently Ohio officers were called on to serve in this capacity while out in the field, but presumably some at least exercised this role. One oath of office specified being commissioned as notary to take a deposition for a specific court case back in Ohio, but other oaths were more open-ended.[41]

"I'm on a Court Martial now. Confound the Court Martials," Charles Wills fumed in May 1863.[42] Like many other officers detailed to serve on a court-martial, Wills registered a dislike for the way the duty separated him from his unit. Most of the duties officers performed related directly to their units. Serving on a court took an officer away from his men and kept him from his usual responsibilities. Jake Ritner's frank view of court duty was typical: "This court-martial is the greatest bore I have come across in the army." [43] He self-deprecatingly wrote that all he did was "sit up on a high bench and look dignified all day—what do you think of that?"[44]

In cases where court-martial service did not separate an officer from his command, he was instead swamped by the combined workload of running his unit while also serving on the court. Active campaigning made it difficult to hold court, so courts-martial often got left behind when the army moved or else had to suspend operation until the army's circumstances became settled again. Some officers had been lawyers before the war, but others had no legal background and awkwardly scrambled to educate themselves when assigned to a court. Many types of accusations came before courts-martial: misconduct in battle, disobedience to orders, disrespect of superiors, breaking and entering, stealing civilian property, desertion, being absent without leave, and drunken brawling. Through it all, officers grumbled at the way this work separated them from their soldiers and kept them from what they regarded as their proper duties.[45]

Throughout much of the summer and fall of 1862, Capt. Luther Howard Cowan found himself wrenched away from his Company B, Forty-Fifth Illinois, to serve on a court-martial. He expressed strong skepticism about the function of such tribunals: "I am still sitting on this tedious court martial inquiring into the whys and wherefores of the shortcomings of our wayward brother soldiers—most of us putting on awful airs of dignity and consequence while investigating other folks action, but as soon as we are done, committing the same or worse acts, only guarding against detection, as that is the measure of guilt in the army as well as in civil life, the innocent and the righteous being those who are lucky enough to escape detection, while those who are caught, though not half so guilty, are awful culprits."[46] Eventually, Cowan did rejoin Company B, though this was not the last time he served on a court during his service.[47]

Edward Jesup Wood, eventually colonel of the Forty-Eighth Indiana, served on at least four different courts-martial throughout 1863–65, with some of those experiences being more positive than others. While serving on a court in August 1863, he wrote that the "genial companionship which has grown up between the members of it—hitherto strangers—has done much to alleviate the tedium of the trials."[48] Wood began a far more frustrating court-martial experience in April 1864. When his regiment moved on without him, Wood wrote darkly, "There is a silence which is deathlike and a stillness which is of the tomb," and said he envied Alexander Selkirk, the real-life castaway who had inspired the novel *Robinson Crusoe*.[49] When it appeared the Forty-Eighth would go to join in the Atlanta Campaign without him, Wood fumed over "the eternal Court Martial" and pronounced himself "real cross, disappointed, lonesome and dismally blue tonight."[50] Wood did manage to rejoin his regiment in time for the Atlanta Campaign. However, after the army reached Savannah, Georgia, in December 1864, Wood again wound up on a court-martial, spending six to eight hours a day sorting through the backlog of cases that accumulated during the march there.[51]

Besides training their men, disciplining them, leading them in battle, and caring for their needs, officers bore constant administrative responsibilities, chiefly bookkeeping but also legal assignments such as courts-martial. Throughout the war, officers grudgingly served on courts, an intersection of their routine role in enforcing discipline with the administrative functions they also performed. When officers detailed to a court-martial had to remain behind while their units moved on, they complained of missing their men, while if their units remained in the same place, they expressed frustration at the difficulty of keeping up with their regular duties while spending so many hours in court. Company and regimental officers also kept records, tracking the status of government property, completing muster rolls and payrolls, writing reports about their battles and expeditions, and documenting sundry other aspects of the war. These men did not start out with expertise navigating government forms, and battlefield conditions made satisfying bureaucratic demands all the more difficult. Consequently, many officers experienced a measure of stress over these duties, and some officers actually fell into serious trouble for failing to keep their records to the War Department's satisfaction. Administrative tasks were neither the most glorious nor the most dangerous aspect of officers' duties, but they were a major facet of their wartime experience. "I think Uncle Sam will have a houseful of documents somewhere when the war is over," William Reid once noted in his diary.[52] He was right.

CHAPTER 7

More Important Than Good Generals

"You could learn more of what an army is in camp one day than you could reading a month or even a year; in fact it is like every other phase of human life, we must *see* it *to fully understand it*," Luther Cowan wrote to his daughter Molly, explaining why he wished she could visit the army.[1] One particular misconception Cowan sought to correct was that the fame of generals might lead one to think that achieving high rank indicated a man possessed special qualities of some kind. "There are some (a good many) good men who are officers, but official uniform is not a sure infallible sign of good sense, good heart, good education or good qualities in any respect," Cowan told Molly.[2] That Cowan wanted his teenaged daughter informed about such matters is fascinating in its own right, but more than that, he was expressing some of his thinking on what qualified a man for a place of authority.

The Army of the Tennessee's officers thought and wrote quite a bit about what made for good or bad leaders and officers. Sometimes this took the form of explicit reflections on the nature of leadership (as in Cowan's comments to Molly), but officers rarely produced philosophical treatises or self-help books on how to be a leader. Instead, officers' thoughts on what qualities made for a good or bad officer typically appear implicitly, embodied in statements praising or censuring the conduct of other officers. To some degree, of course, many of the topics throughout this study pertain to leadership, but this section will examine more directly how the Army of the Tennessee's officers revealed their attitudes regarding leadership. Their chief themes included courage under fire, moral character, good relationships with their men, and avoidance of elitism. Occasionally they also touched on other valuable qualities, such as clarity in communication or physical health.

Especially in the early phases of their service, officers commended displays of courage on the battlefield. George Hunt of the Twelfth Illinois remembered being deeply impressed by the actions of his commander at the Battle of Fort Donelson: "Here I beheld the ideal of all my boyish dreams of soldierly gallantry. It was Colonel John McArthur, riding along the line and holding in place amidst a hail of bullets his hard pressed men. No more knightly or inspiring figure was seen on any battlefield during the war."[3] Before one fight, Henry F. Hole observed the colonel of a nearby regiment ride along his line saying, "Boys don't be afraid. You are on the right side," in response to which the dispirited-looking men stood up straighter and even began to cheer.[4] Recounting how the colonel projected calmness to his men by appearance and speech, Hole concluded, "Simple words spoken boldly and fearlessly before a fight loud enough for the men to hear does good."[5] In parallel to officers' appreciation of courage, they also denounced cowardice, though such comments appeared in their writing less frequently than praise for bravery. Many officers emphasized the need to keep cool under fire to provide an example of courage for their men, and they regarded cowardice as a trait that made a man unfit to lead.[6]

The Vicksburg Campaign furnished many occasions for officers to display bravery and for other officers to see and remark about it. Charles Dana Miller praised the conduct of the Seventy-Sixth's Ohio's commander, Col. Charles R. Woods, at the Battle of Arkansas Post. Woods "exposed himself in the thickest of the fight. His large form was a conspicuous mark, but he was perfectly cool and walked about, twisting his mustache and breaking sticks as was his habit, with an eye on all that was transpiring."[7] After the Battle of Port Gibson on 1 May 1863, Luther Cowan commended his immediate superior, Col. Jasper Maltby, who "rode or walked over the field with his hat off cheering his men and giving orders coolly enough, but showing more fire than most folks thinks he possesses; he is a full team in a fight."[8] In June 1863, Henry A. Kircher defended his commander against charges of cowardice by noting that Col. Hugo Aurelius von Wangelin "has his shortcomings, perhaps too many to make a good colonel, but he doesn't know cowardice."[9] The Army of the Tennessee's officers made fewer references to battlefield courage as the war went on, but they showed no overt signs of discounting its value. Perhaps after the army spent weeks or months under almost daily enemy fire, as it did during the campaigns for Vicksburg and Atlanta, courage under fire might have become more routine than remarkable. Overall, officers' praise for leaders who displayed coolness under fire revealed their attitude that good officers should behave calmly in battle, inspiring their men by their brave example.[10]

Many officers paid tribute to the idea that they and their fellows needed to possess good character and live morally. In a letter to his siblings, Charles Ammack went so far as to claim, "If this government had searched the infernal regions all over for leaders to conduct this war in this locality they would not have found a meaner set of men than they have got here & as for profanity & lying they would beat the devil himself & and whether he ever got drunk or not history don't tell us but if it tells the truth about these men here it will say that they got *drunk*."[11] Captain Ammack's melodramatic laments reflect an underlying assumption that sober, moral officers inspired subordinates' confidence while loose living led men to distrust their leaders. Henry Kircher mused in September 1863 that soldiers seemed to treat their officers with more respect than in the past and speculated that this was because so many of the original officers had been replaced by new ones who "behave themselves better and more like gentlemen, then most of the former ones did on different ocasions."[12] When some of his fellow officers in the Fifth Iowa held a drunken party, John Quincy Adams Campbell railed against their foolish behavior, pointing out the irony that some of these same officers previously punished their soldiers for getting drunk and causing a disturbance. Their hypocrisy, Campbell wrote, would undermine these officers' ability to enforce discipline in the future.[13]

Other officers likewise wrote of the need for officers to lead by example in their conduct and specifically addressed the need for moral courage. While wishing he could go home and "vote for old abe and andy" in the election of 1864, Alphonso Barto made some observations about Democratic candidate George McClellan that display something of Barto's attitude toward leadership.[14] McClellan, Lincoln's opponent, "is not a traitor at heart I dont believe but I think he lacks that moral courage that makes a fighting man or man to lead the people or an army successfully."[15] Barto speculated that when McClellan had led the Army of the Potomac, he had been more focused on setting up future political opportunities than actually subduing the rebellion. Officers like Barto understood that being an effective leader took more than just battlefield courage.[16]

Abstaining from disreputable behaviors such as smoking, drinking, and swearing was something Jake Ritner said he owed his family, but he also penned several condemnations of such activities that show he saw them as having broader leadership implications. He lamented in January 1863 that he was losing his respect "for the Big-bugs in our army," who "all or very nearly all drink and gamble and swear."[17] In another letter, Ritner claimed that he had earned his company's respect through his good conduct. In November of 1863, he reported an evening where about two-thirds of the Twenty-Fifth Iowa's officers acquired whiskey, got drunk, and began "raising Cain generally all over the Camp."[18] Ritner boastfully asserted, "Company B boys are congratulating themselves that their officers are all right and minding their own business. They wouldn't swap officers with any company in the regiment."[19] Beyond rejecting such activities on the basis that they were immoral, Ritner's comments reveal the attitude that officers' misconduct could undercut their ability to command. He saw his own avoidance of such vices as part of being an effective company commander.[20]

Lieutenant Anthony Burton of the Fifth Ohio Light Artillery Battery reported a contrast between how rebel officers related to their soldiers versus the way the Army of the Tennessee's officers and men interacted. On 4 July 1863, after Vicksburg surrendered, Burton took time to visit with the captured Confederate army. He marveled at "the very marked and wide distinction between officers and the men that is made in their army."[21] Burton perceived a great distance between the officers and enlisted ranks: "There is none of that familiarity between them, none of that care for the comfort of the men on the part of the officers that there is in our army."[22] Burton also claimed to have asked some of the rebel soldiers how they felt about the way their officers treated them, and the prisoners consistently responded that their officers treated them poorly. Even if Burton's depiction of the rebel soldiers was exaggerated or otherwise inaccurate, his favorable view of close, caring relationships between officers and soldiers exemplifies another common ideal that officers expressed.

Indeed, many officers indicated that respect for, and personal connections with, one's soldiers went a long way toward getting soldiers to respect and cooperate with their officers. Charles Wills served a stint as a battalion adjutant in the Seventh Illinois Cavalry, during which time he declared, "I'll wager we are the only field and staff that pitch and strike our head quarter's tents without the aid of the men. But I can't bear the idea of making men who are our equals at home do our work here."[23] It seems fair to suppose that Wills's would have maintained this equalitarian outlook on officer-soldier relations when he later became a company commander in the 103rd Illinois.

When Henry Otis Dwight became a second lieutenant, he was transferred to another company that was short a lieutenant, and initially the soldiers there "regarded me as an interloper."[24] Eventually, Dwight forged connections with the men and earned their respect. As part of explaining why the Forty-Sixth Indiana placed such great confidence and trust in Col. Thomas Bringhurst, Alexander Ewing said of his commander, "We all call him pap or that is the term he goes by among the men, they all like him and will do whatever he asks."[25] Other officers also wrote approvingly of colleagues who practiced respect and kindness for their men.[26]

Second Lieutenant Michael Griffin held fond memories of his old commander in Company E of the Twelfth Wisconsin. After characterizing Capt. John Gillispie using a string of adjectives—"impulsive, exceedingly quick of comprehension, of ready decision, forceful and magnetic"—Griffin got more specific about what made his captain a good officer.[27] Gillispie proved himself a stern disciplinarian, yet he balanced this by being "exceedingly kind, gentle, and considerate" toward his men.[28] The captain was able to wield complete authority over the company not by virtue of his rank but because of the soldiers' "regard and esteem for him."[29] Gillispie's subordinates trusted him, believing his orders would help them avoid failure or disgrace and would not put them at pointless risk. Gillispie was also generous with praise, both for the company as a whole and for each of his soldiers individually.[30]

The regimental historians of the Fifty-Fifth Illinois had much to criticize about Col. Oscar Malmborg, but one of the rare anecdotes in the regimental history that cast Malmborg positively centered on a moment when he expressed care for a subordinate. During the Battle of Chickasaw Bayou on 28 December 1862, the Fifty-Fifth Illinois was ordered to cover efforts by another regiment to clear away obstacles to the Union advance. The companies of Illinois volunteers tried to shelter behind swamp vegetation while laying down covering fire for the work. As Capt. Casper Schleich led his company in this task, he was shot in the chest and immediately dropped dead. Moments later, Malmborg, then lieutenant colonel, approached the scene and a man from another company stepped forward and informed him that Captain Schleich had just been killed: "The colonel's lip quivered. In an instant a tear stole down his cheek which he brushed away as though it might seem unsoldierly, and in a tremulous tone gave his directions. . . . It was one of those rare moments when the noise of battle had humanized him, when the every-day turbulent emotions of his being seemed to be suppressed and he could see with a clearer vision. It was an act of feeling on his part which made one inclined to forget the past and hope for the future."[31] The men of the Fifty-Fifth generally viewed Malmborg as an unreasonable authoritarian, and this scene did nothing to salvage his popularity in the long run, but a candid moment of compassion had the power to raise the regiment's esteem for him, at least momentarily. Even officers who intensely criticized Malmborg valued respect and kindness in a commander so much that they favorably acknowledged his heartfelt reaction to Captain Schleich's death.

The counterpart to officers' praise of mutual respect, compassion, and close relationships between leaders and soldiers was their denunciation of elitism, putting on airs of superiority, and disrespectful treatment of subordinates. Jake Ritner condemned generals Frederick Steele and Francis P. Blair Jr. as "supercilious aristocrats" who supposedly felt it beneath their station to speak to volunteer officers.[32] An officer of the Fifty-Fifth Illinois claimed that Col. David Stuart's "autocratic sway and unscrupulous self-seeking . . . inspired fear rather than affection."[33] During an alarm one night in the summer of 1862, Oscar Malmborg called the Fifty-Fifth Illinois to arms and then had his cot and blankets brought from his tent and laid down to sleep right in front of his men, while they stood around on alert. Even Colonel Stuart was upset by this behavior; going to sleep in plain view of the men while requiring them all to stand in line conveyed a deep disrespect of one's inferiors. Richard Howard, who served under Col. Thomas Sloan as both an officer and a chaplain, wrote that Sloan's good qualities were outweighed by his tendency to be "impulsive, conceited and dictatorial."[34] One of Howard's associates explained that Sloan's failing was that he "did not understand human nature, and tried to enforce his school room rules and regulations in his regiment, which rebelled at being treated like a parcel of school boys."[35] Condemnation of elitism and disrespectful treatment appears consistently throughout officers' writings.[36]

Second Lieutenant David Vail had some harsh words for the way his colonel's ambition led him to treat his subordinates poorly. Vail believed that the Sixteenth Wisconsin's first commander, Col. Benjamin Allen, repeatedly put the regiment into dangerous situations, seeking a chance for battlefield glory and a promotion to general. Vail darkly reflected that Allen's ambition cost the Sixteenth serious casualties. "It is my opinion," Vail declared, "that if we had had a different Colonel that many of the old boys who were needlessly put into places of danger and lost their lives in consequence, would be living to day."[37] Vail added that Allen's overweening ambition corrupted other officers. Vail cited his old captain, George Williams, as an example of this. Colonel Allen "'turned' Capt. William's head" with visions of promotion and incited the captain to irresponsible, glory-seeking leadership similar to his own.[38] "War is a terrible thing," Vail concluded, "and to take charge and direct the movements of men on a field of battle is a grave responsibility."[39] Ambition, though not necessarily entirely bad, became a serious problem if it supplanted respect for the lives of one's subordinates.

Tom Taylor of the Forty-Seventh Ohio presented Col. Edward Siber of the Thirty-Seventh Ohio as an exemplar of smug callousness he claimed was typical of European-born officers.[40] Taylor had a theory to explain this purported disparity: "The American officer has from infancy been under the refining and humanizing influences of society; has acted and talked as an equal of every other man; has never been made to . . . bow to others," a way of life that "begets liberal views and feelings."[41] In contrast, "The European officer has been reared under an exactly opposite state of things" and consequently was prone to looking down on his subordinates "as his puppets and instruments" and getting drunk on his sense of authority.[42] According to Taylor, the European-born officer was also used to being on the receiving end of harsh authoritarianism in his home country, and thus as an officer in America he became "an unmitigated tyrant," demanding "slavish obedience" and "humiliating homage" from all.[43] Taylor conceded that Colonel Siber was militarily skilled but nonetheless a "despot."[44] One cannot read Taylor's censure without wondering how much his depiction of Colonel Siber might reflect a bias against European-born officers as much as a factual critique of the man's leadership style. Regardless of how valid the criticism is, Taylor's discourse nonetheless reflects the belief that officers ought to recognize their subordinates as social equals and employ their authority accordingly.

Besides their major themes of what made for a praiseworthy officer, such as battlefield courage, moral character, and respectful relationships with their soldiers, officers' comments regarding their colleagues sometimes suggested other qualities they believed officers needed. In October 1864, Edward Jesup Wood deemed himself "unfit to be a commander any more, because my soul is not in the business."[45] He felt "patriotic as ever" and expected victory for the Union, but he also believed he had done his share of the work and "I want my Jeanie & my *baby*."[46] Wood found he could no longer muster up the energy and focus that a commander ought to have.

Considering various complaints about receiving confusing orders, we can safely assume officers also considered clarity an important quality for good leadership. Anthony Burton, for example, grumbled to his diary during the Siege of Vicksburg that if some of the orders he received were "a little less grandiloquent and a little more explicit and to the point, they would be better understood and would occasionally save much trouble."[47] As Lt. Col. DeWitt Clinton Loudon grieved the death of his subordinate, Maj. John McFerran, he eulogized the late major's reliability: "When I gave him an order and explained to him what I wanted done, I could always be sure that it would be done to suit me & without delay. . . . He was thoroughly *true* & *trusty* & of undoubted courage."[48] Officers' praise, criticism, and self-reflection all suggest qualities they believed a good officer should possess.[49]

Oscar Malmborg filled the starring role in an incomparable anecdote that illustrated both how poorly the men of the Fifty-Fifth Illinois thought of him and why they might have held him in such low esteem. Second Lieutenant John B. Johnson recalled how during the Corinth Campaign, he once received orders to oversee a work detail of fifty men. After he assembled the men, Lieutenant Colonel Malmborg rode up to give him further instructions. The lieutenant colonel gestured to a grove of trees and began to speak, but he paused when he noticed that Johnson was looking in the direction at which he was pointing and gruffly demanded that the lieutenant look at him while he talked. The startled lieutenant hastily saluted, promised he was paying careful attention, and explained that he was looking where Malmborg had pointed for him to go. "'Veil,' Malmborg repeated, 'ven I dalk mit you, I vant you to look to me.'"[50] Feeling irritated, Lieutenant Johnson determined to follow this order precisely, looking straight at Malmborg as he began the speech again: "'Lieutenant Von Johnson, you vill dake your men and tile down de ratine, keeping de men veil sekreded, ondil you come down opposid de glump of dimber vat you see on de poind of land; tin den, you vill durn to de leff, klimb de shteep ascent to de glump of dimber'—and, suddenly looking down at me, he noticed that I was looking straight at him, just as he told me to a moment before."[51] This elicited a new outburst: "'Lieutenant Von Johnson, by Gott, ven I dalk to you I vant you to look ver I poind.'"[52] Johnson saluted and answered that he was obeying the lieutenant colonel's order to look at him, to which he responded, "'ven I dalk mit you, I vant you to look ver I poind.'"[53] Johnson dutifully promised to obey this order. Malmborg began to issue the order for the third time, glancing over partway only to find that Johnson was looking where he was pointing. "'Lieutenant Von Johnson, vat for you shtand like a kettle? By Gott, ven I talk to you, I vant you to look to me,'" the lieutenant colonel burst out.[54] Johnson admitted he lost his temper at this point. The outraged Malmborg ordered the assembled soldiers to escort Lieutenant Johnson to the guardhouse. Johnson countermanded his superior's order. Malmborg again told the men to escort the lieutenant to custody. Again, Johnson told them to remain in line. "Although Malmborg ranked me," Johnson recalled, "his unpopularity rendered his order impotent and gave mine force, so that the men obeyed me and kept their places in the ranks."[55] The sputtering lieutenant colonel finally told Johnson to consider himself arrested and to surrender his sword and return to quarters, and Johnson obeyed. He received a lecture in military etiquette the next day from Colonel Stuart but faced no further consequences from this incident. For Malmborg to be so disrespected by the Fifty-Fifth's soldiers that they would obey a mere lieutenant over him speaks volumes about how Malmborg's behavior undermined his ability to lead his subordinates.

Malmborg's accession to colonel of the Fifty-Fifth Illinois provided an occasion for the regiment's officers to air grievances against him. Even accounting for the possibility of bias against Malmborg for being foreign-born, the details involved make it easy to see why the men of the Fifty-Fifth judged him a poor commander. Soldiers and officers alike were pleased at news that the unpopular Col. David Stuart was being promoted out of their regiment, but they fiercely objected to having Malmborg succeed Stuart. Malmborg's early aura of military expertise had long since evaporated, revealing only "bullying, abusive and insane tyranny."[56] Twenty-one of the company officers signed a petition to Illinois governor Richard Yates begging him for a chance to hold an election to replace Stuart and predicting the regiment would face daily mistreatment and mismanagement if Malmborg took over.[57]

While a large majority of the Fifty-Fifth's company officers condemned Malmborg, a couple of captains aligned themselves with him and informed the outgoing Colonel Stuart of the petition, prompting Stuart to send his own message to the governor. Stuart accused the officers who submitted the first petition of seeking revenge against Malmborg for not promoting them all to major. They were also, Stuart claimed, a bunch of sluggards resentful of Malmborg's strict but fair disciplinary regime. Stuart said these officers (the twenty-one who wrote the petition) suffered from "vanity, selfishness, and that 'prurient ambition for fame not earned,'" which kept them from appreciating all the good that Malmborg had done for them.[58] Stuart predicted that without Malmborg at the helm, the Fifty-Fifth would fall apart within two months. He told the governor that hardly any of his regiment's captains were competent enough to serve even as lieutenants and that the lieutenants were even more inept. The only officers Stuart excluded in this litany of villainy happened to be the same officers who had aligned themselves with him and Malmborg. The colonel and lieutenant colonel had managed to hold the regiment together by doing all the company officers' work for them, Stuart claimed. And this was merely the opening volley in the fight over whether Lieutenant Colonel Malmborg was fit to command the Fifty-Fifth Illinois.[59]

The regiment's officers did not let the matter go. Years later, Lucien Crooker, in his contribution to the Fifty-Fifth's regimental history, unsurprisingly objected to the colonel's portrayal of the line officers. "Every instinct of justice would lead any one at all conversant with the affairs of the Fifty-fifth to indignantly repel the statements contained in the foregoing scurrilous letter," he wrote, pointing out that the officers Colonel Stuart "so glibly vilified" were almost entirely men Stuart himself had appointed to their offices.[60] After the competing letters to Governor Yates, the next flashpoint in the conflict over Malmborg's fitness came months later, as Malmborg's ascendancy finally became definite. When the army began convening courts-martial after the capture of Vicksburg, some in the regiment filed charges against their new colonel. The brigade commander, Gen. Joseph Lightburn, refused to act on the charges, so nothing came of them, but the regimental history preserved a copy of them. They accused Malmborg of drunkenness, as well as "unbecoming" conduct that insulted, cursed, threatened violence against, and otherwise abused various subordinates. During one march, Malmborg reportedly assailed the regiment's officers collectively "using these or equivalent expressions: 'You are a set of damned imbeciles, unfit to command a squad of one man, and claim to be officers!'"[61] The officers also accused Malmborg of undermining order and discipline by, for example, frequently questioning the competence of company officers in the presence of their men.[62] The level of detail to the charges—with names, dates, and eyewitness quotations—lends them a strong sense of veracity, but leaving aside the question of whether Stuart and Malmborg or their opposition were in the right, the arguments put forward by both the anti-Malmborg faction and Colonel Stuart illustrate much about what the Fifty-Fifth's officers believed made for a good or bad leader.[63]

Officers' criticism of fellow officers can reveal a great deal about their assumptions regarding what conduct made one a good or bad officer, but we should not necessarily take all of the criticisms at face value. At times, we have good reason to suspect a more personal conflict lay behind one officer's denunciations of another. Jake Ritner's comments about his subordinate, 2nd Lt. Baron Crane, illustrate how some criticism may not have been strictly professional. Waiting for Crane to return from leave in October 1863, Ritner claimed that he got along just fine with the lieutenant, but the men of their company hated Crane and "are all the time making fun of him and wishing he would never come back."[64] Because of the men's antipathy toward Crane, Ritner said he hoped Crane would resign and thus spare him the trouble of making the men treat Crane respectfully. In November of that year, Ritner declared that he disliked the entire Crane family and especially Baron. Ritner attributed his antipathy to the following faults: "He is too selfish and *snappish*—he sometimes forgets to treat me with the respect which is due from one officer to his *superior*. You know I am *Captain* of Company B and *must be* respected accordingly even by Lieutenants."[65] A couple months later, Ritner complained about Crane again, this time because Crane received more mail than he did! But after grousing about how Crane received many more letters than he did, Ritner petulantly insisted he did not actually care about getting more mail. He claimed Crane received more letters than he did because Crane slacked on his duties in order to write more letters home. Ritner said that instead of working, Crane lounged around the brigade headquarters, before correcting himself to remark, "I said he did not do anything. But when we are in camp he reads novels and plays cards day and night."[66]

Through these letters we can see how Ritner went from claiming to get along fine with Crane to viciously denouncing him. The context and curiously escalating nature of Ritner's accusations undermines the force of the charges. Most instances of officers criticizing other officers do not look nearly as suspicious as this one, but it is fair to acknowledge that other cases where one officer criticized another could have been distorted by personal feelings. However, even if an accusation were untrue, the criticisms still captured the writer's underlying assumptions about how officers ought to conduct themselves.[67]

Among officers' writings, the qualities they most associated with being a worthy leader included battlefield courage, good character, and respectful relationships with their subordinates, though a number of other qualities appear with lesser frequency. Occasionally these attitudes appear in direct comments on leadership, but most of the time officers' views on leadership appear implicitly. When officers praised or criticized other officers, the behaviors and traits they singled out reflected their underlying ideas about proper leadership. The words of critics may not always tell the full story of any particular officer, but the accusations still indirectly reveal their authors' thinking on what made for a good officer. This study focused chiefly on the writings of company and regimental officers, but some sources produced by soldiers or staff officers contained similar views. Soldiers found their officers' courage under fire and dedication to duty inspiring. They appreciated when officers treated them with compassion and kindness. Soldiers loathed elitism and tactless displays of authority and appreciated socializing with their officers. The work of officers, from drill to courts-martial and combat, largely boiled down to different manifestations of leadership, so officers' thoughts on good leadership enhance our understanding of their role within the Army of the Tennessee. Artilleryman Anthony Burton recalled witnessing a fight in which panic and confusion swept through the Fourteenth Illinois because its officers failed to respond effectively. "There was nobody to take command and bring any order out of the chaos," Burton concluded.[68] Bringing order out of chaos is a fitting summary of the work of the Army of the Tennessee's officers.[69]

CHAPTER 8

For the Cause

Charles Dana Miller volunteered to serve in what he characterized as the "War for the Suppression of the Rebellion" because he believed he would feel lasting shame if he did not fight "for the Constitution, the Union and for human liberty."[1] The Army of the Tennessee's officers volunteered for the army, freely choosing to leave home and go to war. Out of a sample of 481 officers, about 77 percent joined the army in 1861, and the remainder enlisted in 1862, all before the Union implemented any meaningful conscription measures. These men gave thought to the nature and purpose of the war and plainly articulated why they volunteered. According to them, an unjustified, immoral rebellion threatened to destroy the wisest, greatest government the world had ever known. The Union represented and enabled their liberty, peace, and prosperity. The traitorous rebellion threatened that Union and therefore was an attack on their rights and those of their families. Officers wrote extensively of ideological and political motivations and of their duty to uphold liberty, justice, and the rule of law. They were passionately invested in the Union cause and disgusted by the rebellion. These officers went to war to defend the Union that safeguarded their rights and liberties and to crush the wicked rebellion that sought to destroy it, and they held to this sense of purpose throughout the war.[2]

Henry Otis Dwight, eventually a first lieutenant in the Twentieth Ohio, shared an especially detailed account of his experiences in the war's early days and how he came to enlist. After the attack on Fort Sumter, Dwight and his brother visited New York City and attended pro-Union rallies, saw former commander of Fort Sumter Maj. Robert Anderson speak, and witnessed a volunteer regiment parading through the streets. He described the Victorian equivalent of the modern twenty-four-hour news cycle: "The bulletin boards of the newspapers were the center of huge crowds; extras were published every hour and between times the people accosted one another on the street to ask and give news."[3] Dwight's brother advised him to wait to enlist, so he went on to Delaware, Ohio, where he planned to start attending Ohio Wesleyan University. Dwight continued to follow the war news and soon joined a militia company formed mostly of fellow students. Eventually, he received a letter from his father (a missionary living in Constantinople) endorsing his desire to enlist. Then news arrived of the First Battle of Bull Run, "with all its shame and broken hopes."[4] Dwight spent the night at the local telegraph office, listening to each news dispatch as the telegraph clerk received it. The Union defeat solidified his choice to enlist. Many of the young men in Dwight's militia unit decided not to enlist yet, and other acquaintances, including the college's president, actively tried to discourage Dwight from enlisting. However, he remained determined to do "that which came to [my] hand toward restoring peace in the land."[5]

Sometimes officers, primarily a regiment's field officers, would give hortatory speeches to their regiments, thereby exhibiting something of their own thoughts on the Union cause. Shortly after the Fortieth Illinois was organized in August 1861, the new colonel, Stephen Hicks, addressed its assembled volunteers and summarized their mission. He declared that with them behind him, he was "willing to meet the rebel crew on the bloody field of conflict who have dared to insult our national standard to deny her sovereignty."[6] Hicks promised his regiment, "We will advance against the foe as a united band of brothers fighting in the same great and righteous cause."[7] The following summer, for Independence Day 1862, the Fortieth's lieutenant colonel, James Boothe, addressed the unit, laying out the importance of good discipline for the sake of "the great responsibility resting upon those whose duty it is to stand by and protect our Government."[8]

Officers in the Fifty-Fifth Illinois shared typical views on the nature of the Union cause. Captain Henry Stedman Nourse framed the war in terms of preserving an inheritance from the past, recalling how volunteers "abandoned ease, possessions, home, youthful aspirations, love, to protect for posterity the constitution which our fathers had built at great cost."[9] In the regimental history they cowrote, Nourse's comrade Capt. Lucien Crooker declared that they went to war for the purpose "of saving a great republic."[10] In March 1863, the Fifty-Fifth Illinois, officers and men alike, responded to news of Copperheads (Northern Democrats thought to sympathize with the Confederacy) back home and a perceived lack of support for the war on the home front by passing a series of resolutions. They affirmed that they volunteered "for the defence of the best government upon the earth" and asserted that "the present rebellion against the rightful authority of the United States of America, is unparalleled for its atrocity in the annals of the world."[11] They expressed willingness to keep fighting "until we witness the death agonies of this godless rebellion."[12]

Early in the war, German immigrant Friedrich Martens tried to explain the situation to his parents back in Europe. "The states that are rebelling are slave states," he wrote in June 1861, "and they want slavery to be expanded, but the northern states are against this, and so it's civil war!"[13] The war would go on "until the last traitor to freedom is lying at our feet, begging for mercy!"[14] Martens expanded on these ideas in August, characterizing the conflict as a fight to protect freedom from slavery "in all its atrociousness."[15] The rebels were "making war on freedom, suppressing the freedom we paid so dearly for. Would I still be worthy of living in this land, enjoying this freedom, if I were not also willing to fight for this freedom, and if need be, to die for it?"[16] Martens requested that if he died, his father would make sure all knew he had fallen in an honorable and sacred cause, fighting in an army full of like-minded volunteers. The value Martens attached to the American government manifested in the wish that his nephew might learn "to hate tyrants, abhor oppressors and . . . to love and venerate freedom, true freedom," because Germany "must someday be free as well, and who knows whether he may need to play his part to make it free."[17] He concluded, "Oh, truly God liveth, and God does not want slaves but free men. God does not appoint a government to oppress the people, but to rule them wisely!"[18] In Martens's view, the US government, then menaced by rebellion, was just such a government.

John Quincy Adams Campbell likewise viewed slavery as the root cause of the war. Campbell denied going to war out of mere enthusiasm or from a desire for honor and glory. To the contrary, he chose to fight "because I believe that duty to my country and my *God,* bid me assist in crushing this wicked rebellion against our government, which rebellion men have instigated to secure their own promotion . . . and to secure the extension of that blighting curse—*slavery*—o'er our fair land."[19] Campbell's subsequent interactions with white Southerners only strengthened his convictions about the war's origin. He wrote to a Northern newspaper in January 1863 that the rebels he met openly admitted "that Slavery is the 'bone of contention' and that the slave question must be settled by this war . . . either the South will succeed in her rebellion and establish slavery on a National basis or the North will whip them and slavery die."[20] Amid a bout of frustrated discouragement in February 1863, Campbell reminded himself, "The Union must stand, undivided, entire, triumphant. Many sacrifices will have to be made, many trials endured. . . . The end, *I believe*, will be the complete triumph of our cause. And such an end is worth the sacrifices and sufferings of a generation."[21]

In contrast to officers such as Martens and Campbell, some officers were quite emphatic that they did not go to war to free slaves. In October 1862, Luther Cowan shared how he made a point of informing white Southerners that he was in their states only "to support and protect the laws of the U. S. in a legal way . . . we proposed to fight for the constitution and laws as long as there [is] a man in arms in the south or any other latitude to fight against them."[22] Several weeks later, he explained to a hometown newspaper that he and other soldiers did not take up arms against the South "to meddle with their 'niggers,'" but rather "to maintain the constitution."[23] He observed that many white Southerners had "been humbugged into the belief that when the northern soldiers entered their territory a scene of murder and rapine would ensue . . . that we were all abolitionists of the deepest dye."[24] Such civilians were repeatedly surprised that the US Army's presence was less horrific than they anticipated.

Late in February 1863, Cowan assured a friend about the army's determination and commitment to "fighting manfully for their rights and the perpetuity of the liberties of the country."[25] Cowan emphasized the sacrifice of personal comfort that army life involved and denied that he or any soldier fought for personal gain: "Anyone who has formed the opinion that the thirteen dollars per month is what the soldiers are soldiers for, is very much mistaken in his conclusion."[26] He reiterated that he fought for the Union, not against slavery, and aimed "to save the union, 'nigger or no nigger'. If it makes him free all right; if it leaves him where it found him, all right; only save the union, and all will be right."[27] Cowan claimed he and his fellow soldiers "are for war, harder and more of it, till the victory is proclaimed, and that for the constitution and laws."[28] They were likewise "for the proclamation and for every other edict that has been or may be issued for the furtherance of our cause."[29] The "proclamation" referred to the Emancipation Proclamation, reflecting how Northerners increasingly came to identify the demolition of slavery as a strategic measure necessary to achieve Union victory. In April 1863, about a month before his death in battle outside Vicksburg, Cowan expressed a "firmly fixed purpose and determination to wage eternal war" against all enemies of the Union "until every infamous, sacrilegious wretch who would butcher his country shall have hidden himself in some loathsome hole or cried for quarter."[30]

Most Army of the Tennessee officers seem to have shared Cowan's dismissal of pay as a motivator, but German immigrant Balzar Grebe was an exception. He enlisted in the Fourteenth Illinois in May 1861 for a three-month term. When the regiment prepared to commit to a three-year term of service, Grebe stopped short. "I did not know what to do. I had a wife and one child at home. My wife lived in hopes that I would not be a long term soldier. So, I concluded I did not want to be a soldier for three years or the duration of the war," he explained.[31] Grebe was discharged and returned home. However, he experienced great difficulties finding work. With his financial situation worsening, Grebe and his wife Christina finally decided that he would rejoin the army to try to feed his family and "that we should have faith and trust in the Lord that He would watch over us."[32] He returned to Company G of the Fourteenth Illinois and subsequently became its second lieutenant.

Some officers exhibited signs that ambition was at least as great a motivator as patriotism in their service. David Stuart, colonel of the Fifty-Fifth Illinois, was a Chicago lawyer who had been accused of adultery with another man's wife and became caught up in a sensational divorce case. Though he had not been found guilty, his social standing never recovered, and he therefore determined to burnish his reputation with martial glory. Being colonel was not enough for Stuart—he aimed to become a general, and when it became apparent that he would not reach that rank, he left the army. The career of Thomas Cavanaugh, colonel of the Sixth Illinois Cavalry, was similar. According to a subordinate, the colonel repeatedly neglected his duties to pursue schemes for obtaining promotion to general. In January 1862, Cavanaugh visited Cairo and Springfield, Illinois, seeking to convince the authorities in each place that he deserved to be a brigadier general. The ambitious colonel "felt so sure he would get it that he provided, and had no better taste than to appear in, the uniform of that grade. The display proved to be decidedly premature, for he ingloriously failed to receive the appointment."[33] Disappointed in his goal, Cavanaugh resigned in March of that year. Some degree of ambition was likely present in the minds of many officers, but for a few, it was a leading motivator of their military service.

Shortly after the Battle of Fort Donelson in February 1862, Oliver Bridgford found time to explore the battleground, an activity that moved him to muse on the cause for which he fought. The area was a gloomy sight, with clothes, hats, boots, and other military gear strewn around haphazardly. "Here and there," Bridgford recounted, "is mounds of Fresh Clay thrown up that plainly Speaks here Lies a Bold Soldier that has Lost his Life for the Love of his Country."[34] In grappling with why his fellow soldiers died, Bridgford revealed his own understanding of the Union cause. These men died "trying to uphold the *Stars and Stripes* the emblem our Forefathers unfurled over the Land of the Free and the Home of the Brave. They Lay there a Sacrifice to union and Liberty."[35] Defending "the union our Fore Fathers Fought for" was worth giving up the comforts of home and family, Bridgford concluded.[36]

From near Corinth, Mississippi, where he was camped in May 1862, Alphonso Barto of the Fifty-Second Illinois outlined his view of the war's greater meaning in a letter to his father. He spoke of his desire to return home to his family once the country was safe and its Republican institutions secured. Already the rebellion threatened those institutions, but recently rumors had spread that France might join the war to aid the Confederacy, prompting Barto to suggest, "The monarchies of the old world are afraid to have this government show that it can put down this rebellion."[37] The Union's triumph was going to establish "beyond question that man is capable of self government and as soon as the World knows . . . the truth of that principal those thrones of the old world will shake to their very center and if we succeed in this struggle I predict that in one hundred years there not be a throne left in Europe."[38] Shortly after the close of the Atlanta Campaign, Barto declared to his father, "Liberty is what we are sacraficing our lives for in the army to day."[39]

Hezekiah Clock, a first lieutenant in the Sixth Iowa, encountered a newspaper editorial claiming that the US Army's efforts were morally equivalent to the John Brown raid. The editorial inspired Clock to share his views on the Union cause with his brother Alonzo. He recalled that Brown "had a *new constitution* which he wrote himself that he hoped to establish, and his followers were sworn . . . to establish a government in opposition to the laws made by our forefathers. The plainest definition I can give is secession. He wanted a new and different government, a new constitution and new laws. So do the rebels."[40] Clock insisted the rebels were murderous, traitorous, and violators of Constitution—just like John Brown. The men fighting "to protect the laws of our Republick" and "to protect the nation that is known throughout the world as the land of Liberty and Freedom" had little in common with John Brown, Clock contended.[41] "Lon if any man in the north thinks this an unjust war and ought to cease," suggested Clock, "let him leave the bad men in which he has been placed and join the good men in the South, and stay among such wicked men no more."[42] Clock fought because he believed only with the rebellion's defeat could peace return to the land.

Alexander Ewing, in a pair of letters from late 1862 and early 1863, explained to his parents why he chose to endure the trials of army life. Rhetorically asking why he would do this, he answered, "Why to defend the Stars and Stripes from being torn and trampled under foot by the hands of traitors who are seeking to destroy our liberties and bring us under the most tyrannical and despotic government the world ever knew."[43] The rebellion represented a grave threat to the rights all Americans enjoyed. "No longer does the Bird of liberty find a Southern home," Ewing waxed poetical, "No longer does freedoms fire burn on Southern soil. But their does wave tyrants dark banner throwing its dark and sombre folds over this once peaceful & happy country."[44] In another missive to his parents, Ewing cited heroes of the past and extolled the Union's merits and his own duty to defend it. "As Old 'Hickory' [i.e., Andrew Jackson] said the Union Right or Wrong."[45] Ewing had no patience for those who complained about the Lincoln administration's actions regarding slavery. "In the words of Stephen Decatur [a famous naval hero] The Union, May she always be right, But the Union Always. This is no time to stop and argue whether it is right."[46] In Ewing's view, people criticizing the Lincoln administration's war policies had misplaced priorities.

Officers' devotion to the Union cause persisted long past the exciting days of enlistment. Henry Kircher of the Twelfth Missouri insisted in July 1863, "The rebs will see into there folly by and by, and play quits, for conquered they will and must be, last it 100 years."[47] Around the same time, Kircher wrote to his mother that good men accepted the need to suffer for their cause, and one "who doesn't want to endure any hardships would not be worth my lifting up my boot to give him a kick in the behind."[48] In mid-November, as he anticipated battle near Chattanooga, Captain Kircher invoked the Union cause as a source of comfort. He wrote to his mother that although many soldiers would die or be wounded in the upcoming fight, their families could "console themselves with the knowledge that they too have done their honest part for freedom, for the preservation of their country."[49]

James Proudfit's sense of duty also remained strong late in the war. While serving as lieutenant colonel of the Twelfth Wisconsin, Proudfit tried in September 1864 to explain to his wife Emelie why he planned to seek promotion to colonel even though it would extend his commitment to the army beyond his original three-year term. "The Government needs the help of good men of military experience," Proudfit declared. "If I am such a man and you will pardon my egotism for thinking I am and probably think so yourself, it is my plain duty as a patriot to stay."[50] He expressed hope that his wife would "lovingly and cheerfully" share his conclusion, asking her, "Write to me and tell what you think and don't forget the great cause that we are struggling for and the duties we owe to our country."[51]

Albert Arndt, a captain in the First Michigan Light Artillery, explained his understanding of the war while conversing with a Southern gentleman in Savannah, Georgia, after Sherman's forces captured the city. According to Arndt, the crux of the matter was "if we could suffer to have this great country broken up, or if it was the duty of every loyal citizen to prevent this."[52] Arndt insisted he had no personal ill will toward Southerners but did hold them responsible for causing the war. "The North surely did not commence this war. The South fired the first shot, determined to destroy this country. Our Government had endeavored to prevent this calamity," but the Southern states "to our great surprise insisted upon this unnatural war."[53] In view of the threat the rebels posed to the country, Arndt felt compelled to fight.

Officers recognized that they might die in the war and judged it an acceptable risk for the sake of the Union. When Capt. Harley Wayne of the Fifteenth Illinois visited the site of the Battle of Wilson's Creek, specifically the place where Gen. Nathaniel Lyon fell, Wayne felt overcome with emotion. "And as I viewed the spot," he reported, "I almost thought that the chance thus to die for the rights and liberties of one's native land was a boon to be ardently desired and sought for."[54] His wife Ellen did not share this feeling, writing to him of her great anxiety about what might happen to her husband. He answered that fear could not take precedence over the duty he owed his country. It pained him to be away from his family, he said, but "your reproaches of want of affection for you and my dear boy (which I need not refute) cannot move me—My own honor—Your honor—Charley's honor and the good name of us all are dependent on my fulfilling my vows and duty to my own native land."[55] To that end, he promised "in the presence of God our master that though I die in conflict or by disease or languish in the prisons dangerous though it cost me all I have and am and are I will try to do my duty so well that you shall not be disgraced or ashamed of my living or dying."[56] One questions whether this oath brought Ellen Wayne much comfort when her husband was killed in action at Shiloh a few months later.

Joseph Stockton, then a captain in the Seventy-Second Illinois, made several observations regarding his sense of duty. After joining the army in July 1862, he wrote, "I trust I may never have occasion to regret the step, as I enlisted from a pure sense of duty toward my country and love for the old flag."[57] Later that summer, he gave voice to a typical expression of soldiers' willingness to die: "God alone knows who will return, but I must not commence thinking of that, as it is a soldier's duty to die if need be."[58] Finally, on a Sunday morning in November 1862, as Stockton thought about the people back home enjoying the privilege of going to church, he wondered, "if any there give their thoughts to the absent ones who loved their country better than all the pleasure and comforts of home and are willing to die for it."[59]

Many officers stated their readiness to die for the Union cause, but Charles Wills was exceptionally vociferous on this point. In September 1861, Wills expressed a desire "to fight the rest of my life if necessary, and die before we recognize them as anything but Rebels and traitors who must be humbled."[60] In August 1862, Wills grimly insisted he would "rather see the whole country red with blood, and ruined together than have this 7,000,000 of invalids (these Southerners are nothing else as a people) conquer, or successfully resist the power of the North. I hate them now, as they hate us."[61] Wills added that he felt little hope for true reunification, predicting "extermination of one or the other of the two parties, and of the two, think the world and civilization will lose the least by losing the South and slavery."[62] Regarding the outcome of the campaign for Vicksburg, he announced in February 1863, "If we get whipped I'd like to die there, for I believe if that army is whipped it will be annihilated; and the cause about lost, which little event I don't care to live to hear."[63] Amid the Atlanta Campaign, in June 1864, Wills told his sister, "I will take the best care I can of myself (and do my whole duty). I yet think that to be connected with such a campaign as this is well worth risking one's life for." [64] Notwithstanding his repeatedly stated willingness to die for the Union, Wills survived the war.

As much as the men who led the Army of the Tennessee valued the Union and felt an obligation to defend their republic from an unjustified rebellion, they recognized other obligations as well, sometimes creating agonizing tension between competing duties. Such conflict arose chiefly when their sense of duty to country took them away from their duty to family. Benjamin Franklin Best, a second lieutenant in the Fortieth Illinois, left his wife Mary and two children to serve in the army. He described in an October 1861 letter his reaction to learning his son was ill: "When i herd he was sick I would have given anything in the world if i could have bin there. Then, and just then, I . . . regretted that I ever volunteered or left home."[65] Despite this, Best retained the conviction that he was serving a worthy cause: "Who could stand with his arms folded and see our glorious liberties trampled opon, Which our fore fathers Fought for, We have enjoyed that glorious Privilege of liberty, and now while life will last we shall stand firm for the Union. If we do not enjoy it our wifes and children, I hope, will." [66] It was the "godforsaken Rebels" who were truly responsible for taking him and his compatriots away from their families, Best declared.[67] "I hope god will speed the time when we will all get home and we still will enjoy the glorious liberty of Freedom," Best concluded.[68]

Henry Ankeny struggled intensely with the feeling that his duty to country was hindering his duty to his family. During his war service, Ankeny had an infant daughter die, a son be born, and another daughter be born and die. These ups and downs prompted him to write at length to his wife Tina about his conflicting obligations to country and family. Ankeny said he joined the army "to fight for the Union and the Constitution and Laws."[69] Reconciling his desire to serve this cause with his duty to his family proved difficult indeed for Ankeny.[70]

Tina was pregnant when he left for the war; Ankeny wrote in August 1861 asking "when you expect to be confined, and if it is possible, I will come home, as it is my desire to be with you then. . . . It is a duty that I owe to you and myself and will fulfill it if possible."[71] In December 1862, he lamented the distress he had caused Tina by joining the army. "Had I have taken your advice and remained at our own peaceful home how much better it would have been," Ankeny concluded.[72] News in March 1863 that his wife and infant son were ill moved him to declare, "I very often think since I received your letter that it was my duty to go to you and our suffering child."[73] In late May of that year, Ankeny contemplated leaving the army once Vicksburg fell: "I feel as if I have done my duty so far and that there is a duty more precious to me to perform to others than my country requires, at least after the next great fight."[74] He received furlough that summer and upon returning to the front, deeply regretted leaving Tina and their son again. "I know I would have been more than happy, but foolishly I have thrown this all away for what is supposed to be my duty to others, that are not mine or yours," Ankeny wrote.[75] He retained a sense of the war's stakes, musing during the Atlanta Campaign "that two great opposing armies are contending the supremacy of what each claims for the right."[76] Despite his qualms, Ankeny served out his full three-year enlistment, then returned home rather than reenlist.[77]

Some officers wrestled with the feeling that responsibility to country conflicted with responsibility to family, but others argued that the two obligations aligned. The epistles of Benjamin Grierson reveal a man who fought to defend his country from rebellion and who believed this was necessary to preserve liberty for his family. Grierson quickly felt a need to participate in the war, informing his wife Alice in May 1861, "I must (to be true to myself & Country) *Stand not idly bye* in this the hour of *trial.*"[78] He reported his reaction to spotting a "Secession Flag" flying across the Ohio River in Kentucky: "As soon as I saw with the Glass (that I had taken along for observation) that contemptible *piece* of *bunting* floating it made my blood boil."[79] He felt duty-bound to oppose the treasonous banner: "I am ready for the fight and believe I will do my duty and I hope to live to see our Country rid of all traitors."[80] If he and others inadequately supported the government during this time, Grierson elaborated in another letter, "we must all submit to the tyranny and despotism of the traitors of the South."[81] Though Grierson said he would feel unworthy of being an American citizen if he held back from serving, he also saw the war's implications for his children. Addressing his son Charlie, Grierson praised "the flag of liberty, the *Stars and Stripes,*" and said he was going to war "so that you and many other little Boys can have a flag of that kind and so that when you get to be men you can see *great big* flags (like it, only larger) floating over this land of Freedom."[82]

Thomas Taylor, then a major of the Forty-Seventh Ohio, was another officer who framed the meaning of his military service in terms of how it benefited his family. In August 1863, he wrote to his wife Margaret (often called "Netta") of envisioning her "on the front porch in your chair and the children playing around. . . . How I would like to sit down on the threshold and have half an hours chat."[83] Taylor quoted from the poem "The Two Homes," by Felicia Hemans, to represent his feelings:

My home! the spirit of its love is breathing
In every wind that plays across my track.

From its white wall the very tendrils wreathing
Seem with soft links to draw the wanderer back.[84]

But all these happy thoughts, according to Taylor, would be meaningless "without the protection afforded by a capable and liberal government."[85] His military service aimed to permanently secure for his family the benefits, and indeed the very existence, of such a good government. "These considerations are what tie me to the army, what induces me to take part in this struggle in which the stakes are human life and peace, order and happiness, against anarchy, miserable tyranny and war," Taylor concluded.[86]

"I have entered the army not for sport or with the hope of benefiting myself," DeWitt Clinton Loudon told his wife Hannah in March 1862, "but simply from a sense of that high duty which every good citizen owes to his country."[87] Writing from Pittsburg Landing, Tennessee, later that month, Loudon expressed a belief that "the politicians & those who wanted to run slavery as a paying concern" had caused the rebellion.[88] Loudon also wanted to make sure his children understood the cause for which he fought, asking that if he died, Hannah would "teach them to love their country" and to understand that he died so that "they among others might enjoy the blessings of Liberty, of Law & order & good government."[89] He also penned a letter to his daughters, Fanny and Betty, trying to explain why he was gone and could not come home. "Wicked men are trying to destroy our government and do great harm to our country," he wrote, "and we have to stay down here & try to put them down."[90] He warned that the rebels would happily raid Ohio and burn their house if the Union did not fight. Consequently, he and many other loving fathers were "staying away from home and living hard and fighting bloody battles in order that their children may continue to have happy homes & all the other blessings which every body had before This cruel war was begun by wicked men."[91]

Throughout the war, Jacob Ritner revealed his commitment to the Union cause through repeated expressions of determination to remain in the army until it secured victory over the rebellion. However, he also acknowledged the tension between duty to country versus duty to family. When a rumor spread in March 1863 that the Twenty-Fifth Iowa would be mustered out that June, Ritner declared that although he was tired of war and eager to go home to his family, he had joined the army to help win the war and wanted to finish the job before he left. Therefore, if he were discharged, he planned to enlist again. "We know that we must all make sacrifices to save our country from this wicked rebellion," he affirmed, explaining that he hoped to leave the army as soon as possible, "but *never* until this unholy rebellion is put down, and the last traitor, both North and South, brought to condign punishment."[92] Ritner insisted he did not desire war, and he lamented its costs, but he held the cause worthy of the sacrifices involved. He bemoaned the terrible war that separated him from his family in a July 1864 letter to his wife Emeline, but he continued to believe that the cause warranted the sacrifice:

> You must not think that I regret that I entered the army, or that I begrudge to my country for a moment all that I have done and suffered in trying to serve her. I have never felt so for a moment. No, my dear, if only through this baptism of blood, our nation, freed and purified from the blighting curse of slavery, shall lift her radiant forehead from the dust, and crowned with the wisdom of freedom go on her glorious way rejoicing. I shall count my past suffering and shattered health only as the small dust in the balance compared with the priceless blessings of peace, freedom, and national unity which they may have contributed however slightly to purchase. Only to have contributed something however little, for the peace, something for the glory, something for the permanence of those beautiful and bright institutions which are the pride of the past and the hope of the future—will be a joy through life and a consolation in death.[93]

Ritner reiterated these themes in a January 1865 letter. Like many of his comrades, he readily acknowledged the trials the war inflicted, but he deemed the cause worth the cost.[94]

Ritner's fervent statements of devotion to the Union cause did not prevent him from considering the impact his military service had on his family. He once tried to explain to his eight-year-old daughter Nellie why he had been gone for so long. He massaged the truth somewhat in his depiction of the Southern states, but his attempt to explain the war to a child still reveals something of his understanding of the war:

> This country is not a bit like Iowa. It's covered with hills and rocks and there are no nice towns and houses. The people live in little old log cabins. I have seen a great many little boys and girls like mine who were dirty and ragged and had nothing to eat and looked very miserable indeed. And then, there are no *schools* in all the country and the children all grow up

without learning anything. I've seen girls and boys a great deal larger than you and Lulie who never were at school in their lives. And I am so thankful that my little girls have a nice home and good clothes and plenty to eat and a good school and Sunday school to go to. Don't you think you ought to be very thankful that you have all these things and such a good, kind mother to take care of you? And then these wicked people down here would like to make our country just as poor and miserable as theirs is. And, if it was not for your pa and the other soldiers, you would soon have no nice homes or schools either. But I expect you think this may be hard to understand. Ask Ma to tell you more about it.[95]

Ritner was trying to reduce the war to terms his young daughter would understand, and in doing so made clear that he saw the rebellion as something that would ultimately menace his own family's wellbeing. Military service took him away from his family, but it was also a measure to protect them.

Ritner's most eloquent discourse on the tension between duty to country and duty to family came at the end of July 1864. "I feel too that I have a duty to discharge to you both [i.e., his wife and mother-in-law] and to our children as well as to our country. But which has the greatest and most pressing claims?" Ritner asked.[96] He answered his own question, "If I were to consult my own feelings and inclinations, without regard to duty or patriotism, I should certainly be at home with you just as soon as possible."[97] However, the question felt more complicated than that: "I am very much attached to my company; I enlisted them all and came out with them with the understanding that I would stand by them and stay with them till their time is out. We have marched and fought and suffered together so far, and seen our ranks gradually thinned out till I have come to feel towards them almost as if they were my brothers. And what excuse could I make to them for leaving them while I am able to stand in my place and at their head and lead them. I don't feel like I could do it."[98] Through the end of the war Ritner wrestled with his conflicting duties and desires. Marching through South Carolina in February 1865, he declared, "I can't help feeling the bitterest hatred towards the wretches who brought on this war. What comfort and happiness I might have enjoyed at home . . . instead of traveling all over creation to force them to respect a government that is intended for a blessing to them."[99]

The men who led the Army of the Tennessee viewed the war in political and ideological terms, seeing it as the attempt of a traitorous rebellion to destroy the best government in history. Many would have shared Edward Wood's assessment of the Confederates as "mad conspirators who have well nigh destroyed our beloved country."[100] Overwhelmingly, officers expressed the belief that the Union they inherited from their ancestors was a force for good—the guarantor of rights, peace, and prosperity for their families—and they had a responsibility to aid in and sacrifice for its defense. As William Burnett put it, they felt duty-bound to serve until "the end of this miserable rebellion and groundless attempt to over throw the best government ever established on earth."[101] Few men voluntarily left their homes and families merely out of social pressure, ambition for rank, financial prospects, or desire for adventure. Over and over officers articulated a more thoughtful outlook on the nature of the war. Many grappled with how duty to country conflicted with duty to family, but their belief that the Union was good meant its preservation ultimately benefited their families. There were of course exceptions, men who enlisted because they needed the pay, sought battlefield glory and prestigious rank, or hoped the war would be a means of destroying the institution of slavery. In general, the Army of the Tennessee's officers plainly described themselves as fighting for the Union and against treasonous rebels, and they retained this outlook throughout the war.

CHAPTER 9

Suffering

"They were going to the front for glory, and I was going to the rear disabled, with no further part in the war and no share in the final victory which awaited us. Then I cried like a child—yes, like a child!" Col. Edward Noyes recalled as he watched his Thirty-Ninth Ohio leave him behind after he lost a leg during the Atlanta Campaign.[1] The Army of the Tennessee's officers both enjoyed and suffered a wide range of experiences during their service. Among the most unpleasant aspects of the war were the dangers of getting captured, falling ill, being wounded, or dying. Notwithstanding the Army of the Tennessee's string of strategically significant victories, there were still plenty of small engagements or chaotic moments within larger battles wherein men could become cut off and taken prisoner. Perhaps about a fifth of the Army of the Tennessee's officers were killed in action or dealt fatal wounds. Many more received wounds that they survived but which led to amputations or long periods of recovery. Sickness, the scourge of armies throughout history, seems to have killed far fewer of the Army of the Tennessee's officers than the rebels did, but even when illness was not deadly, it was miserable. In the context of these perils, numerous officers wrote about death, reflected on their chances of dying, and consistently declared that their cause was worthy of sacrifice. From capture to illness to wounds to death, officers had to confront the worst aspects of wartime experience both personally and in watching their colleagues suffer.

Through various misfortunes, the Army of the Tennessee's officers could find themselves captured by the enemy. Sometimes, the rebels might launch a small raid on an isolated outpost, grab a handful of prisoners during the skirmish, and then withdraw before facing more substantial resistance. Being captured and being wounded are intersecting misfortunes, since a wound could reduce or eliminate a man's mobility and leave him easy prey for advancing Confederate troops. Sometimes an officer just got lost, either at night or in the confusion of battle, and wandered into enemy lines. Throughout the war, both sides exchanged prisoners (although the practice was greatly disrupted by the Confederate refusal to exchange Black US soldiers), and captured officers often rejoined their units once exchanged. Some officers were paroled quickly, but others languished in Confederate prisons for months.[2]

Together with most of his comrades in the Eighth Iowa, 1st Lt. Charles Searle was captured at Shiloh during the first day of the battle: "Everything was in great confusion and hand to hand strife. Being slow of comprehension, it was some time before I fully realized our condition. You may imagine my feelings, but I cannot describe them. My time had come to receive personal attention. A big, burly Rebel captain stepped up to me and said, 'You d—d Yankee, give me your sword!' Oh, how I did want to give it to him point first. But discretion prevailed, and I gave it to him hilt first, which probably saved the burial squad two interments."[3] At the end of day, notwithstanding the fact that he was a prisoner, Searle admitted, "I was thankful to the Almighty God that my wife was not left a widow, or my darling child an orphan; thankful, also, that they could not know my condition."[4] Searle was later exchanged and resumed his service. The Army of the Tennessee's penchant for winning meant its officers faced capture less often than its opponents did, but some like Searle did suffer that fate.

Poor health dogged officers throughout the war. Sick men often got left behind when a regiment moved, potentially adding separation from friends to the inherent discomforts of being unwell. Sickness also meant disruption of officers' regular duties, including missing out on major battles. In a job that relied on giving spoken orders loudly enough to be heard by dozens of men, losing one's voice to a cold was truly debilitating. Attacks of diarrhea were especially problematic during times like the Atlanta Campaign, when men literally spent months constantly in range of enemy fire and could not readily access a latrine. Henry Dwight complained after being left behind sick during one engagement, "I felt like one who has to hear of a picnic to which he might have gone, but which he has missed."[5] Illness was a common reason that lower-ranked officers had to fill in for their superiors. Specific medical issues officers recorded included typhoid, malaria, dysentery, jaundice, headaches, burns, bad teeth, ear infections, hair loss, back injuries, boils, frostbite, rheumatism, and the common cold. Given the ubiquity of sickness, it makes sense why officers' letters home so frequently included assurances that they were in good health—such as Luther Cowan's colorful declaration: "I am all right, tough as an owl's gizzard and an appetite like a saw mill."[6] If a surgeon believed it essential to save a man's life, he could write a certificate recommending a sick man get a leave of absence, but most of the time sick officers just had to endure poor health where they were. Even when officers could obtain a furlough, if they were not near a river or railroad, they might be too sick to travel home.[7]

If their complaints can be believed, in many cases officers seem to have received poor medical care. Oscar Jackson claimed medical care providers (specifically the US Sanitary Commission and US Christian Commission) were biased against officers and treated common soldiers far better: "Every one takes it for granted that officers have money and friends and if these things are illusionary you fare badly."[8] Jake Ritner likely had something similar in mind when he blasted the Sanitary Commission's practices as "the most stupendous humbug, the most damnable imposition, and the most outrageous rascality."[9] Oliver Bridgford angrily declared, "If there ever was a Lot of men in the world that aught to be gibbetted it is the Doctors in the army they think no more of a mans Life or Comfort than they would of a dogs."[10] Warren Gray speculated in his diary that the doctors "don't care much whether a man lives or dies."[11] Ephraim Brown recorded a rare positive healthcare experience, but notably, it came from his comrades rather from doctors: men throughout the 114th Ohio brought him "Chicken Soup and pieces of chicken and all kinds of the best things they could get" while he was ill.[12] In short, many officers criticized the medical care they received.[13]

Evidence to how bad medical care could be is that a hospitalized Jake Ritner claimed he preferred being on the front lines of the Atlanta Campaign to being in an army field hospital: "I shall go to the front just as soon as I can, and so would you if you were in such a hole as this is."[14] He told of sick and wounded patients being crowded together onto dirty freight cars and left unattended, going unfed at times, and being crowded into rooms with dozens of other casualties. During Ritner's convalescence, Gen. James B. McPherson ordered all unwell officers sent back to Chattanooga, which entailed another protracted, miserable train trip for Ritner: "We nearly melted in the dirty cars."[15] Ritner finally reached Chattanooga, but according to him, the doctor sent along to supervise the patients was drunk and failed to make proper accommodations for the new arrivals. They were sent to Crutchfield House (a hotel in Chattanooga where Ritner had stayed the previous December), but there was no room and thus many officers literally had to spend the night in the street. Eventually Ritner was transferred to a hospital for officers atop Lookout Mountain.[16] The hospital was a lovely place, "where the air feels as pure and cool and bracing as it does in Iowa," and "we can see 'all over creation' almost, sleep under two blankets at night, and feel comfortable in the daytime, when persons in the valley below are sweltering and almost suffocating in the heat and dust."[17] Ritner later expressed eagerness to get away from the hospital, this time not from frustration with the care provided, but because of the isolation and a desire to get news and return "to the *front* where there is something going on and some excitement."[18]

James Compton, a captain of the Fifty-Second Illinois, contributed to a somewhat unconventional story of care for one injured officer in the fall of 1863. The Fifty-Second was stationed in Pulaski, Tennessee, and one morning a young man showed up claiming to be clerk for one Captain Owens of an Indiana regiment in another division of the Army of the Tennessee. This Owens had been thrown from his horse a couple weeks prior, injured, and left at a plantation when his regiment moved on; the clerk remained behind to care for him. Unfortunately, indecisive rebel guerillas had visited, taken the captain and clerk prisoner, paroled them, then threatened to return and kill them. A Union division commander had previously threatened the planter in whose home they were staying, telling him that if Owens were harmed, the general would return and burn every house in a radius of five miles. Thus their host was quite eager to be rid of Captain Owens before the guerrillas returned to make good on their threat. The clerk also claimed the plantation was under surveillance and he had to sneak out after dark and travel through the night to reach Pulaski. Most of the Fifty-Second's officers thought the story sounded sketchy and doubted the unfamiliar young man's veracity. However, 1st Lt. Lucien S. Kinney, eager for a break from routine, begged permission to investigate the matter. He obtained authorization, if he could find volunteers for the job. At this point, Compton got involved, helping Kinney collect a dozen volunteers. The regiment was short of fresh meat, so as part of the deal for them to go with Kinney, it was agreed that they would apprehend any rebel pigs they saw on the way. Collecting three ambulances and some medical supplies, the expedition departed.[19]

Kinney put the clerk who brought the information in the front wagon and sat behind him and the driver with a sergeant whom he ordered to "remove all the head of the guide above the ears" at the first sign of a trap.[20] It was not a trap; they found Owens just as the clerk described, collected him, and headed back to the Fifty-Second's camp.[21] When they reached a major road and felt relatively safe, they spotted some "razor backs" and halted to fulfill the aforementioned commitment to kill rebel hogs.[22] Ironically, Owens was outraged by this adventure. Lieutenant Kinney later claimed he "never heard such an accomplished swearer as Owens. His vocabulary of cuss-words was something wonderful."[23] The captain was fearful and impatient to reach Union lines, "so he lifted up his voice and swore, going, the boys said, 'through the whole scale from high C. to seven flats.'"[24] He denounced Kinney as "an idiot, a pretty thing to be an officer in the United States Army: told him that he was not fit to wear the uniform of a private and ending by ordering the whole outfit to move on."[25]

Lieutenant Kinney gamely admitted that he obviously was an idiot, for otherwise he would have left Owens "to die where he had found him, for the good of the service."[26] He explained that Owens was not the sole goal of the expedition and that he had to bring other pigs to camp, too, but that if Owens did not like the situation, he was free to get out and walk back to the plantation while they dealt with the other hogs. The expedition returned safely, and Compton, Kinney, and another officer of the Fifty-Second cared for Owens until he was well enough to return home for further rest. The conclusion to the adventure came months later, when the Fifty-Second passed through Rome, Georgia, during the Atlanta Campaign. As Kinney was walking down the road, an officer rode up and declared, "I told you once, sir, that you were not fit to be an officer in the United States Army and I have not changed my mind a d—d bit. I suppose you are looking for hogs as usual. I have a little account to settle with you, and you will come with me."[27] It was Owens, returned to duty and now in charge of the commissary department in Rome. His harsh greeting proved to be in jest, and he treated the officers who had cared for him to what Compton called "mighty smooth" supplies, although Compton recalled they had "possibly a little too much mint to suit an Irishman," and Owens requested that Kinney's company receive the privilege of serving as guard for his stores.[28]

Combat injuries ranged from minor scratches to mortal wounds, and even when a wound was not itself fatal, there was grave risk of infection that might kill a man. Hopeful predictions that a man would recover were commonly disappointed. Even so, plenty of officers suffered wounds that they survived. Sometimes the damage was severe enough to keep them from returning to active duty, but many did rejoin their units after convalescing. When possible, the wounded received immediate care during or just after the battle, and then they were sent by steamboat or train back to a hospital in some more secure area. Severely injured officers might procure a surgeon's certificate authorizing them to go home to rest and heal, if the surgeon deemed it necessary to save their life or prevent permanent disability. Officers also received truly minor injuries. A ball might pass through their coat, cut a canteen strap, or graze their skin, leaving a painful mark and a hole in their clothes but not threatening their lives or interfering with their ability to perform their duties. One artillery captain recounted being hit and feeling certain he would die, until closer examination revealed that the ball had glanced off the pipe in his coat pocket, bounced downward into his belt buckle, and been deflected by it away from him, leaving him shaken and bruised but otherwise unharmed. On the spectrum between fatal wounds and those that healed were those that inflicted irreparable damage. Many officers lost appendages, from thumbs to arms and legs, either completely blown off by enemy fire or amputated.[29]

A couple days after the Battle of Shiloh, a wounded Capt. Oliver Bridgford wrote to his wife Eliza that he was "shattered all over I have to go on cruches."[30] Two weeks after the battle, he sent his family an update on his condition: "My wound is getting along fine I am so I can get around on cruches first Rate."[31] He hoped and expected he would rejoin his company soon. Bridgford obtained a surgeon's certificate recommending a thirty-day leave of absence, but his regimental commander, Col. John E. Smith, did not provide authorization for him to go. Consequently, Bridgford reported, "I cannot come home without Running the chances of meeting the Displeasure of *Col Smith* So I have to be content where I am If he had attended to it as he Said he would I might have been gone long before this time."[32] Bridgford felt frustrated over this outcome, "but we must expect Disapointments and Troubles and thank god it is no worse."[33] He also mentioned encountering Mrs. Mary Ann Bickerdyke and praised the care she provided soldiers: "She is the Best women in the world except *wives and mothers* She is So Kind to the Boys that are sick."[34] A series of letters in July 1862 chronicled Bridgford's ongoing recovery; he continued to struggle to walk, which greatly hindered his ability to perform military duties. The continuing pain and reduced mobility led him to resign in September 1862.[35]

David Vail, a lieutenant of the Sixteenth Wisconsin, was wounded in the leg at Shiloh and sent back to a hospital in Iowa. He spent almost two weeks there without receiving medical attention and became desperate to get out and find someone to tend to his wound. Since it was a military hospital, there were guards keeping soldiers from just walking out without a pass. However, Vail talked some civilians into lifting up his cot, with him on it, and simply carrying him right out the door of the hospital. The move was so bold that the guards assumed the men must have had permission and let them go. Vail soon found a civilian surgeon, and the doctor claimed that if Vail had not gotten out of the hospital, he would almost certainly have lost his leg. The man with whom Vail had shared a room in the hospital did die, a fate Vail blamed on the neglectful hospital staff. He felt little doubt he would have wound up just as dead if he had left himself in their care rather than escaping the hospital.[36]

Henry Kircher of the Twelfth Missouri left behind a fascinating example of the effect of being wounded. Captain Kircher was wounded on 27 November 1863 at Ringgold, Georgia, during the pursuit that followed the Union victory in the Battle of Missionary Ridge. That morning, Kircher made a mundane note in his diary: "Have no coffee this morning. only crackers and some bacon."[37] The text that followed this entry differed dramatically from the usual script that came previously, as Kircher recorded that after his note that morning, he was shot in the left leg and right arm. The loss of Kircher's right arm is plainly visible in the roughly scrawled text of the diary, as he struggled to write with his nondominant left hand. Kircher was never able to return to duty after his debilitating injuring.[38]

Even serving as part of the American Civil War's most victorious army was a risky endeavor, and the Army of the Tennessee's officers accepted the risk of death, deeming the Union worthy of sacrifice. In a sample of 481 men who served as lieutenants, captains, majors, lieutenant colonels, and colonels in the Army of the Tennessee, 89 of them died during their service—approximately 19 percent or one-fifth of the sample. Of those 89 dead, 50 were killed in action, 21 died of wounds received in combat, and 11 perished from illness. There were a handful other rare causes of death, such as friendly fire or murder, but combat and illness were by far the leading killers. Thirty-five of these officers died in 1862, 23 in 1863, and 27 in 1864. In this study's sample, only four men died in either 1861 or 1865; the vast majority of deaths took place from 1862 through 1864. These numbers should suggest some sense of the trends in the deaths of the Army of the Tennessee's officer corps. (For comparison, out of this study's sample of 481 officers, 49 percent left the army before the war's end without dying and 32 percent were still serving the army in some capacity when the war ended.)[39]

In September 1861, Harley Wayne sent home some pictures of himself, asking his wife Ellen that if he died, his photograph be preserved "as of one who did not fear to die in the cause of our glorious country."[40] Along with many other officers, Wayne was killed at the Battle of Shiloh, 6–7 April 1862. Some officers died instantly, without even opportunity for last words; others lingered for hours or into the next day before dying, giving them time to exhort their men to fight on. Theodore W. Hodges was shot while kneeling on one knee and leaning on his sword, which he had stuck point first into the ground. Hodges was struck in the head mid-sentence as he ordered a soldier to take a wounded comrade to the rear. He clung to his sword as he keeled over, bending it double until the blade snapped and flew into the air. Hodges died a few days later; once or twice he muttered the word "father," but otherwise he never awoke.[41] After one bullet struck Nesbit Baugher in the leg above the knee, another struck his hip, and yet another his shoulder. He started to crawl toward the rear, leaning on his sword for support, and along the way he was shot again. Then yet another ball struck his sword and ricocheted into his forehead. Eventually, with excruciating difficulty, and barely avoiding capture, Baugher reached medical care. The doctors did what they could for him, but his body was greatly weakened and in mid-May 1862 he took a sudden turn for the worse and died.[42]

The Vicksburg Campaign witnessed the deaths of many officers. On 16 May 1863, the Army of the Tennessee evacuated Jackson, Mississippi, and continued toward Vicksburg. About half an hour after pulling out, Col. John Nelson Cromwell of the Forty-Seventh Illinois returned to Jackson, despite the knowledge that rebel forces were approaching the city. Accounts differ as to why he went back; he might have been trying to round up stragglers, seeing to the care of wounded men who had been left behind or making sure none of his men had been accidently left behind on guard duty. Whatever the reason, Cromwell ventured back without any bodyguard after the Union rear guard had withdrawn. Cromwell entered a hotel where he hoped to find some of his men. Moments later, he heard the shouts of rebel cavalry approaching. He rushed out, sprang onto his horse, and started to flee. The enemy scouts quickly surrounded him and demanded his surrender. Cromwell had been taken prisoner once before, and after the ill treatment he faced had determined never to be captured again. The colonel killed one of the rebels with his pistol before the others shot him.[43]

Some of the officers who died fighting for Vicksburg penned fascinating comments on the possibility of dying prior to doing so. In March 1863, 1st Lt. Sylvester Gridley Beckwith of the Twenty-Third Iowa wrote to his wife, "We are all anxious to be there [i.e., Vicksburg] for if we fall in a great fight it will be no worse than in a little one & if we Survive it will be a great gain to us when we can tell that we were in the great battle of Vixburg."[44] He expounded further on the risk of death in another letter a few days later: "We all go with the expectation of getting through the great battle unhurt & come out all safe. yet many of us . . . fall on the battle field & if we do we are Shure & know that we fall in a good & noble cause as thousands of our fellow soldiers have fell, who were as good as we are."[45] Later he responded to a letter from his wife by saying, "I cannot see why you do not wish me to go to Vixburg, for there is no more danger of being hurt there than in any other battle."[46] This was probably not the most comforting message for her.

At the Battle of Big Black River Bridge, on 17 May 1863, the Army of the Tennessee drove rebel forces out of some field fortifications and across the Big Black River. From a field hospital near the battleground, Beckwith reported to his wife that he had been shot. "We made one of the most daring & despert bayonet charges that ever was made" he boasted.[47] Beckwith "was wounded within about 200 yards of the fortifications & I tied up my leg & rushed on over the breastworks & nearly to the railroad bridge & then I gave out & could not keep up."[48] He was struck in the right leg just below the knee; he claimed to feel relatively well, was able to get around on crutches, and hoped to return home soon. By mid-June, Beckwith had moved to a hospital in Keokuk, Iowa, whence he wrote to his wife that his wound had worsened and he was unable to travel farther. On 22 June, a frustrated and frantic Beckwith wrote home again describing the pain in his leg and complaining about not receiving any letters from his wife. "I am beginning to think that you are all dead or else you have forsaken me in an hour of affliction and many a tear have I shed while lying in bed reflecting over these things," Beckwith declared, adding a threat not to write again until he received mail from home.[49] Three letters from his wife arrived in quick succession, prompting an apologetic response from Beckwith on 28 June. He still longed to get home to see her but could not leave the hospital until the head surgeon issued him a leave of absence. That never happened. Beckwith's condition worsened, and he died in the hospital on 5 July without ever reaching home.[50]

Major Luther Howard Cowan of the Forty-Fifth Illinois pondered the possibility of death on a couple of occasions early in the war, and his words acquire added significance in hindsight. He informed his wife Harriet in January 1862 that he had taken out a life insurance policy on himself worth $1000, explaining, "I don't intend to come up missing but if I do this will help some."[51] Like many officers, Cowan expressed unfounded

138   MORE IMPORTANT THAN GOOD GENERALS

confidence that he would survive: "I don't feel any concern about bullets for I have a presentiment that I am not to be hurt in battle, though ever so much exposed, and am not afraid at all."[52] He also stated on multiple occasions that he would rather die than live as a coward who failed to defend his country when it needed him. Notwithstanding Cowan's boastful predictions, only a few steps into leading the Forty-Fifth in a charge during the assault on Vicksburg of 22 May 1863, Cowan fell to the enemy's first volley. One of his soldiers lamented, "The saddest news that I have got to write is that we have lost our Major. . . . I am very sorry Major Cowan was killed for he was as brave a man as ever lived and made a good officer, but the brave are as apt to get killed as any."[53] Cowan's brother, also serving in the Forty-Fifth, recovered his body and arranged for his burial.[54]

Even after the Siege of Vicksburg began, officers continued to fall. Near the end of May, while he was observing an artillery bombardment, an enemy rifle ball hit 1st Lt. Charles Luther of the Seventy-Sixth Ohio in the mouth and passed out the back of his neck. He lingered in pain for about twenty minutes before dying. Lieutenant Colonel Melancthon Smith was shot three times, including once in the head, as he led the Forty-Fifth Illinois to storm the breach created by a mine the Union troops exploded on 25 June. Smith endured for three days before dying. His immediate subordinate, Maj. Leander Fiske, also perished in the 25 June assault, shot through the heart. First Lieutenant Julius A. Pratt of the 124th Illinois was sitting in his tent in apparent safety when he was struck and killed instantly. The ball that slew him apparently glanced off a branch of a tree atop the hill in front of his tent and plunged downward to pass through the back of his neck and emerge out of his face. Pratt's brother Norman, a lieutenant in the same regiment, obtained a furlough and casket to take his brother's remains home to Illinois. Eight days after Pratt's death, the months-long struggle for Vicksburg, with its many casualties along the way, came to a close.[55]

The Army of the Tennessee spent months under fire during the Atlanta Campaign, but one of the campaign's deadliest moments occurred on 27 June 1864. Through much of that campaign, Gen. William T. Sherman skillfully employed his superior numbers to repeatedly turn the flank of the rebel army, prompting Confederate general Joseph E. Johnston to withdraw each time. At Kennesaw Mountain, however, Sherman undertook an atypical direct assault on a fortified rebel position. The attack failed and many Union troops perished. The Thirtieth Ohio's Lt. Col. George H. Hildt described the fate of one of his officers in dramatic detail: "Captain

Chamberlain had his head blown off by a percussion shell which exploded afterwards & tore off his arms, blowing his brains over his first Sergt & Capt Brooks near & also burnt Capt Brooks shirt."[56] Hildt lost other officers at Kennesaw Mountain, but even for that bloody day, Captain Chamberlain's death was shocking.[57]

Prior to the great wars of the twentieth century, throughout history disease was regularly a deadlier wartime killer than actual combat. The Army of the Tennessee's officers seem to have been exceptions to that norm, but they weren't immune to death by disease. Major John W. McFerran went from seeming perfectly well to having a chill in a single day in the fall of 1862. His regiment departed on a brief, unfruitful pursuit of rebel guerrillas, and McFerran remained in camp to rest. Lieutenant Colonel DeWitt Clinton Loudon, McFerran's superior, stated, "When we started up the river he was not very well & was left behind. On our return we found him in his coffin."[58] Loudon lamented, "His death is an irreparable loss to his poor wife & his little children who are not yet old enough to know how much they have lost."[59] Second Lieutenant Townsend P. Heaton left a remarkable account of how the Seventieth Ohio escorted Major McFerran's body to a boat to send it back home: "Every company formed on the color line, one company with their guns to fire the salute all the others without. The Captains were the pall bearers, they all had their Sashes without their Swords, his horse was then led in the rear of the hearse his Shoes & Spurs in the Stirrup and his Sword hung on the Saddle, then came the Lieutenants, after them the regiment, each company in charge of the orderly sergeant. All seemed to feel they had lost a friend and a noble officer."[60] Many officer deaths occurred in circumstances that were not conducive to such formal mourning, which makes this display of grief exceptional.[61]

On at least one exceptional occasion, an officer in the Army of the Tennessee murdered a colleague. The night of 3 November 1863, Maj. Thomas Herod of the Sixth Illinois Cavalry appeared at the regimental headquarters at Germantown, Tennessee, and asked where the commander was. Herod went to the house where Lt. Col. Reuben Loomis was boarding and accosted his superior in a hallway. Loomis had earlier reprimanded Herod for abuse of authority, and now Herod demanded that Loomis retract that criticism or else he would kill him. According to witnesses, Loomis calmly answered, "Major Herod, you have got a pistol in your hand and I am unarmed. If you want to kill me, kill me."[62] Herod fired five times, hitting Loomis twice and killing him immediately. Herod was court-martialed but used influential friends to get the sentence reduced to just ten years imprisonment. After serving only one year for murdering his commander, Herod obtained a pardon from President Andrew Johnson in 1866.[63]

Officers were very conscious of the possibility that they might die at any time and wrote frankly of the risks involved, of their fears, and of whether death would be worthwhile. Contemplating the possibility of death, 2nd Lt. Friedrich Martens exhorted his parents to weep if he fell, "but after you have done that, then unite in a prayer of praise to the good Helmsman of the world, and thank Him that He gave you a son who was man enough to fight for a sacred cause and to die."[64] In December 1862, Robert Steele wrote to his parents expressing his acceptance of the possibility of death and framing his willingness to risk death in religious terms: "Our stay in this world is short at the longest let us live so we can welcome death and be prepared to meet when wars and sin and parting are no more."[65] Live or die, all officers had to reach some kind of acceptance of death.[66]

Jake Ritner revealed his fears of death to his wife Emeline after a skirmish in late October 1863, as the Army of the Tennessee proceeded to Chattanooga. He had experienced a greater than usual sense of dread before a recent fight: "I believe I am about as brave as the most of men, but I thought . . . anxiously that night about my dear sweet wife at home. And felt for the first time, that perhaps I might never kiss you again, and a good deal more of the same sort."[67] Ritner felt embarrassed to admit to such feelings, declaring, "I am ashamed of this foolish letter—if I had time I would tear it up and write another. I'll be real 'spunky' if you let anybody see it."[68] He worried about what would happen to his wife and children if he never returned and concluded, "If I fall it will be in a good cause and at my post doing my duty, and may God protect and comfort and provide for you and the children."[69] Other officers likewise pondered the prospect of death throughout the war.[70]

DeWitt Clinton Loudon, the Seventieth Ohio's lieutenant colonel, discussed his feelings about dying with his wife Hannah on a few occasions. As the army inched toward Corinth, Mississippi, in early May 1862, Loudon raised the topic, though he began by insisting that he fully expected to return home safely:

> If I should not return do the best you can for our children. Teach them to love their country & not to forget that their father gave his life for his country they among others might enjoy the blessings of Liberty, of Law & order &

good government. For myself, I am not afraid to die. If my life can be of service to my country, it is freely given. Here as when at home I often think of Death & the world to come. Death is the certain end of all & at most is but a question of time. But for the thought of you & my children I could lie down & sleep sweetly tonight, tho I was certain that I was to die on the morrow.[71]

At the close of this reflection, Loudon explained to Hannah that though he did not often write to her about such concerns, he had given them much thought. Near the end of the month, he wrote again that as much as he hoped and prayed he would survive the war, he felt compelled to prepare for the alternative. "God may require as the price of the reestablishment of our noble government that yet more lives be sacrificed & still other hearth-stones be made desolate. We may be called on to bear our share of the awful burden as thousands of others have already done. The price whatever it may be must not be withheld. 'Let us bow & trust,'" he declared (quoting from the poem "The Lexington" by John Lofland).[72] Looking back over his life, Loudon said he was "thankful that I had the moral courage to stand by my convictions" rather than be guided only by what would bring him immediate gain.[73] Great as the consolations of a good conscience and good reputation were, Loudon added that his one regret for his life lay in not having done more to assure the financial security of his family. He feared Hannah would face such slander and harassment over his unpaid debts that she might need to leave town and suggested that his pension would be enough to support her and the children comfortably if they went to live with her mother. Loudon concluded by reiterating the hypothetical nature of this advice and his earnest hope that it would never be relevant. He revisited the specter of his death once more in November 1862, focusing this time on how Hannah would raise their daughters. "Rear them up to be industrious & economical. I would like to have them educated as well as our meager means will allow," Loudon wrote.[74] He also wanted the girls to understand why their father died, asking that Hannah "teach them to despise & hold in detestation" those who did not support their country.[75]

Even in an army as unused to defeat as the Army of the Tennessee, the officers still faced all the perils of war, chief among them being captured, getting sick, being wounded, and dying. Lieutenant Colonel Loudon survived his term of service, returning home in 1864, but that did not make his concerns about dying any less weighty. He and every other officer had to come to terms with the possibility of dying, and perhaps a little less than a fifth of them did die during their service. A vastly larger share of officers suffered nonfatal wounds or illnesses over the course of the war. All officers, even those who ultimately emerged completely unscathed by death or injury, had to come to terms with the risks they faced and cope with the reality of suffering in the lives of colleagues and subordinates. Officers were never eager to die nor to endure any other kind of suffering, but they framed such risks as worthy sacrifices to uphold the Union. The grim realities of war were a major part of officers' wartime experience, though army life also contained many elements besides suffering.

CHAPTER 10

A Dawning Day of Liberty

After some slaves guided Capt. Joseph Stockton and his men to a stash of meat and sugar their master had hidden in the woods, Stockton reported that as the party returned and passed the owner's house, "I never heard a man curse as he did at what were in the morning his slaves, but now free men. We took the darkies off with us, as the man would have killed them."[1] Few Union soldiers went to war expecting to end slavery, though they fully recognized slavery's centrality to the conflict. Racism in mid-nineteenth-century America was pervasive and systemic in a way difficult for twenty-first-century Americans to comprehend. Even people who condemned slavery could be thoroughgoing racists.

Despite their racism, the Army of the Tennessee's officers increasingly turned against slavery. The Army of the Tennessee traversed more of the Deep South than any other Union army, giving its members an unparalleled opportunity to see the practice of slavery. Some witnessed slavery in person for the first time and were appalled by its brutal reality. Others found it absurd to return runaway enslaved people to masters who were in rebellion against the government. A number of officers identified slavery as a lynchpin of the rebel war effort that ought to be taken away. Still others came to appreciate the unfailingly reliable aid that Black people gave the US Army, noting how this contrasted with the implacable hostility white Southerners commonly displayed. For all these causes, officers' writings suggest that over the course of the Civil War, they came to oppose slavery and favor emancipation, and some also developed a noticeably more positive opinion of Black people.

Officers' thoughts on slavery and emancipation cannot be understood without grasping their racism. Like most white people in the United States in the mid-1800s, the Army of the Tennessee's officers would be considered racist by twenty-first-century standards, routinely using language and expressing attitudes shocking to present-day sensibilities. Black people were a frequent subject of ridicule. Second Lieutenant Joseph S. Reynolds jested to his brother Willie, "How would you like to plow corn with forty or fifty negro boys & girls in the field as there is here? You would not get lonesome then. I would rather be in a field alone than where such baboons are."[2] James W. Kays wrote in October 1862 to some friends condemning abolitionism, "I was very sorry to learn that the negroes was about to run the white working class out the Boys say for you to dislodge the abolitionist and kill the d d negroes."[3] Harlow Waller suggested in May 1863, "Those that are fond of the nigger ought to come down here and see them I think they would get their fill they are a filthy supusticious race it is hard to believe some of them is human."[4] In March 1864, Henry Miller Culbertson disdainfully observed, "There are some very good churches in [Vicksburg] . . . but the negro meetings beats them all. There is a host of these abolitionists that think that a negro is better than a white man, and they have great times praying for their 'colored brothers.'"[5] Throughout the war, many officers displayed such negative or demeaning attitudes toward Black people.[6]

However, alongside their obvious disdain for African Americans, many officers expressed support for major changes regarding slavery's place in the war, such as President Abraham Lincoln issuing the Emancipation Proclamation or the US Army starting to raise regiments of Black soldiers. Their comments mostly focused on the strategic advantages to freeing enslaved people or permitting Black men to become soldiers. An officer of the Forty-Fifth Illinois recognized as early as July 1862 how freeing slaves would undermine the rebel war effort: "If the war is desired to be finished soon, there is one short cut to that result—tell all the niggers to come in."[7] Henry Hole told his sister Minerva that the Emancipation Proclamation was necessary to save the country, prevent needless bloodshed, end further conflict over the question of slavery, keep the Confederate government from freeing its slaves first and using them against the Union, and forestall foreign meddling in the war. "I am for the Presidential Proclamation teeth and toe nails," Hole declared, "Because it is right, it is necessary, it is expedient, it is just, it is what the whole civilized world expected us to do, and last I am for it because C. L. Vanlaningham . . . and a host of others are against it."[8] (He presumably meant notorious Copperhead Clement L. Vallandigham.) Other officers similarly saw emancipation as a crucial step to Union victory and peace. These officers were not primarily concerned with the moral issues surrounding slavery, but they still turned against the institution because they regarded its destruction as key to winning the war.[9]

Luther Howard Cowan was another officer whose writings made clear that although he did not go to war to end slavery, he fully supported President Lincoln's antislavery policies. Cowan strongly endorsed the Emancipation Proclamation, declaring in February 1863 that any man who "won't fight for the nigger" was in truth "a coward and traitor."[10] Ironically, later that month he also declared that the enslaved people he saw around Young's Point, Louisiana, were "but a grade above a beast, manifest no signs of human intelligence scarcely."[11] His racism and antislavery attitudes coexisted. Cowan explained how he and his comrades did not go to war to free the enslaved, but they fully accepted the addition of emancipation to the Union cause: "The soldiers know that the war, on the part of the Administration, was not begun for the purpose of interfering with the 'Favored institution' but that it was thrust in our way at every step, and that the slave holders south, and their abbetors in the north, have compelled the administration to make that an issue, and then as soon as this is done they raise the howl that the war is only to free the negro. This position comes of the devil, and is as false as himself. . . . Every honest and sane man knows it is false."[12] Notwithstanding his earlier racist comments, by April 1863 Cowan showed no doubts about Black people's ability to be soldiers. "We are now about to enter the time in history which will show the fallacy of the long entertained notion that the negro could not be made to fight as a soldier," he declared.[13] He felt confident their performance under fire would dispel any stigma associated with Black soldiers.[14]

A month before the president issued the preliminary Emancipation Proclamation, Jasper A. Maltby forcefully laid out the strategic, punitive, and racist case for freeing slaves in a letter to a friend. He began by recounting how a recent order had permitted Union forces to hire fugitive slaves as cooks, personal servants for officers, teamsters, and so on. The lieutenant colonel set forth his view on this new policy:

> I go this, "the whole hog." I go for employing him in all manner of menial positions. I am not for the heroes of Donelson and Shiloh wasting their lives, when that can be done by negroes. I go in for the *hurt* principle hereafter. Temporizing with traitors might have been a good policy once, but even that is "played out." I go in for the confiscation of every dollar's worth

of property held by rebels, and until that is the policy the war will last. Let traitors from this time henceforward feel that it is dangerous to be disloyal. I am in command of this post, and you can bet high, that all fugitives that come into these lines *of their own free will* shall be employed in such a manner as to *save the white man*.[15]

Despite his obvious racism, Maltby recognized the advantages to undermining the South's prized institution. Maltby apparently anticipated disagreement from his interlocutor and preemptively countered the criticism. "I expect," he continued, "that you will call me an 'abolitionist.' Well, if you do, we are all abolitionists. We are unanimous for conducting the war in such a manner as to save ourselves and *hurt* the enemy, and to save him in the pocket is the fatal mistake."[16] Even someone avowing racist attitudes could see merit in freeing the slaves and make a case for doing so out of strategic and punitive reasons.

Second Lieutenant Alexander K. Ewing vigorously endorsed the Emancipation Proclamation and any other methods the president deemed necessary to win the war. "I see the President has announced his 1st Jany Proclamation in the face of a strong opposition which I had my doubts about his doing[.] He has knocked out the cornerstone and may he prove successful in his undertaking," Ewing declared in January 1863.[17] He denounced all who refused to support emancipation as traitors, and believed many in the North would rather see the Union destroyed than slavery ended. "This aforesaid institution has been a draw back and a disgrace to our government ever since its foundation and now when the opportunity is at hand for its overthrow I say Pitch it overboard," he declared.[18] Writing in early March 1863, Ewing again identified a gap between the army and folks back home on the topic of slavery: "What man that told you the army is all turning to be democrats tells a *dam Lie* I call myself a democrat, but the party called now democrat would style me an abolitionist."[19] The runaway enslaved people Ewing met left a favorable impression on him, often bringing "some valuable intelligence as some are very intelligent and are capable of knowing considerable and can be looked upon as generally reliable."[20]

A few officers acknowledged the immoral nature of slavery in addition to the practical or strategic factors around it. One evening in July 1862, Z. Payson Shumway remarked at how lovely and quiet the night was, except "that in the distance I hear the . . . baying of hounds perchance on the back of some flying fugitive. Alas for what little of pity or philanthropy there is in man. God pity that poor downtrodden race wronged as they are in this land of *freedom!!*"[21] Friedrich Martens explained to his parents that slavery was central to the war, framing the conflict as arising from the fact that "we didn't want to believe that slavery is a godly institution."[22] Not all of Martens's comrades shared his concern with whether slavery was godly, but his comments at least reflect his own feelings. Shortly after resigning from the army in the summer of 1863 due to poor health, a recuperating Martens wrote to his family, "We will have finished off the rebellion soon, and I hope that slavery will come to an end as well."[23] Daniel L. Ambrose also found deeper moral significance to the issue of slavery, characterizing the Emancipation Proclamation as "one of the most powerful blows against rebellion; the freedom of the slave paving the way for the advance of free thought."[24] Officers who found slavery morally objectionable were a minority, but they did exist.[25]

Other officers made clear that they supported emancipation for both moral and strategic reasons. As early as May 1862, Henry Giesey Ankeny called for the Union to raise regiments of Black troops. He wrote to his wife Tina about his frustration over the government's slow progress at putting down the rebellion and called for an end to what he regarded as useless efforts to conciliate the rebels. "The Slaves should be armed at once. . . . The policy of protecting the rebels in what they call their constitutional right, that means the nigger, is absurd—perfectly so," he declared.[26] He identified the right to keep enslaved people as central to the rebel cause and saw depriving rebels of their slaves as key to victory. In another letter from August 1862, Ankeny reiterated his support for arming Black soldiers and praised the army's decision to employ contrabands as laborers, but he found this step inadequate. "We have gained a great victory on the slave question. By employing contrabands we increased the fighting force many thousand," he wrote, "but we *must* still go *farther* with them—it is not enough."[27] In the same letter, he wrote in glowing terms of an expedition in which he took part: "We sent in 8 or 900 bales of king cotton, some 50 mules, and worse than all, about 400 contrabands followed us and are now safe from their master, at least for the present. It was the greatest sight I ever saw, but there will no doubt be many more of the same kind. Several slaves were killed by the overseers to intimidate the others. They drive them into the canebreaks and hills as we advanced, but when left they came by the hundreds singing, crying and dancing for joy. They think their day of liberty is dawning and I hope it may be so."[28] Ankeny acknowledged both the ill treatment enslaved people faced and their obvious desire for liberty. The day after the June 1863 Battle of Milliken's Bend (in which Black soldiers successfully defended a Union outpost from rebel attack), Ankeny responded, "Good for the darkies! I wish there were more of them in the army."[29] His early endorsement of Black soldiers appeared vindicated.[30]

The Twenty-Fifth Iowa's Jacob B. Ritner also showed consistent sympathy toward the enslaved and support for emancipation. One night in the late fall of 1862, Ritner's Company B camped on a cotton plantation. The plantation owner was still present, but there did not appear to be any slaves or livestock left. After dark, however, one of Ritner's men found a young Black boy, perhaps about ten years old, out in the cotton field:

> We brought him in, and he told us that he was nearly starved and frozen. He said his master had chained two of his Negro men out in the cane break to keep them from going off with us, and that the mules were tied out the same place. He said that he and the other Negroes, mostly women and children, 25 in number, had been driven out into a swamp about two miles, and made to stay there for fear we would take them along. We determined to investigate the matter. A squad went to each place. We found the two men handcuffed and tied with a . . . chain, in the cane break, and the other lot in a swamp where the water was half-knee deep in shallow places. They had been in this condition for forty-eight hours without *fire* or *food*. They were the most miserable looking lot I ever saw. They had scarcely any clothing at all, ragged, dirty and bare-footed; it had snowed that morning and that night it froze hard.[31]

According to Ritner, this encounter "made an abolitionist" out of several Democrats in his company.[32] He had his company bring in all the former slaves and mules, made a point of burning the plantation's cotton gin, "and would have shot the owner if we had been allowed."[33] Ritner also urged his wife to hire the formerly enslaved as farmhands on multiple occasions and encouraged one Black family to move to his hometown—a level of acceptance on his part that was exceptional for the era.[34]

Opposition to slavery seems to have been a family affair for the Ritners. Jake Ritner never referred to himself as an abolitionist in his letters, but his father Henry Ritner was an avowed abolitionist, and it seems probable that the elder Ritner's attitudes would have shaped his son's views. In January 1863, Henry Ritner observed in a letter to his son that abolitionists were too lacking in numbers and influence to have ever caused the war, and instead imputed a divine cause to the conflict: "It is . . . God's war, and the object is to abolish slavery and punish the nation for its sins, especially that of slavery and to install the black man in to his natural and inalienable rights, and the sooner the government and the army recognize this aspect and act upon it the sooner we will have peace . . . if we as a nation refuse to acknowledge the rights of the black man then it may cost us our national existence."[35] It is difficult to imagine that hearing such sentiments from his father did not shape Jake Ritner's own attitudes toward slavery and African Americans. Captain Ritner also sought to pass on his antipathy for slavery to his own children. He wrote to his wife Emeline in November 1863 advising her on how to instruct their children. "You must teach them all to love God and their country, and to *hate* a lie, the devil, and all traitors and copperheads; teach them to honor and respect the flag of our country, its rulers and institutions, and to love freedom and hate slavery, and everything and everyone that has caused this wicked war," he exhorted.[36] Notably, in addition to declaring slavery hateful, he also numbered it among the causes of the war.

Captain Ritner also supported the raising of Black regiments. From Greenville, Mississippi, he wrote in April 1863 of how swiftly the former slaves learned to be soldiers. This approach "is the quickest way to end the war," he insisted.[37] Ritner called out the coexistence of racism with antislavery views, pointing out that although "universal sentiment" favored freeing the slaves and training them as soldiers, "yet there is just as much prejudice against them as there ever was. There is always someone trying to abuse, insult, and impose upon them."[38] For his part, Ritner asserted, "I have a great deal more respect for a Negro than for anyone who will misuse them."[39] He believed that most soldiers had recognized that the faster rebels lost use of their slaves, the sooner the war would end and they could all go home.[40]

Ritner also attended a sort of antislavery rally held while he was stationed in Greenville. General Frederick Steele's whole division gathered for a mass meeting, and Steele delivered a stirring, patriotic address that endorsed the government's policies for freeing and arming African Americans and called on all soldiers to fully support these efforts. Steele declared that the time for gentle, conciliatory measures had passed and that the government should pursue all options to crush the rebellion. The general's speech greatly elevated him in Ritner's eyes: "I have always considered him rather too pro slavery and too much disposed to protect rebel property."[41] After the division commander spoke, officers from every regiment present made additional speeches in support of the administration. Some of the officers claimed they had always favored such measures, but others admitted "that if it had been adopted a year or more ago they would have opposed it, but now supported it heartily."[42] Ritner gained great encouragement from the unanimity officers and men showed in support of emancipation and arming the formerly enslaved.[43]

Ritner's comments about former slaves reflected a distinct sense of sympathy rarely found in the writings of most of his counterparts. He repeatedly remarked on the way Black people indicated their desire for freedom. Whether he was traveling up the river on a steamboat, venturing into the countryside on foot, or guarding some outpost, he saw former slaves flock to the presence of Union troops. Often freedmen brought with them intelligence on the location of cotton or other goods that their erstwhile masters had hidden. Early in 1865, Ritner discovered that the Union-held enclave of Beaufort, South Carolina, had become a gathering point for "a great many refugees from slavery" who had constructed a functioning society.[44] In contrast to the "poor, ragged, starved wretches we see on the plantations," the free Black people at Beaufort all looked "contented, industrious, and doing well . . . generally clean and decently clothed."[45] They farmed, engaged in commerce, and went to schools, all "just like white folks."[46] He marveled at one unusual sight: "I saw the other day a northern school-marm, 'young and pretty,' ride through town in a buggy with a buck negro. What do you think of that?"[47] It is illustrative of Captain Ritner's unconventional attitudes on race that he responded merely with bemusement, but no outrage, to the sight of a Black man escorting a white woman. As the army marched through South Carolina late in the war, Ritner remarked at the vast number of former slaves following after the army in pursuit of liberty, despite the great hardship that this caused them. "I never felt as much pity for any one as I have for those poor Negroes," he declared in March 1865.[48] He also expressed concern for the freedmen's future: "I do hope the people of the north will endeavor to supply their wants."[49] Ritner also perceived the fear white Southerners held toward their slaves: "One of the beauties of the 'peculiar institution' was brought prominently to my notice" on the night Columbia, South Carolina, burned.[50] He realized that the white Southerners "were more afraid of their own Negroes than they were of our soldiers. They did not dare to go into the street without a guard. 'Why' they said, 'the niggers will kill us' and were dreading what the negroes would do after we left."[51] Throughout the war, Ritner consistently displayed a sympathetic view of the enslaved and their efforts to enjoy liberty.[52]

John Quincy Adams Campbell was another rare sort of officer: an open abolitionist. He was especially prone to quoting from the Bible when discussing the issue. As the Fifth Iowa advanced southward in April 1862, Campbell reported "frequent evidences of the existence of slavery, in the miserable looking dwellings and farms of the poor whites."[53] In April 1863, Campbell reported that after seeing "the despotic sway" planters wielded over their plantations, "I am not surprised that they should be aristocrats, nor do I wonder that they cling to their 'pet institution.' 'Where their treasures are, there will their heart be also.' 'Give me neither poverty nor riches'" (references to Matthew 6:21 and Proverbs 30:8).[54] The Army of the Tennessee's officers rarely expressed themselves in terms of class consciousness, but on the few occasions that they used such language, it was usually in reference to white Southerners, as when Campbell here distinguished between "poor whites" and elite planters. Campbell's readiness to denounce slavery as a moral evil and attribute problems in the Southern states to slavery's influence were typical attitudes for abolitionists, but they were not so common among Northerners generally.

Campbell avidly followed shifts in the Lincoln administration's policy toward slavery and rejoiced at new developments. He was pleased to learn of the preliminary Emancipation Proclamation in September 1862, declaring that emancipation should have come a year earlier, "But better late than never."[55] He crowed that 1 January 1863 would be "the day of our nation's second birth" and prayed that "God bless and help Abraham Lincoln— help him to 'break every yoke and let the oppressed go free.' The President has placed the Union pry under the corner stone of the Confederacy and the structure *will* fall."[56] With this observation (which contains an echo of Isaiah 58:6), Campbell embraced emancipation as both a moral and strategic good. Following the implementation of the Emancipation Proclamation in January 1863, Campbell wrote to a Northern newspaper praising it as "an effective agent in crushing out the rebellion" that all true Unionists would support.[57] He argued although rebels and Copperheads might ridicule it as a useless gesture, "Behind this laughing mask, they wear a serious, anxious face. Despite their wish that it may be harmless, they 'believe and tremble' that Slavery is doomed and the Union is saved."[58] This time, he not only identified emancipation with Union victory but also went out of his way to promote its merits to the community back home (as well as making yet another biblical allusion, this time to James 2:19).[59]

One area where Campbell did not differ from his fellow officers was in recognizing that Black Southerners were overwhelmingly pro-Union and desirous of liberty. Writing to a Northern newspaper in July 1862, he reported that one group unfailingly welcomed Union forces and showed sympathy for their cause: "Of course, I mean the slaves. Universally, we find them loyal, ready to aid us by word or deed. No love of master holds them back, but they give us any desired information they can . . . Is it anything but fair our government should lend a helping hand to these Union men of Mississippi?"[60] Other officers appreciated Black support for the Union war effort, but Campbell's characterization of slaves as "Union men" was an unusually respectful accolade. Campbell penned another letter to the paper to address the question of how loyal slaves were to their masters:

> My eyes were greeted by a strange, an unusual, an interesting sight yesterday. "What was it?"—"A beast of the earth, a fowl of the air, or a fish of the sea?" Neither! Was it a Secesh General? Not that. "A Union man in Mississippi?" No. "What then, was it, a ghost or hobgoblin?" No. It was—(though it may be doubted)—it was a secesh nigger! Let John Van Buren, Fernando Wood, and Chilton A., rejoice that there is one, at least, who will not listen to the voice of Abraham, and "go out FREE," on the first day of next January, I say again, let them rejoice.[61]

Campbell's mocking levity indirectly acknowledged enslaved people's desire for liberty and reflects how vanishingly rare pro-Confederate Black people really were.

When January 1863 came around and the Emancipation Proclamation went into effect, Campbell wrote yet again to the newspaper, further exploring the question of whether Black people wanted liberty or were content in slavery:

> Do they desire to be free? I answer emphatically, they do. Nothing but the innate love of liberty in man could have caused the wide spread desire for freedom that is manifested among the slaves wherever our army goes. In regions where an Abolitionist was never heard of, the Yankees are hailed by the darkies as their deliverers. And their masters as far as they are able (though they talk loudly about the happiness and contentment of their slaves) keep

shoving them farther south as our army advances. The darkey is not to be trusted (contented or discontented) where Freedom is in question.[62]

He reported that slaves commonly traveled for days, at risk of their lives, to reach the Union lines and secure their freedom. People who had never visited the Confederacy might fall for the lie that the enslaved were content in slavery, Campbell concluded, "but it won't go down with one who has been with our army and seen for himself."[63] He had witnessed far too many slaves seek freedom at the first opportunity to believe they were happy in slavery.

Benjamin Henry Grierson also had a background of opposition to slavery, though it would be too much to call him an abolitionist. Grierson campaigned for John C. Frémont, the very first Republican presidential candidate, in 1856, and also campaigned for Abraham Lincoln's senatorial bid in 1858, during which he met Lincoln. His first comments on slavery during the war came in a November 1861 letter to his wife Alice, provoked by an order from Gen. Henry W. Halleck enjoining officers not to permit fugitive slaves to enter their lines. If the government attempted to make the army into "*Slave Catchers for the south* there will be no little *kicking out of the traces.*"[64] Grierson promised to quit the army rather than do anything to recapture and return runaway slaves. He later recalled that Halleck's edict "met the supreme disgust and contempt of a large majority of the officers and soldiers of the Union army," who thought it absurd for the army to provide such a service to those rebelling against the government.[65] By July 1862, now Colonel Grierson reported that when Black people approached his lines, he wrote them passes and asked no questions about where they were going. "Any quantity of '*Niggers*' in this country and very many of them are *giving leg Bail* . . . and while I never expect to steal any of them from their owners I am very certain that I will not hunt or Catch the darkies for them." he explained.[66] Grierson also praised the Emancipation Proclamation.[67]

Oscar Lawrence Jackson was another officer who opposed slavery prior to the war. The day before his twentieth birthday in September 1860, he gave a speech "in favor of Abe Lincoln and the principles of the Republican party, which I claimed to be: opposition to the extension of slavery, favoring a homestead bill, protective tariff, etc., and opposed to S. A. Douglas and the sham Democratic party."[68] In another speech to local Republicans that October, Jackson extolled the "fight for the rights of freemen against slavery extensionists."[69] His enmity toward slavery went well beyond this prewar anti-expansion rhetoric, however. In April 1862, as Jackson traveled by steamboat, he witnessed a Black man run along the riverbank and beg the boat to take him aboard. The steamboat could not stop and soon left him behind, but the man made an impression on Jackson. "How I pitied this son of Africa," he wrote, "striving for that which we all love so well, 'liberty,' and thus far unsuccessfully. God grant him success yet."[70] While convalescing back in Ohio in January 1863 after being wounded at the Battle of Corinth in October 1862, locals asked Jackson to give a speech. He recalled that his discourse was not eloquent, but that he "lashed Copperheads and sympathizers and proclaimed myself an unconditional abolitionist to a crowded house."[71] Few officers openly identified themselves as abolitionist, but Jackson embraced the label, and his subsequent comments confirm his stance.

Jackson displayed his respect for African Americans in a variety of encounters later in the war. After praising a Black man named Aleck who served as his guide while on a foraging mission during the Savannah Campaign, Jackson observed, "I have never seen a negro, old or young, male or female, that did not appear willing and even anxious to leave master and follow our army. They hail us as deliverers and are true and loyal under all circumstances."[72] Seeing Black soldiers at Beaufort, South Carolina, prompted Jackson to marvel, "I am surprised what a change two years drilling and campaigning has made on the rude field hands. . . . Without doubt they are the equal if not superior in soldierly qualities to the average of our white regiments and their families are really genteel."[73]

As the army advanced through South Carolina in March 1865, Major Jackson movingly described the privations former slaves endured as they followed in the wake of the Union army. He recalled one elderly Black Southerner: "She kept repeating, 'Thank the Lord, I have lived to see the day.' But she much regretted that as her eyes beheld it she must feel that she was dying. She blessed her children and told them they would enjoy liberty after she was gone. The Children of Israel never were more fully convinced that the destruction of their enemies was intended for their deliverance than these black people are that our success is for their liberty. Sooner would I lose my right arm than do aught to disappoint their expectations."[74] Jackson lamented that even this late in the war, many Union soldiers did not share this desire and "have as yet no idea of treating the oppressed race with justice."[75] He believed Northerners collectively were complicit in the oppression of Black people and that the national suffering the war inflicted was a penalty for them as much as for white Southerners. "The north is not guiltless in this question and for its guilt it seems to me it is now bearing its share of this terrible affliction," he declared.[76] Still, former slaves won over most potential detractors in the army by their oft-displayed loyalty to the Union cause. "Never," Jackson wrote, "have I heard of a black man hesitating to peril his life for the comfort of any Union soldier that was placed in his way and hundreds of our men when prisoners have been indebted to them for means of escape from the enemy, though that help was given under peril of certain death if detected."[77] Men such as Ritner, Campbell, and Jackson make clear that although racism was ubiquitous in nineteenth-century America, officers could and did rise above it, at least to some degree, and practice compassion and respect toward Black Southerners.

DeWitt Clinton Loudon was one of a number of officers who evinced clear signs of changing his views regarding Black people and slavery, generally due to a combination of firsthand encounters and wartime realities. In a July 1862 letter to his wife Hannah, Loudon reported that the African Americans he encountered proved themselves both helpful and intelligent. "They come often to our pickets & outposts & give information & what they communicate is found to be true & reliable. They have much more intelligence than we up north are taught to [illegible]. You would be surprised to learn how much they know of what is going on," he explained.[78] Besides discovering that he had been misinformed about enslaved people's purported lack of intelligence, Loudon also realized that claims he had read and heard about how much slaves loved their masters were "all bunk."[79] Loudon dismissed the idea that they would ever use Black men as Confederate soldiers: "The South will never put arms in the hands of their slaves. They are afraid to trust them for they know that if they do so, the arms will first be used at home against themselves."[80] Venturing into the South and seeing slaves and slavery in person at least partially overturned Loudon's preconceptions. This was hardly a full embrace of racial equality, however, as revealed in another letter praising the government's use of contrabands as laborers for the army. He said he would much rather the government use Black men to dig ditches than wear out himself and his soldiers on such tasks. Regarding "secession sympathizers at home who have so high an idea of the sanctity of the institution of slavery & so much to say about the constitutional rights of the slave holders," Loudon thought that if they spent some time in the sun digging trenches or repairing roads and bridges, they "would soon experience a 'change of heart'" about employing contrabands.[81] He was no abolitionist, but he could see the benefit to freeing fugitive slaves instead of returning them to their masters.

156 MORE IMPORTANT THAN GOOD GENERALS

From meeting slaves and discovering they were both more intelligent and less happy with slavery than he had always heard to finding practical value in freeing slaves rather than enforcing slavery, Loudon moved to outspoken opposition to slavery and support for emancipation. In October 1862, he explained to Hannah his understanding of slavery's place in the war:

> You remember that among the Egyptians the cat was a sacred animal. The Roman army once captured her capital. The inhabitants quietly submitted to the rule of the invaders, incurring loss of property change of rulers & all the ills attending the state of a conquered people. One day a soldier killed a cat in the street. The mob set upon him & tore him to pieces & his General found the city so exasperated he dare not avenge his death. Slavery is the "sacred cat" of our butternut brethren. They can bear to see the Union soldiers die of disease in the deadly swamp, & along the weary road, to wear away their strength in the hardships & toils of warfare. They can endure that happy homes shall be made desolate, that the land be filled with orphans & widows. The flower of our young men may fall in battle & no outcry. But let any body touch a hair of slavery & the devil's is to pay at once.[82]

Encountering white Southerners and seeing slavery in person convinced Loudon that slavery was central to the Confederate cause and turned him against the institution on practical grounds.

Loudon wrote on New Year's Day 1863 to express his support for the Emancipation Proclamation. "I am anxious to see what he [i.e., the president] will do. God grant that he may stand firmly by the policy he has indicated," Loudon declared.[83] Instead of giving pragmatic reasons to free slaves, as he did the previous summer when describing how the use of contrabands made life easier for himself and his men, Loudon addressed the long-term moral significance of emancipation:

> It is high time, the world should know whether a great nation is for or against the Christianity & civilization of the age, whether a people who have loudly boasted of their humanity, their freedom, their civilization, their intelligence, their high regard for the mandates of the Prince of Peace, are willing to stand by their government in the struggle for self preservation, to be true to the behests of Eternal Justice & to the teachings of humanity, whether while they profess to be loyal citizens of the Republic of the United States, they are willing to be loyal citizens of the Grand

Republic of all mankind, or whether they will shrink back appaled by the prejudices of caste & the barbarism of a thousand years.[84]

He concluded that the war would have profound consequences for the future: "Let these questions be settled now that they are upon us; and may they be so settled that when the future historian shall record the unprejudiced judgment of mankind our children may not feel their faces tingle with shame as they read the solemn record."[85] Rather, Loudon desired that America's descendants would someday read the history of those times and see "that their ancestors lived in the full blaze of the civilization of the nineteenth century & were not a pagan people."[86] This was not full-fledged abolitionism, but it was certainly a profound recognition that there was a moral issue at stake with slavery.

Alphonso Barto also reported changing his views regarding slavery. When Captain Barto's father asked his opinion of the recently implemented Emancipation Proclamation, Barto responded in February 1863, "I go in strong for any thing that will *hurt* these rebels & if there are rebels at home I go in for hanging them out & out."[87] That July, Barto explained his views on slavery at greater length: "It is awful to think of a people so prosperous as we were at the beginning of this war and that a government had done so much as ours had for us and then to see a portion of our own people try to tear that government to pieces it is too horrible to think of. And then the worse idea of founding a government of their own upon that *accursed* institution of Slavery."[88] Clearly, by the summer of 1863, Barto viewed slavery as central to the Confederate cause and fully supported emancipation as a war measure. He emphasized that this was not always the case and that abolitionism was not the reason he went to war. "You know Father that I started in this war with no real abolition sentiment and I even believed in inforcing the fugitive slave law as far as could be and I believed it constitutional . . . a little more than a year ago I saw some fugitives delivered up to their master and thought it right," Barto declared.[89] He explained that firsthand encounters with slavery had wrought a conversion from his initial attitude, calling special attention to slaveholders' propensity to rape their female slaves and then treat the resulting offspring, their own flesh and blood, as slaves. Barto began the war without any particular desire to end slavery, but seeing it in practice persuaded him that it was an evil institution and made him a wholehearted supporter of the Emancipation Proclamation. He now favored "*Death to the Man* be he *North* or South that

158   MORE IMPORTANT THAN GOOD GENERALS

will oppose the measure taken by our beloved President to *annihilate* the institution."[90] The war made Captain Barto into an opponent of slavery, a fact he fully recognized.[91]

Occasionally, an officer's shifting attitudes toward race and slavery are visible through a survey of his writings over time. He might not have explicitly acknowledged a conversion in the way that Captain Barto did, but more subtle signs of change sometimes appear as well. Charles W. Wills's Civil War participation started when he joined a three-month regiment in April 1861. Afterward, he signed on with a cavalry regiment, then transferred to a different cavalry regiment, and finally helped raise what became Company G of the 103rd Illinois. He became Company G's captain and eventually rose to be major of the 103rd. Over the course of this service, Wills underwent a distinct softening of his racial attitudes. Early in the war, Wills gave frequent voice to all manner of racist expressions. He mentioned seeing "the ugliest, dirtiest niggers I ever saw . . . Awful nasty!" in June 1861.[92] He declared in April 1862, "I don't care a damn for the darkies, and know that they are better off with their masters 50 times over than with us," though he qualified this slightly by adding, "but of course you know I couldn't help to send a runaway nigger back. I'm blamed if I could."[93] Wills unquestionably began the war with little regard or sympathy for Black people, but his wartime writings reveal substantial adjustments.

In August 1862, Wills penned a slew of comments indicating a negative view of African Americans. He noted that for the first time he witnessed slaves "that have marks of severe punishment. They were man and wife. . . . The man I think is made a cripple for life from blows by a club on his ankles and knees, the woman is badly cut on the arms and shoulders, as with a horsewhip, but she's all right yet."[94] He followed this observation with unsympathetic perplexity: "How a man can be fool enough to so abuse such valuable property as this is more than I can understand."[95] Wills complained later that month, "My pet negro got so lazy and worthless I was compelled to ship him. I'll take back, if you please, everything good that I ever said of free negroes"—not that the written record shows he had ever said anything nice about them prior to that point.[96] Next, he rejoiced at a report that the government was not going to accept Black men as soldiers, claiming, "Aside from the immense disaffection it would create in our army, the South would arm and put in the field three negroes to our one," and "Hundreds of the officers who are emancipationists, as I am . . . would resign."[97] This is a puzzling statement, since nothing in Wills's previous comments would have led one to suspect he had any interest in emancipation. Still later in August, Wills produced a philippic on the worthlessness of Black people, with a little criticism of slavery woven in:

> You have no idea what a miserable, horrible-looking, degraded set of brutes these plantation hands are. Contempt and disgust only half express one's feelings toward any man that will prate about the civilizing and christianizing influence of slavery. The most savage, copper savage, cannot be below these field hands in any brute quality. Let them keep their negroes though, for we surely don't want our Northern States degraded by them, and they can't do the Southerners any good after we get them driven a few degrees further down. These nigs that come in now, say that their masters were going to put them in the Southern Army as soldiers. I'm sure the Southerners are too smart for that, for a million of them aren't worth 100 whites.[98]

Impressively, Wills managed to simultaneously attack Southern claims about the positive effects of slavery while also viciously disparaging Black people. The obvious disdain for African Americans he shows here makes his later comments all the more striking.

By November 1862, now Captain Wills of the recently organized 103rd Illinois wrote approvingly of the government employing Black people to collect cotton.[99] Later that month, he wrote to his sister about his Black servant:

> My colored boy, Dave, went into the country 20 miles last night and returned this P.M. with his wife, a delicate looking black woman, neat and much above the ordinary slave. She has been a sewing girl all her life, and I think would be worth something to a family that has much plain sewing to do. I think I will try to send her to Mrs. S. C. Thompson. "Dave" is a first rate cook and waiter, and I'll keep him with me until the war closes (if he don't spoil) and then take him to his woman. How'd you like a good colored woman for your kitchen? This woman mended my pants (I have two pairs) as neatly as any tailor could.[100]

Wills looked down on African Americans but did not mind letting them do work for him. In a January 1863 letter to his sister, he joked, "I can send you a nigger baby if it would be acceptable. They are more 'antic' than either a squirrel or a monkey. I have two he niggers, two she's and three babies, mess property. I think I will either have to drown the babies, or sell them and the women, whom I endure because their husbands are such good hands."[101] However, Wills's condescension toward Black people and willingness to make cruel jests at their expense did not keep him from supporting the Emancipation Proclamation, which had taken effect on the first of the month. He reported that when some other officers in the 103rd Illinois murmured about resigning in protest over the proclamation, "we were too strong for the d—d compromising lickspittles and to-day you can't hear a whimper against it. The major and adjutant were strongly opposed to it, but they dare not say so to-day."[102] Racist as he was, Wills had shifted from claiming that slaves were better off staying with their masters (as he did back in 1862) to defending emancipation.

Though Wills got on board with emancipation, his overall attitudes toward race and slavery remained largely unchanged, as seen in a story he shared in March 1863. The departure of a Black man named Bob, whom Wills had been employing as a servant, occasioned a rant that turned into a broader discussion of race:

> I have lost my negro, Bob. . . . There is some kind of a scare along the line, and the authorities this morning shipped to Memphis some 600 negroes, to get them out of the way of the trouble. I made my Bob send his wife and children, and the scamp, when it came to the party, couldn't resist her pleading, and so he joined the party. It is beautiful to see such an exhibition of love and constancy in the brute species. All of these Africans will undoubtedly be sent to Illinois or somewhere else. I declare I don't like to see them introduced into our State, for they increase like rabbits. I believe will eventually outnumber the white race, in any country in which they are planted. This matter of slavery is an awful sin and I'm satisfied debases the governing race, but if we have to keep these negroes in the country, I say keep them as slaves. Take them from secesh and turn them over to Unionists, but don't free them in America. They can't stand it. These negroes don't average the ability of eight-year-old white children in taking care of themselves. There are exceptions of course; arm all the latter and make them fight Rebels. They will probably be fit for freedom after a few years as soldiers.[103]

Much of this diatribe matches Wills's previous racist expressions. However, pronouncing slavery "an awful sin" was a stronger criticism of the institution than any he previously made (even if his chief concern seemed to be with its effects on whites and he still found slavery preferable to having free

Black people). Another element of this statement that hints at Wills's changing views was the limited approbation he gave to the idea of Black soldiers.

A further discussion of Black soldiers in May 1863 did much to elucidate how Wills (and others like him) could be so racist and yet also support emancipation. In an unusual move, Wills expressed genuine concern for Black people. He felt troubled that good men were not being chosen to serve as officers in a nearby regiment of Black soldiers:

> I think poor Sambo should be allowed a fair chance, and that he certainly will never get under worthless officers. I suppose that the regiment organization here numbers some 800 now, and will soon be full. I don't know whether I wrote it to you or not, but a year ago I sincerely thought that if the negro was called into this war as a fighting character, I would get out of it as quickly as I could, honorably. I am by no means an enthusiast over the negro soldiers yet. I would rather fight the war out without arming them. Would rather be a private in a regiment of whites than an officer of negroes; but I don't pretend to set my voice against what our President says or does; and will cheerfully go down to Mississippi and forage for mules, horses and negroes and put muskets in the hand's of the latter. I have no trouble believing that all these Rebels should lose every slave they possess; and I experience some pleasure in taking them when ordered to.[104]

On this occasion, Wills stated plainly something he had only hinted at before: he might despise Black people, but his support for President Lincoln and the Union war effort took precedence. Moreover, he admitted to finding satisfaction in the punitive aspect of emancipation, in the way that it deprived rebels of the "property" that was so precious to them. Wills thus typified the sort of Union officer who could support emancipation for strategic and punitive reasons without actually caring about Black people or giving much heed to slavery as a moral problem.

Strategic concerns and a desire to punish the rebels helped begin a shift in Wills's attitude toward slavery and race, and his firsthand observation of African Americans also seemed to affect him. He revealed another step in his conversion story in late June 1863, writing to his sister:

> I was over to the negro camps yesterday and have seen a good deal of them since I last wrote you. An honest confession is good for the soul. I never thought I would, but I am getting strongly in favor of arming them, and

am becoming so blind that I can't see why they will not make soldiers. How queer. A year ago last January I didn't like to hear anything of emancipation. Last fall accept confiscation of Rebel's negroes quietly. In January took emancipation readily, and now believe in arming negroes. The only objection I have to it is a matter of pride.[105]

Wills's admission that his greatest objection to Black soldiers stemmed from pride is impressively introspective. He followed up this statement with an acknowledgement a few days later that the two Black regiments he had seen "really look right well in their uniforms."[106] Notably, from this point onward, derisive remarks and cruel jokes about African Americans became much less frequent in Wills's writing. He never went so far as to be an abolitionist, but if his cessation of derogatory comments is any indication, he apparently developed at least a limited sense of respect for Black people that he had not possessed before.

Some of Wills's later encounters with slaves stand out for the absence of the condescension that typified his references to Black people in the first couple years of the war. In October 1863, he paid a social call to an Arkansas plantation owned by a man named Worthington. Worthington's son and daughter were "quadroons" (one-quarter Black by descent). Wills wrote: "They are the best educated persons of color I ever met. The young man was educated in France and the young woman in Oberlin, Ohio. She played the piano quite well and sings beautifully. A negro lady is something of a novelty, and if I did not conduct myself exactly right in her presence, I think I am somewhat excusable, for I could see the others were equally puzzled. She is well informed, sensible and talks with animation, using very pretty language."[107] He later learned that Worthington had sold off the mother of his two children. The tone of the entire encounter is strikingly different from the style Wills used early on. It's notable how he dropped the use of the pejoratives "nigger" and "darkey" in favor of the (for the time) more respectful "negro." Other references to Black people from later in the war continued to reflect this pattern of Wills's comments becoming more sympathetic and less insulting.[108]

Wills's evolution to at least slight appreciation or respect for African Americans continued down to the waning days of the war. His improved opinion of Black soldiers, and the concern that they have good officers to lead them, appeared implicitly in October 1864 when he responded to news that a Union outpost at Dalton, Georgia, had surrendered. "Eight hundred of the prisoners captured by them were negroes, who could not have been taken but for the cowardice of their Colonel," Wills fumed.[109] By blaming defeat on the white commanding officer, he tacitly acknowledged the fighting ability of the African American soldiers. Wills still found Black people strange, remarking early in the Savannah Campaign, "It is most ludicrous to see the actions of the negro women as we pass. They seem to be half crazy with joy, and when a band strikes up they go stark mad."[110] Even so, this nonplussed comment is noticeably less pejorative in tone than his early observations about Black people. Later during the March to the Sea, Wills reported, "An immense number of 'contrabands' now follow us, most of them able-bodied men, who intend going into the army."[111]

On 5 December 1864, Wills told of one runaway slave in particular who caught his attention: "A nice yellow girl came to our regiment about an hour after dark. She is the property of Milly Drake, who lives 30 miles back. The girl showed our men where Milly hid her horses and mules, in return for which, after the column had passed, gentle Milly took half a rail and like to wore the wench out. Broke her arm and bruised her shamefully. That was all the reason that the girl had for running away."[112] His sarcastic reference to "gentle Milly" and explicit condemnation of Ms. Drake for beating her slave girl contrasts with Wills's first encounter with enslaved people who had been beaten. Back then, he seemed more focused on the foolishness of misusing valuable property, but by the fall of 1864, his comments instead contain sympathy for the former slave. During the march through the Carolinas, he reported how joyful former slaves swarmed the army to follow in its wake. Surveying Charles Wills's comments about Black people throughout the war, a distinct trajectory emerges, where his initial racism and disinterest in the plight of slaves was gradually supplanted by a limited degree of regard and sympathy. His willingness to support President Lincoln's war strategy and desire to punish rebels appear to have made Wills open to emancipation, but his encounters with African Americans also seem to have increased his solicitude for them.[113]

A similar conversion narrative emerges from the writings of 2nd Lt. Henry Adolph Kircher of the Twelfth Missouri. Kircher left behind extensive expressions of racism and criticism of the idea of Black troops but seemed to grow more accepting of Black soldiers over time. In January 1863, he told his mother, "Now come what may, I am willing to wade through thick and thin in blood up to my knees if thereby the last Negro and the last traitor finds his death."[114] He also wished that President Lincoln would "pray less and guide more, and garnish the halls more with secesh and traitors than with our own people."[115] Elaborating on this, Kircher criticized a recent incident in which a white teamster who shot a Black man was sentenced to be hung. "Is a Negro more than our Fatherland?" he railed.[116] Kircher said he would rather have dead Black than dead white people. His disdain for racial equality appeared in a diary entry from March 1863 during the Yazoo Pass expedition, as he sarcastically recorded seeing many "Negroes, or as it pleases some to say 'Free americans of african descent.'"[117] The arming of African Americans troubled Kircher deeply. He informed his mother that he "don't like the idea of fighting side-by-side with a Negro. That's asking a little too much. If the colored and others do government work, I don't have anything against it. But to see him fighting with weapons in his hand at my better side, hey now, no sirree bob. If we 20,000,000 whites can't force, stamp out not even 10 million rebels, then we don't deserve any better than to be ruled by them, amen."[118] In other words, Kircher claimed he would rather lose the war than win it with the help of Black soldiers.

He shared a similar sentiment with his father in April 1863, although this time he noticeably hedged his opposition to Black soldiers. Speaking of fighting alongside Black men, Kircher said he "wouldn't like to be a slave boss, a slave driver, and fight at his side, mix my blood with his, perhaps be wounded by the same bullet that first traffics with a Negro and then pays me a visit. I am not far enough advanced in civilization that I don't know the difference between white and black anymore."[119] However, he insisted that far from opposing the raising of Black regiments, he favored it (a striking departure from his earlier willingness to lose the war rather than win with Black soldiers). He could tolerate Black regiments so long as they "don't come into any contact with the white ones."[120] Fighting alongside Black soldiers would be an insult to white troops, Kircher claimed. He also feared that if white and Black soldiers fought side by side, "Gradually the difference between white and black will show less and less until it has disappeared."[121] Such a development would be a travesty in Kircher's eyes. "What is a white who forgets that he stands above the African? Then he is no better," he declared.[122] Kircher considered African Americans impudent, proud, vain, greedy, and unappreciative, asking for too much and needing to be put in their place. And yet, notwithstanding the many faults he attributed to them, Kircher reluctantly conceded "that the Negroes make tolerable soldiers. . . . Their courage is not up to much, but not every soldier is courageous by a longshot, he just is when he has to be."[123] This discourse to his father was no embrace of racial equality, but it still hinted that his views on Black people were softening compared to the ones he enunciated to his mother six weeks earlier.

In April 1863, adjutant general of the army Lorenzo Thomas visited the Army of the Tennessee to make the administration's case for arming Black as soldiers. Kircher found the whole presentation deeply underwhelming. In a letter to his mother, Kircher criticized Thomas's speech for being weak, "as if he or the government didn't have the courage simply to command obedience," to the policy of raising Black regiments.[124] All the speeches and cheering and playing of "The Star-Spangled Banner" were contrived and unnecessary, Kircher complained. Soldiers "are long since accustomed to obedience, to the 'must,' and prefer that to a timidity that is just laughable."[125] Interestingly, Kircher's criticism here was no longer in opposition to the idea of Black soldiers, but instead it was only deriding the style in which the government marketed the policy—small change but still noticeable in the broader context of his various comments on the topic. Besides the reaction to Adjutant General Thomas's presentation that Kircher described to his mother, he recorded a somewhat different response in the privacy of his diary. In his diary entry for the day of Thomas's speech, Kircher wrote that the policy of arming Black men "when carried out as proposed will be the hardest blow that yet was struck at the rebs. May it be their grave."[126] That is an impressive shift in attitude for a man who less than three months earlier claimed he preferred to lose the war than employ Black men as soldiers.

Further evidence of Kircher's changing racial attitudes appeared in a diary entry from June 1863. In its siege works surrounding Vicksburg, the Army of the Tennessee had received news that rebel troops had attacked Union outposts at Young's Point and Milliken's Bend over in Louisiana (the Battle of Milliken's Bend). Kircher's reaction to the news is telling: "It gives me pleasure to hear the darkies had don so well. May they be successful in all aid they give in restoring piece to the once happiest and strongest nation in the world. And freeing themselves for a Republic with slavery is no republic and will never stand the cornerstone being Freedom, liberty! to white or black."[127] Kircher's pronouncement that the enslaved people ought to be free and that the cornerstone of the republic was liberty for both Black and white represents a dramatic alteration over about a sixth-month span.

Racism was ubiquitous among the Army of the Tennessee's officers, but their experiences during the war tended to increase their opposition to slavery and their acceptance of emancipation. A fringe minority of abolitionists already desired to end slavery when they enlisted, but most came to see the value of emancipation because of the war. Their relationships to African Americans changed over time. Early in the war, some officers dutifully attempted to enforce orders against harboring or assisting runaway slaves and handed over fugitives when their masters showed up to claim them. Later, they accepted the employment of contrabands as laborers. A number of officers hired former enslaved people as servants, paying them for such tasks as cooking or caring for their horses. By the time the Emancipation Proclamation went into effect, the overwhelming majority rallied behind it (this study found only one officer who expressed definite opposition to the proclamation). Officers, even when openly racist, generally supported raising regiments of Black troops and acknowledged after seeing the results that Black men were indeed capable of making fine soldiers. Some also expressed concern for enslaved people's well-being. Officers' exact views on slavery and race fell on a spectrum. Some condemned slavery as immoral and sympathized deeply with oppressed Black people. Others identified emancipation as a way to punish the traitors who had started the war. Many recognized freeing the enslaved and letting them become soldiers as sound strategic measures that would help win the war. The Army of the Tennessee's officers were largely racists who did not go to war to get rid of slavery, but their experiences in the war turned them against the "peculiar institution" and softened racist attitudes.[128]

CHAPTER 11

The Very Life of the Country

The Army of the Tennessee's officers were politically engaged—and not just regarding the question of slavery. They showed signs of caring about politics prior to the war, and they remained as politically aware and active as they could throughout the conflict. They appreciated that political questions held a central place in the causes of the war and that political choices in Washington, in the state capitals, and among their fellow citizens back home had bearing on ultimate Union victory. The place of slavery and African Americans in America was of course the greatest political question of the day, but politics entered into officers' wartime experience in other ways as well. One notable issue was conscription, but a much greater one was the existence of so-called "Copperheads"—Democrats in favor of making peace with the Confederacy—and other people who did not support the war effort wholeheartedly. Starting early in the war, but especially from late 1862 through early 1863, officers condemned anyone seen as undermining the war effort, be they politicians, generals, or Democrats. Especially in the context of elections, officers looked to the civilian population of the North as allies against the Copperheads. However, officers' fears that Copperheads would somehow snatch defeat from the jaws of victory diminished as time went on, and they grew increasingly certain of winning the war. Officers' most common forms of political expression included messages to newspapers and voting.[1]

Besides the question of slavery, one issue on which officers strongly expressed themselves was conscription. Those who commented on the topic were consistently in favor of the federal government implementing a draft to strengthen the army and end the war more quickly. Some began to endorse a draft as early as the fall of 1862. Likely in response to the Enrollment Act passed by Congress in February 1863 and signed by Lincoln at the

167

beginning of March, many officers expressed support for a draft in March 1863. The officers of the Fifty-Fifth Illinois wrote a resolution declaring, among other provisions, "*Resolved,* That we will heartily sustain the administration in each and every effort put forth consistent with the laws of civil warfare, for the suppression of rebellion, and we hail with gladness the Conscript Laws of Congress, hoping thereby all vacant ranks will be filled, treason speedily annihilated and the majesty of the law vindicated."[2]

Officers in other regiments similarly expressed interest in the draft, showing the hope that the additional men would bring about a speedier conclusion to the war. They also fumed that the government was not more vigorously replenishing the army's depleted ranks. The Enrollment Act did not yield the results officers expected, leading to complaints and criticism. Edward Jesup Wood wrote in the summer of 1863 that the army needed more men "to oppose the rebel hordes," and he fretted over the "weakness of the Administration" and the "blatherings of traitorous demagogues" that were obstructing proper implementation of the conscription law.[3] Wood also critiqued New York governor Horatio Seymour's handling of the antidraft riots that summer as "a base concession to a traitorous inhuman fiendish mob."[4] Through August and September 1864, Jake Ritner especially dwelled on the draft and hopes that strict enforcement of conscription would hasten Union victory. "I have no doubt," he wrote on 9 September, "but that there are a great many cowards and copperheads in the north who wish they had been born a girl, or had died when they were young. But I say go on with the draft. If Old Abe doesn't enforce it this time I won't vote for him."[5] Ritner repeated in two further letters that if Lincoln did not carry out conscription, he and many other soldiers would not vote for him in the upcoming election, and then in a fourth letter he declared, "I see that the draft is to be enforced, and the army will support Lincoln."[6] Officers wanted to win the war and saw conscription as a legitimate political tool to do so.[7]

The Army of the Tennessee's officers were volunteers who went to war because they believed in their cause. Many officers expressed grave concerns over how the Copperheads back home might hinder them and bring their sacrifices to naught. Such people were, in officers' eyes, as treasonous as the men in Confederate uniforms—or, if possible, even worse. Copperheads inspired more fear than rebel soldiers did. Officers felt keenly the need for the support of the Northern people for them to achieve ultimate military victory. Officers fulminated against perceived mismanagement of the war by Northern political and military elites, whether those leaders and politicians were Democrats. One common refrain was that the war could have been won far more quickly if only the politicians had the will to act decisively and support the soldiers properly. It is worth noting that officers did not regard the home front exclusively as a source of anxiety or a domain of traitors. The folks back home could and did hold patriotic gatherings, organize soldier aid societies, and bestow gifts and attention on the volunteers, powerfully encouraging officers' morale. Nonetheless, officers devoted far more ink to the problems they perceived, producing numerous tirades against those who would not support the Union cause and praising those who opposed Copperheads and supported the army.[8]

Officers displayed irritation with political leadership and directed wrath toward those they felt undermined the Union cause throughout the war, but most of all in 1862 and 1863. To judge by their writings, late 1862 and early 1863 were the darkest days of the war, the time when the Army of the Tennessee's officers felt most troubled about traitorous, pro-rebel Northerners and most frustrated about dithering by the US government. From Pittsburg Landing, Tennessee, days after the Battle of Shiloh, Erasmus Ward fumed against the men "who stay at home and find fault with our Generals and form plans for us to follow. . . . We despise them in our harts men who are to Cowardly to fite and have nothing to do only to sit around town talk of soldier."[9] In February 1863, Alphonso Barto declared that the "Traitors at home" had been "handled . . . with silk gloves too long."[10] He proclaimed his love for free speech and a free press, "but in all civilized countries Treason is punishable with death and I would like to see it enforced in this country."[11] Barto's response to "cowards" who "howl . . . about the suspension of the write of Habeas corpus and say it is unconstitutional to suspend it," was that *any thing that protects the Constitution is* constitutional."[12] In May 1863, Bennet Grigsby told his family that when the soldiers came home, the Copperheads would "call upon the rocks and mountains to fall on them and hide them from the face of him that sitteth upon the throne: viz. Abraham the Just. I am of the opinion that a great many of them will receive bloody noses for their wages when the boys get home."[13] Many officers similarly wrote about traitors on the home front and failures of political leadership.

As early as January 1862, Henry F. Hole was blaming the lack of progress in the war on politicians. "What does Mister Sumner and Wilson's splendid orations about the rights of man accomplish?" Hole asked his sister Minerva.[14] The country needed politicians who "advocated war and war now."[15] Politicians' constant meddling with the army "scares everybody. There is not an officer in the army from McClellan down but is afraid to make a movement or order a scout afraid that Congress will appoint a committee to investigate the matter."[16] In October that year, Hole turned his wrath from busybody congressmen to rebel-sympathizing Democrats. He suggested the people of his home county should raise a militia and hang all rebel sympathizers. Such men were traitors who "would rather that Jeff Davis and his rebel hordes of uncombed, unwashed, poor whites, would gain the day than that Abram Lincoln with his fine array of men should once more restore the country to its old accustomed ways."[17] Hole said he prayed that "every rebel sympathizer, every northern doughface democrat . . . could experience a night march to the Hatchie, or that the 'three days around Donelson's grim works' could be felt by some."[18] Hole had seen men die or suffer crippling wounds for the cause that Northern Democrats were undermining, and he had no tolerance for them.

DeWitt Clinton Loudon wrote especially eloquently about the failings of Northern politicians and the dangers of Northern traitors. In July 1862, he fumed over the government's misguided sympathy for Southerners and foolish reluctance to wage war with the necessary ferocity. Up to that time, Loudon said, the Union had only fought a "miserable sort of half war & half missionary society business."[19] The government was "all the time too lenient too tender of the feelings of the infernal miscreants who have clothed the land in mourning & brought sorrow to so many hearts & distress & misery to so many firesides."[20] Politicians needed to recognize "that a terrible rebellion is waged against the very life of the country,"[21] and the government needed to exert its power to "crush the rebel cause to atoms."[22] Loudon believed that if the Northern people took the war as seriously as did the rebels, then they could win the war within a few months. He wrote of despair over the country's fate due to Northern traitors and their sympathy for the South. His frustration is evident:

> Great God! I am sick of hearing senators & representatives talk about our mistaken brethren & prating of constitutional rights & habeas corpus & trial by jury & days in court & all that in behalf of a set of scoundrels & villains who have violated every law human or divine. I tell you it's but poor encouragement to the soldiers who are daily & hourly risking their lives in the camp or on the battle field to see men of ability who fill respectable positions in the government giving aid & comfort to the enemy & doing their utmost to

weaken the hands of their own government & to render vain the sacrifices of the noble lives & gallant blood which has been so freely laid upon the altar of our country. The Lord have mercy on the traitorous curs & their aiders & abettors. They will find none at the hands of the loyal soldiers.[23]

With that thunderous outburst, Loudon's fury abated, at least in this particular letter, but he was by no means done excoriating what he considered weak Northern political leadership.

A few weeks later, Loudon returned to the topic, proposing a solution for the "secession sympathizers at home who have so high an idea of the sanctity of the institution of slavery & so much to say about the constitutional rights of the slave holders."[24] He wished that such men could be forced to spend some time with the army: "If they were obliged to go out in the hot sun & dig trenches or repair roads & bridges my opinion is they would soon experience a 'change of heart'. Lying in the ranks without tents, among 'chiggers' eating fat pork & short iron crackers marching barefooted over the hot dusty roads with clothes all ragged & lousy would soon convert Saul of Tarsus if he belonged to the Vallandingham democracy though I don't believe he was so bad as that, Pharisee & bigot as he was, before his journey to Damascus."[25] He optimistically claimed that if the government just ended its "temporizing rosewater missionary policy" and prosecuted the war aggressively, Union victory would take only a few months.[26] Hope of peaceful conciliation was "not even respectable nonsense."[27] Loudon said he had seen no pro-Union sentiment in the rebel states he had visited and declared, "If the rebellion is put down, it must be done by force of arms & by war waged in earnest & carrying suffering destruction over the land. If rebels are not to be treated as criminals they must at least be treated as enemies with whom we are at war."[28] Shifting to a more moderate tone, Loudon noted that it might actually be good that the government was slower than the people in recognizing the need for hard war; had it attempted hard war at the start, rebel sympathizers might have been able to win over people who had not yet recognized the need for stern measures. Now the people were ready to fully support the war effort. Despite all his frustrations with the government, Loudon still believed God would grant the Union victory: "Sooner or later, Providence in the end will beat all the politicians. God's work is never left undone & whenever the people of the loyal states show that they are worthy of the blessings of the noble government of our fathers & are willing to suffer for it to give their money & their lives for it, it will . . . be restored in all the majesty of its original proportions."[29] He felt that if Northerners were not willing to sacrifice and exert the necessary effort, then they deserved to lose their country. "People in this world only get good government so long as they deserve it."[30]

Loudon produced further lengthy treatments on these themes in a pair of January 1863 letters to his wife Hannah. On New Year's Day, he reported favorably on the way the army had been living off the land during its abortive venture into Mississippi, and he explained why this was a profound shift from the conduct of the war up to that point: "It now looks like we were making *war*. Gen Grant is pursing a policy which has already made itself felt by the citizens ... What he is doing now, our whole army should have done a year ago. I am heartily rejoiced that the policy of respecting & protecting property of known & avowed rebels & rebel sympathizers ... is 'played out'. The country we occupy must be made to feel all the rigors of war authorized by the usages of civilized nations. Handling rebels with kid gloves must be stopped or this infernal rebellion will not be crushed."[31] Loudon predicted that the "traitors at home" would fuss about the new approach to war, and he wished they "had the manliness" to fight for the side where their loyalty truly lay so that he would be free to shoot them.[32] Despite this important change, final victory still seemed distant to Loudon. The Northern people were still not as unified around the cause of preserving the Union as the rebels were in trying to destroy it, Loudon believed, and he feared the country "was drifting into the condition of France, at the time of her first revolution," and would end up with military despotism.[33] Thus far, however, he saw no signs of a general like Oliver Cromwell or Napoleon Bonaparte who would exploit the war in that way. Still, he thought it possible that corrupt politicians could so bungle the war that the army would revolt against civilian authority: "Unfortunately for the country, too many of those charged with administering the government are more concerned in laboring for the success of this party, or their pet candidate, or policy, or enabling some grocery keeper to swindle the government & cheat the soldiers by a good contract, than they are in looking after the public welfare & the success of the national arms."[34] The country would put up with such behavior for a long time, but eventually, "The last feather which breaks the camel's back may finally be laid on."[35]

Later in January 1863, Loudon again reflected on the perceived failings of Northern leaders. The army had just endured a blast of wintry weather, including sleet, snow, and a hard freeze. Loudon had seen many soldiers endure "through it all without tents, their clothing is ragged & many of them stood picket with their barefeet in the snow. I cant tell you with what admirable patience & fortitude they endured it. No sullenness & grumbling; but cheerfulness & good humor."[36] Loudon believed the army lacked proper tents and clothing because of government negligence and misplaced priorities. He reiterated his proposal to educate the Union's elite on the common soldier's experience. He advocated that congressmen, generals, and newspaper editors should spend a week living "under dog kennel shelters" like the average soldier, "who has left a comfortable home, standing out all night with ragged pants & shoes & no other lodging than a 1/5th interest in a rotten Sibly & the comfort of knowing, perhaps, that his wife & little ones are starving at home, for want of the wages . . . which are yet unpaid."[37] The nation's leaders needed to take better care of the common soldier "& stop their infernal quarreling about party concerns."[38] Loudon predicted that many prominent men would face a stern reckoning one day when the soldiers returned home.

The winter of 1862–63 saw Charles W. Wills produce a torrent of philippics against the Copperheads. In January, he declared, "If any part of this army is ever called home to quell those Illinois tories, orders to burn and destroy will not be necessary. . . . It would make your blood run cold to hear the men in this army, without regard to party, curse those traitors."[39] He named off specific Copperheads or other figures seen as rebel sympathizers, including the editors of the *Chicago Times*. These purported advocates of treason discouraged the army greatly, and imprisoning them would do much to bolster morale, he believed. In February, Wills hailed an order from Brig. Gen. Jeremiah C. Sullivan prohibiting the sale of the *Chicago Times* in the area under his command. Wills found the move a pleasant surprise that gave him hope for additional strong measures. Wills said he had ten men in mind he would personally hang. Northern traitors were not limited to newspaper editors; Wills reported that some duplicitous Northerners lowered morale by sending soldiers letters condemning the war. "I assure you," he told his sister, "that it is by no means the lightest portion of an officer's duties now, to counteract the effects of these letters. I know that I put in a good deal more of my time than I wish to, in talking patriotism at the boys and doing good, round, solid cursing at the home cowardly vipers, who are disgracing the genus, man, by their conduct."[40] Wills called for strong actions within the army: "I have advised my men to whip any enlisted man they hear talking copperheadism, if they are able, and at all hazards to try it, and if I hear any officer talking it that I think I can't whale, I'm going to prefer charges against him."[41] In early March, Wills continued to lament the problems of "wicked copperheadism" and wished the Northern people would give the army the support it needed.[42] Hilariously and hypocritically, he claimed at the same time that there was no political talk in his company and, "Above all things I dislike to hear it."[43] Such a claim hardly seems consistent with his lengthy discourses on the matter. By the middle of the month, the situation seemed to have improved, for Wills declared, "I think copperheadism is not worth quite the premium it was a few months since . . . though 'tis mortifying to think we have such dirtcatchers in our State."[44] His invective against Copperheads tapered off after this time.[45]

Like other officers, the winter of 1862–63 seems to have been the time when Alexander K. Ewing felt the greatest concern over rebel supporters in the Northern states. In November 1862, he believed, "In Northern States they have sympathizers men who would to day if the opportunity presented itself go in the Southern army. And these are not a few they are hundreds and thousands."[46] The existence of such legions of pro-rebel Northerners is dubious, but that didn't stop Ewing from claiming they demoralized the army. In February 1863, he wrote to his parents about how he despised the traitors of Indiana even more than those of the South. If pro-Confederate Northerners just had the guts to take up arms, the army could act against them, whereas when Copperheads fought only with words, they could harm the war effort without fear of retaliation. The Democrats needed to be destroyed as a party, Ewing colorfully insisted:

> I predict that that so called Democratic Party will before 6 Mos be so dead, that if Gabriel were to sound his trumpet they could not hear it, for we have to refer us to the fall of a party in oposition to the War of 1812, also of a party in oposition to the Mexican War. If they died after opposing these wars what an awfull death is awaiting these Butternuts. I have just one wish for them all and I tell it to all both great small. That they may all be sunk so low in the infernal regions that the resurrection day cannot find them, and then they have not got half what they deserve.[47]

Ewing marveled that intelligent people could go along with the antiwar movement and threatened to kill anyone he heard speak traitorously, explaining, "A traitor in the Northern States is worse to us then those armed and equiped under the control of Jeff Davis."[48] No denunciation or punishment was too harsh for such traitors. In April he grumbled that while soldiers risked their lives to show the world that the US government was "the best on the face of gods earth," traitors at home were trying to undermine their efforts.[49] Cass County, Indiana, ought to feel ashamed of itself, he declared.[50]

In a January 1863 letter, Robert B. Latham revealed his distress over the activities of the Copperheads. Speaking about some resolutions that a group of Illinois Democrats recently published, he declared, "I never was so dumbfounded in my life as when I saw those resolutions and the speeches that were made at the meeting."[51] He added that he believed most Democrats were staunch patriots. He attributed the antiwar activities to a small segment of the party who was seeking personal advancement and trying to mislead more honorable fellow citizens. Such antiwar speeches and resolutions "gave more aid to the rebels than an army of ten thousand men. It is Treason, and the men that got up those resolutions and made those vindictive speeches are traitors, for they that knowingly aid the rebels are traitors."[52] Latham said that when speaking with a "cesesh" recently, "My cheek burned with shame" as the man predicted the war "would close soon by the dissensions of the north, and said to me that the action of the legislature of your own Illinois is evidence of it. And that is the *hope* and *belief* of the south."[53] Latham's ire toward Copperheads persisted several months later, when he stated the army bore more enmity toward Copperheads than toward rebel soldiers and concluded, "I hope the day of reckoning is near at hand."[54]

The winter and spring of 1863 were likewise the time when Henry Adolph Kircher most vehemently expressed ire toward antiwar Democrats and general political mismanagement of the war. In December 1862, he declared it was "high time that the secesh find their end so that we can provide the *Dumbo*crats a similar fate."[55] In January 1863, he lamented that good soldiers were dying while disloyal Northerners remained safe at home; such men deserved harsh punishment. Free speech was no object to Kircher; those who supported the rebellion should hang.[56] He feared a treasonous uprising might occur in Illinois, in which case he promised to hasten home "to establish in the State of Illinois a butcher shop where there is only flesh of traitors to the State of Illinois and the United States."[57] Anticipating a surprised reaction from his father at his cannibalistic furor, Kircher explained, "the experiences that I have collected so far have served to embitter me against all who think otherwise from the way I think, and especially against those who refuse to defend their Fatherland."[58] In February, he shared a hope that Illinois Democrats, "the miserable, underhanded traitors," would soon "wear a hempen necklace."[59] After the office of a Democrat-aligned newspaper editor was ransacked, Kircher declared in April that the event would "make every reasonable man more happy than sad, for if someone can't work any better with letters of the alphabet he doesn't need any."[60] He predicted that when the soldiers could go back home, Democrats, such as the unfortunate editor, would require substantial protection.[61]

During the fall of 1862 and the winter of 1862–63, Luther Cowan showed the most concern over the danger that political ineptitude and treachery back home would undermine the Union war effort. Too many of the men in the highest ranks of the army and civil government seemed not to care for the good of the country, Cowan wrote. The "ignorant and deluded masses" were clearing the way for the government to waste lives and treasure by electing such men into high office.[62] The country was "*irretrievably ruined*" unless the army and the people "take the war into their own hands," attack the rebels aggressively, and "take these quarrelling and seditious politicians and hang them."[63] In November, Cowan sniffed disdainfully at the "quack doctors, pettifogging lawyers and newspaper writers" who quibbled over politics.[64] Later in the month, Cowan wrote to his hometown newspaper to blame "political prejudice" and "a set of bungling unprincipled demagogues" for the continuation of the war.[65] "As long as the gusty speeches of these heartless speculating office-seekers are listened to, there is no end to the war, no peace, no hope, for our country," he thundered.[66] He was convinced the army could win the war in a month if only the politicians stopped interfering. In January 1863, he again said that between the rebels and the Northern Democrats, the country was in deep trouble. In February, he cynically speculated that little would come of attempts to capture Vicksburg except maybe a little fighting to give a pretext to hand out commissions for some more generals. Cowan feared the rebel sympathizers in the North would soon become strong enough to force Lincoln to make peace. However, by March he seemed more optimistic about the Copperhead problem, expressing satisfaction at various signs that the Northern people were rallying behind the effort to save the Union. He also said any man who claimed he would not fight for the Emancipation Proclamation was just a coward grasping for an excuse.[67]

Most of the letters that officers wrote were to their families, but they also reached out to wider audiences by writing to hometown newspapers. News about one's regiment helped maintain a sense of connection between a unit and the folks back home, but messages to newspapers often had a specifically political aim. On a number of occasions, one regiment or another drafted resolutions on various political matters and sent them to newspapers to make clear the soldiers' view on recent developments or current debates. In January 1863, officers from several Illinois regiments stationed around Corinth, Mississippi, appointed a committee to express their views on Copperheads and the Democratic Party in Illinois. They desired to make clear to the people and politicians of Illinois that the state's soldiers favored "a vigorous prosecution of the war" and fully supported "our President and our Governor in all their efforts to crush the rebellion and restore the Union."[68] Officers representing seven different Illinois regiments made up the committee. The whole group of officers then endorsed the resolutions, which called on everyone at home to support the president's war measures in the "struggle for the perpetuation of every right dear to us as American citizens."[69] They condemned the "traitorous conduct of those members of the Illinois Legislature . . . who have been proposing a cessation of the war . . . to give time for the exhausted rebels to recover strength" and pronounced such efforts the "damnable work of treason."[70] The Illinois officers also proclaimed that they "despise a sneaking, whining traitor in the rear much more than an open rebel in front."[71] They denounced anyone who opposed the state or national government's "measures for the vigorous prosecution of the war for the suppression of this godless rebellion."[72] The only terms of peace they found acceptable were a return of all states to the Union "under the constitution as our fathers made it."[73] After the officers approved the committee's resolutions, they submitted them to their respective regiments, where the resolutions received wide approval.[74]

The Fifty-Fifth Illinois produced another set of resolutions for newspapers. In response to news of Copperhead activity, a perceived lack of popular support for the war back in Illinois, and a letter published by a newspaper, the regiment passed a set of resolutions on 3 March 1863. People must unite amid the national crisis, they declared. "Diabolical agencies" pursuing "dastardly ends" were attempting to persuade the Northern people that the army was ready to give up. The men of the Fifty-Fifth Illinois were especially outraged by a letter published in an Illinois paper, the

Fulton County Ledger, from one "D. H.," claiming the regiment was ready to quit fighting.[75] They thanked the person who sent them a copy of the paper, making them aware of its "falsehood and its cowardly truckling" and enabling them to refute the "highly discreditable" image of the regiment that was being spread among the towns from which the regiment's men came.[76] The resolutions began thus:

> *Resolved,* That we have left our homes and separated from our avocations for the defence of the best government upon the earth.
>
> *Resolved,* That the present rebellion against the rightful authority of the United States of America, is unparalleled for its atrocity in the annals of the world.
>
> *Resolved,* That all sympathizers with armed traitors are our enemies, and, in proportion to the sympathy rendered, they are weakening our hands, nerving the rebel aims and making our conflict prolonged and terrible.[77]

The men of the Fifty-Fifth recalled fighting at such battles as Shiloh and Chickasaw Bayou and stated their determination to keep fighting until they "witness the death agonies of this godless rebellion."[78] They called out Daniel Hedges (author of the letter claiming the Fifty-Fifth Illinois was turning against the war) as a vulgar drunk and a regrettable blot on the regiment. The resolutions concluded by thanking all those back home who supported the regiment and expressing an intention to send a copy of the resolutions to several newspapers to make sure the message got out. This statement represented the entire regiment, not just the officers, but the clear implication is that it certainly included their sentiments.

The most significant election of the war was the presidential election of 1864, in which Abraham Lincoln ran for reelection against Democrat George B. McClellan, erstwhile commander of the Army of the Potomac. After hearing about Lincoln's nomination in June 1864, Charles Dana Miller wrote approvingly, "all the soldiers say 'amen.' There will be but few soldiers who will not vote for 'Old Abe.'"[79] Charles Wills was likewise glad for the news, noting, "The unanimity of the convention does us more good than anything else."[80] Wills also took note of the Illinois governor's race, stating his belief that every Illinois soldier would support Republican candidate and former Army of the Tennessee general Richard J. Oglesby. Officers also took note of the Democrats' convention, held in Chicago, 29–31

August. "Oh yes, we are here surrounded with rebels," wrote Jake Ritner, "But I assure you we have thought and talked more about the rebels that meet at Chicago today than about these, and we hate them worse and fear them more. The sentiment of the army is universally for Lincoln."[81] Captain Wills overheard some rebel prisoners discussing the Northern election: "Every pup of them has hopes that the Chicago Convention will do *something* for them, they hardly know what."[82]

Many officers expressed pro-Lincoln opinions during the election season. One way they did this was showing their satisfaction over regimental polling that invariably seemed to show strong pro-Lincoln majorities. Jake Ritner was an especially prolific commentator on the election of 1864. Discussing his intention to vote for Lincoln, Ritner explained to his wife, "I was a Fremont man once but I am not now. He has turned out to be nothing but a selfish demagogue. Every soldier feels that the only way to end the war and save the country is to elect Lincoln."[83] In mid-September, Ritner declared, "If the north is going to be divided and McClellan elected, we have already done enough for nothing. All our labor and fighting and suffering will then be for nothing; all the blood that has been shed and the lives that have been lost will be in vain."[84] However, with the army voting for the president, he believed Lincoln would win, and if Lincoln were reelected, "The war will not last much longer."[85] He retained this conviction a month later: "I believe Lincoln will be re-elected, as he ought to be, and that will have a good effect, and tend greatly to shorten the war, and hasten an honorable peace."[86] However, Ritner also predicted that before the election the rebels would do everything in their power to encourage the Copperheads and help McClellan win.[87]

Officers' support for Lincoln was not universal, although it came close. Major Thomas Taylor's atypical statements of opposition to Lincoln during the election season illustrate the feelings of the minority that opposed the president. During a conversation at dinner one day, Taylor (a Democrat) pointedly implied that Lincoln should be removed from office, declaring, "When a man becomes higher than the Constitution he should be hung."[88] After dinner, a general present called Taylor and "asked if I was a constitutional man—gave me a cigar & had slight talk from which I inferred that he disliked my remark & wished me to keep silence in future."[89] Taylor recorded in August that while chatting with a colonel, he had "called Lincoln a usurper & despot &c. Farce of comdng."[90] A couple days later, Taylor added, "I am no peace man, yet I am opposed to the policy enunciated by the Republican party in their platform."[91] On 8 November 1864, Election Day, he recorded that while he organized the election for his regiment, he refrained from voting.[92]

In many cases, officers not only voted but facilitated the election process for their units. Captain Oscar Lawrence Jackson illustrated the nature of this work when he described supervising the voting for the Sixty-Third Ohio in Ohio's October 1864 congressional election. The army was on the march in northwestern Georgia: "We are in Cass County, Georgia, and it is election day. We have polls opened at my headquarters. 1:00 P.M. Move and carry election with us. Have a camp kettle with paper pasted over it for a poll box. The officers march at head of the regiment and every few minutes halt and take in tickets. We are in the same county still, and as my headquarters are in the saddle the voting is strictly legal being at the quarters of the commanding officer."[93] They continued the process throughout the day until time for the polling place to close. A week and a half later, they received news that the elections had gone well for the Republicans.[94]

Unlike Major Taylor, most officers found a great deal of satisfaction in the results of the election of 1864. Jake Ritner reported that his Twenty-Fifth Iowa "elected Old Abe with a perfect rush," with Lincoln winning 323 of the regiment's votes and McClellan only 15.[95] To Ritner's special pleasure, no one in his own company voted for McClellan. "We are all highly pleased with the result and hope the folks at home have done their duty as well," he concluded.[96] News of Lincoln's electoral victory arrived on 11 November, prompting celebration. The Fifty-Fifth Illinois's regimental historians interpreted the election outcome as "a proclamation from the popular heart, declaring that the war must be energetically prosecuted to a speedy end," and also "a vote of confidence that forever silenced the copperhead accusation—'the war is a failure.'"[97] Oscar Jackson noted that on the day of Lincoln's second inauguration, soldiers began joking that the president was now a veteran.[98]

While not on the level of Lincoln's reelection, another prominent election during the war was Ohio's 1863 gubernatorial race. Outspoken Copperhead Clement Vallandigham had been expelled from the Union and sent to the Confederacy, which did not want him either, so he ended up running for governor of Ohio from exile in Canada. The election was held in October 1863, but as early as January of that year, a lieutenant in the Thirty-Third Wisconsin named George B. Carter was appalled at the thought of Vallandigham potentially becoming governor. He gloomily predicted, "If he is elected it will be worse than any defeat we have suffered yet."[99] Even Democrats could dislike Vallandigham. The cantankerous Tom Taylor not only wrote of "how intensely I despise Mr. Vallandigham"[100] but also claimed all other Democrats in the army also opposed him: "Val. won't obtain a corporals guard in our regiment, nor in Grants army. All who can vote look upon his nomination as showing a total disregard of the feelings of the Democrats who are in the army—as an outrage upon them. I hunt out the Democrats and we talk together . . . among ourselves and when I speak for them I know whereof I am speaking."[101] Taylor felt much better after seeing a list of other Democrats running for state or local offices that year, praising several candidates with whom he was acquainted.[102] Taylor believed Vallandigham needed to be stopped "at all hazards" and planned to canvass his Forty-Seventh Ohio to drum up opposition.[103] After talking with many of his soldiers, he found very few Vallandigham voters, "and before the election we shall truly have none."[104] He also wrote to friends and relatives back home urging them to oppose the Copperhead. Other Ohioan officers shared similar, albeit less verbose, anti-Vallandigham sentiments.[105]

Politically engaged officers also took note of other less prominent elections throughout the war. In May 1862, Illinois held an election to vote on changes to the state constitution. Benjamin H. Grierson was quite pleased that only two of his soldiers voted in favor of the changes, despite being part of what he called "this *Egyptian Democratic Regt.*"[106] Grierson had worked hard for this result: "It took *considerable talk* in the right way and to the right persons to bring about such a vote."[107] (The Southern counties of Illinois, a region nicknamed "Little Egypt," were predominately Democrat and heavily settled by immigrants from the South. The convention that produced the proposed new constitution had been Democrat controlled, and Republicans strongly opposed the proposal.) This was just one of a variety of elections that occurred throughout the war. Jake Ritner praised the results of Iowa's October 1863 election as "another victory over the rebels," because of how Iowans rejected Copperhead candidates.[108] Of special interest to Ritner was that John Allison Smith, formerly captain of Ritner's company, won reelection to superintendent of public schools in Ritner's district. Officers' leading concern throughout wartime elections was to ensure continued political support for the Union war effort. As Alexander K. Ewing put it, "We do not want any man who is in favor of making peace while the Enemy is in open arms or is in favor of even an armistice."[109] Officers participated in elections by voting and by seeking to persuade both fellow soldiers and folks back home of how to vote, as well as by simply seeking to stay informed on political matters.[110]

DeWitt Clinton Loudon was an example of officers who showed political interest throughout the war. In the summer of 1862, he sought information about candidates for county offices back home in Ohio. Loudon contemplated running for office himself, though a bout of ill health convinced him not to hazard the effort. On Election Day that October, he wrote, "How I hope the '*copperheads*' are beaten."[111] Loudon feared that "a triumph of the butternut sympathizers at the polls would cost the life of many a gallant soldier, & strengthen the rebellion more than a battle won."[112] Later in the month, he learned through newspapers that "it seems the butternuts have made a pretty sweep in Ohio."[113] Loudon had an explanation for this:

> The Union party may thank themselves for this result, by refusing last winter to pass a law allowing the soldiers to vote. If the soldiers could have voted the result would have been different. Our brigade is all Ohio troops; & the boys would have thrown nearly a solid vote for the Union ticket. A great many of them are democrats, or rather were; but there is no difference of opinion among them. Soldiers have no politics, except to stand by their country & her glorious old flag; & they are almost to a man for standing by the party & the men at home who are for standing by the soldiers in the field & prosecuting the war with vigor & to the "bitter end."[114]

(This situation had changed by the time of the presidential election two years later, as various states implemented voting laws that would permit soldiers in the field to participate.) Loudon showed continued engagement with even local elections throughout the war, inquiring about contested results and celebrating Democrat defeats. He closed one letter to his wife Hannah with "P. S. I forgot to tell you how delighted I was to hear that the copperhead rats are at last smoked out of the Court house. I hope our county will never be disgraced by putting any of them back."[115] Part of how officers such as Loudon remained connected to home was in following local politics.[116]

The Army of the Tennessee's officers showed signs of political engagement throughout the war, and they displayed the greatest concern over Copperheads, Northern traitors, and political mismanagement of the war from the fall of 1862 to the spring of 1863. Thereafter, although officers remained interested in elections and other political developments, they did not express fears that perfidious Northerners would undermine the Union cause with anywhere near the same frequency or intensity. Slavery was the greatest political issue of the war, but officers also took note of everything from gubernatorial elections to constitutional referendums. They knew victory in the war depended on support from Northern civilians and political leaders and through both voting and writing letters to the public sought to marshal support for aggressive prosecution of the war.

CHAPTER 12

That Class of Generals Who Think That War Means Fighting

Officers freely and frequently expressed opinions about their commanding generals. They did not interact personally with their commanders on a day-to-day basis but saw them enough to form strong impressions and occasionally even develop some degree of personal relationships with them. Still, most junior officers dealt with their generals infrequently enough that personal encounters with a general were noteworthy. Officers had definite ideas about what made for good or bad generals, and in the privacy of their letters and diaries they felt free to share both laudatory and scathing reviews of their commanders. Occasionally, rather than editorialize on a general's leadership or competence, they simply remarked at his appearance, as if they had just encountered a celebrity. Unsurprisingly, officers had more to say about Ulysses S. Grant and William T. Sherman than any of their other generals. For both Grant and Sherman, officers' trust grew over time, until by the latter portions of their service under each general, the commander was a great source of confidence for officers. In addition to the Army of the Tennessee's two most prominent generals, though, officers doled out praise, criticism, or simple observations on many other army, corps, division, and brigade commanders they encountered. Generals exerted tremendous power over the war experience of junior officers, whether inspiring confidence or inflicting frustration.[1]

All generals could, at any time, wield great influence over the fates of junior officers. Charles W. Wills illustrated the power generals could exert

184

when, on the day Wills's 103rd Illinois set out to join the Siege of Vicksburg, Gen. Richard J. Oglesby "gobbled me without a moment's warning," attaching Wills to his staff and leaving him "almost demoralized over the matter."[2] Wills was literally pulled off the train just before the 103rd departed for the front. He hated being separated from his comrades as they headed toward danger. Oglesby had been wounded at the Battle of Corinth back in October 1862 and thus was on duty in the rear rather than with a command at the front, and Wills was stuck with him. He actually admired Oglesby, calling the general "the very ideal of a chivalric, honorable, gallant, modest, high-spirited, dignified, practical, common-sense, gentleman. Nobody can help loving him."[3] Wills added, "There is such a big rolling river of fun and humor in his conversation. Such a hearty honest laugh; I know his heart is big enough to hold a regiment."[4] But his regard for General Ogelsby did not stop Wills from fretting all through June, July, and August 1863 over his involuntary separation from his regiment. By September, he felt determined to get back and essentially begged Oglesby to let him go, to which the general assented.

Any general could wield significant power over the status of company and regimental officers, but Ulysses S. Grant and William T. Sherman stand out far above the others in terms of shaping the experiences of the entire Army of the Tennessee officer corps.[5] Above all else, the Army of the Tennessee was Grant's army, profoundly shaped by his leadership in its formative days; even after he left it to assume command of the full US war effort, his influence remained. Many officers recorded having personal encounters with Grant at some point in their service. Charles Dana Miller remembered the general amid the tedious canal-digging days during the winter of 1862–63 as "a man of ordinary stature, rather square built, but not fleshy: his beard and hair were cut close; plainly dressed with hardly a mark of his high rank. He wore a slouched black felt hat and smoked a cigar most of the time."[6] Miller also observed that Grant seemed fond of horses and appeared to enjoy talking to others about them. Anthony B. Burton, lieutenant of an Ohio artillery battery, described seeing Grant on 17 June 1863 during the Siege of Vicksburg: "Gen. G. is a smaller man than I had supposed from having always heretofore seen him on horseback; has gray eyes and whiskers cut short; is a little stoop shouldered; is very quiet in his manner and of unchangeable countenance; was smoking a cigar and had on a blouse and a low crowned hat."[7] Captain Charles W. Wills chanced to travel down the Mississippi in September 1863 aboard the same steamboat as Julia Grant, or as Wills referred to her, "Mrs. General Grant."[8] He wrote, "I think Mrs. Grant a model lady. She has seen not over thirty years, medium size, healthy blonde complexion, brown hair, blue eyes (cross-eyed) and has a pretty hand. She dresses very plainly, and busied herself knitting during nearly the whole trip. Believe her worthy of the general."[9] While this description chiefly pertains to Julia Grant, Wills's final comment nonetheless hints at something of a positive view of the general too. Physical appearance plays an important role in overall perceptions of other people, but officers had much to say about Grant in addition to how he looked.[10]

Despite early doubts and occasional later moments of frustration, officers developed firm confidence in General Grant, valuing his aggressiveness and willingness to fight in contrast to other commanders they judged inferior. Early impressions of Grant after the Battle of Shiloh were not favorable. Major John Hancock concluded, "I have not got confidence in Grant's executive ability—he fights well but is not cautious enough."[11] Henry F. Hole told his sister Minerva, "Where the blame rests: Most certainly on Major General Ulysses S. Grant commander in chief and Brig. Gen. W. T. Sherman."[12] Sherman, Hole thought, was "either a traitor or a fool. I don't know which but it is charitable to suppose the latter."[13] Had almost anyone but Grant and Sherman been in command, the battle would have gone far better, Hole claimed. It is not surprising that some questioned Grant's leadership in the aftermath of such a costly (and nearly disastrous) battle. However, criticisms such as those of Hancock and Hole did not remain the norm among officers throughout the war. Even after Shiloh, not everyone lost faith in Grant; one officer remembered, "We thanked God for the arrival of the army of the Ohio, but we never thanked God for Don Carlos Buell when he rode across the Tennessee and spoke lightly of the great Grant."[14]

By the fall of 1862, officers expressed more satisfaction with Grant's leadership. Captain Luther Howard Cowan revealed a broadly positive view of Grant in a series of epistles from that period. Reporting to his hometown newspaper about the Battle of Corinth, Cowan outlined the army's situation: "Grant is watching [Confederate general Sterling Price] while Rosencrans, McPherson, Ord, Lawlin, and Hurlbert are thrashing him. If the western army is not managed with so much West Point 'science' as that of the East the people will begin to see that they can fight. It is my opinion that if there was a little more 'good horse sense' and less of 'red tape' and political favoritism used, the war would move faster. The rebels as usual here in Tenn. run away and leave their wounded for us to take care of."[15]

This commentary on army leadership, while thought-provoking, is slightly ambiguous as to Cowan's view of Grant, but subsequent letters clarified Cowan's confidence in Grant as a fighting general. The second week of December, Cowan informed his daughter Molly that Price was trying to escape, but "Grant will not let him stop and rest and build fortifications as our Generals have usually done in the past."[16] Captain Wills shared a similar view of Grant, remarking that although Gen. William S. Rosecrans might be the most popular general overall and many generals disliked Grant, "the whole line believe in him, mostly, because he is for going ahead and will fight his men."[17] On a related note, 2nd Lt. Henry Otis Dwight recalled Grant's eagerness to advance during the army's abortive attempt to reach Vicksburg, Mississippi, in December 1862. As the army marched toward Grenada, Mississippi, Dwight's Twentieth Ohio led the column: "Our cavalry was scouring the country some fifteen or twenty miles in advance, so that there was no great risk of sudden attack on the head of the column. A small squad of cavalry men marched a short distance in front of us, and then came Gen. Grant with his staff and the Twentieth right behind him. Gen. Grant was at this a very ordinary looking man, dressed in old clothes and without a sign of rank about him. He was always wanting to go, and had much ado to let the men rest for five or ten minutes in the hour."[18] Dwight noted appreciatively that despite the general's keen desire to keep on the move, Grant took care not to push the army more than fifteen or twenty miles a day, so that men did have opportunity to rest well at night. Overall, then, by the close of 1862, officers displayed a growing appreciation for Grant's aggressive leadership.[19]

Views of Grant remained mixed heading into the new year, as a pair of contrasting comments from January 1863 show. Following the failure of the overland expedition toward Vicksburg, Lt. Col. DeWitt Clinton Loudon had occasion to visit Grant's headquarters at Holly Springs, Mississippi, on New Year's Eve 1862. Loudon spent more than an hour chatting with the commanding general and wrote to his wife Hannah regarding his impression of Grant, "The Gen shows that he appreciates his great responsibility. He is a good officer, careful & industrious & belongs to that class of generals who think that war means fighting, & fighting means injury & destruction to whatever is in the way. If more of our high officers had been of this same notion, we should have more to show in the way of results."[20] Again, Grant's willingness to fight appeared as a key part of what officers appreciated about him. Writing a few weeks later, though, James Kerr Proudfit did not share Loudon's optimistic appraisal of the commanding general's competence, telling his sister: "I don't believe in Genl. Grant or any of the other generals who have inflicted so much unnecessary misery upon an army as we have endured lately. They may succeed but only because there is greater imbeciles on the other side and that I don't think is possible. You may think I am bitter but I cannot help it. I love my country & her cause but I abhor the fools and villains in high places who are doing the utmost to ruin all."[21] Proudfit concluded his polemic by declaring that the only enemy he feared was "the forces of Genl. Mismanagement," which he doubted whether the army could defeat.[22]

Once the cold, dark, muck-digging days of the winter of 1862–63 passed and the Vicksburg Campaign began in earnest, officers showed consistent confidence in Grant. Early in the campaign, Captain Wills declared, "We think that Grant is going to beat them all yet. But his army is more responsible for his good fortune than himself."[23] Although the campaign itself was brilliant, it concluded with one of Grant's most regrettable decisions, the disastrous 22 May assault on Vicksburg. In the immediate aftermath of the slaughter, Lt. Henry Adolph Kircher reacted to news that Grant had decided there would be no more attempts to storm the city by exclaiming derisively, "When the child falls in the well, then cover it! By the way, all the generals were supposedly greatly opposed to this last storm, but Grant wouldn't let himself be stopped and still gave the order for the entire line to charge."[24] However, even Kircher's frustrations over the 22 May assault did not destroy his overall high regard for Grant. He affirmed to his mother a few weeks later, "I say that nobody can reproach General Grant, whether he is responsible for it or not, at all about the entire campaign since Milliken's Bend on May 2d until the 22d."[25]

Likewise, the failed assault does not seem to have crippled Grant's standing in the eyes of 1st Lt. Richard W. Burt of the Seventy-Sixth Ohio. Burt wrote a couple of letters to a newspaper back home during the siege, declaring in one, "Our army has unlimited confidence in Gen. Grant, and think there is no such thing as failing in taking Vicksburg and the whole rebel army inside its works, prisoners of war."[26] He maintained this confidence in a follow-up letter on 21 June, reporting that everyone expected the rebels "must put up the white flag and submit finally to an unconditional surrender. There is the greatest confidence in Gen. Grant's ability to prevent the siege from being raised by Johnston, Bragg, or anybody else who may attempt it."[27] Although Burt spoke of the army collectively, it seems fair to assume he included himself in the number that trusted Grant. Major Edward Jesup Wood observed during the siege, "The greatest confidence is felt in Gen Grant's ability to defeat him [Johnston] should he come."[28] Shortly after beginning the Siege of Vicksburg, 1st Lt. Henry Miller Culbertson boldly claimed, "Grant is sure of taking the place this week. Would take it sooner, but does not want to lose the men."[29] General Grant did not quite live up to Culbertson's prediction, but he did eventually capture the city. While visiting the captured stronghold in August, Culbertson told his family, "If I had seen this place before the boats ran the blockade, I should have said that General Grant was crazy to attempt anything of the kind, but the old fellow has a long head and works to win. Let General Grant have his army in here, and I defy the World to take the place in seven years."[30] If rough battles or hard times gave some officers pause in their evaluation of Grant as leader, by the time Vicksburg fell, he had solidly earned their respect.

Vicksburg was the last major campaign in which Grant had direct command of the Army of the Tennessee, and thus the frequency of officers' references to him tapered off after the siege, though a few late observations stand out. Days after Grant's victory at Chattanooga, Jake Ritner declared, "No one man here knew what has been done, except the general result which is that the rebels have been out-generaled by Grant, and defeated, routed, demoralized, and the whole army gone to the devil where it belongs."[31] That December, Captain Wills expressed some doubts as to what Grant was doing. "I don't like to slander so great and noble a man as Grant," he began, before saying that the way Grant was dividing his forces looked disturbingly reminiscent of the way Gen. Henry W. Halleck had strewn his army across the countryside after capturing Corinth in the spring of 1862.[32] Officers also pondered how Grant would perform in the eastern theater. Even before Grant headed east, Capt. George B. Carter worried, for Grant's sake, about the possibility that the general would be called to take command of the Army of the Potomac. Carter wrote to his brother George late in July 1863: "I see there is a probability that Grant will be called to the command of that army. If I were he I'd rather resign than take it. There is too damn much doubters in that army, and too much jealously to allow any man to be successful. If Grant goes I hope they will let him take his army or least a part of it."[33] Writing in May 1864, Colonel Wood apparently did not share Carter's fears about how Grant would fare. "The brave old Grant more than holds his own on the Potomac, & *we* know that he has the gift of *tenacity* in a wonderful degree. He never lets go, when he has fastened on his victim, & tho' he may suffer delay & perhaps temporary defeat, he will not fail of his purpose," Wood wrote confidently in May 1864.[34] Later in the month, Wood remarked, "The situation looks critical for Grant in Virginia—if the Govt only supports him, he is bound to succeed—he will do as he says, 'fight it out on that line if it takes all summer' and in that is the key to his character."[35] The Army of the Tennessee's officers experienced their moments of doubt or intense frustration with Grant, but their comments about him suggests that he earned their confidence and that they particularly appreciated his aggressiveness.

William T. Sherman was prominently associated with the Army of the Tennessee for almost the entirety of its service, rising from division commander to corps commander to army commander to commander of all US armies in the western theater. Junior officers had relatively little to say about Sherman prior to his command of the ill-fated Chickasaw Bayou expedition at the close of 1862. Unlike Grant, whose departure to the east made him less directly relevant to officers still serving in the western theater, even when Sherman was promoted out of direct personal command of the army, he remained closely connected to it. Benjamin Grierson reported one of the earliest instances of an officer meeting Sherman, when he called on the general while passing through Paducah, Kentucky, in February 1862. Having heard "all the stories that had been in circulation as to his being 'crazy,'" Major Grierson said he "naturally scrutinized him quite closely."[36] Grierson deemed Sherman "a very courteous and agreeable gentleman . . . a man of marked ability, and it was a real pleasure to me to hear him talk," though he noted the general paced nervously throughout their conversation.[37] Charles W. Wills called Sherman "certainly the most peculiar-looking man I ever saw" and curiously noted that the general perpetually seemed to have a half-gone yet unlit cigar in his mouth.[38] Oscar Jackson spotted the general during the Savannah Campaign and recorded, "He is a very plain, unassuming man and today is in undress uniform but has that big shirt collar on as usual."[39] Finally, late in March 1865, Sherman reviewed John Nilson's Twenty-Fifth Indiana as it passed through Goldsboro, North Carolina, and Nilson remarked, "He was in a joyful mood, which is the 1st time I have ever seen him look so gleeful. He generally wears a sad look as if in deep study."[40] Such were the impressions of Sherman's physical presence that officers recorded. Throughout the war, Sherman had his detractors, but as with Grant, the majority view seemed to be a strong sense of confidence in his leadership, and like with Grant, confidence in Sherman solidified as the war continued, until he was consistently esteemed in the war's latter phases.[41]

The failed Chickasaw Bayou expedition at the end of 1862 definitely hurt Sherman's image among officers. Henry Kircher declared that attacking the rebel defenses atop the Walnut Hills above the bayou was "complete madness" on Sherman's part.[42] Kircher believed the general "would have just sacrificed us all, because Mr. Sherman believed that he could take Vicksburg with such a handful of men. . . . Then he would be the great hero; not those, those really courageous and brave soldiers who happily looked into the jaws of death and went into the gaping jaws."[43] Around this same time, Robert Steele proclaimed Sherman's attempt to reach Vicksburg "a complete failure" and blamed "crazy Sherman" for planning it poorly.[44] In fact, Steele asserted, Sherman had "displayed good generalship once in his life in planning his retreat."[45] Immediately after the battle, Henry G. Ankeny deplored the "useless sacrifice of life" and admitted he felt "very much discouraged and disheartened" because the generals (obviously including Sherman) "do not understand their business and do not appear to care for the loss of life no more than were we so many brutes."[46] Ankeny's criticism of Sherman remained just as fierce weeks later. After explaining to his wife Tina his views on how Vicksburg could be taken, Ankeny claimed, "But for the incompetency of Sherman and the jealousy of his brigadiers, it would have been done. Now in Grant, I hope we may hope, although I don't see that he has been very successful in his generalship."[47] Officers continued to hold Sherman in low esteem later in the Vicksburg Campaign, for Kircher (in addition to blaming Grant) also lambasted Sherman for the bloody 22 May assault. "A third of the entire 12th regiment murdered, only because Sherman thinks everything can be forced by the stormers without knowing the terrain or testing it out," Kircher lamented.[48] However, George H. Hildt dissented from officers' typically poor assessments of Sherman during this period, telling his parents in April 1863 that Sherman "is a good man, and has the confidence of all."[49] Hildt's comment aside, it does appear that many officers initially felt unhappy with Sherman's leadership.

A year after the Battle of Chickasaw Bayou, however, officers began to hint that sentiments toward Sherman were shifting. Some still thought poorly of the general. John Quincy Adams Campbell claimed, "I am not now (nor ever was) an admirer of Gen. Sherman for he has only succeeded at failing. In every expedition and undertaking he has tried during the war he has sacrificed more lives than any other general in the Western Army."[50] Charles W. Wills exhibited a resigned annoyance with some of Sherman's choices, though he did not go so far as to pronounce the general an utter failure. Conversely, Captain Ankeny's previously negative opinion had begun to turn, for in November 1863 he told his wife, "I like him [i.e., Sherman] as a general and patriot."[51] This was no ringing endorsement, but, compared to his previous declaration that Sherman was incompetent, it hinted that Ankeny was reassessing Sherman's leadership ability. After calling on General Sherman in Nashville in December 1863, Lt. Col. DeWitt Clinton Loudon reported, "He was very cordial & treated me very kindly. He is one friend I can count on in case of trouble for he knows me & thinks I am a good soldier."[52] In April 1864, Loudon again enjoyed a cordial visit at Sherman's Nashville headquarters, after which he predicted that Sherman "will make things move in this dept. Somebody will have to run or be hurt when he starts."[53] Loudon offered his wife Hannah a measured evaluation of the western theater's new senior commander: "Sherman is not free from faults; but he is a man of wonderful energy & terribly in earnest in this war work. If we should ever get whipped, which I guess wont happen when he is with us there will be a good many of us who wont get home to tell about how it happened. His old division is very proud of him. We all feel glad he is to succeed Gen Grant as commander of this great Military Division. And he has not forgotten who stood by him through the bloody days of Shiloh's fight."[54] That last comment alludes to the way Sherman had commended Loudon's Seventieth Ohio for its good conduct after the Battle of Shiloh. Later that summer, Loudon fondly recalled Sherman's praise for their performance at Shiloh as evidence of their prowess. Sherman's post-battle compliment to the Seventieth stuck with Loudon not merely for months but years later in the war. By the winter of 1863–64, Sherman was not yet deeply beloved by the Army of the Tennessee's officers, but there were clear signs that officers' poor opinion of him was improving.[55]

During the Atlanta Campaign, officers began to manifest more consistently favorable views of Sherman—very similar to the way positive opinions of Grant seemed to solidify during the Vicksburg Campaign. In contrast to the past, by the summer of 186–64, Sherman inspired a sense of confidence in his officers. Jake Ritner admitted in June that he had no idea how the rest of the army was deployed or what they were doing, but "I suppose General Sherman knows all about it and that is enough."[56] Owen Stuart boldly declared, "I am sure that Sherman will Flank him [Joseph E. Johnston] again. He is as able a Flanker as Johnston is a *Retreater*."[57] Later in June, Stuart noted, "The whole Army have confidence in Sherman & McPherson and admire the cautiousness in which they move and the pains they take in saving life."[58] Edward Jesup Wood believed, "There seems no doubt of Sherman's ability to enter Atlanta with his present force."[59] Charles W. Wills remarked frequently about Sherman's popularity in the army. He declared in June, "If we get to Atlanta in a week all right; if it takes us to months you won't hear this army grumble. We know that 'Pap' is running the machine and our confidence in him is unbounded."[60] He also shared a marvelous anecdote: "They credit a prisoner with saying that Sherman will never go to hell, for he'll flank the devil and make heaven in spite of all the guards."[61] On 29 August, referring to the Democratic Party's national convention occurring that day, Wills wrote: "I would like to know what the Chicago Convention is doing to-day. We hear there is a possibility they may nominate Sherman. How we wish they would. He would hardly accept the nomination from such a party, but I would cheerfully live under Copperhead rule if they would give us such as Sherman. Sherman believes with Logan, 'that if we can't subdue these Rebels and the rebellion, the next best thing we can do is to all go to hell together.'"[62] Officers' comments at the victorious close of the Atlanta Campaign indicated their ongoing confidence in him. Oscar Jackson remarked approvingly at how the army now cheered for the man once decried as "'Crazy' Sherman."[63] Charles Wills basked in the satisfaction that his trust in Sherman was vindicated. Alphonso Barto said of Sherman, "I like his style," and confessed, "I don't know but we all think almost as much of Sherman as we ever did of Grant but who belonged to Grants old army still swear by Grant."[64] The Atlanta Campaign seemed to mark a turning point in officers' view of Sherman, a time in which he fully secured their respect.[65]

The Army of the Tennessee enjoyed two further campaigns under Sherman's overall direction, marching from Atlanta to the sea and then across the Carolinas. Sherman continued to inspire optimism and confidence throughout these closing campaigns of the war. Charles Wills continued to report Sherman as finding widespread favor in the army, and with Sherman in charge, everyone (implicitly including himself) "seems to think the idea of these Rebels being able to do us any permanent harm is perfectly preposterous."[66] In between the Savannah and Carolinas Campaigns, Wills declared, "Thinking nothing impossible if Sherman goes with us, and go he will."[67] On Christmas Day 1864, Jake Ritner assured his wife, "You need not be uneasy about General Sherman going on a 'wild goose chase' and getting his men into trouble. He is all right, and knows what he is about!"[68] Hearing in January 1865 that Secretary of War Stanton and Quartermaster General Meigs had come to visit Savannah, Ritner declared, "We don't want to see either one of them. If they will stay at Washington and mind their own business, General Sherman can run this concern without any of their help."[69] At Beaufort, South Carolina, Owen Stuart wrote, "Well now about the Army, no body Knows where we are going. Pap Sherman has not arrived yet he keeps his own Secrets, and leaves us all in the Dark, but we are all Satisfied with his decision and I trust in God."[70] Having gained officers' confidence, Sherman apparently continued to enjoy their approbation through the Army of the Tennessee's last two campaigns. With the war over, at the close of April 1865, Charles Wills offered a final assessment of his commander: "We all think the world of him. I'd rather fight under him than Grant, and in fact if Sherman was Mahomet we'd be as devoted Musselmen as ever followed the former prophet."[71]

Sherman made his share of mistakes as a general, but officers' wartime comments about him suggest they came to respect and trust him as they grew more familiar with him. One exception to this norm is Col. Thomas Worthington of the Forty-Sixth Ohio. Worthington conceived himself a military mastermind who fell victim to Sherman's bitter enmity. Worthington ended up cashiered on (according to him) trumped-up charges of misconduct, and after the war he launched volley after literary volley against his purported nemesis. For example, Worthington judged Sherman's performance at Shiloh to be "blunders, and nothing else but blunders, and far worse."[72] Worthington claimed the army's movements early in 1862 "had their origin in Washington, having several purposes—one to supplant McClellan, one to prolong the war, and beyond this to put Halleck, Grant, and Sherman into the positions they attained, at the sacrifice of hundreds of millions and myriads of lives. Treacheries—not blunders."[73] Moreover, the battleground at Shiloh was "selected by Sherman with demoniac sagacity and approved by Grant."[74] Meanwhile, Worthington delusionally affirmed that the value of his own leadership during the Battle of Shiloh "availed the government more than the expenses of West Point for centuries."[75] According to Worthington, he could not get the authorities to investigate Sher-

THAT CLASS OF GENERALS WHO THINK THAT WAR MEANS FIGHTING 195

man's misconduct at Shiloh, so he deliberately engaged in insubordinate actions in order to provoke a court-martial where he could expose Sherman's perfidy. Colonel Worthington was the exception that proved the rule: the incomparable and absurd nature of his rancor highlights the extent to which the overwhelming majority of the Army of the Tennessee's officers eventually grew to appreciate Sherman, at least once they saw more of his leadership than the rough moments at Shiloh and Chickasaw Bayou.[76]

Grant and Sherman were easily the most prominent commanders of the Army of the Tennessee, but the army served under several other commanders throughout the war. After Shiloh, Gen. Henry W. Halleck assumed command until after capturing Corinth, Mississippi, at the close of May 1862. Captain Lucien B. Crooker remembered that during this time the army mocked their commander as "Grandmother Halleck" because of his "timid hesitation and fear of a general engagement."[77] Henry Otis Dwight's memory concurred that the army imputed Halleck's glacial slowness to fear. "He had no power of infusing enthusiasm into his men and was regarded as a meddler who would be better away from his army than with it," Dwight explained.[78] He further declared his ongoing distaste for Halleck: "I have always felt a sense of regret that it was Gen. Halleck . . . who recommended me to be appointed 2d Lieutenant. I therefore felt under obligations to one whom I could not point to with pride as having perceived my superior abilities. I would have valued the appointment ten fold more had it come from a fighting soldier."[79] Halleck left the western theater later in the summer of 1862 to take command in the east, at which time Grant resumed command of the Army of the Tennessee.

After Grant left for the east in the winter of 1864 and Sherman became overall commander of the western theater, James B. McPherson took command of the Army of the Tennessee. Lieutenant Dwight shared a story from McPherson's days as a lieutenant colonel on Grant's staff, which had given officers and men a favorable view of McPherson before he ever became their commander:

> It was at Corinth or Burnsville [Mississippi], that a sutler had several barrels of onions some of the barrels had braken, and as the troops marched by the men helped themselves from the loose and scattered vegetables. Now sutlers, like the Surgeons of the Regiments are held in great contempt by the soldiers, as men who make a good living out of the war without any of the risks. The feeling toward this particular sutler was not improved when

he stepped up to Gen. Grant who was standing by, and said "General, just see how your men are stealing my onions. Wont you give me a guard to stop them?" Gen. Grant looked at the man a moment and then replied "Well if they did not need those onions I guess they would not take them." The amusement on the face of Col. McPherson at this reply struck a chord in the hearts of the soldiers, and although they regarded him as somewhat of a fop, because of his "biled" shirts when he was appointed to the command of the right wing of the army, they were already prepared to give him the devotion which they afterwards yielded to his abilities.[80]

McPherson did indeed earn officers' respect and recognition as "a fighting general"—the same quality officers praised Grant and Sherman for demonstrating and criticized Halleck for lacking.[81] To the great sadness of the army, McPherson was killed during the Battle of Atlanta on 22 July 1864. Alphonso Barto lamented McPherson's death, suggesting he was the third-best general in the entire US Army (presumably after Grant and Sherman) and declared, "We loved McP. Peace to his ashes."[82] Edward Jesup Wood claimed, "The army could not have sustained a severer loss" than the death of General McPherson. "Brave as a lion, chivalric as a knight of old, modest, unassuming, warm & generous in his praise of others, a courteous gentleman in all the relations of life, he was the idol of his soldiers—the most *beloved* of all the Generals in the army," Wood opined.[83] With the pain of the general's loss fresh in his mind, Wood felt that "the sacrifice of the whole rebel army would scarcely atone for the death of McPherson."[84] Jake Ritner wrote, "We feel his loss deeply. We all loved him and had confidence in his ability and courage."[85] If their eulogies are any indication, McPherson may have acquired officers' respect more quickly than Grant or Sherman did.[86]

McPherson had two successors as commander of the Army of the Tennessee. John A. Logan assumed command of the army during the Battle of Atlanta, but thereafter Sherman choose another to command the Army of the Tennessee through the Atlanta, Savannah, and Carolinas Campaigns. However, Logan did reprise his role as army commander for the Grand Review in Washington after the war. Officers praised Logan's bravery and his effectiveness as a fighting general, and they defended him against criticism. They found him warm and friendly, "a very jolly sort of a general."[87] Beyond his combat leadership skills, Logan proved himself a proficient orator with a keen understanding of the men he led. In the spring of 1863, adjutant general of the army Lorenzo Thomas visited the Army of the

Tennessee to promote the government's plans to raise regiments of Black soldiers. He spoke at length to Lieutenant Dwight's division, threatening serious discipline against any who opposed the government's new policy and making a poor impression on his audience. Dwight believed that at the end of Thomas's speech, the audience was against him and the plan of arming Black men. Then, however, General Logan began to speak:

> In a few mildly expressed phrases he state to Gen. Thomas that the soldiers of this army were men accustomed to think for themselves, and could not be driven by threats to accept anything which they candidly believed to be wrong. Hence there was no use in uttering threats to them. They were not afraid to take the consequences of their honest opinions. Then he launched out in a stirring exposition of the reasons why we were in the army, and of our determination to see it through and to support the government in the use of any means to put down the rebellion. "Why," said he "if the Government can use elephants to good purposes to put down the rebellion we are willing. The rebellion must be crushed out at any cost. Of course we have no objection to the use of negroes for soldiers if that will aid in the great object for which we are all laboring and risking our lives."[88]

Dwight concluded that by displaying understanding of the common soldier's point of view and accompanying it with humor, Logan won over the division on the issue of Black regiments. In deed and in word, John A. Logan earned his men's respect.[89]

The man Sherman appointed to lead the Army of the Tennessee after McPherson's untimely demise, supplanting Logan, was Oliver O. Howard. Shortly after Howard assumed command, Jake Ritner declared, "General Howard commands our department now and Logan the Fifteenth Army Corps as before. I think we will like Howard very well. He managed the engagement yesterday admirably."[90] Not long after, Charles Wills shared a similarly optimistic take on the new commander: "I think we'll like Howard first rate. If he is as good as McPherson, he'll do."[91] After visiting with General Howard in December 1864, Colonel Wood found him "a very agreeable, pleasant gentleman."[92] Ritner's hopes in Howard from July 1864 were apparently not in vain. He wrote from Beaufort in January 1865, "I have just heard that Major General Howard is to preach in town this P.M. If I had known it in time I should certainly have gone to hear him. We all think a great deal of Howard. There is not a man in the army that does not love him."[93] Like McPherson and Logan, Howard did not lead the Army of the Tennessee long enough to garner nearly the number of comments that Grant and Sherman did, but such references as officers made to him indicate he gained their fondness and respect. That Howard did this is especially remarkable, for while McPherson and Logan served as corps commanders and were familiar to many officers even before they took command, Howard was a general from the eastern theater whose first association with the Army of the Tennessee was when he took charge of it.[94]

Edward Jesup Wood's mocking nickname of division commander Gen. John E. Smith as "His Mysterious Highness" is one of the many comments one finds when surveying officers' comments regarding brigade, division, and corps commanders.[95] Tom Taylor in particular had a lot to say about generals of the Fifteenth Corps. After a meeting in July 1863, Taylor provided a fascinatingly detailed description of Gen. Francis P. Blair Jr., who served variously as a brigade and division commander before eventually leading the Fifteenth Corps:

> I found him to be an affable gentleman, true to his scotch instincts and blood and extending 'a real highland welcome' to his guests, his manners are easy and perfectly natural; no formalities, no studied grace, his actions mirror the man, his language that which is used in the ordinary walks of life and his conversation adapted to his visitors and that without appearing to be case. In height he will measure about five feet ten inches, broad shouldered, which gives massiveness to his appearance, very slightly bowed . . . large feet & hands, forehead hard high and full, large face, high broad nose eyes well set in the head, light blue, at times keen, almost to piercing, complexion sandy, hair light, whiskers sandy sprinkled with gray. His pants fitted very poorly & in fact his dress showed that he paid but little attention to the toilette.[96]

One can only wonder why Major Taylor thought it worthwhile to record such a thorough report of the man, but obviously General Blair made an impression. Meanwhile, Taylor criticized Gen. William B. Hazen for requiring his troops to entrench and construct an abatis (a defensive obstruction made of felled timber) one evening late in August 1864. "A wise general, I think, would prefer to take chances of a fight and give his soldiers a nights good repose, than exhaust their strength in constructing works to repel an imaginary foe," Taylor groused.[97] Taylor also ridiculed Hazen as a "Miserable plagiarist!" for supposedly publishing portions of the army regulations as if they were his own invention, moving Taylor to paraphrase from Shakespeare's *Measure for Measure:*

Vain man
Drest in little brief authority
Play such fantastic tricks before his heaven
As makes the angels weep.[98]

Taylor must have liked this passage, for he also used it when denouncing General Logan regarding resignations. Brigade commander Gen. Joseph A. J. Lightburn also got on Taylor's nerves, as evidenced by the complaint, "Annoyed with Lightburns manner of asking for details."[99]

General Peter J. Osterhaus, a division commander who rose to lead the Fifteenth Corps for a time, was the subject of many comments by officers. Osterhaus replaced Gen. Frederick Steele as a division commander, which Henry Kircher believed benefited the health of the whole division, since Osterhaus ensured the camps were cleaner and more orderly than before. Kircher had also once complained that Osterhaus's predecessor "rather is a fool or tries to kill us, marching allwas in the greatest heat of day" and exhausting the men needlessly.[100] In contrast, under Osterhaus, Kircher felt confident that even though he had no idea where they were marching, "It doesn't matter at all. Wherever the Red One (Osterhaus) can go, we can go too."[101] Another time, Kircher recorded that Osterhaus's presence made the men feel "sure of victory."[102] It seems plausible to wonder if Kircher, who was of German ancestry, did not feel some special affinity with Osterhaus because of the general's Prussian ancestry. However, Jake Ritner also shared the sentiment that Osterhaus was far superior to Steele. If Osterhaus was a better leader than Steele, though, he was not better than General Logan in Ritner's eyes, for he wrote in January 1865, "General Logan has got back and takes command of the corps again. We are all glad of that. 'Old hell-smell' as we call General Osterhaus goes to St. Louis."[103] Charles Wills also liked Osterhaus. To Wills's great irritation, "two or three insulting puppies" in the 103rd Illinois once began crying "Kraut!" as Osterhaus rode by, irritating the general and, Wills feared, tarnishing the 103rd's reputation in his eyes.[104]

Wills supplied anecdotes on some of the Fifteenth Corps' other generals too. Division commander Gen. William Harrow was likely "the most unpopular officer with his corps that there is in the West. I never knew his match for meanness."[105] Wills criticized various harsh disciplinary measures Harrow imposed, found Harrow unlikeable and hard to get along with, and, in contrast to his mortification when soldiers insulted Osterhaus, wrote with approving amusement about how men made fun of Harrow and the general's overbearing discipline. Wills also captured a humorous moment involving division commander Gen. Charles R. Woods. In January 1865, General Hazen was promoted to full major general, to the displeasure of his fellow division commanders in the Fifteenth Corps who were only brevetted. One day, an aide of General Woods remarked at a turkey buzzard flying overhead, "There is a turkey," to which Woods retorted "I think that it is a turkey by brevet."[106] In short, among officers of the Fifteenth Corps, General Osterhaus seems to have been most appreciated, with several of the corps' other generals being distinctly unpopular.[107]

The Sixteenth Corps had a shorter existence than the Fifteenth and did not even serve together as a coherent unit all the way through the war, but a couple of its division commanders stood out in officers' writings. General Jacob G. Lauman came in for criticism, with artillery lieutenant Anthony B. Burton complaining during the Siege of Vicksburg that General Lauman's "worst fault . . . the want of energy—a love of ease" led him to cede all oversight of the division to an upstart engineering captain, Henry C. Freeman.[108] Lauman was dismissed for failure to follow orders in the summer of 1863, and Z. Payson Shumway's account of his final departure in early October implied that few missed him. Shumway bemusedly noted that Lauman had no command since July "& how he came or what he is doing here I dont know."[109] Lauman gave a brief a speech and "rode away while three *rather faint* cheers followed him."[110] In September 1863, Charles Wills heard there had been some conflict between William S. Smith and Gen. Williams S. Rosecrans in the Army of the Cumberland, and he feared this might cause Smith's division to be left behind rather than join the rest of the army in marching to relieve Rosecrans at Chattanooga. Wills said that although the division liked Smith, it "would ten times rather lose him than have to, on his account, again go to guarding railroads."[111] While hardly the strongest of endorsements, the anecdote does reveal Wills maintained an overall favorable view of Smith.

Officers reported several comical incidents in which generals in the Seventeenth Corps figured prominently. The first occurred in December 1862, during Grant's abortive overland drive on Vicksburg (soon to be curtailed

THAT CLASS OF GENERALS WHO THINK THAT WAR MEANS FIGHTING 201

due to the loss of his supply base at Holly Springs, Mississippi). Henry Otis Dwight recalled how his Twentieth Ohio, part of the Third Division of the Seventeenth Corps, was marching at the head of the column one day. Leading the column was a privilege that rotated among the divisions (the division at the front did not have to do extra work guarding the wagon train and always reached the evening campsite first, thus enjoying the longest rest). As the army left Oxford, Mississippi, heading for Grenada, the Third Division under General Logan enjoyed the privilege of leading the day's march. Somehow, Gen. Isaac F. Quinby's Seventh Division also received orders to lead the march, and Quinby began trying to maneuver his troops to pass the Twentieth Ohio. Dwight proudly recalled his regiment's fleetness, and Quinby's efforts to snatch the lead proved vain until the road narrowed to a point where only one column could pass at a time. The Twentieth Ohio was in the lead when General Quinby personally rode up and ordered Col. Manning F. Force to halt his regiment and let Quinby's division pass. Force refused to do so without an order from his own division commander, General Logan, so Quinby arrested the colonel on the spot. Force turned over command of the Twentieth to Maj. John C. Fry, and upon declining to accept Quinby's order to halt the regiment, Quinby arrested him too. Command of the Twentieth devolved on the senior captain, and Quinby was about to arrest him when General Logan rode up. According to Dwight, "The two generals had some pretty hot words on the subject, and Gen. Logan told Gen. Quinby in a few concise phrases what he thought of him."[112] The entire column halted as both generals went to appeal the case to General Grant: "Gen. Grant heard them both and then said to Gen. Quimby, 'how many days rations have you?' 'Three days rations' was the answer. 'Gen. Logan, how many days' rations have you?' 'Ten days,' said Gen. Logan. 'Very good,' said Gen. Grant, 'Gen. Logan, you will take the advance.' Gen. Logan turned to Col. Force and said 'Colonel, move on.' We moved on and shouted until the woods re-echoed with the jubilation over our victory over Quimby's Division."[113] Logan's forceful defense of his men no doubt earned him favor in their eyes on this occasion.

Another humorous anecdote starring a Seventeenth Corps general involved John Wallace Fuller, a brigade commander. Captain Oscar Lawrence Jackson's Sixty-Third Ohio was not even part of Fuller's brigade, but on 16 June 1864, during the Atlanta Campaign, General Fuller took it upon himself to approach Jackson and sharply criticize him for not aligning his men with Fuller's own skirmish line, as well as for letting his men waste ammunition shooting though there was no enemy nearby. Jackson countered that Fuller was the one who had deployed his skirmish line poorly. As the huffy general prepared to depart, he peeked through a crack in the logs sheltering Jackson's men and asked who was occupying the rifle pits a few yards out in front. Jackson answered that those were the rebels' rifle pits. Just about that moment the rebel troops opened fire all along Jackson's line. Fuller was forced to ask Jackson what the safest path would be to get away. Jackson was gratified to have the rebels contradict Fuller's charge that his men were firing when there was no enemy, and not long afterward he and his men watched with even more amusement as Fuller's brigade shifted positions to align with their own.[114]

Officers took great interest in their own commanders, and they also kept track of the war beyond their front and formulated opinions of more distant generals. Henry F. Hole wrote hopefully to his sister Minerva in August 1861, "Now there is 300,000 armed men in the field, now under command of the best Generals in the world, McClellan in the east and Fremont in the West."[115] By the following March, his expectations for McClellan had evaporated, for Hole told Minerva, "I do not expect much from McClellan's . . . army."[116] Harley Wayne wondered why Grant had halted at Pittsburg Landing and speculated it involved some byzantine scheme to let McClellan have the glory of winning the war. "It would not do to have the army of the west do all the fighting & win all the victories and therefore they are used to draw off Enemy from the East & let them take the empty fortifications & wooden guns," Wayne huffed.[117] Not every officer distrusted McClellan. Charles H. Floyd argued that McClellan, who had his army taken away in the summer of 1862, should have retained command a while longer and blamed other eastern generals for focusing on selfish gain over the interests of the Union. Floyd judged McClellan's successor, Gen. John Pope, fit only for brigade or division command and thought McClellan deserved another chance to prove himself. McClellan got that chance but did not make much use of it, leading to Alexander Ewing's observation in November, "Late Papers bring us the news of the overthrow of Genl Buel (the slow coach) and the Fighting Genl Rosecrans substituted. A wise change. I am in hopes McClelland will take warning and go in on his muscle."[118] Charles Wills shared this concern for McClellan's unwillingness to fight, observing around the same time, "Nobody in this country seems to care a cuss whether McClellan is removed or not."[119] Wills also shared Ewing's affection for General Rosecrans, stating, "Believe I would rather we would be whipped here than see 'Rosy' beaten. There will be somebody awfully hurt though, before that latter item takes place, and Rosecrans himself will never live to read an account of it."[120] In practice, Rosecrans's generalship did not live up to Captain Wills's expectations. Wills also maintained respect for Pope, even after Pope's defeat at the Second Battle of Bull Run. He hoped Pope would return to the western theater: "I don't believe there is a regiment in this army that would not cheer him as its corps commander. Everybody seems to be willing to bet something on Pope."[121] In September 1863, Henry Kircher mused, "If only [General George G.] Meade will dare and attack Lee energetically. The rebels are defeated by their own persuasion and are just wrestling in their last death throes."[122] Kircher was disappointed in this wish; Meade was no U. S. Grant.[123]

As demonstrated by the comments about General Rosecrans, the Army of the Tennessee's officers took note of generals in their fellow western army, the Army of the Cumberland. Famous general Joseph "Fighting Joe" Hooker, erstwhile commander of the Army of the Potomac but subsequently a corps commander in the Army of the Cumberland, generated much interest, although chiefly in his personal appearance. As the Army of the Tennessee moved into position around Chattanooga in mid-November 1863, 2nd Lt. James A. Woodson recorded of Hooker, "He is quite a tall man, much more so than I had formed an idea he was. Has gray hair and whiskers—he is a very ordinary looking man, does not look like there was much fighting in him."[124] In contrast, Edward Jesup Wood deemed Hooker "a splendid-looking man—he *looks* the General more than any man I have seen."[125] Likewise, John Quincy Adams Campbell pronounced "Fighting Joe" to be "the finest looking Major General I have seen. He is over 6 feet high—well built—good looking—florid complexion—'Presbyterian whiskers'—and looks 'every inch a soldier.' His hair and whiskers are very gray—nearly white."[126] George H. Hildt's Thirtieth Ohio had served in the Army of the Potomac before transferring to the Army of the Tennessee in January 1863. Having seen Hooker earlier in the war, Hildt remarked in July 1864, "Saw Gen. Hooker today he looks ten years older than when we were in the Potomac Army."[127] General George H. Thomas, who succeeded Rosecrans as commander of the Army of the Cumberland, also caught officers' attention. Oscar Jackson spotted Thomas one day in September 1864, "standing very unconcernedly at the church near the center of the village. He is a tall, spare, greyhaired veteran. Looks like a very good man and every one says he is."[128] On 18 April 1865, while Sherman and

Confederate general Joseph E. Johnston negotiated the war's end, Charles Wills claimed Thomas was underappreciated in the North: "We have as much confidence in him as in Grant or Sherman, and then he never writes any letters or accepts valuable presents, or figures in any way for citizen approbation, or that of his army. The only objection I ever heard against him is the size of his headquarters or 'Thomasville' as it is called by the army. That comes from his West-Pointism."[129] Arguments continue to this day as to whether Thomas is underrated among US generals of the war.

The Army of the Tennessee's officers showed a marked preference for generals who were aggressive and tenacious (albeit tempered by respect for the lives their men). Officers voluntarily left their homes and joined the army because they believed fighting was necessary and because they wanted to get that fighting over with, win the war, and go home as soon as possible. They had little interest in spending weeks or months garrisoning isolated hamlets or tiptoeing around the Confederacy trying to avoid meeting the enemy. Harley Wayne began complaining in October 1861 about the lack of offensive action in the western theater. The soldiers in the field were ready to fight, "to quell this rebellion . . . but with Such leaders—Such weak Kneed imbicility as seems to characterize even the President and all his political military appointees we can never succeed."[130] Wayne believed too many men received high command for purely political reasons, when they lacked the qualifications even to be corporals leading a squad. Other officers early in the war similarly wished for more active campaigning and praised leaders they saw as willing to forcefully prosecute the war. Hearing in November 1862 that Confederate General Price was active nearby, Luther Cowan reported approvingly: "As nearly as I can learn it is Grant's intention not to let him have his own *time* to *come get ready* and fight us as best suits his own views. It is high time I think to begin to take part of the management of the war in our own hands, it has thus far been managed just to suit the Secesh, not to interrupt them in their camping, marching, or plan of battles, and let them have all the advantages all the time."[131] Henry Kircher believed in March 1863 that it would have been easy to capture Vicksburg the previous summer, if only the army had bold leadership: "There is nothing to blame but the stupidity of our generals for the fact that the South is not farther advanced in its defeat."[132] If the Union had "just half as many generals and they were real generals, real patriots and not speculators and cowardly, conceited sleepyheads! Half a dozen [Franz] Siegels and Rosecrans's at the head of our armies and the war would be at an end inside a few months. Various [Benjamin] Butlers would also not be anything to sneeze at."[133] Kircher's list of generals seems laughable in hindsight, considering how dismally they all performed, but the point remains that he was one of many officers who favored aggressive, active leadership. Writing after the war, Benjamin Grierson noted that Army of the Potomac commanders neglected "taking greater risks with the greater chances for that success which is rarely attained except by prompt and decisive action."[134] The Army of the Tennessee, from U. S. Grant to the lowliest second lieutenant, showed an affinity for such action, and Grant's successors carried on his legacy.[135]

CHAPTER 13

Nothing but Victory

Perhaps in some wars, soldiers who began as naively overconfident civilians had their optimism crushed by the bloody realities of battle, after
which they grew ever more cynical, hopeless, and apathetic as the war
dragged on. Certainly, some scholars have claimed this was the case with
the Civil War's combatants. However, the Army of the Tennessee's junior
officers were different. Despite their often-admitted ignorance of what was
happening at any given time, officers retained confidence in themselves
and in the Army of the Tennessee as a whole throughout the war, and their
confidence and optimism grew stronger as the war continued. They faced
trials and setbacks and suffered moments of discouragement and frustration, but they retained their self-confidence and expectation of victory
on the battlefield and in the war as a whole. The winter of 1862–63 was a
uniquely despondent period for the Army of the Tennessee's officers (par-
alleling this study's findings that officers worried most about Copperheads
during the same period), but outside that exceptional time, they were consistently sanguine about their prospects for victory throughout the war
and grew more so the longer the war went on.

Officers' sense of certainty about the war's long-term future stands in
contrast to their frequent admissions that they had no idea what was going
on in the present or what would happen in the near future. They speculated
extensively on matters such as how long the army would stay in one place,
where it would go next, why it might go there, and when the next battle
might be. Officers endured much uncertainty about the immediate future,
but this did not keep their initial sense of confidence in themselves and in
Union victory from strengthening over the course of the war, a pattern that
deviated only during the dismal opening months of the Vicksburg Campaign before coming back strong for the last two years of the war.

206

When officers discussed the future, they emphasized their own igno-rance and uncertainty, and yet they could not seem to resist attempting to predict where they would go, what their generals were planning, and when the war would end. Above all, they expected ultimate victory. The question was when and how victory would occur. On these points, they often endeavored to guess. In the first few months of 1862, several officers predicted the war would be finished by summer, sometimes mentioning being home in time to celebrate Independence Day with their families. Even after the Battle of Shiloh, there were still occasional predictions that the war would end soon. Officers' propensity for predicting how long it would take to crush the rebellion declined by the summer of 1862, though a few predictions about how much longer the war would last did pop up later in 1864 and 1865. Through the summer of 1864, Jake Ritner showed unshakeable optimism not only about capturing Atlanta but also about fin-ishing the war before the year's end. Just before the Carolinas Campaign, Adam W. McLane told his sister Eliza, "The spring campaign is going to tell heavy on the confederacy and I think that their heart will fail them ere six months pass by and they will return to Father Abrahams bosom."[1] Lieutenant McClane was correct; that final campaign brought an end both to the war and to the uncertainties of army life.[2]

Officers' speculations usually dealt with where they would go next, how long they would stay in their current location, when the next big battle would occur, or how long it would take to capture a strategic target. Sur-veying officers' comments throughout the war reveal a string of sometimes correct, but often wrong, guesses about the army's activities. For example, near the close of 1863, Henry G. Ankeny offered a prediction of Union vic-tory (while casually poking fun at the Army of the Potomac): "One more ac-tive and successful campaign will end the war, but it will require another to teach the Southern chivalry that they must and can do without slavery; thus, must the war last until 1864. This is in consequence of Meade's failure in defeating Lee, or in giving him battle, but then we must never expect much from the Potomac army, for they can't fight."[3] The war lasted longer than Ankeny expected, but he turned out to be right that the Army of the Tennes-see's next major venture—the Atlanta Campaign—would effectively secure Union victory without persuading the rebels to give up. All through the war, junior officers tried to figure out what was happening around them.[4]

In February 1863, while at Helena, Arkansas, 2nd Lt. Alexander K. Ewing analyzed the course of the war. He explained that when he joined the army back in November 1861, he figured the rebellion would be over within a year. However, Ewing continued, "Him who rules on high and has our destiny in his hands has willed otherwise and we as true soldiers to our country must abide our time and with fortitude."[5] Ewing's answer to the question of when the war would end was that "no one knows but we can give our opinion."[6] His guess was that it would take another six months "for this unholy rebellion to end and peace be restored as in days gone by."[7] Ewing looked forward to peace, but he insisted that the Union make no concessions to the Confederacy to get it. "With peace I want to hear the clamoring notes of liberty wafted upon every breeze and see the old Ensanguined flag of Washingtons blood-bought Government again wave in proud triumph over every foot of American Soil, peace upon any other terms would be at no far distant day our death warrant."[8] He felt confident that the traitors would receive "the Vengeance of a just God."[9]

Officers tried to look for clues to the army's next move, but these were often unreliable. Riding aboard a steamboat up the Tennessee River toward an unfamiliar place named Fort Henry, Luther Cowan wrote to his wife Harriet, "We don't know what one hour will bring forth. . . . But in war as in private life the big fishes boss the little ones. Eat them or not, just as their stomachs feel."[10] When Henry Ankeny and the Fourth Iowa reached Milliken's Bend, Louisiana, he expected to remain there "until we get reinforcements or something. God only knows what."[11] Charles Ammack told his siblings facetiously, "That is one of the beauties of a soldiers life he never knows one night where he will sleep the next."[12] At the start of the Carolinas Campaign, James Kerr Proudfit told his wife Emilie he was not sure where exactly they were going, but that they "will probably turn up somewhere to the dismay and disgust of all rebeldom."[13] Officers regularly expressed the belief that people back home received news about the overall course of the war much sooner than the soldiers at the front ever did, and they sometimes attributed this to generals deliberately keeping their men in the dark. The pervasive uncertainty clearly weighed on these men.[14]

Officers' numerous declarations regarding their ignorance of the army's operations and goals betrayed frustration, but they could also contain humor (both intentional and unintentional). "Where we are going God knows, or perhaps only our generals and the enemy, but we certainly don't," Henry Kircher jested to his mother at the start of 1863.[15] He had no better idea at the end of January, when he joked, "Like God's way, those of our generals are also marvelous."[16] A staff officer in the Army of the Tennessee recalled how after the Yazoo Pass Expedition, Maj. Daniel Chase, a regular army officer commanding a battalion of the Thirteenth US Infantry, "came to my room, carefully closed the door, looked around to see that we were alone, and in a manner that indicated that he had a great secret to impart, whispered to me, 'I command a battalion of regulars,—I have been on an expedition,—I must write a report,—I want you to tell me where I have been, how I went there, what I did, and if I came back the same way I went, or if not, how I did get back.'"[17] The staff officer cited this comical incident as an example of how little junior officers knew what was going on. On that note, Luther Cowan told his family, "A soldier never knows anything ahead of time and but little afterward."[18] Officers' numerous declarations of ignorance about how the war was going were sometimes laced with humor.[19]

When pondering the uncertainty of the future, officers' thoughts sometimes ranged beyond the conflict at hand to optimistic predictions about what would come after the war. Henry Kircher provides an interesting example of this. He made plans with a couple of comrades to save as much of their pay as possible, with the plan that after the war they would "travel to Europe and journey to every place that was worth seeing."[20] He asked his mother, "Wouldn't that be nice, to sail around the world as a young clover until the wind blows all the sails away and we then will calmly and complacently burden our necks again with the bourgeois yoke as satisfied and well-traveled young people?"[21] In another letter, Kircher said he would take as his guide the proverb "Kommt Zeit, Komm Rath."[22] Accounting for some misspelling on Kircher's part, this translates to "comes time, comes advice" and is a German saying conveying the idea that "things have a way of working themselves out."[23] Though many officers viewed the postwar future hopefully, they, too, had to wait as the war played out.[24]

The Army of the Tennessee's officers shared a confident expectation of victory that rarely wavered, but this pertained to their chances on the battlefield and in the war as a whole and did not keep them from experiencing moments of personal despondency. Charles Wills supplied a deliberately humorous reflection on one period of malaise. In a letter to his sister, Wills reported, "Without any earthly cause I am troubled with a small fit of the blues this evening. I can't imagine what brought it on."[25] Though disgruntled and irritable, he remained self-aware enough amid this funk to find a kind of humor in his glum feelings:

Guess the trouble must be in the fact that I have no trouble. Everything moves too smoothly. No pushing in my family to knock down a looking-glass balanced on a knitting needle. Nothing in my precious life to keep me awake one minute of my sleeping time, and nothing in the future that I now care a scrap for. All of that is certainly enough to make one miserable. I'm convinced that my constitution requires some real misery, or a prospect for the same, in order to keep me properly balanced. If you can furnish me any hints on the subject, that will induce distress, trouble, or care, in a reasonable quantity to settle on my brain, I will be obliged.[26]

He followed this with an observation that despite having numerous interesting experiences since joining the army, when he was alone his mind skipped over them all to dwell on memories of home. Captain Wills's bout of melancholy exemplifies the fact that officers were by no means incessantly and unfailingly chipper. However, homesickness caused them depression far more often than fears about the course of the war ever did.[27]

Officers' statements on the course of the war, with the exception of one bout of widespread discouragement during the winter of 1862–63, brimmed with confidence from the beginning of the war to its end. At the outset of his service in August 1861, Henry F. Hole announced, "I have no fears for the result of the war. We will surely conquer because we are right."[28] Meanwhile, Friedrich Martens informed his parents early in February 1862, "I look like a little rebel-eater, and as far as courage goes, I can say that I know the words *fear* or *coward* only from dictionaries."[29] Martens wrote these words just prior to the Army of the Tennessee's first major campaign. Late in March, while camped at Pittsburg Landing, Oliver Bridgford predicted to his wife Eliza a big fight was imminent, "and if these two armies come together they will make a terrible Battle I have every confidence of our Success but it may take some hard Fighting to accomplish it."[30] Just a few days before the Battle of Shiloh, DeWitt Clinton Loudon boasted, "Finer *materiel* never filled the ranks of any army in Christendom," and confidently observed, "Our men don't count on anything else than threshing them someday."[31] Rough as it was, the Battle of Shiloh did not undermine Loudon's confidence. A few days afterward, as he contemplated the chances of another battle occurring, he claimed, "I have no doubt of our success but it may cost us dearly in the blood of brave soldiers."[32] During the Corinth Campaign, Luther Cowan predicted a major battle was imminent and told his daughter Molly, "Nothing but victory will do the army that is here now."[33] Near the end of the Corinth Campaign, Loudon cautioned his wife Hannah that the end of the war was yet distant and outlined some possible setbacks the Union cause might face, but he said he had "no doubt of the ultimate success of the Federal arms."[34] A couple days later, Cowan noted while he could not predict the future, "I don't believe that the union army *will be* whipped, they will *die* almost to a man first—it won't *do* to be whipped here now."[35] Such thoughts were typical of officers' confidence early in the war.[36]

Officers' confident outlook continued through the summer and fall of 1862. In July, Loudon remarked proudly at how much his Seventieth Ohio had improved as soldiers and declared, "If we have another fight, we'll slay them worse than we did before—when [Gen. William T.] Sherman specially complimented us."[37] While the Forty-Fifth Illinois was on guard duty in Tennessee, rumors began to arrive of what turned out to be the Second Battle of Corinth. Luther Cowan expressed disappointment at missing the fight and had no doubts about the outcome: "We whip them everytime we can get a fight out of them here in Tenn. I can't see why they don't do better in the east."[38] Cowan erroneously believed the rebels outnumbered the Army of the Tennessee two to one, but he had no doubts the Union army would win anyway, though he did worry that "the casualties must necessarily be great as they have to fight against such superior numbers, yet we feel sure that the Illinois boys *Can't Be Whipped*."[39] Second Lieutenant Henry Otis Dwight of the Twentieth Ohio recalled his outlook in late October 1862: "We had now been a year in the service, and had learned to march at a swinging pace that covered the ground rapidly, had learned to live on rich food or poor, and had acquired the belief that we were invincible in battle."[40] Speculating at the end of November 1862 on the army's next course of action, Henry Kircher remarked, "It is probably a deep, anxious lull before a storm, a mighty eruption that will flood the South not with lava, but significantly with Dutchmen and Yankees."[41] At the start of December 1862, Charles Wills boasted, "I never saw men in as good spirits and so confident as this army now appears."[42] Up through the end of the year, officers continued expecting victory.[43]

The winter of 1862–63 stands out as a time of uncharacteristic pessimism about the course of the war. As Sherman's forces withdrew from their repulse at Chickasaw Bayou, Warren Gray noted on 2 January that retreating always hurt morale and said that while he was willing to suffer for his country, he would rather not suffer pointlessly. Charles Wills wrote that many officers, himself included, harbored doubts about the Union's prospects, though they had no intention of giving up the attempt. Wills thought that even if they could not crush the entire rebellion, "we can confine the Rebels to Virginia (Eastern), the Carolinas, Georgia and Florida. Alabama, I believe, we can hold if we get Mississippi."[44] Henry Ankeny reported that he had "lost all my enthusiasm, a large portion of my patriotism and all my confidence in those who are at the head of the different departments of the army."[45] He feared that because the Northern people were not unified, "unless some unforeseen power should very soon be demonstrated in our favor, the Southern Confederacy will be a fixed fact."[46] At the end of January, Robert Steele told his wife, "Things look dark and gloomy,"[47] and he feared there would be a "dishonorable peace or the dissolution of the Union."[48]

The rest of that winter remained a dark time. Ankeny reiterated his lack of confidence in the Union's leadership, though he insisted he had not given up all hope and still thought if the Northern people came together they could win relatively quickly. Charles Wills declared, "The regiment is going to the d—l as fast as time will let it. . . . It almost gives me the blues."[49] In the Sixty-Ninth Indiana, the discouragement grew so pervasive that Col. Thomas W. Bennett, despite being ill, dragged himself from his sickbed to call out his regiment and "poured forth a denunciation of copperheads and cowards . . . and made such a magnificent appeal to the patriotism of the men that current was completely turned, and the old spirit of ''61' possessed them."[50] Officers' stated concerns during the winter of 1862–63 pertained to political and military leadership and to disunity and pro-rebel sentiment on the home front—not to the army's fighting ability, with one even suggesting a battle might be just the thing to raise morale. One also wonders to what extent the army's dreary circumstances played a part in officers' discouragement at this time. The Army of the Tennessee did not suffer any major defeats during the winter of 1862–63. However, the year had closed with a withdrawal in Mississippi and the defeat and retreat at Chickasaw Bayou, and 1863 opened with months spent fruitlessly digging in the Louisiana mud and mucking about in the swamps of Yazoo Pass—hardly activities that would sustain morale. Coming after one of the Army of the Tennessee's rare experiences with defeat and retreat, such physically uncomfortable and strategically unsuccessful pursuits likely contributed to officers' demoralized state.[51]

Over the course of February, March, and April 1863, Jake Ritner provided an interesting series of snapshots of morale and concerns about

Copperheads. In February, he claimed many officers were trying to resign. Describing the situation on the home front as the source of officers' discouragement, he explained: "The army here is not very enthusiastic—on the contrary a great many are discouraged and homesick. What disheartens us more than anything else is that we learn from the papers that the North is becoming divided. The cowardly, sneaking, traitorous Democrats are throwing off the cloak and taking sides openly with the rebels, and are in favor of disunion!!"[52] Throughout March, Ritner continued to express concern about Copperheads in the army, suggesting that this minority's pernicious influence was great. He also raised another obvious reason for soldiers' pessimism, noting that some had sent home discouraged letters when the regiment first arrived in Louisiana, "when we were nearly all sick, and knee-deep in mud."[53] At one point his regiment, the Twenty-Fifth Iowa, tried to pass some pro-Union resolutions, and Ritner was appalled by how many abstained or voted against them; there were not many, but there were still more than he expected. In Ritner's own Company B, sixty-nine voted in favor of the resolutions, one voted against them, and six abstained. Ritner offered various theories to explain the voting and ultimately concluded that the outcome reflected the influence of each company's officers. In the past, some had "misrepresented the objects of the war and the intentions of the government," creating a climate in which their men were less ready to fully support the Union cause.[54] Ritner still believed the Twenty-Fifth's soldiers, regardless of how they voted, would fight well against the rebels if given the chance.[55]

Despite the discouragement some officers experienced during the opening months of the Vicksburg Campaign, a strong thread of confidence remained. Henry Ankeny declared in late December 1862, "In a week or two you may expect to hear from us and I believe that we will not fail for I have great faith in our western troops. Would to God that the East could come up to their great work."[56] Stuck guarding Memphis, Lt. George B. Carter boasted to his brother Bill in May 1863, "It is the universal wish of the Western army to be permitted to meet their vaunted army of the East," a clear expression of confidence in the army's prowess.[57] Jake Ritner, who wrote about his discouragement in the winter of 1862–63, had displayed cautious optimism in January, calling Vicksburg "a pretty hard place to take, but I believe we can take it."[58] As noted, after this confidence Ritner grew more doubtful in February and March, but by mid-June he clearly felt much more positive about the Army of the Tennessee's endeavor: "We have received large reinforcements from the North and could whip 100,000 on the rear, besides leaving enough here to hold those in the city. You need not doubt but that the victory will be on our side. We are certain to take the place—there aren't men enough in the Southern Confederacy to save it now."[59] Near the end of June, Ritner described the slow but steady progress of the siege and repeated his confidence the city would soon fall. He dismissed the possibility that outside interference—that is, the rebel army under Gen. Joseph E. Johnston—posed any threat or held any hope of breaking the siege. Just over a week later, Vicksburg did indeed surrender.[60]

Major Thomas Thomson Taylor perpetuated this self-assured tone in some of his letters in the summer of 1863. "We hardly know how to contain ourselves over the unequalled flow of good news. Every body is electrified with it. The army is on fire, as irresistible as an avalanche, it will stop at no difficulties," Taylor affirmed in mid-July.[61] In response to turmoil brought on by Copperheads in the North, Taylor declared in September, "I have an abiding faith that the cause of Union will triumph."[62] He derisively compared the supporters of Clement Vallandigham to an annoying itch, necessary to be scratched but not a serious threat to the nation's health. Rebel sympathizers in the North were growing shriller, Taylor believed, precisely because they recognized the imminent destruction of the rebellion.

As the Army of the Tennessee approached Chattanooga and prepared to assist the Army of the Cumberland, officers continued to share bold expectations of success. Around this time, Maj. Edward Jesup Wood told his wife Jeanie, "I have suggested that our *Division* be *divided*—so as to give each Brigade a chance to be in the front. If one Brigade was put in front of Rosecrans & one in front of the Army of the Potomac, I think our troubles would be at an end—for we have always been in the front and *never* have been defeated."[63] About a week before the series of battles that drove rebel forces away from Chattanooga, Capt. Henry Ankeny predicted a decisive battle would occur soon. He wrote, "Should victory crown us with its glory, it will give us Georgia and Alabama, and with them the Confederacy. If we are defeated, it will prolong the war another campaign or two, but we will not be beaten here again; it can't be done."[64] About the same time, Jake Ritner made a similar pronouncement: "Our army never was in better spirits or more enthusiastic in the cause than at present. We all expect a hot fight before long, but we expect nothing but *victory*."[65] (Fascinatingly, the phrasing "nothing but victory" parallels that used by Luther Cowan back in May 1862.) Ritner noted that his company was in far better spirits than back in the "dark days" of the previous winter and that his men were committed to suppressing the rebellion.[66] John Quincy Adams Campbell reported that confidence in the Army of the Tennessee had spread beyond its members to other Union armies. He wrote to his hometown newspaper, "The arrival of Sherman's army is hailed by the troops here with a great deal of pleasure. Some of the Potomac boys remarked as we passed 'there goes Sherman's army—they have never been whipped.'"[67] Captain Ritner also addressed a rumor that the Army of the Tennessee might face the Confederacy's greatest general: "It is reported that [Robert E.] Lee has command of the rebel forces at Chattanooga. If he has, he will find that he has not the 'Army of the Potomac' to contend with, and if he doesn't look sharp we will come Vicksburg over him."[68] What exactly Ritner meant by using "Vicksburg" as a verb is unclear, but he certainly did not fear General Lee.[69]

After the Chattanooga Campaign came to the victorious conclusion that officers anticipated, the western theater experienced a lull over the winter of 1863–64, before ramping up into the Atlanta Campaign the following spring. Morale remained high. Near the end of winter, Charles Wills reported being "in high feather" over rumors that the army was going to the eastern theater, and he confidently stated, "If the 15th and 17th corps reach the Rapidan, we doubt your hearing anything more about recrossing the Rapidan and taking positions inside the Washington fortifications."[70] From a camp in northeastern Alabama, along the Tennessee River, the Seventieth Ohio's Lieutenant Colonel Loudon smirked that even if the Army of the Tennessee built bridges over the river to make it convenient for the Confederates to come attack, they would still easily trounce the rebel forces. After a division review by Gen. John A. Logan near the end of April, Loudon observed, "The men are a different looking kind of troops to what they were two years ago. It will take mighty good soldiers to whip us certain."[71] About the same time, but at a different camp a little farther down the Tennessee River, Captain Wills likewise observed the army's preparations for what he expected to be a bloody campaign. Confederate general Joseph E. Johnston "will have a large force. But ours will be perfectly enormous. . . . We have no doubt of our ability to whip Johnston most completely, but . . . of course somebody will stand a remarkably good chance of being hurt in the proceedings," Wills declared.[72] The Army of the Tennessee's officers embarked upon the Atlanta Campaign with high hopes.[73]

Sherman's quest to take Atlanta dragged on through May, June, July, August, and into September, making it not quite as lengthy as Grant's effort to capture Vicksburg, but it was still a long campaign. Jake Ritner asserted in mid-May, "I don't know how much longer it will last. But it will be till the rebels are completely whipped, which they are sure to be."[74] Captain Wills issued a series of similarly confident statements throughout May 1864; at one point he noted that even if things went badly for Grant in the east, "it won't keep us from whaling Johnston."[75] At the end of May, Alphonso Barto declared that he was "like all the rest of our army of the west *confident of victory.*"[76] On 2 June, Ritner observed that it had been a couple weeks since he heard any news of how Grant's campaign was doing, but "I hope he will succeed and I am certain that we will and that will surely crush the rebellion."[77] Owen Stuart declared near the middle of June, "We have a superior army."[78] On 7 July, Captain Wills recorded, "This is the 68th day of the campaign. We hope to end it by August 1st, though if we can end the war by continuing this until January 1st, '65, I am in."[79] Ritner wrote at the end of July that "I can't tell anything about when Atlanta will be taken, but believe it will surely fall."[80] Responding to news about a fresh wave of reinforcements on its way to join Sherman, Wills boasted, "I don't think we need them, but the more, the merrier."[81] Finally, at the beginning of September 1864, Atlanta did fall, just as officers believed it would. When the news reached the 103rd Illinois, the regiment received orders to clean arms, "and the boys, showing their contempt of the enemy's power to do harm, took their guns all to pieces and set to polishing the should-be bright parts, right in view of the enemy's pickets," Wills gloated.[82] There were moments of frustration throughout the four-month campaign, but officers' confidence endured and proved justified.[83]

Officers' morale remained high in the weeks after the fall of Atlanta, as Sherman's forces and those of John Bell Hood (who had replaced Joe Johnston as Confederate commander) danced around northwestern Georgia. Hood failed to disrupt Union supply lines but succeeded in keeping Sherman at arm's length and avoiding a general engagement. Early in October, Wills confidently noted that although he did not know what the rebels were up to, "'Pap' [Sherman] knows all about it," and if a battle occurred, "It can have but one result, and cannot fail to be a disastrous one for them."[84] In mid-October, Oscar Lawrence Jackson sneered at rebel efforts to halt Sherman by blocking the Snack Creek Gap: "We have a fine example here of the folly of attempting to stop an army by obstructing roads. I think I never saw another as fine chance to block up a road with timber as this was, yet so soon did our Pioneer Corps open the way that our artillery and ambulances got through by midnight."[85] The following week, Wills wrote to his sister, "It tickles us to see that you home folks are uneasy about us because Hood has got into our rear. I tell you that I have not seen a man uneasy for a minute, on that subject, and that Hood has to run like a hound to get away from us. If Hood's army was to-day, twice as strong as it is, we would be too many for him."[86] As they tromped after the elusive rebels, Edward Jesup Wood remarked at the army's self-confidence, as well as his own: "I believe they are the best soldiers in the world. Four months of incessant fighting & marching have made them invincible—they have the utmost confidence in Sherman & in themselves, and went by here at a killing pace, eager to meet the 'Johnny Rebs' & 'clean them out.'"[87] Eventually, Sherman turned his army toward a more profitable task than chasing Hood, but one about which they felt no less confident.[88]

"Treason fled before us, for resistance was in vain," claimed the song "Marching through Georgia," written by Henry Clay Work to commemorate the way the US Army swept across the state to Savannah. Though written after the fact, the lyrics accurately reflect the feelings of Army of the Tennessee officers as they marched "from Atlanta to the sea." As Charles Wills observed preparations for a major new campaign during the first week of November 1864, he wrote that whatever their destination turned out to be, "We are going to shake up the bones of the rebellion. I would not miss this campaign for anything."[89] Captain Joseph S. Reynolds informed his brother Charles that the army was about to start a long march. "Gen Sherman says it will be the grandest move of the war," he explained, "I have command of the 64th Ills and will during the trip. I am well and feel tip top at the head of so noble a Regiment."[90]

Unlike Captain Wills, Edward Jesup Wood knew his destination, perhaps a result of having risen to be colonel of the Forty-Eighth Indiana. He shared with his wife that the army was about to march on Savannah and guessed that Sherman planned to leave Gen. George Thomas to take care of Hood. Wood doubted the army would encounter any meaningful opposition on the way to Savannah besides "annoyance" from the Georgia militia.[91] "I am afraid you will be alarmed at news of this expedition," he wrote to Jeanie, "but I assure you it is attended with no more hazard & indeed with not so much as many we have already undertaken successfully and in fact it involves no more peril than common camp life."[92] Wood concluded optimistically, "I expect to take my Christmas dinner near Savannah and wishing Uncle Sam a 'Happy New Year' return to spend it with my dear Jean."[93]

Thinking about the upcoming campaign, Jake Ritner explained to his wife: "General Thomas has plenty of men there [i.e., in Tennessee] to attend to his [i.e., Gen. John Bell Hood's] case while we turn the thing wrong side out, without much opposition down here. He [Hood] can do no harm in Tennessee, while we can ruin their country here. I think Hood and Beauregard have been completely out-generaled again. The only thing that can prevent us from dealing the rebellion a mortal blow is the weather."[94] The weather did not save the Confederacy, however. Captain Wills recorded several confident assertions during the march across Georgia. He derided the rebel effort to defend Macon by reporting on 21 November that they "scraped together some ten or a dozen *things* to defend the town with."[95] A few days later, he heard that these same rebel troops were trying to pass up the army. "Suppose they want to get in our front to annoy us again. They had better keep out of our way," Wills jeered.[96] By mid-December, he wrote confidently from outside Savannah that the city was certain to fall. And indeed it did.[97]

After advancing victoriously through much of the Confederacy over the course of 1862–1864, in February 1865 the Army of the Tennessee embarked on its final campaign. The army's officers undertook the march through the Carolinas with the same self-confidence they had showed everywhere else. During the January interlude between campaigns, Maj. Oscar Jackson's three-year term of service expired. He was not permitted to leave because the Sixty-Third Ohio was too short on officers, but Jackson admitted he did not mind because he was so eager to see the war to its end and share in the campaign that was about to begin. Meanwhile, Jake Ritner advised Emeline, "Have no fears at all for our army, it can't be whipped, and whatever point we start for will be reached and taken—if it is Richmond itself."[98] Owen Stuart wrote to his wife Margaret that soldiers never knew what was going on, but considering how near they were to "the Rebel of all Rebel cities that is Charleston," he expected, "ere long you will hear of it tumbling to the ground in ashes before the best army in the world and that is Sherman's."[99] In another letter, Stuart reported that "W. T. or 'old Billy' [i.e., Sherman] in his order to his command says that the Campaign will be short and decisive," and Stuart predicted the army would "meet with very little resistance, from the Enemy as they are nearly plaid out except Lee's army."[100] Officers began their final campaign optimistically.[101]

Sherman's army moved out at the beginning of February. A regimental historian of the Twelfth Wisconsin recalled a "a universal sentiment" among the army "that we could not be beaten; hence, whatever we undertook we *expected to accomplish*—did not regard any other result as at all probable."[102] Charles Wills actually worried the army might be "too conceited," acting "more like schoolboys, having a holiday, than the veterans they are," and he suggested maybe the army needed a small defeat to restore its sobriety.[103] However, Wills shared in the unflinching self-confidence, for not long after, when he heard that a corps of Hood's army might try to halt the army's advance, he blithely declared, "We whipped them July 28, '64, and can do it again."[104] In March, Major Jackson expressed amusement at the rebels' "silly custom" of burning bridges. "Pontooning a river delays us scarcely any. It makes that part of the command work a little harder is all," he noted.[105] On 14 March, near Fayetteville, North Carolina, Jackson reported, "I believe we can go any place or do anything we please. We wade swamps and creeks waist deep, march through mud and rain, day and night, sleep out on the wet ground with clothes and blankets wet through and through, eat nothing but 'slap-jacks' and meat—yet no one gets sick or discouraged."[106] At the beginning of April, rumors swirled that Lee might evacuate Richmond and rush to join Joe Johnston (restored to command) in an attempt to crush Sherman's army. First Lieutenant Laurens W. Wolcott fearlessly assured his father that "we don't think there are Johnnies enough in the rebel states to pen this army very closely within their works, & if they undertake the job of driving us out it will be just as good a thing as we want."[107]

Instead of combining with Johnston, Lee's defeated army surrendered to Grant on 9 April, leaving Johnston's troops as the last major rebel military force. On 15 April, Charles Wills affirmed that Johnston's surrender was also imminent, "and if he don't surrender we will go for him in a way that will astonish him."[108] Wills also took this time to query his sister, "We consider our cause gained and are searching each other's records to see who was ever doubtful of success. I don't remember at any time being despondent over the war or being doubtful of the issue. Was I? I did think the war might last for years yet, but take that back."[109] Overall, Wills's recollection was not far off. The Army of the Tennessee's officers displayed confidence in themselves and in the army from their earliest campaigns down to the denouement in North Carolina. Various issues—their generals, politicians, Copperheads at home—frustrated them, but their basic confidence in their ability to overcome any opponent and win the war rarely wavered. Far from collapsing in discouragement and cynicism as the war dragged on, officers' optimism grew more certain as the war moved into its last couple years.

Officers' confidence in their army and their sense of accomplishment manifested not just in statements about current events but obliquely in the form of comments about the Army of the Potomac, the Union's major army in the eastern theater. Unimpressed by the Army of the Potomac's performance, Charles H. Floyd of the Fiftieth Illinois suggested in September 1862, "I think they had better send the western Army on to Virginia, 'which has never been defeated yet' and let them have A chance with the taking of Richmond and the whipping of the rebles there."[110] Charles Wills wrote in the fall of 1862 "that the Potomac Army is only good to draw greenbacks and occupy winter quarters."[111] During the siege of Vicksburg, Harlow Waller predicted that the Army of the Tennessee would have to finish the war because the eastern army did not fight nearly as well as Grant's army (perhaps their officers were just incompetent, he mused). The Chattanooga Campaign provided the Army of the Tennessee new opportunities to see and interact with soldiers from the Army of the Potomac, and "we are all proud of belonging to the Army of the West," Jake Ritner affirmed.[112] The men of each theater boasted of having the better army, Ritner noted, before mocking, "For my part I don't see what the Army of the East has to be proud of. If I belonged to it, I should be ashamed to own it."[113] When Oscar Jackson visited the rebel fortifications around Richmond and Petersburg, Virginia, in May 1865, he expressed surprise at how inferior they were to the rebel fieldworks he had seen in the western theater—clearly a jab at the Army of the Potomac. Jackson did concede he might be biased, however. (Notably, Captain Wills also visited the works at Petersburg and drew a different conclusion. "I'll take back all I ever said against the Potomac Army. I have been down to Fort Steadman to-day and troops who will work up to an enemy as they did there, will do anything if handled right," he wrote.[114]) Officers' feeling that the Army of the Tennessee was superior to other Union armies was a practical display of their self-confidence.[115]

The Army of the Tennessee's officers faced much uncertainty regarding when and where they might fight next, but from the beginning of the war to its end they maintained a strong sense of self-confidence and anticipation of victory that only grew as the war went on. The winter of 1862–63 was the only period in which officers showed signs of widespread pessimism about the war. Probably not coincidentally, this was the same period in which fears ran highest that Copperheads would sabotage the war effort. It was also a time of exceptional physical discomfort, as cold, wet officers led their men digging Louisiana swamp muck or getting lost in the jungles of Yazoo

Pass. Prior to this episode, officers showed confidence in their ability to win battles and to win the war, and afterward their expectations of victory grew even stronger. Officers frequently guessed when and where the army would move next and what the rebels might be doing. Perhaps their overriding expectations of winning no matter where they went made it easier to deal with the uncertainties of army life. The end of the war did not bring an end to uncertainty, of course. Postwar life could, in its own way, be intimidating. With the war effectively over, Captain Wills reflected on 15 April 1865: "To-day makes four years soldiering for me. It is a terrible waste of time for me who have to make a start in life yet, and I expect unfits me for civil life. I have almost a dread of being a citizen, of trying to be sharp, and trying to make money. I don't think I dread the work. I don't remember of shirking any work I ever attempted, but I am sure that civil life will go sorely against the grain for a time. Citizens are not like soldiers, and I like soldier ways much the best."[116] Whatever the postwar future held, wartime uncertainty was over and officers could at least look back with satisfaction on a long string of military triumphs. The Army of the Tennessee's victorious record validated its officers' confidence, and the work of company and regimental officers played a significant part in those successes.

Conclusion

The surrender of the rebel armies under Robert E. Lee in Virginia and Joseph E. Johnston in North Carolina marked the end of the American Civil War. On 8 April 1865, Owen Stuart received "Glorious news" about Gen. Ulysses S. Grant, most likely regarding how Grant had broken the rebel lines at Petersburg, Virginia.[1] Stuart noted, "I do hope he whipped Lee as bad as is reported, and if so the War is near at an end what a Blessing that will be."[2] His regiment fired a salute in honor of the report, and Stuart hoped the salute might be the regiment's final shots of the war. News of Lee's surrender on 9 April reached Charles Wills three days later, on the morning of 12 April. "This is an army of skeptics, they won't believe in Lee's surrender," he wrote later in the day, "I do, and I tell you it makes this one of my brightest days. His surrender makes sure beyond any chance that what we have been fighting for for four years is sure."[3] Oscar Jackson described the moment that news arrived on 14 April that Johnston was also ready to surrender: "The men are throwing away their guns and officers their hats and such wild excitement I never saw anything like a comparison to. I cannot describe it but no one who witnessed it will ever forget it."[4] Jackson was especially pleased that Sherman and Johnston implemented an armistice until the surrender terms were settled: "It would be a pity if any more lives are lost."[5] Johnston surrendered the remaining rebel forces on 26 April. The Army of the Tennessee started for Washington not long after, which brought it through Virginia, its ninth Confederate state to visit (missing out only on distant Texas and irrelevant Florida).

"Thus closes this diary of one of the most memorable year's campaigns in the history of modern times. We remained in camp between Alexandria and Arlington until the 23d [of May, 1865], when we crossed the Potomac river, of which we had heard so much, and the next day (the 24th), participated in the Grand Review of the Grandest Army that ever was created," Charles Wills wrote.[6] The Grand Review was one of the Army of the Tennessee's last acts as an organization, and Wills's accolade of "the Grandest Army" remains eminently deserved. The Army of the Tennessee's victories at Fort Henry, Fort Donelson, Vicksburg, Chattanooga, Atlanta, Savannah, and so many other places were indispensable to Union victory, as well as to the implementation of the Emancipation Proclamation. The conflicts associated with the Civil War did not cease with the surrender of the rebel armies, of course. The turbulence of Reconstruction began immediately, as unrepentant rebels worked to preserve white supremacy even after the loss of slavery. Decades of Jim Crow lay ahead. Only a century after the war did the civil rights movement effectively secure the rights of African Americans. The Army of the Tennessee's officers made tremendous sacrifices for the cause of liberty, and even if their generation did not fully complete that task, their efforts laid an indispensable foundation for further advances toward putting into practice the ideal that "all men are created equal."

The Army of the Tennessee's company and field grade officers endured the war's trials with their moral and political worldview intact. Throughout all their struggles and successes, they resisted undergoing any significant ideological disillusionment. In key areas of life that helped define them—family and faith—they remained consistent. Their work as officers included diverse challenges, but their emphasis on treating subordinates with care and respect and their sense of what made one a good officer endured. Officers faced many other forms of hardship during their service, through which such ideological motivations as patriotism and faith helped sustain them. They continued to champion the Union cause as a just one and to regard the rebellion as a moral evil. Many officers turned against slavery because of the war, a striking change, but their reasons for doing so—the needs of the Union war effort and basic compassion—highlight the continuance of their core values. Officers followed Northern politics as best they could, with their concerns reflecting their dedication to the Union cause. Likewise, their marked preference for boldness and tenacity in their generals evinced their desire to go out and win the war for the Union. Officers began the war confident in themselves and their men, and their expectations of victory grew stronger as the war proceeded. The Army of the Tennessee's unparalleled record of successes suggests their confidence was well founded. Moreover, while these officers were overcoming the rebellion militarily, their worldview was overcoming the stresses that war imposed on their characters. These lieutenants and captains and majors and lieutenant colonels and colonels—ordinary men who voluntarily left their homes and families to defend their country and along the way helped end slavery in America—truly were part of the "the Grandest Army."

Notes

ABBREVIATIONS

In citing works in the notes, short titles have generally been used. Works frequently cited have been identified by the following abbreviations:

ALPL   Abraham Lincoln Presidential Library
IHS   Indiana Historical Society
MOLLUS   *Papers of the Military Order of the Loyal Legion of the United States*
OHC   The Ohio History Connection
WHS   Wisconsin Historical Society

INTRODUCTION

1. William T. Sherman to Halleck, 4 Sept. 1864, in *War of the Rebellion*, ser. 1, 38:5.
2. This organization was not formally designated "the Army of the Tennessee" until October 1862, but for clarity's sake I will refer to it by that name throughout this work.
3. Wiley, *Life of Billy Yank*, 38.
4. Wiley, *Life of Billy Yank*, 38.
5. Wiley, *Life of Billy Yank*, 24–26, 37–40, 43–44, 67–68, 80–81,128, 198–99, 209, 211–13, 218, 223, 230–31.
6. Linderman, *Embattled Courage*, 2.
7. Linderman, *Embattled Courage*, 240.
8. Linderman, *Embattled Courage*, 241.
9. Linderman, *Embattled Courage*, 3, 8, 16, 83, 156, 158–59, 180–81, 183, 188–91, 216–20, 229–30, 250–55, 266; Bledsoe, *Citizen-Officers*, x–xi, xiii, 2, 35–38, 42–46, 59–64, 66, 68, 70, 75–76, 78–79, 81, 83, 86, 94, 96, 98–99, 103–5, 146–48, 158, 160–61, 164, 167–68, 174, 180–82, 185–86, 190–91, 193, 219.
10. Haughton, *Training, Tactics and Leadership*, 2, 54, 86–88; Robertson, *Soldiers Blue and Gray*, 126–30, 140.
11. McPherson, *For Cause and Comrades*, 53–60, 80–82; Hess, *Union Soldier in Battle*, 21, 75, 95–98, 101–4, 111, 117, 120–22, 138, 156–57, 192, 194–95, 197.
12. Woodworth, *Nothing but Victory*, ix.
13. Woodworth, *Nothing but Victory*, 56, 82, 91, 120, 184, 192, 589.

225

226   NOTES TO PAGES 9–11

1. DOING ALL THINGS WELL

1. Crooker, Nourse, and Brown, *Story of the Fifty-Fifth Regiment,* 180–81.

2. Crooker, Nourse, and Brown, *Story of the Fifty-Fifth Regiment,* 143, 221; "Diary," John Nilson Diary and Papers, IHS; Warren Gray, "Diary, 1862–1863," SC 531, WHS; A. A. General W. Randall, "Special Orders No. 151," 11 Sept. 1863, in Sylvester, Daniel Robbins, "Papers," 1858–1901, Wis Mss 51S, WHS; Howard, *History of the 124th Regiment Illinois Infantry Volunteers,* 136; Luther Cowan Diary, Letters and Diary of Luther H. Cowan, Wis Mss 218S, WHS; Miller, *Struggle for the Life of the Republic,* 168, 194; Campbell, *The Union Must Stand,* 70; Edward Jesup Wood to Wife, 13 Dec. 1862, Edward Jesup Wood Papers, IHS; Rood, *Story of the Service of Company E,* 241–43; Henry Dwight, "My War Experiences," Henry Otis Dwight Papers (Microform), 1861–1900, Mic 127, OHC.

3. John A. McLaughlin to Sister, 15 June 1863, McLaughlin-Jordan Family Papers, IHS; Alphonso Barto to Sister, 2 Sept. 1863, SC 2627 Barto, Alphonso, ALPL; Henry Kircher, "Diary," Engelmann Kircher Family Papers, ALPL; William VanMeter, "A Condensed History of the 47th Regiment of Illinois Vol. Infantry," SC 357 Cromwell, John Nelson, ALPL; Harley Wayne to Ellen, 23 Sept. 1861, SC 2824 Wayne, Harley, ALPL; Luther H. Cowan to Harriet, 21 Jan. 1863, Letters and Diary of Luther H. Cowan, Wis Mss 218S, WHS; Benjamin Grierson to Alice, 15 Dec. 1861, Grierson Box 1, Benjamin Grierson Family Papers, ALPL; Grierson to Alice, 26 Jan. 1862, Grierson Box 1, Benjamin Grierson Family Papers, ALPL; Rood, *Story of the Service of Company E,* 267, 377–78; DeWitt Clinton Loudon to Hannah, 31 May 1862, DeWitt Clinton Loudon Papers, Mss 610, OHC; Loudon to Hannah, 9 June 1862, DeWitt Clinton Loudon Papers, Mss 610, OHC; Loudon to Hannah, 23 June 1862, DeWitt Clinton Loudon Papers, Mss 610, OHC; DeWitt Clinton Loudon to Dr. J. W. Gordon, 31 July 1862, DeWitt Clinton Loudon Papers, Mss 610, OHC; Loudon to Hannah, 8 Oct. 1862, DeWitt Clinton Loudon Papers, Mss 610, OHC; Loudon to Hannah, 14 Oct. 1862, DeWitt Clinton Loudon Papers, Mss 610, OHC; Loudon to Hannah, 19 Oct. 1862, DeWitt Clinton Loudon Papers, Mss 610, OHC; Loudon to Hannah, 25 Nov. 1862, DeWitt Clinton Loudon Papers, Mss 610, OHC; Loudon to Hannah, 23 Jan. 1863, DeWitt Clinton Loudon Papers, Mss 610, OHC; Z. Payson Shumway to Hattie, 14 Feb. 1863, SC 1388 Shumway, Z. Payson, ALPL; "Diary of Z. Payson Shumway," SC 1388 Shumway, Z. Payson, ALPL; Thomas T. Taylor, "Diary," Roll 21, Mic 17 Civil War Collection, OHC; Thomas Thomson Taylor to Wife, 18 Sept. 1863, Thomas Thomson Taylor papers, 1861–1865, Mss 7, OHC; Taylor to Wife, 15 Aug. 1863, Thomas Thomson Taylor papers, 1861–1865, Mss 7, OHC; Taylor to Wife, 19 Aug. 1863, Thomas Thomson Taylor papers, 1861–1865, Mss 7, OHC; Taylor to Wife, 23 Aug. 1863, Thomas Thomson Taylor papers, 1861–1865, Mss 7, OHC; Taylor to Wife, 31 Aug. 1863, Thomas Thomson Taylor papers, 1861–1865, Mss 7, OHC; Taylor to Wife, 3 Sept. 1863, Thomas Thomson Taylor papers, 1861–1865, Mss 7, OHC; Wills, *Army Life of an Illinois Soldier,* 214, 215, 220, 224, 226; "Army Correspondence," *Galena Daily Advertiser,* 6 Dec. 1861; Jackson, *The Colonel's Diary,* 152, 159–60; Hart, *History of the Fortieth Illinois Inf.,* 72, 77–78, 81, 91; Barto to Sister, 27 Apr. 1862, SC 2627 Barto, Alphonso, ALPL; Owen Stuart to Wife, 20 Jan. 1865, SC 2406 Stuart, Owen, ALPL.

4. David McKee Claggett, "Diary," SC 2689 Claggett, David McKee, ALPL; George H. Hildt to Parents, 26 Feb. 1864, Typescripts of George H. Hildt letters and diary, 1862–1865, vol. 548, OHC; Loudon to Hannah, 11 Apr. 1864, DeWitt Clinton Loudon Papers, Mss 610, OHC; Miller, *Struggle for the Life of the Republic,* 59, 120; Rood, *Story of the Service of Company E,* 35, 40, 142, 145–46, 229, 496; John Eugene Smith to Capt. Dickey, 17 July 1862, SC 771–45 Smith, John Eugene, ALPL; Benjamin Franklin Best to Wife, 6 Jan. 1862, SC 2478 Best, Benjamin Franklin, ALPL; "Personal," *Galena Daily Advertiser,* 2 Dec. 1863; "Recruits Wanted for the 45th Ill. Vol., Lead Mine Regiment," *Galena Daily Advertiser,* 7 Dec. 1863; "More Recruits," *Galena Daily Gazette,* 16 Feb. 1864; Howard, *History of the 124th Regiment Illinois Infantry Volunteers,* 2, 3, 5, 7, 8; Henry G. Ankeny to Tina, 30 Sept. 1861, in Cox, *Kiss Josey for Me!,* 33; Hart, *History of the Fortieth Illinois Inf.,* 7–11; Henry A. Kircher to Mother, 17 Feb. 1863, in Hess, *A German in the Yankee Fatherland,* 69–71; Oliver A. Bridgford to Eliza, 12 Nov. 1861, Oliver A. Bridgford Papers; Crooker, Nourse, and Brown, *Story of the Fifty-Fifth Regiment,* 24.

5. Jackson, *The Colonel's Diary*, 41.

6. Edward Gee Miller, "History of Company G," in "Civil War Papers, 1861–1906," Wis Mss 62S, WHS.

7. Jacob B. Ritner to Wife, 22 Apr. 1864, in Larimer, *Love and Valor*, 267.

8. Ritner to Wife, 22 Apr. 1864, in Larimer, *Love and Valor*, 267.

9. Jackson, *The Colonel's Diary*, 40–41; Edward Gee Miller, "Captain Edward Gee Miller of the 20th Wisconsin: His War, 1861–1865," in "Civil War Papers, 1861–1906," Wis Mss 62S, WHS; Miller, "History of Company G," in "Civil War Papers, 1861–1906," Wis Mss 62S, WHS.

10. Wills, *Army Life of an Illinois Soldier*, 210.

11. Henry Giesey Ankeny to Wife, 22 Jan. 1864, in Cox, *Kiss Josey for Me!*, 208.

12. Jackson, *The Colonel's Diary*, 109.

13. Rood, *Story of the Service of Company E*, 233, 235, 236; War Department Adjutant General's Office, "General Orders No. 376," 21 Nov. 1863, Thomas Thomson Taylor papers, 1861–1865, Mss 7, OHC; Jackson, *The Colonel's Diary*, 104–5, 107–8; Loudon to Hannah, 10 Jan. 1864, DeWitt Clinton Loudon Papers, Mss 610, OHC; Ankeny to Wife, 6 Jan. 1864, in Cox, *Kiss Josey for Me!*, 205; Ankeny to Wife, 23 Jan. 1864, in Cox, *Kiss Josey for Me!*, 209–10; Ankeny to Wife, 28 Feb. 1864, in Cox, *Kiss Josey for Me!*, 214; Hildt to Parents, 7 Feb. 1864, Typescripts of George H. Hildt letters and diary, 1862–1865, vol. 548, OHC; Hildt to Parents, 26 Feb. 1864, Typescripts of George H. Hildt letters and diary, 1862–1865, vol. 548, OHC.

14. Wood to Wife, 20 Dec. 1863, Edward Jesup Wood Papers, IHS.

15. Wood to Wife, 17 Jan. 1864, Edward Jesup Wood Papers, IHS.

16. Wood to Wife, 10 Dec. 1863, Edward Jesup Wood Papers, IHS; Wood to Wife, 4 Jan. 1864, Edward Jesup Wood Papers, IHS; Wood to Wife, 24 Apr. 1864, Edward Jesup Wood Papers, IHS; Crooker, Nourse, and Brown, *Story of the Fifty-Fifth Regiment*, 296–97, 299–300, 304, 306–13, 320, 361–64; Wills, *Army Life of an Illinois Soldier*, 224.

17. Ritner to Wife, 1 Nov. 1863, in Larimer, *Love and Valor*, 235.

18. Loudon to Hannah, 10 Apr. 1862, DeWitt Clinton Loudon Papers, Mss 610, OHC; Hart, *History of the Fortieth Illinois Inf.*, 25, 34; "Worth Promotion," *Galena Daily Advertiser*, 4 Mar. 1862; Frank and Reaves, *"Seeing the Elephant,"* 2–3; William VanMeter, "What I Know of the Life of John N. Cromwell, Colonel of the 47th Regiment of Illinois Vol. Infantry," SC 357 Cromwell, John, ALPL.

19. Luther Cowan to Harriet, 1 Feb. 1862, Letters and Diary of Luther H. Cowan, Wis Mss 218S, WHS.

20. James Balfour to Louisa, 26 Mar. 1862, SC 2451 Balfour, James, ALPL.

21. Loudon to Hannah, 3 May 1862, Mss 610, DeWitt Clinton Loudon Papers, OHC.

22. Loudon to Hannah, 24 May 1862, Mss 610, DeWitt Clinton Loudon Papers, OHC.

23. Loudon to Hannah, 24 May 1862, Mss 610, DeWitt Clinton Loudon Papers, OHC.

24. Cowan to Harriet, 27 May 1862, Letters and Diary of Luther H. Cowan, Wis Mss 218S, WHS.

25. Luther Cowan to Molly, 28 June 1862, Letters and Diary of Luther H. Cowan, Wis Mss 218S, WHS.

26. Campbell, *The Union Must Stand*, 71.

27. Stuart to Wife, 23 June 1863, SC 2406 Stuart, Owen, ALPL.

28. John Quincy Adams Campbell to the *Ripley Bee*, 21 Nov. 1863, in Grimsley and Miller, *The Union Must Stand*, 223–24.

29. Campbell to the *Ripley Bee*, 21 Nov. 1863, in Grimsley and Miller, *The Union Must Stand*, 223–24.

30. Campbell to the *Ripley Bee*, 24 Sept. 1862, in Grimsley and Miller, *The Union Must Stand*, 211.

31. Campbell to the *Ripley Bee*, 24 Sept. 1862, in Grimsley and Miller, *The Union Must Stand*, 211.

32. Force, "Personal Recollections of the Vicksburg Campaign," in *MOLLUS*, 1:305.

33. Miller, *Struggle for the Life of the Republic*, 160.

228   NOTES TO PAGES 15–21

34. Stuart to Wife, 17 Jan. 1865, SC 2406 Stuart, Owen, ALPL; John Hancock, "Special Order No. 18," 13 Oct. 1862, "Colonel John Hancock Papers, 1862–1889," File 1862 Feb. 14, WHS; Luther Cowan to Dear Ones, 30 Mar. 1862, Letters and Diary of Luther H. Cowan, Wis Mss 218S, WHS; James Balfour to William Balfour, 4 Apr. 1862, SC 2451 Balfour, James, ALPL; Strayer and Baumgartner, *Echoes of Battle: The Atlanta Campaign*, 140; Campbell to the *Ripley Bee*, 24 Sept. 1862, in Grimsley and Miller, *The Union Must Stand*, 211–12; Morton, "Opening of the Battle of Shiloh," in *MOLLUS*, 45:308.

35. Arndt, "Reminiscences of an Artillery Officer," in *MOLLUS*, 50:290.

36. "Letter From Capt. Cowen," *Warren Independent*, 4 Mar. 1862.

37. "Letter From Capt. Cowen," *Warren Independent*, 4 Mar. 1862.

38. Gray, "Diary," 1862–1863, SC 531, WHS.

39. Friedrich Martens to Dear Ones, 12 June 1862, in Kamphoefner and Helbich, *Germans in the Civil War*, 320.

40. Martens to Dear Ones, 12 June 1862, in Kamphoefner and Helbich, *Germans in the Civil War*, 321.

41. Martens to Dear Ones, 12 June 1862, in Kamphoefner and Helbich, *Germans in the Civil War*, 321.

42. Jacob Ritner to Wife, 1 Nov. 1863, in Larimer, *Love and Valor*, 235.

43. Ritner to Wife, 1 Nov. 1863, in Larimer, *Love and Valor*, 235.

44. Ritner to Wife, 1 Nov. 1863, in Larimer, *Love and Valor*, 236.

45. Ritner to Wife, 1 Nov. 1863, in Larimer, *Love and Valor*, 236.

46. Dwight, "My War Experiences," Henry Otis Dwight Papers (Microform), 1861–1900, Mic 127, OHC; Henry A. Kircher, "Diary of Henry Kircher," Engelmann Kircher Family Papers, ALPL; Ritner to Wife, 1 Nov. 1863, in Larimer, *Love and Valor*, 234; "The Fight at Medon, Tenn.; Report of Lt. Col. Maltby; Heroic Conduct of the 'Lead Mine Regiment'; Desperate Fighting of Capt. Rouse; List of Killed, Wounded and Prisoners," *Galena Daily Advertiser*, 18 Sept. 1862.

47. Grierson to Alice, 23 June 1862, Grierson Box 1, Benjamin Grierson Family Papers, ALPL.

48. Grierson to Alice, 23 June 1862, Grierson Box 1, Benjamin Grierson Family Papers, ALPL.

49. Grierson to Alice, 7 Sept. 1862, Grierson Box 1, Benjamin Grierson Family Papers, ALPL.

50. Jackson, *The Colonel's Diary*, 110.

51. Jackson, *The Colonel's Diary*, 109–11.

2. WIVES AND CHILDREN DEAR

1. Henry G. Ankeny to Wife, 29 Mar. 1863, in Cox, *Kiss Josey for Me!*, 139–40.

2. Benjamin Franklin Best to Wife, 10 Nov. 1861, SC 2478 Best, Benjamin Franklin, ALPL; Troy Moore to Alice, 21 Oct. 1863, SC 2757 Moore, Troy, ALPL; Moore to Alice, 8 Oct. 1863, SC 2757 Moore, Troy, ALPL; James Kerr Proudfit to Wife, 16 Oct. 1863, Proudfit, James Kerr, "Correspondence, 1861–1865," Wis Mss 158S, WHS; "Personal," *Galena Daily Advertiser*, 12 Nov. 1861; Charles Brush to Sister, 1 Apr. 1865, Brush Box 1, Folder 10, ALPL; Wills, *Army Life of an Illinois Soldier*, 359; Proudfit to Wife, 4 Mar. 1864, Proudfit, James Kerr, "Correspondence, 1861–1865," Wis Mss 158S, WHS; Proudfit to Sister, 24 Sept. 1863, Proudfit, James Kerr, "Correspondence, 1861–1865," Wis Mss 158S, WHS; Ritner and Ritner, *Love and Valor*, 373; Jacob B. Ritner to Emeline, 15 Feb. 1863, in Larimer, *Love and Valor*, 117; Ritner to Emeline, 17 Apr. 1863, in Larimer, *Love and Valor*, 154; Robert Steele to Wife, 31 Jan. 1863, "Papers, 1827–1891," Wis Mss 113S, WHS; Owen Stuart to Wife, 28 Jan. 1865, SC 2406 Stuart, Owen, ALPL; Stuart to Wife, 4 Oct. 1864, SC 2406 Stuart, Owen, ALPL; Stuart to Wife, 23 Dec. 1864, SC 2406 Stuart, Owen, ALPL; Steele to Wife, 8 Feb. 1863, "Papers, 1827–1891," Wis Mss 113S, WHS; Steele to Wife, 4 Jan. 1863, "Papers, 1827–1891," Wis Mss 113S, WHS; Robert Steele to Washington, 3 Dec. 1862, "Papers, 1827–1891," Wis Mss 113S, WHS; Steele to Wife, 9 Nov. 1862, "Papers, 1827–1891," Wis Mss 113S, WHS; Robert Steele to Father and Mother, 18 Dec. 1862, "Papers, 1827–1891," Wis Mss 113S, WHS; Steele to Wife, 14 Feb. 1863, "Papers,

NOTES TO PAGES 21-22   229

1827–1891," Wis Mss 113S, WHS; Harley Wayne to Ellen, 22 May 1861, SC 2824 Wayne, Harley, ALPL; Wayne to Ellen, 31 May 1861, SC 2824 Wayne, Harley, ALPL; Wayne to Ellen, 13 July 1861, SC 2824 Wayne, Harley, ALPL; Wayne to Ellen, 26 July 1861, SC 2824 Wayne, Harley, ALPL; Wayne to Ellen, 14 Dec. 1861, SC 2824 Wayne, Harley, ALPL; Wayne to Ellen, 22 Dec. 1861, SC 2824 Wayne, Harley, ALPL; Wayne to Ellen, 18 Feb. 1862, SC 2824 Wayne, Harley, ALPL; Thomas Thomson Taylor to Wife, 15 Aug. 1863, Thomas Thomson Taylor papers, Mss 7, OHC; Taylor to Wife, 19 Aug. 1863, Thomas Thomson Taylor papers, Mss 7, OHC; Alexander K. Ewing to Parents, 25 Mar. 1863, SC 2667 Ewing, Alexander K., ALPL; Ewing to Parents, 29 Mar. 1863, SC 2667 Ewing, Alexander K., ALPL; James Balfour to Louisa, 26 Mar. 1862, SC 2451 Balfour, James, ALPL; Ephraim Brown to Drusilla, 22 Sept. 1862, Ephraim Brown Papers, Mss 76, OHC; Brown to Drusilla, 27 Nov. 1862, Ephraim Brown Papers, Mss 76, OHC; Brown to Drusilla, 8 Dec. 1862, Ephraim Brown Papers, Mss 76, OHC; Brown to Drusilla, 18 Jan. 1863, Ephraim Brown Papers, Mss 76, OHC; Brown to Drusilla, 25 Jan. 1863, Ephraim Brown Papers, Mss 76, OHC; Brown to Drusilla, 20 Jan. 1863, Ephraim Brown Papers, Mss 76, OHC; Brown to Drusilla, 21 Dec. 1862, Ephraim Brown Papers, Mss 76, OHC; Brown to Drusilla, 20 Jan. 1863, Ephraim Brown Papers, Mss 76, OHC; Brown to Drusilla, 27 Oct. 1862, Ephraim Brown Papers, Mss 76, OHC; Luther H. Cowan to Harriet, 17–19 Mar. 1863, Letters and Diary of Luther H. Cowan, Wis Mss 218S, WHS; Ankeny to Wife, 10 Dec. 1862, in Cox, *Kiss Josey for Me!*, 109–10; Ankeny to Tina, 26 Dec. 1862, in Cox, *Kiss Josey for Me!*, 114; Ankeny to Wife, 4 Jan. 1863, in Cox, *Kiss Josey for Me!*, 39–40; Ankeny to Wife, 8 Jan. 1864, in Cox, *Kiss Josey for Me!*, 207; Ankeny to Wife, 26 May 1863, in Cox, *Kiss Josey for Me!*, 158; Ankeny to Wife, 15 July 1863, in Cox, *Kiss Josey for Me!*, 175; Margaret Stuart to Sisters and Brothers, 17 Dec. 1862, SC 2406 Stuart, Owen, ALPL; Owen Stuart to Father and Mother, 12 Apr. 1863, SC 2406 Stuart, Owen, ALPL; Stuart to Father and Mother, 20 May 1863, SC 2406 Stuart, Owen, ALPL; Margaret Stuart to Husband, 9 Sept. 1863, SC 2406 Stuart, Owen, ALPL; Henry Miller Culbertson to Mother, Brother, and Sister, 1 June 1863, "Civil War Letters," 1861–1864, Wis Mss 216S, WHS; Culbertson to Mother, Brother, and Sister, 5 Aug. 1863, "Civil War Letters," 1861–1864, Wis Mss 216S, WHS; Henry Miller Culbertson to Sister, 3 Mar. 1864, "Civil War Letters," 1861–1864, Wis Mss 216S, WHS; George H. Hildt to Parents, 3 June 1864, Typescripts of George H. Hildt letters and diary, 1862–1865, vol. 548, OHC; Hildt to Parents, 19 June 1863, Typescripts of George H. Hildt letters and diary, 1862–1865, vol. 548, OHC; Henry F. Hole to Minerva, 24 Feb. 1862, SC 2427 Hole, Henry F., ALPL; Henry A. Kircher, "Diary of Henry Kircher," Engelmann Kircher Family Papers, ALPL; Ewing to Parents, 9 Nov. 1862, SC 2667 Ewing, Alexander K., ALPL; Ewing to Parents, 22–23 Nov. 1862, SC 2667 Ewing, Alexander K., ALPL; Ewing to Parents, 4 Jan. 1863, SC 2667 Ewing, Alexander K., ALPL; Henry F. Hole to Sister Mine, 13 Oct. 1862, SC 2427 Hole, Henry F., ALPL; Alexander K. Ewing to Mother, 23 Dec. 1862, SC 2667 Ewing, Alexander K., ALPL; Alexander Ewing to Parents, 29 Mar. 1863, SC 2667 Ewing, Alexander K., ALPL; Ewing to Parents, 24 Apr. 1863, SC 2667 Ewing, Alexander K., ALPL.

3. Jackson, *The Colonel's Diary*, 147–48.

4. Jackson, *The Colonel's Diary*, 212.

5. Henry F. Hole to Sister, 25 Mar. 1862, SC 2427 Hole, Henry F., ALPL.

6. Hole to Sister, 25 Mar. 1862, SC 2427 Hole, Henry F., ALPL.

7. Grierson, *A Just and Righteous Cause*, 86.

8. Henry A. Kircher to Mother, 12 Sept. 1862, in Hess, *A German in the Yankee Fatherland*, 22; Benjamin H. Grierson to Alice, 12 May 1862, Grierson Box 1, Benjamin Grierson Family Papers, ALPL; Benjamin H. Grierson to Father, 21 May 1862, Grierson Box 1, Benjamin Grierson Family Papers, ALPL; Benjamin H. Grierson to Father and John, 31 May 1862, Grierson Box 1, Benjamin Grierson Family Papers, ALPL; Grierson to Alice, 6 Apr. 1862, Grierson Box 1, Benjamin Grierson Family Papers, ALPL; T. H. Cavanaugh to Brig. Gen. U. S. Grant, 30 Jan. 1862. Grierson Box 1, Benjamin Grierson Family Papers, ALPL; Grierson to Father, 20 Sept. 1862, Grierson Box 1, Benjamin Grierson Family Papers, ALPL; Grierson, *A Just and Righteous Cause*, 83–85; Grierson to Alice, 10 Aug. 1862, Grierson Box 1, Benjamin Grierson Family Papers, ALPL.

230 NOTES TO PAGES 22–26

9. John Nelson Cromwell to Wife, 11 Dec. 1862, SC 357 Cromwell, John Nelson, ALPL.

10. Zachariah Dean to Emily, 19 June 1863, Zachariah Dean Papers, IHS.

11. James Kerr Proudfit to Emelie, 30 Sept. 1864, Proudfit, James Kerr, "Correspondence, 1861–1865," Wis Mss 158S, WHS; George Harvey to Wife, 13 Jan. 1862, Captain George Harvey Papers, IHS; Sylvester G. Beckwith to Wife, 25 Mar. 1863, SC 2078 Beckwith, Sylvester Gridley, ALPL; Sylvester G. Beckwith to Dear & beloved wife & children, 6 Apr. 1863, SC 2078 Beckwith, Sylvester Gridley, ALPL; Steele to Wife, 31 July 1863, "Papers, 1827–1891," Wis Mss 113S, WHS; Steele to Wife, 12 June 1863, "Papers, 1827–1891," Wis Mss 113S, WHS; Steele to Wife, 8 Feb. 1863, "Papers, 1827–1891," Wis Mss 113S, WHS; Steele to Wife, 14 Feb. 1863, "Papers, 1827–1891," Wis Mss 113S, WHS; Steele to Wife, 18 June 1863, "Papers, 1827–1891," Wis Mss 113S, WHS.

12. Edward Jesup Wood to Wife, 23 Mar. 1863, Edward Jesup Wood Papers, IHS.

13. Wood to Wife, 2 Apr. 1863, Edward Jesup Wood Papers, IHS.

14. Wood to Wife, 17 Jan. 1864, Edward Jesup Wood Papers, IHS.

15. Wood to Wife, 17 Apr. 1864, Edward Jesup Wood Papers, IHS.

16. Wood to Wife, 29–30 May 1864, Edward Jesup Wood Papers, IHS.

17. Wood to Wife, 13 Dec. 1862, Edward Jesup Wood Papers, IHS; Wood to Wife, 18 Dec. 1862, Edward Jesup Wood Papers, IHS; Wood to Wife, 2 Jan. 1863, Edward Jesup Wood Papers, IHS; Wood to Wife, 28 Dec. 1863, Edward Jesup Wood Papers, IHS; Wood to Wife, 25 Mar. 1864, Edward Jesup Wood Papers, IHS; Wood to Wife, 21 June 1863, Edward Jesup Wood Papers, IHS; Wood to Wife, 20 Dec. 1863, Edward Jesup Wood Papers, IHS; Wood to Wife, 8 May 1863, Edward Jesup Wood Papers, HIS; Wood to Wife, 16 Oct. 1863, Edward Jesup Wood Papers, IHS; Wood to Wife, 23 Mar. 1863, Edward Jesup Wood Papers, IHS.

18. Edward Jesup Wood to Jeanie, 26 Nov. 1862, Edward Jesup Wood Papers, IHS.

19. Wood to Wife, 25 Oct. 1863, Edward Jesup Wood Papers, IHS.

20. Wood to Wife, 9 Nov. 1864, Edward Jesup Wood Papers, IHS; Wood to Wife, 17 Apr. 1864, Edward Jesup Wood Papers, IHS; Wood to Wife, 17 Jan. 1864, Edward Jesup Wood Papers, IHS.

21. DeWitt Clinton Loudon to Hannah, 25 May 1862, DeWitt Clinton Loudon Papers, Mss 610, OHC.

22. Loudon to Hannah, 25 May 1862, DeWitt Clinton Loudon Papers, Mss 610, OHC.

23. Loudon to Hannah, 3 Apr. 1864, DeWitt Clinton Loudon Papers, Mss 610, OHC; Loudon to Hannah, 16 Nov. 1862, DeWitt Clinton Loudon Papers, Mss 610, OHC; Loudon to Hannah, 8 Dec. 1863, DeWitt Clinton Loudon Papers, Mss 610, OHC; Loudon to Hannah, 1 Jan. 1863, DeWitt Clinton Loudon Papers, Mss 610, OHC.

24. Grierson to Alice, 19 Dec. 1861, Grierson Box 1, Benjamin Grierson Family Papers, ALPL.

25. Grierson to Alice, 23 Dec. 1861, Grierson Box 1, Benjamin Grierson Family Papers, ALPL.

26. Grierson to Alice, 29 Dec. 1861, Grierson Box 1, Benjamin Grierson Family Papers, ALPL.

27. Grierson to Alice, 25 Jan. 1862, Grierson Box 1, Benjamin Grierson Family Papers, ALPL.

28. Grierson to Alice, 3 Apr. 1862, Grierson Box 1, Benjamin Grierson Family Papers, ALPL.

29. Grierson to Alice, 3 Apr. 1862, Grierson Box 1, Benjamin Grierson Family Papers, ALPL.

30. Grierson to Alice, 5 Jan. 1862, Grierson Box 1, Benjamin Grierson Family Papers, ALPL; Grierson to Alice, 11 Jan. 1862, Grierson Box 1, Benjamin Grierson Family Papers, ALPL; Grierson to Alice, 10 Jan. 1862, Grierson Box 1, Benjamin Grierson Family Papers, ALPL; Grierson to Alice, 21 Dec. 1861, Grierson Box 1, Benjamin Grierson Family Papers, ALPL.

31. Jacob B. Ritner to Wife, 10 Aug. 1864, in Larimer, *Love and Valor*, 333.

32. Ritner to Emeline, 30 Mar. 1863, in Larimer, *Love and Valor*, 143.

33. Ritner to Emeline, 4 Apr. 1863, in Larimer, *Love and Valor*, 147.

34. Ritner to Wife, 20 Sept. 1863, in Larimer, *Love and Valor*, 209.

35. Ritner to Wife, 16 Sept. 1864, in Larimer, *Love and Valor*, 359.

36. Ritner to Wife, 2 Oct. 1864, in Larimer, *Love and Valor*, 369.

37. Ritner to Wife, 1 Feb. 1863, in Larimer, *Love and Valor*, 110; Ritner to Emeline, 15 Mar. 1863, in Larimer, *Love and Valor*, 134; Ritner to Emeline, 20 Mar. 1863, in Larimer, *Love and*

Valor, 140; Ritner to Emeline, 12 Apr. 1863, in Larimer, *Love and Valor,* 151; Ritner to Emeline, 2 Dec. 1862, in Larimer, *Love and Valor, 72.*

38. Ritner to Wife, 4 Oct. 1863, in Larimer, *Love and Valor,* 216.

39. Ritner to Wife, 2 Oct. 1864, in Larimer, *Love and Valor,* 369.

40. Ritner to Wife, 10 Aug. 1864, in Larimer, *Love and Valor, 333.*

41. Ritner to Emeline, 12 Apr. 1863, in Larimer, *Love and Valor, 151.*

42. Ritner to Wife, 4 Oct. 1863, in Larimer, *Love and Valor,* 216–17; Ritner to Emeline, 22 Dec. 1862, in Larimer, *Love and Valor,* 82; Ritner to Wife, 20 Sept. 1863, in Larimer, *Love and Valor,* 209.

43. Ritner to Emeline, 23 Nov. 1862, in Larimer, *Love and Valor,* 65.

44. Ritner to Wife, 22 Apr. 1864, in Larimer, *Love and Valor,* 267.

45. Ritner to Wife, 24 Aug. 1864, in Larimer, *Love and Valor,* 342.

46. Ritner to Wife, 19 Sept. 1864, in Larimer, *Love and Valor,* 360.

47. Ritner to Wife, 13 Oct. 1864, in Larimer, *Love and Valor,* 372.

48. Ritner to Wife, 13 Oct. 1864, in Larimer, *Love and Valor,* 372.

49. Z. Payson Shumway, "Diary," SC 1388 Shumway, Z. Payson, ALPL.

50. Z. Payson Shumway to Hattie, 1 Apr. 1862, SC 1388 Shumway, Z. Payson, ALPL.

51. Shumway to Hattie, 2 Mar. 1863, SC 1388 Shumway, Z. Payson, ALPL.

52. Shumway to Hattie, 17 Sept. 1863, SC 1388 Shumway, Z. Payson, ALPL; Shumway to Hattie, 3 Oct. 1863, SC 1388 Shumway, Z. Payson, ALPL; Shumway to Hattie, 16 Nov. 1862, SC 1388 Shumway, Z. Payson, ALPL; Shumway to Hattie, 2 Mar. 1863, SC 1388 Shumway, Z. Payson, ALPL; Shumway to Hattie, 14 Feb. 1863, SC 1388 Shumway, Z. Payson, ALPL.

53. Wayne to Ellen, 29 Dec. 1861, SC 2824 Wayne, Harley, ALPL.

54. Taylor to Wife, 23 Sept. 1863, Thomas Thomson Taylor papers, Mss 7, OHC.

55. Taylor to Wife, 23 Sept. 1863, Thomas Thomson Taylor papers, Mss 7, OHC.

56. Steele to Wife, 22 Dec. 1862, "Papers, 1827–1891," Wis Mss 113S, WHS.

57. James Leeper to Mary, 28 Mar. 1863, James Leeper Papers, IHS; Balzar Grebe, "Autobiography and Civil War Diary," SC 2681 Grebe, Balzar, ALPL; Beckwith to Wife, 1 Mar. 1863, SC 2078 Beckwith, Sylvester Gridley, ALPL; Beckwith to Wife, 25 Mar. 1863, SC 2078 Beckwith, Sylvester Gridley, ALPL; Best to Wife, 6 Jan. 1862, SC 2478 Best, Benjamin Franklin, ALPL; Proudfit to Emelie, 30 Sept. 1864, Proudfit, James Kerr, "Correspondence, 1861–1865," Wis Mss 158S, WHS; Oliver A. Bridgford to Eliza, 1 Dec. 1861, Oliver A. Bridgford Papers; Bridgford to Eliza, 29 July 1862, Oliver A. Bridgford Papers; Brown to Drusilla, 19 Dec. 1862, Ephraim Brown Papers, Mss 76, OHC; Brown to Drusilla, 26 Feb. 1863, Ephraim Brown Papers, Mss 76, OHC; Brown to Drusilla, 18 Mar. 1863, Ephraim Brown Papers, Mss 76, OHC; Wood to Wife, 18 Dec. 1862, Edward Jesup Wood Papers, IHS; Wood to Wife, 13 May 1864, Edward Jesup Wood Papers, IHS; Robert B. Latham to Wife, 9 Nov. 1862, SC 895 Latham, R. B., ALPL; Latham to Wife, 22 Jan. 1863, SC 895 Latham, R. B., ALPL; Latham to Wife, 11 May 1863, SC 895 Latham, R. B., ALPL; Steele to Wife, 24 May 1863, "Papers, 1827–1891," Wis Mss 113S, WHS; Steele to Wife, 3 Mar. 1863, "Papers, 1827–1891," Wis Mss 113S, WHS; Steele to Wife, 31 Jan. 1863, "Papers, 1827–1891," Wis Mss 113S, WHS; Benjamin H. Grierson to Charlie Grierson, 10 Aug. 1862, Grierson Box 1, Benjamin Grierson Family Papers, ALPL; Ankeny to Wife, 20 Dec. 1862, in Cox, *Kiss Josey for Me!,* 111; Ankeny to Wife, 4 Jan. 1863, in Cox, *Kiss Josey for Me!,* 39; Ankeny to Wife, 28 June 1863, in Cox, *Kiss Josey for Me!,* 169; Henry G. Ankeny to Tina, 24 May 1864, in Cox, *Kiss Josey for Me!,* 156; Ankeny to Tina, 9 Aug. 1863, in Cox, *Kiss Josey for Me!,* 180; Loudon to Hannah, 11 May 1862, DeWitt Clinton Loudon Papers, Mss 610, OHC; Loudon to Hannah, 8 Oct. 1862, DeWitt Clinton Loudon Papers, Mss 610, OHC; Loudon to Hannah, 25 Apr. 1864, DeWitt Clinton Loudon Papers, Mss 610, OHC; Loudon to Hannah, 2 Apr. 1862, DeWitt Clinton Loudon Papers, Mss 610, OHC; Loudon to Hannah, 24 May 1862, DeWitt Clinton Loudon Papers, Mss 610, OHC; Loudon to Hannah, 1 Jan. 1863, DeWitt Clinton Loudon Papers, Mss 610, OHC; DeWitt Clinton Loudon to Fanny and Betty, no date [filed in the presence of other letters dated in early November 1862], DeWitt Clinton Loudon Papers, Mss 610, OHC.

232 NOTES TO PAGES 30–32

58. Ritner to Emeline, 7 Jan. 1863, in Larimer, *Love and Valor*, 99.

59. Ritner to Wife, 26 June 1863, in Larimer, *Love and Valor*, 190–91.

60. Ritner to Wife, 4 Oct. 1863, in Larimer, *Love and Valor*, 217.

61. Ritner to Wife, 21 May 1864, in Larimer, *Love and Valor*, 274.

62. Ritner to Wife, 18 Oct. 1863, in Larimer, *Love and Valor*, 226.

63. Ritner to Emeline, 24 May 1863, in Larimer, *Love and Valor*, 172.

64. Jacob B. Ritner to Nellie, 11 July 1864, in Larimer, *Love and Valor*, 306–7.

65. Ritner to Emeline, 2 Dec. 1862, in Larimer, *Love and Valor*, 75.

66. Ritner to Wife, 1 Feb. 1863, in Larimer, *Love and Valor*, 111; Ritner to Wife, 22 Jan. 1865, in Larimer, *Love and Valor*, 412; Ritner to Emeline, 19 Dec. 1862, in Larimer, *Love and Valor*, 80; Ritner to Emeline, 15 Feb. 1863, in Larimer, *Love and Valor*, 118–19; Ritner to Emeline, 22 Feb. 1863, in Larimer, *Love and Valor*, 121; Ritner to Emeline, 15 Mar. 1863, in Larimer, *Love and Valor*, 134; Ritner to Emeline, 7 May 1863, in Larimer, *Love and Valor*, 166; Ritner to Emeline, 30 May 1863, in Larimer, *Love and Valor*, 175; Ritner to Wife, 17 Nov. 1863, in Larimer, *Love and Valor*, 240; Ritner to Wife, 9 Sept. 1864, in Larimer, *Love and Valor*, 350; Ritner to Wife, 19 Sept. 1864, in Larimer, *Love and Valor*, 361; Ritner to Wife, 7 Nov. 1864, in Larimer, *Love and Valor*, 379; Ritner to Emeline, 2 Dec. 1862, in Larimer, *Love and Valor*, 75; Ritner to Emeline, 12 Apr. 1863, in Larimer, *Love and Valor*, 152; Ritner to Wife, 25 Dec. 1864, in Larimer, *Love and Valor*, 395.

67. Luther H. Cowan to Children, 12 Apr. 1863, Letters and Diary of Luther H. Cowan, Wis Mss 218S, WHS.

68. Luther H. Cowan to Mollie, 21 Nov. 1862, Letters and Diary of Luther H. Cowan, Wis Mss 218S, WHS; Cowan to Mollie, 10 Dec. 1862, Letters and Diary of Luther H. Cowan, Wis Mss 218S, WHS; Luther H. Cowan to Phine and George, 20 Apr. 1863, Letters and Diary of Luther H. Cowan, Wis Mss 218S, WHS; Luther H. Cowan to Josephine, 13 Feb. 1863, Letters and Diary of Luther H. Cowan, Wis Mss 218S, WHS; Cowan to Harriet, 7–8 Dec. 1862, Letters and Diary of Luther H. Cowan, Wis Mss 218S, WHS; Cowan to Harriet, 2 Sept. 1862, Letters and Diary of Luther H. Cowan, Wis Mss 218S, WHS; Luther H. Cowan to Family, 1 Mar. 1863, Letters and Diary of Luther H. Cowan, Wis Mss 218S, WHS; Cowan to Harriet, 18 Nov. 1862, Letters and Diary of Luther H. Cowan, Wis Mss 218S, WHS; Cowan to Molly, 28 June 1862, Letters and Diary of Luther H. Cowan, Wis Mss 218S, WHS; Cowan to Family, 27 Apr. 1862, Letters and Diary of Luther H. Cowan, Wis Mss 218S, WHS; Cowan to Family, 27 Apr. 1862, Letters and Diary of Luther H. Cowan, Wis Mss 218S, WHS; Cowan to Harriet, 16 Apr. 1862, Letters and Diary of Luther H. Cowan, Wis Mss 218S, WHS.

69. Cowan to Molly, 28 June 1862, Letters and Diary of Luther H. Cowan, Wis Mss 218S, WHS.

70. Cowan to Molly, 3 May 1862, Letters and Diary of Luther H. Cowan, Wis Mss 218S, WHS.

71. Cowan to Molly, 25–26 Jan. 1862, Letters and Diary of Luther H. Cowan, Wis Mss 218S, WHS.

72. Cowan to Molly, 6 May 1862, Letters and Diary of Luther H. Cowan, Wis Mss 218S, WHS.

73. Cowan to Molly, 6 May 1862, Letters and Diary of Luther H. Cowan, Wis Mss 218S, WHS.

74. Cowan to Harriet, 13 Jan. 1862, Letters and Diary of Luther H. Cowan, Wis Mss 218S, WHS; Cowan to Harriet, 9 Dec. 1861, Letters and Diary of Luther H. Cowan, Wis Mss 218S, WHS; Cowan to Family, 27 Apr. 1862, Letters and Diary of Luther H. Cowan, Wis Mss 218S, WHS.

75. William K. Barney to Sam, 17 Feb. 1863, Barney, William K., "Papers, 1845–1874," Wis Mss 123S, WHS.

76. Wood to Wife, 10 Sept. 1864, Edward Jesup Wood Papers, IHS.

77. Taylor to Wife, 10 Sept. 1863, Thomas Thomson Taylor papers, Mss 7, OHC.

78. George B. Carter to Bill, 12 May 1863, Carter, George B., Civil War Letters, 1861–1864, Wis Mss 140S, WHS; Alexander K. Ewing to Dave, 26 Apr. 1863, SC 2667 Ewing, Alexander K., ALPL; Erasmus D. Ward to Sister, 12 Apr. 1862, SC 3110 Ward, Erasmus D., ALPL; "Diary," SC 2812 Reid, William M., ALPL; Edward Jesup Wood, "Letter to Wife," 6 Dec. 1862, Edward Jesup Wood Papers, IHS; Wood to Wife, 17 Dec. 1864, Edward Jesup Wood Papers, IHS;

NOTES TO PAGES 33–35 233

Taylor to Wife, 11 Sept. 1863, Thomas Thomson Taylor papers, Mss 7, OHC; Taylor to Wife, 18 Sept. 1863, Thomas Thomson Taylor papers, Mss 7, OHC.

79. Henry Otis Dwight, "My War Experiences," Henry Otis Dwight Papers (Microform), 1861–1900, Mic 127, OHC.

80. Dwight, "My War Experiences," Henry Otis Dwight Papers (Microform), 1861–1900, Mic 127, OHC.

81. Dwight, "My War Experiences," Henry Otis Dwight Papers (Microform), 1861–1900, Mic 127, OHC.

82. Ritner to Emeline, 10 Mar. 1863, in Larimer, *Love and Valor*, 126.

83. Ritner to Emeline, 17 Apr. 1863, in Larimer, *Love and Valor*, 153.

84. Ritner to Emeline, 17 Apr. 1863, in Larimer, *Love and Valor*, 153.

85. Ritner to Emeline, 30 May 1863, in Larimer, *Love and Valor*, 173.

86. Jacob B. Ritner to Ma, 14 Aug. 1864, in Larimer, *Love and Valor*, 335.

87. Ritner to Emeline, 10 Mar. 1863, in Larimer, *Love and Valor*, 126; Ritner to Emeline, 22 Apr. 1863, in Larimer, *Love and Valor*, 157–58; Ritner to Emeline, 29 Apr. 1863, in Larimer, *Love and Valor*, 162; Ritner to Emeline, 23 May 1863, in Larimer, *Love and Valor*, 169; Ritner to Emeline, 24 May 1863, in Larimer, *Love and Valor*, 171–72; Ritner to Wife, 29 July 1864, in Larimer, *Love and Valor*, 321; Ritner to Ma, 14 Aug. 1864, in Larimer, *Love and Valor*, 335.

88. Ritner to Emeline, 24 Jan. 1863, in Larimer, *Love and Valor*, 107; Ritner to Emeline, 22 Feb. 1863, in Larimer, *Love and Valor*, 121; Ritner to Emeline, 2 Dec. 1862, in Larimer, *Love and Valor*, 74–75; Ritner to Emeline, 30 Mar. 1863, in Larimer, *Love and Valor*, 142; Ritner to Wife, 15 June 1863, in Larimer, *Love and Valor*, 184; Ritner to Wife, 10 Aug. 1864, in Larimer, *Love and Valor*, 333; Ritner to Emeline, 15 Feb. 1863, in Larimer, *Love and Valor*, 117; Ritner to Wife, 8 Jan. 1865, in Larimer, *Love and Valor*, 404; Latham to Wife, 18 Dec. 1862, SC 895 Latham, R. B., ALPL; Latham to Wife, 22 Jan. 1863, SC 895 Latham, R. B., ALPL; Latham to Wife, 23 Apr. 1863, SC 895 Latham, R. B., ALPL; Sylvester G. Beckwith to Wife and Children, 24 Apr. 1863, SC 2078 Beckwith, Sylvester Gridley, ALPL; Beckwith to Wife, 8 May 1863, SC 2078 Beckwith, Sylvester Gridley, ALPL; Cowan to Harriet, 22 Apr. 1863, Letters and Diary of Luther H. Cowan, Wis Mss 218S, WHS; Cowan to Children, 12 Apr. 1863, Letters and Diary of Luther H. Cowan, Wis Mss 218S, WHS; Luther Cowan Diary, Letters and Diary of Luther H. Cowan, Wis Mss 218S, WHS; Luther H. Cowan to Dear Ones, 30 Mar. 1862, Letters and Diary of Luther H. Cowan, Wis Mss 218S, WHS; Ritner to Emeline, 22 Dec. 1862, in Larimer, *Love and Valor*, 82; Samuel J. Nasmith to Louisa, 8 Feb. 1863, Nasmith, Samuel J. "Letters," 1861–1863, Wis Mss 66S, WHS; Grierson to Alice, 18 Dec. 1861, Grierson Box 1, Benjamin Grierson Family Papers, ALPL; Wood to Wife, 29–30 May 1864, Edward Jesup Wood Papers, IHS; Wood to Wife, 26 Feb. 1863, Edward Jesup Wood Papers, IHS; Ritner to Emeline, 30 May 1863, in Larimer, *Love and Valor*, 173; Ankeny to Wife, 31 May 1863, in Cox, *Kiss Josey for Me!*, 159; Ankeny to Tina, 5 June 1863, in Cox, *Kiss Josey for Me!*, 161–62; Ankeny to Tina, 10 June 1863, in Cox, *Kiss Josey for Me!*, 164; Ankeny to Wife, 28 June 1863, in Cox, *Kiss Josey for Me!*, 169; Ankeny to Wife, 3 June 1863, in Cox, *Kiss Josey for Me!*, 160; Ritner to Emeline, 30 May 1863, in Larimer, *Love and Valor*, 176; Shumway to Hattie, 8 Jan. 1863, SC 1388 Shumway, Z. Payson, ALPL; Shumway to Hattie, 10 Dec. 1862, SC 1388 Shumway, Z. Payson, ALPL; Shumway to Hattie, 4 Jan. 1863, SC 1388 Shumway, Z. Payson, ALPL.

89. Balfour to Louisa, 26 Mar. 1862, SC 2451 Balfour, James, ALPL; Beckwith to Wife, 12 Mar. 1863, SC 2078 Beckwith, Sylvester Gridley, ALPL; Beckwith to Wife and Children, 24 Apr. 1863, SC 2078 Beckwith, Sylvester Gridley, ALPL; Beckwith to Wife, 25 Mar. 1863, SC 2078 Beckwith, Sylvester Gridley, ALPL; Proudfit to Wife, 16 Oct. 1863, Proudfit, James Kerr, "Correspondence, 1861–1865," Wis Mss 158S, WHS; Grierson to Father, 21 May 1862, Grierson Box 1, Benjamin Grierson Family Papers, ALPL; Bridgford to Eliza, 12 Nov. 1861, Oliver A. Bridgford Papers; Bridgford to Eliza, 22 Feb. 1862, Oliver A. Bridgford Papers; Best to Wife, 2 Feb. 1862, SC 2478 Best, Benjamin Franklin, ALPL; Ankeny to Wife, 18 June 1863, in Cox, *Kiss Josey for Me!*, 166; Ankeny to Wife, 9 Feb. 1864, in Cox, *Kiss Josey for Me!*, 211; Ankeny to Wife, 7 Aug. 1864, in Cox, *Kiss Josey for Me!*, 233; Loudon to Hannah, 13 Mar. 1862, DeWitt

234   NOTES TO PAGE 35

Clinton Loudon Papers, Mss 610, OHC; Loudon to Hannah, 2 Apr. 1862, DeWitt Clinton Loudon Papers, Mss 610, OHC; Loudon to Hannah, 24 May 1862, DeWitt Clinton Loudon Papers, Mss 610, OHC; Loudon to Hannah, 9 July 1862, DeWitt Clinton Loudon Papers, Mss 610, OHC; Loudon to Hannah, 23 Jan. 1863, DeWitt Clinton Loudon Papers, Mss 610, OHC; Loudon to Hannah, 1 Jan. 1863, DeWitt Clinton Loudon Papers, Mss 610, OHC; Hildt to Parents, 2 Jan. 1864, Typescripts of George H. Hildt letters and diary, 1862–1865, vol. 548, OHC; Hildt to Parents, 7 Feb. 1864, Typescripts of George H. Hildt letters and diary, 1862–1865, vol. 548, OHC; Hildt to Parents, 17 May 1864, Typescripts of George H. Hildt letters and diary, 1862–1865, vol. 548, OHC; Hildt to Parents, 26 Feb. 1864, Typescripts of George H. Hildt letters and diary, 1862–1865, vol. 548, OHC; Hildt to Parents, 22 Sept. 1864, Typescripts of George H. Hildt letters and diary, 1862–1865, vol. 548, OHC; Hildt to Parents, 15 Aug. 1864, Typescripts of George H. Hildt letters and diary, 1862–1865, vol. 548, OHC; Taylor to Wife, 11 Sept. 1863, Thomas Thomson Taylor papers, Mss 7, OHC; Taylor to Wife, 15 July 1863, Thomas Thomson Taylor papers, Mss 7, OHC; Taylor to Wife, 26 July 1863, Thomas Thomson Taylor papers, Mss 7, OHC; Taylor to Wife, 23 Aug. 1863, Thomas Thomson Taylor papers, Mss 7, OHC; Taylor to Wife, 23 Sept. 1863, Thomas Thomson Taylor papers, Mss 7, OHC; Taylor to Wife, 18 Sept. 1863, Thomas Thomson Taylor papers, Mss 7, OHC; Cowan to Family, 1 Oct. 1862, Letters and Diary of Luther H. Cowan, Wis Mss 218S, WHS; Cowan to Harriet, 11 Oct. 1862, Letters and Diary of Luther H. Cowan, Wis Mss 218S, WHS; Cowan to Harriet, 16 Oct. 1862, Letters and Diary of Luther H. Cowan, Wis Mss 218S, WHS; Cowan to Harriet, 1 Mar. 1862, Letters and Diary of Luther H. Cowan, Wis Mss 218S, WHS; Cowan to Harriet, 9 Dec. 1861, Letters and Diary of Luther H. Cowan, Wis Mss 218S, WHS; Cowan to Harriet, 27 May 1862, Letters and Diary of Luther H. Cowan, Wis Mss 218S, WHS; Cowan to Harriet, 16 Apr. 1862, Letters and Diary of Luther H. Cowan, Wis Mss 218S, WHS; Luther H. Cowan to Josephine and Harriet, 3 Aug. 1862, Letters and Diary of Luther H. Cowan, Wis Mss 218S, WHS; Cowan to Harriet, 9 Aug. 1862, Letters and Diary of Luther H. Cowan, Wis Mss 218S, WHS; Cowan to Harriet, 29 Oct. 1862, Letters and Diary of Luther H. Cowan, Wis Mss 218S, WHS; Cowan to Molly, 3 May 1862, Letters and Diary of Luther H. Cowan, Wis Mss 218S, WHS; Cowan to Harriet, 7 Mar. 1862, Letters and Diary of Luther H. Cowan, Wis Mss 218S, WHS; Ritner to Wife, 7 Nov. 1864, in Larimer, *Love and Valor*, 383; Ritner to Wife, 18 Oct. 1863, in Larimer, *Love and Valor*, 226; Ritner to Emeline, 16 Nov. 1862, in Larimer, *Love and Valor*, 64; Ritner to Emeline, 25 Nov. 1862, in Larimer, *Love and Valor*, 67; Ritner to Wife, 1 Feb. 1863, in Larimer, *Love and Valor*, 111; Ritner to Emeline, 15 Feb. 1863, in Larimer, *Love and Valor*, 117; Ritner to Emeline, 1 Mar. 1863, in Larimer, *Love and Valor*, 123–24; Ritner to Emeline, 20 Mar. 1863, in Larimer, *Love and Valor*, 139–40; Ritner to Emeline, 30 May 1863, in Larimer, *Love and Valor*, 176; Ritner to Wife, 26 June 1863, in Larimer, *Love and Valor*, 191; Ritner to Emeline, 2 Dec. 1862, in Larimer, *Love and Valor*, 74; Ritner to Emeline, 8 Feb. 1863, in Larimer, *Love and Valor*, 115; Ritner to Emeline, 30 Mar. 1863, in Larimer, *Love and Valor*, 142; Ritner to Emeline, 22 Apr. 1863, in Larimer, *Love and Valor*, 157; Ritner to Wife, 17 Nov. 1863, in Larimer, *Love and Valor*, 240; Ritner to Wife, 21 May 1864, in Larimer, *Love and Valor*, 274; Ritner to Wife, 26 Sept. 1864, in Larimer, *Love and Valor*, 364; Ritner to Emeline, 22 Feb. 1863, in Larimer, *Love and Valor*, 121; Ritner to Wife, 2 Oct. 1864, in Larimer, *Love and Valor*, 369; Ritner to Wife, 18 Oct. 1863, in Larimer, *Love and Valor*, 226.

90. Wood to Wife, 7 June 1863, Edward Jesup Wood Papers, IHS; Charles W. Wills to Sister, 12 Jan. 1863, in Wills, *Army Life of an Illinois Soldier*, 145; Cowan to Harriet, 1 Feb. 1862, Letters and Diary of Luther H. Cowan, Wis Mss 218S, WHS; Cowan to Harriet, 7 Mar. 1862, Letters and Diary of Luther H. Cowan, Wis Mss 218S, WHS; Cowan to Harriet, 1–2 Feb. 1862, Letters and Diary of Luther H. Cowan, Wis Mss 218S, WHS; Joseph S. Reynolds to Lottie, 20 Jan. 1865, Joseph S. Reynolds Papers, #5060-z, Wilson Library, Univ. of North Carolina at Chapel Hill; Charles C. Ammack to Brother and Sister, 21 Mar. 1863, Ammack and Howland Family Letters, Wis Mss 123S, WHS; Wayne to Ellen, 20 Oct. 1861, SC 2824 Wayne, Harley, ALPL; Wayne to Ellen, 2 Aug. 1861, SC 2824 Wayne, Harley, ALPL; Taylor to Wife, 7 Sept. 1863, Thomas Thomson Taylor papers, 1861–1865, Mss 7, OHC; Taylor to Wife, 11 Sept. 1863, Thomas Thomson Taylor papers, 1861–1865, Mss 7, OHC; Stuart to Wife, 23 June 1863, SC

2406 Stuart, Owen, ALPL; Moore to Alice, 4 Oct. 1863, SC 2757 Moore, Troy, ALPL; Moore to Alice, 24 July 1863, SC 2757 Moore, Troy, ALPL; Loudon to Hannah, 25 Apr. 1864, DeWitt Clinton Loudon Papers, Mss 610, OHC; Loudon to Hannah, 23 Jan. 1863, DeWitt Clinton Loudon Papers, Mss 610, OHC; Loudon to Hannah, 14 Oct. 1862, DeWitt Clinton Loudon Papers, Mss 610, OHC; Loudon to Hannah, 23 Mar. 1862, DeWitt Clinton Loudon Papers, Mss 610, OHC; Bridgford to Eliza, 29 July 1862, Oliver A. Bridgford Papers; Bridgford to Eliza, 27 July 1862, Oliver A. Bridgford Papers; Bridgford to Eliza, 25 Mar. 1862, Oliver A. Bridgford Papers; Bridgford to Eliza, 15 Mar. 1862, Oliver A. Bridgford Papers; Bridgford to Eliza, 22 Feb. 1862, Oliver A. Bridgford Papers; Hildt to Parents, 28 Apr. 1863, Typescripts of George H. Hildt letters and diary, 1862–1865, vol. 548, OHC; Jackson, *The Colonel's Diary*, 152; Henry Giesey Ankeny to Wife, 7 May 1863, in Cox, *Kiss Josey for Me!*, 149; Steele to Wife, 14 Feb. 1863, "Papers, 1827–1891," Wis Mss 113S, WHS; Ritner to Emeline, 25 Nov. 1862, in Larimer, *Love and Valor*, 66; Henry Giesey Ankeny to Tina, 9 Aug. 1863, in Cox, *Kiss Josey for Me!*, 180; Wood to Wife, 17 June 1864, Edward Jesup Wood Papers, IHS; Shumway to Hattie, 6 Apr. 1863, SC 1388 Shumway, Z. Payson, ALPL; Ritner to Wife, 1 Nov. 1863, in Larimer, *Love and Valor*, 234; Ritner to Wife, 16 Sept. 1864, in Larimer, *Love and Valor*, 357; Ritner to Wife, 4 Oct. 1863, in Larimer, *Love and Valor*, 215; Ritner to Wife, 21 May 1864, in Larimer, *Love and Valor*, 273; Taylor to Wife, 11 Sept. 1863, Thomas Thomson Taylor papers, 1861–1865, Mss 7, OHC; Loudon to Hannah, 2 Apr. 1862, DeWitt Clinton Loudon Papers, Mss 610, OHC; Loudon to Hannah, 24 Apr. 1862, DeWitt Clinton Loudon Papers, Mss 610, OHC; Ira Merchant to Henry Yates, 26 Feb. 1862, SC 1033 Merchant, Ira, ALPL; Bridgford to Eliza, 20 July 1862, Oliver A. Bridgford Papers; Culbertson to Mother, Brother, and Sister, 1 June 1863, "Civil War Letters," 1861–1864, Wis Mss 216S, WHS; Wills to Sister, 11 Dec. 1863, in Wills, *Army Life of an Illinois Soldier*, 205; Miller, *Struggle for the Life of the Republic*, 196; Ritner to Wife, 7 July 1864, in Larimer, *Love and Valor*, 304.

91. Kircher to Mother, 8 Sept. 1862, in Hess, *A German in the Yankee Fatherland*, 19.

92. Cowan to Family, 26 Oct. 1862, Letters and Diary of Luther H. Cowan, Wis Mss 218S, WHS.

93. Ritner to Wife, 18 Oct. 1863, in Larimer, *Love and Valor*, 226.

94. Wills, *Army Life of an Illinois Soldier*, 362; Wills to Sister, 18 Mar. 1865, in Wills, *Army Life of an Illinois Soldier*, 363; Cowan to Family, 26 Oct. 1862, Letters and Diary of Luther H. Cowan, Wis Mss 218S, WHS; Wills to Sister, 22 Mar. 1865, in Wills, *Army Life of an Illinois Soldier*, 366–67; Stuart to Father and Mother, 20 May 1863, SC 2406 Stuart, Owen, ALPL; Stuart to Wife [date unknown, but since it is written from Savannah it must be late December 1864 or early January 1865], SC 2406 Stuart, Owen, ALPL; Stuart to Wife, 20 Jan. 1865, SC 2406 Stuart, Owen, ALPL; Loudon to Hannah, 6 Mar. 1862, DeWitt Clinton Loudon Papers, Mss 610, OHC; Bridgford to Eliza, 20 July 1862, Oliver A. Bridgford Papers; Bridgford to Eliza, 1 Dec. 1861, Oliver A. Bridgford Papers; Loudon to Hannah, 5 Nov. 1862, DeWitt Clinton Loudon Papers, Mss 610, OHC; Alphonso Barto to Father, Sister, Mother, & Brother, 24 July 1864, SC 2627 Barto, Alphonso, ALPL; Bridgford to Eliza, 9 Mar. 1862, Oliver A. Bridgford Papers; Loudon to Hannah, 2 Nov. 1862, DeWitt Clinton Loudon Papers, Mss 610, OHC; Bridgford to Eliza, 5 Feb. 1862, Oliver A. Bridgford Papers; Bridgford to Eliza, 21 Feb. 1862, Oliver A. Bridgford Papers; Bennet Grigsby to Wife & Children, 18 May 1863, Bennet Grigsby Civil War Letters, IHS; Brown to Drusilla, 18 Jan. 1863, Ephraim Brown Papers, Mss 76, OHC; Wayne to Ellen, 18 Oct. 1861, SC 2824 Wayne, Harley, ALPL; Grebe, "Autobiography and Civil War Diary," SC 2681 Grebe, Balzar, ALPL; Loudon to Hannah, 16 Nov. 1862, DeWitt Clinton Loudon Papers, Mss 610, OHC; Grierson to Alice," 23 Dec. 1861, Grierson Box 1, Benjamin Grierson Family Papers, ALPL; Ankeny to Tina, 20 Feb. 1863, in Cox, *Kiss Josey for Me!*, 132; Ritner to Emeline, 10 Mar. 1863, in Larimer, *Love and Valor*, 127; Cowan to Molly, 18 Jan. 1862, Letters and Diary of Luther H. Cowan, Wis Mss 218S, WHS; Ritner to Emeline, 15 Jan. 1863, in Larimer, *Love and Valor*, 106; Grierson to Alice," 23 Dec. 1861, Grierson Box 1, Benjamin Grierson Family Papers, ALPL; Ritner to Wife, 18 Oct. 1863, in Larimer, *Love and Valor*, 224; Ritner to Wife, 25 July 1864, in Larimer, *Love and Valor*, 317; Shumway to Hattie, 2 Mar. 1863, SC 1388 Shumway, Z. Payson, ALPL; Ritner to Wife, 20 Nov. 1863, in Larimer, *Love*

236   NOTES TO PAGES 36–37

and Valor, 242–43; Bridgford to Eliza, 15 Mar. 1862, Oliver A. Bridgford Papers; Balzar Grebe to Wife and Children, 22 Jan. 1863, SC 2681 Grebe, Balzar, ALPL; Culbertson to Mother, Brother, and Sister, 21 Mar. 1862 in "Civil War Letters," 1861–1864, Wis Mss 216S, WHS; Ritner to Wife, 25 Dec. 1862, in Larimer, *Love and Valor*, 84; Ritner to Emeline, 24 Jan. 1863, in Larimer, *Love and Valor*, 107; Loudon to Hannah, 27 Feb. 1862, DeWitt Clinton Loudon Papers, Mss 610, OHC; Ewing to Parents, 22 Mar. 1863, SC 2667 Ewing, Alexander K., ALPL.

95. Shumway to Hattie, 24 July 1863, SC 1388 Shumway, Z. Payson, ALPL.

96. Alphonso Barto to Sister, 17 June 1864, SC 2627 Barto, Alphonso, ALPL.

97. Loudon to Hannah, 28 Oct. 1862, DeWitt Clinton Loudon Papers, Mss 610, OHC; Moore to Alice, 22 Oct. 1863, SC 2757 Moore, Troy, ALPL; Charles Palmetier to Brother & Sister, 28 Jan. 1863, "Civil War Letters, 1861–1864," Wis Mss 168S, WHS; Thomas Thomson Taylor to Margaret, 29 July 1863, Thomas Thomson Taylor papers, 1861–1865, Mss 7, OHC; Wills to Sister, 22 Jan. 1863, in Wills, *Army Life of an Illinois Soldier*, 149; Ankeny to Wife, 22 Feb. 1863, in Cox, *Kiss Josey for Me!*, 132; Sylvester Gridley Beckwith to Wife, 25 Mar. 1863, SC 2078 Beckwith, Sylvester Gridley, ALPL; Grierson to Alice, 21 Dec. 1861, Grierson Box 1, Benjamin Grierson Family Papers, ALPL; Ritner to Wife, 19 Sept. 1864, in Larimer, *Love and Valor*, 361; Alphonso Barto to Father, 27 May 1862, SC 2627 Barto, Alphonso, ALPL; Wood to Wife, 13 May 1864, Edward Jesup Wood Papers, IHS; Taylor to Wife, 18 Sept. 1863, Thomas Thomson Taylor papers, 1861–1865, Mss 7, OHC; Taylor to Wife, 31 Aug. 1863, Thomas Thomson Taylor papers, 1861–1865, Mss 7, OHC; Loudon to Hannah, 3 Apr. 1864, DeWitt Clinton Loudon Papers, Mss 610, OHC; Ritner to Emeline, 2 Dec. 1862, in Larimer, *Love and Valor*, 72; Proudfit to Wife, 16 Oct. 1863, "Correspondence, 1861–1865," Wis Mss 158S, WHS; Taylor to Wife, 23 Aug. 1863, Thomas Thomson Taylor papers, 1861–1865, Mss 7, OHC; Grierson to Alice," 23 Dec. 1861, Grierson Box 1, Benjamin Grierson Family Papers, ALPL; Ritner to Wife, 16 Sept. 1864, in Larimer, *Love and Valor*, 357; Wills to Sister, 1 Sept. 1864, in Wills, *Army Life of an Illinois Soldier*, 295; Taylor to Wife, 23 Aug. 1863, Thomas Thomson Taylor papers, 1861–1865, Mss 7, OHC.

98. Ankeny to Wife, 10 July 1864, in Cox, *Kiss Josey for Me!*, 227; Ankeny to Wife, 6 Dec. 1863 [book gives date of 6 October 1863, but this is clearly an error], in Cox, *Kiss Josey for Me!*, 184; Ankeny to Wife, 3 Aug. 1864, in Cox, *Kiss Josey for Me!*, 231; Ankeny to Tina, 22 Mar. 1863, in Cox, *Kiss Josey for Me!*, 138; Bridgford to Eliza," 7 July 1862, Oliver A. Bridgford Papers; Ritner to Emeline, 25 Nov. 1862, in Larimer, *Love and Valor*, 67; Ritner to Wife, 20 Sept. 1863, in Larimer, *Love and Valor*, 209; Ritner to Wife, 2 Oct. 1864, in Larimer, *Love and Valor*, 368; Ritner to Emeline, 24 May 1863, in Larimer, *Love and Valor*, 172; Ritner to Wife, 2 Oct. 1864, in Larimer, *Love and Valor*, 366; Bridgford to Eliza, 20 July 1862, Oliver A. Bridgford Papers; Bridgford to Eliza, 20 Apr. 1862, Oliver A. Bridgford Papers; Ritner to Emeline, 25 Nov. 1862, in Larimer, *Love and Valor*, 66; Ritner to Wife, 22 Jan. 1865, in Larimer, *Love and Valor*, 415; Ritner to Wife, 19 Sept. 1864, in Larimer, *Love and Valor*, 359–60; Ritner to Wife, 14 Mar. 1865, in Larimer, *Love and Valor*, 429; Wills to Sister, 9 Mar. 1863, in Wills, *Army Life of an Illinois Soldier*, 161; Wills to Sister, 6 June 1864, in Wills, *Army Life of an Illinois Soldier*, 255–56; Wills to Sister, 6 Mar. 1864, in Wills, *Army Life of an Illinois Soldier*, 216; Wills to Sister, 5 May 1864, in Wills, *Army Life of an Illinois Soldier*, 234; Wills to Sister, 21 Oct. 1864, in Wills, *Army Life of an Illinois Soldier*, 314; Stuart to Husband, 26 Sept. 1863, SC 2406 Stuart, Owen, ALPL; Stuart to Wife, 4 Oct. 1864, SC 2406 Stuart, Owen, ALPL; Stuart to Wife, 25 June 1864, SC 2406 Stuart, Owen, ALPL; Loudon to Hannah, 9 July 1862, DeWitt Clinton Loudon Papers, Mss 610, OHC; Wills to Sister, 26 June 1864, in Wills, *Army Life of an Illinois Soldier*, 267; Latham to Wife, 11 May 1863, SC 895 Latham, R. B., ALPL; Loudon to Hannah, 23 June 1862, DeWitt Clinton Loudon Papers, Mss 610, OHC; Miller, *Struggle for the Life of the Republic*, 178; Taylor to Wife, 15 July 1863, Thomas Thomson Taylor papers, 1861–1865, Mss 7, OHC; Grierson to Alice, 23 Dec. 1861, Grierson Box 1, Benjamin Grierson Family Papers, ALPL; Erasmus D. Ward to Mary, 28 Oct. 1862, SC 3110 Ward, Erasmus D., ALPL; Ritner to Wife, 31 Jan. 1865, in Larimer, *Love and Valor*, 417; Taylor to Wife, 23 Aug. 1863, Thomas Thomson Taylor papers, 1861–1865, Mss 7, OHC; Loudon to Hannah, 18 Nov. 1862, DeWitt

Clinton Loudon Papers, Mss 610, OHC; Wills to Sister, 11 Feb. 1865, in Wills, *Army Life of an Illinois Soldier*, 344; Ankeny to Wife, 1 Oct. 1864, in Cox, *Kiss Josey for Me!*, 244; Ankeny to Wife, 13 Oct. 1864, in Cox, *Kiss Josey for Me!*, 246; Ankeny to Wife, 16 Jan. 1863, in Cox, *Kiss Josey for Me!*, 119; Ankeny to Wife, 19 Dec. 1863, in Cox, *Kiss Josey for Me!*, 200; Ankeny to Wife, 8 June 1864, in Cox, *Kiss Josey for Me!*, 220; Ankeny to Wife, 18 Sept. 1864, in Cox, *Kiss Josey for Me!*, 243; Grierson to Alice, 22 Jan. 1862, Grierson Box 1, Benjamin Grierson Family Papers, ALPL; Kircher to Mother, 19 Jan. 1863, in Hess, *A German in the Yankee Fatherland*, 57; Shumway to Hattie, 4 Jan. 1863, SC 1388 Shumway, Z. Payson, ALPL; Hildt to Parents, 7 Feb. 1864, Typescripts of George H. Hildt letters and diary, 1862–1865, vol. 548, OHC; Loudon to Hannah, 13 Dec. 1863, DeWitt Clinton Loudon Papers, Mss 610, OHC; Ritner to Emeline, 24 May 1863, in Larimer, *Love and Valor*, 172; Ritner to Wife, 13 Oct. 1864, in Larimer, *Love and Valor*, 373; Ritner to Wife, 31 Jan. 1865, in Larimer, *Love and Valor*, 418; Barto to Father, 9 Feb. 1863, SC 2627 Barto, Alphonso, ALPL; Ritner to Emeline, 17 Apr. 1863, in Larimer, *Love and Valor*, 153; Loudon to Hannah, 19 Oct. 1862, DeWitt Clinton Loudon Papers, Mss 610, OHC.

99. Kircher to Mother, 10 Mar. 1863, in Hess, *A German in the Yankee Fatherland*, 77.

100. Barney to Sam, 17 Feb. 1863, Barney, William K., "Papers," 1845–1874, Wis Mss 123S, WHS; Culbertson to Mother, Brother, and Sister, 21 Nov. 1863, "Civil War Letters," 1861–1864, Wis Mss 216S, WHS; Ewing to Parents, 8 Dec. 1862, SC 2667 Ewing, Alexander K., ALPL; Ewing to Parents, 25 Mar. 1863, SC 2667 Ewing, Alexander K., ALPL.

101. Kircher to Mother, 30 Jan. 1863, in Hess, *A German in the Yankee Fatherland*, 63.

102. Wood to Wife, 13 Dec. 1862, Edward Jesup Wood Papers, IHS.

103. Loudon to Hannah, 15 Apr. 1862, DeWitt Clinton Loudon Papers, Mss 610, OHC; Loudon to Hannah, 5 Nov. 1862, DeWitt Clinton Loudon Papers, Mss 610, OHC; Loudon to Hannah, 17 Apr. 1864, DeWitt Clinton Loudon Papers, Mss 610, OHC; Loudon to Hannah, 19 Oct. 1862, DeWitt Clinton Loudon Papers, Mss 610, OHC; Loudon to Hannah, 28 Oct. 1862, DeWitt Clinton Loudon Papers, Mss 610, OHC; Loudon to Hannah, 28 Apr. 1862, DeWitt Clinton Loudon Papers, Mss 610, OHC; Loudon to Hannah, 1 Jan. 1863, DeWitt Clinton Loudon Papers, Mss 610, OHC; Kircher to George, 2 Sept. 1862, in Hess, *A German in the Yankee Fatherland*, 16–17; Kircher to Mother, 17 Feb. 1863, in Hess, *A German in the Yankee Fatherland*, 71; Culbertson to Mother, Brother, and Sister, 21 Nov. 1863, "Civil War Letters," 1861–1864, Wis Mss 216S, WHS; Ewing to Parents, 8 Dec. 1862, SC 2667 Ewing, Alexander K., ALPL; Ewing to Parents, 25 Mar. 1863, SC 2667 Ewing, Alexander K., ALPL; Ammack to Brother and Sister, 31 Jan. 1863, Ammack and Howland Family Letters, Wis Mss 123S, WHS; Wayne to Ellen, 21 June 1861, SC 2824 Wayne, Harley, ALPL; Stockton, *War Diary*, 3; Latham to Wife, 29 May 1863, SC 895 Latham, R. B., ALPL; Taylor to Wife, 15 Aug. 1863, Thomas Thomson Taylor papers, 1861–1865, Mss 7, OHC; Thomas Thomson Taylor to Wife, 4 July 1863, Thomas Thomson Taylor papers, 1861–1865, Mss 7, OHC; Wood to Wife, 21 Nov. 1863, Edward Jesup Wood Papers, IHS; Wood to Wife, 13 May 1864, Edward Jesup Wood Papers, IHS; Taylor to Wife, 2 July 1863, Thomas Thomson Taylor papers, 1861–1865, Mss 7, OHC; Stuart to Wife, 13 June 1864, SC 2406 Stuart, Owen, ALPL; Proudfit to Wife, 10 Nov. 1862, "Correspondence, 1861–1865," Wis Mss 158S, WHS; Moore to Alice, 22 Oct. 1863, SC 2757 Moore, Troy, ALPL; Hildt to Parents, 20 June 1864, Typescripts of George H. Hildt letters and diary, 1862–1865, vol. 548, OHC; Bridgford to Eliza, 21 Feb. 1862, Oliver A. Bridgford Papers; Sylvester Gridley Beckwith to Wife and Children, 24 Apr. 1863, SC 2078 Beckwith, Sylvester Gridley, ALPL; Ankeny to Tina, 8 Feb. 1863, in Cox, *Kiss Josey for Me!*, 129; Leeper to Mary, 28 Mar. 1863, James Leeper Papers, IHS; Dwight, "My War Experiences," Henry Otis Dwight Papers (Microform), 1861–1900, Mic 127, OHC; Miller, *Struggle for the Life of the Republic*, 179; Kircher to Mother, 3 Sept. 1862, in Hess, *A German in the Yankee Fatherland*, 17–18; Loudon to Hannah, 5 Mar. 1862, DeWitt Clinton Loudon Papers, Mss 610, OHC; Ritner to Emeline, 30 Mar. 1863, in Larimer, *Love and Valor*, 141; Kircher to Mother, 30 Jan. 1863, in Hess, *A German in the Yankee Fatherland*, 63.

104. Crooker, Nourse, and Brown, *Story of the Fifty-Fifth Regiment*, 137.

105. Cowan to Harriet, 16 Apr. 1862, Letters and Diary of Luther H. Cowan, Wis Mss 218S, WHS.

238   NOTES TO PAGES 38–39

106. Cowan to Harriet, 27 May 1862, Letters and Diary of Luther H. Cowan, Wis Mss 218S, WHS.

107. Ritner to Wife, 22 Jan. 1865, in Larimer, *Love and Valor,* 412

108. Wills to Sister, 10 Jan. 1865, in Wills, *Army Life of an Illinois Soldier,* 336; Taylor to Wife, 15 July 1863, Thomas Thomson Taylor papers, 1861–1865, Mss 7, OHC; Bridgford to Eliza, 9 Mar. 1862, Oliver A. Bridgford Papers; Cowan to Harriet, 13 Jan. 1862, Letters and Diary of Luther H. Cowan, Wis Mss 218S, WHS; Cowan to Family, 27 Apr. 1862, Letters and Diary of Luther H. Cowan, Wis Mss 218S, WHS; Cowan to Molly, 3 May 1862, Letters and Diary of Luther H. Cowan, Wis Mss 218S, WHS; Cowan to Harriet, 1 Feb. 1862, Letters and Diary of Luther H. Cowan, Wis Mss 218S, WHS; Ritner to Emeline, 20 Mar. 1863, Ritner, in Larimer, *Love and Valor,* 138–39.

109. Wayne to Ellen, 29 Dec. 1861, SC 2824 Wayne, Harley, ALPL.

110. Cowan to Molly, 25–26 Jan. 1862, Letters and Diary of Luther H. Cowan, Wis Mss 218S, WHS; Beckwith to Wife and Children, 24 Apr. 1863, SC 2078 Beckwith, Sylvester Gridley, ALPL; Brown to Drusilla, 27 Oct. 1862, Ephraim Brown Papers, Mss 76, OHC; Brown to Drusilla, 8 Dec. 1862, Ephraim Brown Papers, Mss 76, OHC; Brown to Drusilla, 26 Feb. 1863, Ephraim Brown Papers, Mss 76, OHC; Best to Wife, 3 Sept. 1861, SC 2478 Best, Benjamin Franklin, ALPL; Gray, Warren, "Diary," 1862–1863, SC 531, WHS; George H. Hildt, "Diary of the Siege of Atlanta, May 28–Oct. 7 1864," Typescripts of George H. Hildt letters and diary, 1862–1865, vol. 548, OHC; Cowan to Harriet, 6 July 1862, Letters and Diary of Luther H. Cowan, Wis Mss 218S, WHS; Grierson to Alice, 30 May 1861, Grierson Box 1, Benjamin Grierson Family Papers, ALPL; Hildt to Parents, 20 June 1864, Typescripts of George H. Hildt letters and diary, 1862–1865, vol. 548, OHC; Loudon to Hannah, 10 Nov. 1863, DeWitt Clinton Loudon Papers, Mss 610, OHC; Loudon to Hannah, 2 Apr. 1862, DeWitt Clinton Loudon Papers, Mss 610, OHC; Loudon to Hannah, 17 Apr. 1864, DeWitt Clinton Loudon Papers, Mss 610, OHC; Moore to Alice, 29 Sept. 1863, SC 2757 Moore, Troy, ALPL; Moore to Alice, 22 Oct. 1863, SC 2757 Moore, Troy, ALPL; Shumway to Hattie, 2 Mar. 1863, SC 1388 Shumway, Z. Payson, ALPL; Shumway to Hattie, 6 Apr. 1863, SC 1388 Shumway, Z. Payson, ALPL; Shumway to Hattie, 12 May 1863, SC 1388 Shumway, Z. Payson, ALPL; Steele to Wife, 31 July 1863, Steele, Robert, "Papers, 1827–1891," Wis Mss 113S, WHS; Robert Steele to Father, 9 Apr. 1863, Steele, Robert, "Papers, 1827–1891," Wis Mss 113S, WHS; Taylor to Wife, 18 Sept. 1863, Thomas Thomson Taylor papers, 1861–1865, Mss 7, OHC; Wayne to Ellen, 20 Oct. 1861, SC 2824 Wayne, Harley, ALPL; Wills to Sister, 9 Apr. 1864, in Wills, *Army Life of an Illinois Soldier,* 223; Wood to Wife, 10 Dec. 1863, Edward Jesup Wood Papers, IHS; Wood to Wife, 13 May 1864, Edward Jesup Wood Papers, IHS; Wood to Wife, 19 May 1864, Edward Jesup Wood Papers, IHS; Ritner to Emeline, 15 Mar. 1863, in Larimer, *Love and Valor,* 134; Ewing to Parents, 24 Apr. 1863, SC 2667 Ewing, Alexander K., ALPL; Ritner to Wife, 2 Aug. 1863, in Larimer, *Love and Valor,* 202; Loudon to Hannah, 15 May 1862, DeWitt Clinton Loudon Papers, Mss 610, OHC; Ritner to Wife, 12 Jan. 1865, in Larimer, *Love and Valor,* 409; Ritner to Wife, 4 Oct. 1863, in Larimer, *Love and Valor,* 217; Latham to Wife, 11 May 1863, SC 895 Latham, R. B., ALPL; Wood to Wife, 18 Dec. 1862, Edward Jesup Wood Papers, IHS; Harlow M. Waller to Slott, 23 Sept. 1862, "Harlow M. & Henrietta Waller Letters, 1861–1869," SC 2952, WHS; Campbell, *The Union Must Stand,* 120; Hildt to Parents, 17 May 1864, Typescripts of George H. Hildt letters and diary, 1862–1865, vol. 548, OHC.

111. Ritner to Wife, 21 May 1864, in Larimer, *Love and Valor,* 273.

112. Ritner to Wife, 21 May 1864, in Larimer, *Love and Valor,* 273.

113. Ritner to Wife, 31 July 1864, in Larimer, *Love and Valor,* 326.

114. Ritner to Emeline, 25 Nov. 1862, in Larimer, *Love and Valor,* 67; Ritner to Emeline, 3 Jan. 1863, in Larimer, *Love and Valor,* 95; Ritner to Emeline, 24 Jan. 1863, in Larimer, *Love and Valor,* 108; Ritner to Wife, 2 July 1864, in Larimer, *Love and Valor,* 301; Ritner to Wife, 25 July 1864, in Larimer, *Love and Valor,* 316; Ritner to Wife, 11 Sept. 1864, in Larimer, *Love and Valor,* 351; Ritner to Wife, 13 Oct. 1864, in Larimer, *Love and Valor,* 373; Ritner to Wife, 7 Nov. 1864, in Larimer, *Love and Valor,* 379; Ritner to Wife, 17 Nov. 1863, in Larimer, *Love and Valor,* 237–38;

NOTES TO PAGES 40–43   239

Ritner to Wife, 31 Jan. 1865, in Larimer, *Love and Valor,* 421; Ritner to Wife, 7 July 1864, in Larimer, *Love and Valor,* 304; Ritner to Emeline, 19 Dec. 1862, in Larimer, *Love and Valor,* 80.

115. While it would no doubt be interesting and eminently worthwhile to explore the perspectives of officers' family members on the home front, doing so here would have been beyond the scope of this book, so that topic is one of many left for future researchers. Any scholars undertaking such a project should be warned of the practical difficulties of finding appropriate sources. Letters sent *from* officers are vastly more common in archival collections than letters *to* them. Perhaps this is because letters to family could be stored safely at home, whereas the rigors of military campaigning meant that letters to officers were much more susceptible to being lost or damaged.

3. PRAYER AND PROVIDENCE

1. Ephraim Brown to Drusilla, 15 Feb. 1863, Ephraim Brown Papers, Mss 76, OHC.

2. Campbell, *The Union Must Stand,* 12; DeWitt Clinton Loudon to Hannah, 17 Apr. 1864, DeWitt Clinton Loudon Papers, Mss 610, OHC; Jacob B. Ritner to Emeline Ritner, 7 May 1863, in Larimer, *Love and Valor,* 166; Oliver A. Bridgford to Eliza, 3 Feb. 1862, Oliver A. Bridgford Papers; Bridgford to Eliza, 5 Feb. 1862, Oliver A. Bridgford Papers; Bridgford to Eliza, 25 Mar. 1862, Oliver A. Bridgford Papers; Bridgford to Eliza, 1 Dec. 1861, Oliver A. Bridgford Papers; James Compton, "The Second Division of the 16th Army Corps, in the Atlanta Campaign," in *MOLLUS,* 30:121; Thomas T. Taylor, "Diary," Roll 21, MIC 17 Civil War Collection, OHC; Edward Jesup Wood to Wife, 29 May 1864, Edward Jesup Wood Papers, IHS; Wills, *Army Life of an Illinois Soldier,* 153; Charles W. Wills to Sister, 16 Jan. 1863, in Wills, *Army Life of an Illinois Soldier,* 148; Henry F. Hole to Sister, 25 Mar. 1862, SC 2427 Hole, Henry F., ALPL.

3. Robert Steele to Wife, 3 Dec. 1862, "Papers, 1827–1891," Wis Mss 113S, WHS.

4. Wood to Wife, 8 May 1863, Edward Jesup Wood Papers, IHS.

5. Troy Moore to Alice, 21 Oct. 1863, SC 2757 Moore, Troy, ALPL.

6. Zachariah Dean to Emily, 19 June 1863, Zachariah Dean Papers, IHS; Warren Gray, "Diary, 1862–1863," SC 531, WHS; Brown to Drusilla, 20 Jan. 1863, Ephraim Brown Papers, Mss 76, OHC; James Balfour to William Balfour, 4 Apr. 1862, SC 2451 Balfour, James, ALPL; Steele to Wife, 17 Mar. 1863, "Papers, 1827–1891," Wis Mss 113S, WHS; Steele to Wife, 14 Feb. 1863, "Papers, 1827–1891," Wis Mss 113S, WHS; Steele to Wife, 4 Jan. 1863, "Papers, 1827–1891," Wis Mss 113S, WHS; Steele to Wife, 22 Dec. 1862, "Papers, 1827–1891," Wis Mss 113S, WHS; Moore to Alice, 8 Oct. 1863, SC 2757 Moore, Troy, ALPL; Thomas Thomson Taylor to Wife, 29 July 1863, Thomas Thomson Taylor papers, 1861–1865, Mss 7, OHC; Net Hymnal, "God Moves in a Mysterious Way," accessed 21 June 2016, http://cyberhymnal.org/; Taylor to Wife, 23 Aug. 1863, Thomas Thomson Taylor papers, 1861–1865, Mss 7, OHC; Wood to Wife, 21 Apr. 1863, Edward Jesup Wood Papers, IHS; Brown to Drusilla, 21 Dec. 1862, Ephraim Brown Papers, Mss 76, OHC; Wood to Wife, 13 Dec. 1862, Edward Jesup Wood Papers, IHS; Z. Payson Shumway to Hattie, 8 May 1862, SC 1388 Shumway, Z. Payson, ALPL; Steele to Wife, 31 July 1863, "Papers, 1827–1891," Wis Mss 113S, WHS; Benjamin Grierson to Alice, 29 Dec. 1861, Grierson Box 1, Benjamin Grierson Family Papers, ALPL; Taylor to Wife, 23 Sept. 1863, Thomas Thomson Taylor papers, 1861–1865, Mss 7, OHC; Brown to Drusilla, 15 Feb. 1863, Ephraim Brown Papers, Mss 76, OHC; Sylvester Gridley Beckwith to Wife, 25 Mar. 1863, SC 2078 Beckwith, Sylvester Gridley, ALPL.

7. Jackson, *The Colonel's Diary,* 211.

8. Loudon to Hannah, 28–30 Apr. 1862, DeWitt Clinton Loudon Papers, Mss 610, OHC; Loudon to Hannah, 25 May 1864, DeWitt Clinton Loudon Papers, Mss 610, OHC; Robert Steele to Father and Mother, 5, 14, 15 Jan. 1863, "Papers, 1827–1891," Wis Mss 113S, WHS; Benjamin H. Grierson to Alice, 7 Sept. 1862, Grierson Box 1, Benjamin Grierson Family Papers, ALPL; Azel Grover to Aurelia, 3 July 1863, "Letters, 1858, 1861–1865," SC 1153, WHS; Wills, *Army Life of an Illinois Soldier,* 133, 159; Henry A. Kircher to Mother, 3 Jan. 1863, in Hess, *A German in the Yankee*

240   NOTES TO PAGES 43–45

Fatherland, 48; Owen Stuart to Wife, 17 Dec. 1864, SC 2406 Stuart, Owen, ALPL; Warren Gray, "Diary, 1862–1863," SC 531, WHS; Kircher to Mother, 26 May 1863, in Hess, *A German in the Yankee Fatherland*, 101; Erasmus D. Ward to Sister, 12 Apr. 1862, SC 3110 Ward, Erasmus D., ALPL; Friedrich Martens to Dear Ones, 24 Sept. 1862, in Kamphoefner and Helbich, *Germans in the Civil War*, 321; Steele to Wife, 24 May 1863, "Papers, 1827–1891," Wis Mss 113S, WHS; Campbell, *The Union Must Stand*, 10; Alphonso Barto to Sister, 4 Oct. 1863, SC 2627 Barto, Alphonso, ALPL; Thomas T. Taylor, "Diary," Roll 21, MIC 17 Civil War Collection, OHC; Luther Cowan to Mollie, 5 May 1863, Letters and Diary of Luther H. Cowan, Wis Mss 218S, WHS; Cowan to Mollie, 14 Jan. 1863, Wis Mss 218S, WHS; Jacob Ritner to Emeline, 22 Dec. 1862, in Larimer, *Love and Valor*, 83; Wood to Wife, 25 May 1863, Edward Jesup Wood Papers, IHS; Charles Wills to Sister, Cape Girardeau, 9 Feb. 1862, in Wills, *Army Life of an Illinois Soldier*, 61; Jacob B. Ritner to Wife, 20 Aug. 1864, in Larimer, *Love and Valor*, 339; Jackson, *The Colonel's Diary*, 144; John Hancock to Henry, 13 Apr. 1862, "Colonel John Hancock Papers, 1862–1889," File 1862 Feb. 14, WHS; Martens to Dear Ones, 19 Sept. 1863, in Kamphoefner and Helbich, *Germans in the Civil War*, 323; Henry Miller Culbertson to Mother, Brother, and Sister, 10 Apr. 1862, "Civil War Letters," 1861–1864, Wis Mss 216S, WHS; Jacob B. Ritner to Emeline, 13 Jan. 1863, in Larimer, *Love and Valor*, 102; Ritner to Emeline, 25 May 1863, in Larimer, *Love and Valor*, 168–69; Ritner to Wife, 11 Sept. 1864, in Larimer, *Love and Valor*, 351–52; Charles Wills to Sister, 16 Apr. 1865, in Wills, *Army Life of an Illinois Soldier*, 371; Campbell, *The Union Must Stand*, 98; Henry Ankeny to Brother, Sister, and Mother, 9 Apr. 1862, in Frank and Reaves, *"Seeing the Elephant,"* 125; Ritner to Wife, 7 June 1864, in Larimer, *Love and Valor*, 284–85; Stuart to Wife, 17 Dec. 1864, SC 2406 Stuart, Owen, ALPL.

9. "Diary of Z. Payson Shumway," SC 1388 Shumway, Z. Payson, ALPL.

10. Stuart to Wife, 20 Jan. 1865, SC 2406 Stuart, Owen, ALPL.

11. Loudon to Hannah, 25 May 1864, DeWitt Clinton Loudon Papers, Mss 610, OHC.

12. Loudon to Hannah, 6 Mar. 1862, DeWitt Clinton Loudon Papers, Mss 610, OHC; Ritner to Emeline, 7 May 1863, in Larimer, *Love and Valor*, 166; Ritner to Wife, 4 Jan. 1865, in Larimer, *Love and Valor*, 402–3; Shumway to Hattie, 2 Nov. 1862, SC 1388 Shumway, Z. Payson, ALPL; Benjamin Franklin Best to Wife, 6 Jan. 1862, SC 2478 Best, Benjamin Franklin, ALPL; Steele to Wife, 31 Jan. 1863, "Papers, 1827–1891," Wis Mss 113S, WHS; Steele to Wife, 25 Apr. 1863, "Papers, 1827–1891," Wis Mss 113S, WHS; Steele to Wife, 3 Mar. 1863, "Papers, 1827–1891," Wis Mss 113S, WHS; Grierson to Alice, 18 May 1861, Grierson Box 1, Benjamin Grierson Family Papers, ALPL; Wood to Wife, 21 Nov. 1863, Edward Jesup Wood Papers, HIS; Grierson to Alice, 8 July 1862, Grierson Box 1, Benjamin Grierson Family Papers, ALPL.

13. Campbell, *The Union Must Stand*, 120.

14. "Diary of Z. Payson Shumway," SC 1388 Shumway, Z. Payson, ALPL; Grierson to Alice, 15 Dec. 1861, Grierson Box 1, Benjamin Grierson Family Papers, ALPL; Best to Wife, 2 Sept. 1861, SC 2478 Best, Benjamin Franklin, ALPL; Dean to Emily, 30 Apr. 1863, Zachariah Dean Papers, IHS; Miller, *Struggle for the Life of the Republic*, 146; Bridgford to Eliza, 20 July 1862, Oliver A. Bridgford Papers; Bridgford to Eliza, 27 July 1862, Oliver A. Bridgford Papers; Bridgford to Eliza, 7 July 1862, Oliver A. Bridgford Papers; Campbell, *The Union Must Stand*, 4, 5, 12, 13, 15, 16, 19, 20, 42, 43, 47, 66, 67, 71, 75–77, 79, 82, 84–87, 102, 105, 106, 109, 117, 119, 122, 123, 126, 144; Shumway to Hattie, 3 Oct. 1863, SC 1388 Shumway, Z. Payson, ALPL; Wood to Wife, 24 Apr. 1864, Edward Jesup Wood Papers, IHS; Wood to Wife, 1 Jan. 1865, Edward Jesup Wood Papers, IHS; Erasmus D. Ward to Mary, 28 Oct. 1862, SC 3110 Ward, Erasmus D., ALPL; Wills, *Army Life of an Illinois Soldier*, 223; Stockton, *War Diary*, 2–3, 8. Loudon to Hannah, 19 Oct. 1862, DeWitt Clinton Loudon Papers, Mss 610, OHC; Grierson to Alice, 10 Aug. 1862, Grierson Box 1, Benjamin Grierson Family Papers, ALPL; Grierson to Alice, 6 July 1862, Grierson Box 1, Benjamin Grierson Family Papers, ALPL.

15. Bridgford to Eliza, 1 Dec. 1861, Oliver A. Bridgford Papers.

16. Moore to Alice, 21 Oct. 1863, SC 2757 Moore, Troy, ALPL.

17. Shumway to Hattie, 18 May 1862, SC 1388 Shumway, Z. Payson, ALPL.

18. Campbell, *The Union Must Stand*, 40; Steele to Wife, 14 Feb. 1863, "Papers, 1827–1891," Wis Mss 113S, WHS; Stockton, *War Diary*, 2–3, 6–7, 9–10, 17; Rood, *Story of the Service*

of Company E, 220–21; Miller, *Struggle for the Life of the Republic,* 213–14; "Diary of Z. Payson Shumway," SC 1388 Shumway, Z. Payson, ALPL; Loudon to Hannah, 2 Nov. 1862, DeWitt Clinton Loudon Papers, Mss 610, OHC; Warren Gray, "Diary, 1862–1863," SC 531, WHS; Stockton, *War Diary,* 5; Charles W. Stanton to Mr. Day, 5 Feb. 1863, SC 2379 Joshua Day Family, ALPL; Ritner to Emeline, 1 Feb. 1863, in Larimer, *Love and Valor,* 111; Shumway to Hattie, 16 Nov. 1862, SC 1388 Shumway, Z. Payson, ALPL; Campbell, *The Union Must Stand,* 10; Ritner to Emeline, 8 Feb. 1863, in Larimer, *Love and Valor,* 114–15.

19. Howard, *History of the 124th Regiment Illinois Infantry Volunteers,* 402–3.

20. Howard, *History of the 124th Regiment Illinois Infantry Volunteers,* 395–98, 400, 401, 408, 414.

21. Campbell, *The Union Must Stand,* 77.

22. Grierson to Alice, 18 May 1861, Grierson Box 1, Benjamin Grierson Family Papers, ALPL; Ritner to Emeline, 16 May 1861, in Larimer, *Love and Valor,* 20; Kircher to Mother, 6 Sept. 1863, in Hess, *A German in the Yankee Fatherland,* 119; Luther Howard Cowan to Molly, 5 Oct. 1862, Letters and Diary of Luther H. Cowan, Wis Mss 218S, WHS; Campbell, *The Union Must Stand,* 25, 41, 46; Ritner to Wife, 2 July 1864, in Larimer, *Love and Valor,* 300–301; Henry Otis Dwight, "My War Experiences," Henry Otis Dwight Papers (Microform), 1861–1900, Mic 127, OHC; Martens to Dear Ones, 24 Sept. 1862, in Kamphoefner and Helbich, *Germans in the Civil War,* 322; Robert Steele to Sam, 23 Jan. 1865, "Papers, 1827–1891," Wis Mss 113S, WHS.

23. Steele to Wife, 31 July 1863, "Papers, 1827–1891," Wis Mss 113S, WHS.

24. Beckwith to Wife, 25 Mar. 1863, SC 2078 Beckwith, Sylvester Gridley, ALPL.

25. Beckwith to Wife, 25 Mar. 1863, SC 2078 Beckwith, Sylvester Gridley, ALPL.

26. Beckwith to Wife, 25 Mar. 1863, SC 2078 Beckwith, Sylvester Gridley, ALPL.

27. Sylvester Gridley Beckwith to Dear & beloved wife & children, 6 Apr. 1863, SC 2078 Beckwith, Sylvester Gridley, ALPL.

28. Bridgford to Eliza, 21 Feb. 1862, Oliver A. Bridgford Papers; Loudon to Hannah, 1 Jan. 1863, DeWitt Clinton Loudon Papers, Mss 610, OHC; Ritner to Wife, 4 Jan. 1865, in Larimer, *Love and Valor,* 402–3; Best to Wife, 10 Nov. 1861, SC 2478 Best, Benjamin Franklin, ALPL.

29. Friedrich Martens to Most Dearly Beloved Parents, 3 Feb. 1862, in Kamphoefner and Helbich, *Germans in the Civil War,* 320.

30. Zachariah Dean to E. J. Dean, 26 Jan. 1863, Zachariah Dean Papers, IHS.

31. Steele to Wife, 8 Feb. 1863, "Papers, 1827–1891," Wis Mss 113S, WHS.

32. Ritner to Emeline, 23 May 1863, in Larimer, *Love and Valor,* 170; Campbell, *The Union Must Stand,* 78–79; Hymnary.org, accessed 20 June 2016, http://www.hymnary.org/text/ when_shall_we_meet_again_meet_neer_to_se; Grierson to Alice, 22 Jan. 1862, Grierson Box 1, Benjamin Grierson Family Papers, ALPL; Stockton, *War Diary,* 16; Kircher to Mother, 12–13 Sept. 1862, in Hess, *A German in the Yankee Fatherland,* 23; Kircher to Mother, 18 Nov. 1863, in Hess, *A German in the Yankee Fatherland,* 139; Stuart to Wife, 17 Jan. 1865, SC 2406 Stuart, Owen, ALPL; Taylor to Wife, 29 July 1863, Thomas Thomson Taylor papers, 1861–1865. Mss 7, OHC; *The British Controversialist, and Literary Magazine,* 158; Steele to Wife, 3 Dec. 1862, "Papers, 1827–1891," Wis Mss 113S, WHS.

33. Charles C. Ammack to Brother and Sister, 31 Jan. 1863, Ammack and Howland Family Letters, Wis Mss 123S, WHS.

34. Ammack to Brother and Sister, 31 Jan. 1863, Ammack and Howland Family Letters, Wis Mss 123S, WHS.

35. Ammack to Brother and Sister, 31 Jan. 1863, Ammack and Howland Family Letters, Wis Mss 123S, WHS.

36. Ammack to Brother and Sister, 31 Jan. 1863, Ammack and Howland Family Letters, Wis Mss 123S, WHS.

37. Ammack to Brother and Sister, 16 Feb. 1863, Ammack and Howland Family Letters, Wis Mss 123S, WHS.

38. Henry Giesey Ankeny to Wife, 21 Sept. 1861, in Cox, *Kiss Josey for Me!,* 28–29.

39. Ankeny to Wife, 21 Sept. 1861, in Cox, *Kiss Josey for Me!,* 29.

40. Ankeny to Wife, 21 Sept. 1861, in Cox, *Kiss Josey for Me!,* 29.

242   NOTES TO PAGES 48–54

41. Ankeny to Wife, 21 Sept. 1861, in Cox, *Kiss Josey for Me!*, 30.

42. "A Ritual Phrase Used by Freemasons," Wikipedia, "So Mote It Be," accessed 6 June 2017, https://en.wikipedia.org/wiki/So_mote_it_be.

43. Henry Giesey Ankeny to Tina, 22 Sept. 1861, in Cox, *Kiss Josey for Me!*, 30–31.

44. Ankeny to Tina, 22 Sept. 1861, in Cox, *Kiss Josey for Me!*, 30–31.

45. Ankeny to Tina, 23 Sept. 1861, in Cox, *Kiss Josey for Me!*, 32–33.

46. Shumway to Hattie, 13 Apr. 1862, SC 1388 Shumway, Z. Payson, ALPL.

47. Wood to Wife, 25 May 1864, Edward Jesup Wood Papers, IHS.

48. DeWitt Clinton Loudon to Dr. J. W. Gordon, 31 July 1862, DeWitt Clinton Loudon Papers, Mss 610, OHC.

49. "Diary of Z. Payson Shumway," SC 1388 Shumway, Z. Payson, ALPL; Loudon to Hannah, 28 Oct. 1862, DeWitt Clinton Loudon Papers, Mss 610, OHC.

50. Campbell, *The Union Must Stand*, 65.

51. Campbell, *The Union Must Stand*, 131.

52. Campbell, *The Union Must Stand*, 131.

53. Ritner to Emeline, 7 June 1864, in Larimer, *Love and Valor*, 286.

54. Ritner to Emeline, 7 June 1864, in Larimer, *Love and Valor*, 286.

55. Ritner to Emeline, 7 July 1864, in Larimer, *Love and Valor*, 303.

56. Ritner to Emeline, 7 July 1864, in Larimer, *Love and Valor*, 303.

57. Ritner to Emeline, 7 July 1864, in Larimer, *Love and Valor*, 303.

58. Jacob B. Ritner to Ma [mother-in-law Eleanor Bereman], 14 Aug. 1864, in Larimer, *Love and Valor*, 335.

4. A GREAT BIG HEART

1. Rood, *Story of the Service of Company E*, 130–31.

2. "From the Lead Mine Regiment," *Galena Daily Advertiser*, 6 June 1862; Henry Ankeny to Wife, 11 Dec. 1863, in Cox, *Kiss Josey for Me!*, 198; "Personal," *Galena Daily Advertiser*, 8 Oct. 1861; "The Regiment," *Galena Daily Advertiser*, 12 Oct. 1861; "Clothing for the Regiment," *Galena Daily Advertiser*, 18 Oct. 1861; "Independent Lead Mine Regiment," *Galena Daily Advertiser*, 2 Nov. 1861; Edward Jesup Wood to Wife, 11 Apr. 1864, Edward Jesup Wood Papers, IHS; Wood to Wife, 28 June 1864, Edward Jesup Wood Papers, IHS; Wood to Wife, 1 June 1863, Edward Jesup Wood Papers, IHS; Stockton, *War Diary*, 7–9; Howard, *History of the 124th Regiment Illinois Infantry Volunteers*, 19–21, 68; Hart, *History of the Fortieth Illinois Inf.*, 31, 67, 109–10, 117–18; "Diary of Lieut. Anthony B. Burton, Commanding 5th Ohio Independent Battery, from May 18, to July 4, 1863, Inclusive," SC 2401 Burton, Anthony B.; ALPL; Charles A. Willison to Sister, 1 July 1863, 76th Ohio Volunteer Infantry Correspondence, Vfm 4626, OHC; "Diary of John A. Griffin," Griffin Box 1, Folder 2 BV, Griffin, John Alexander, ALPL; Crooker, Nourse, and Brown, *Story of the Fifty-Fifth Regiment*, 31; Thomas Thomson Taylor to Wife, 31 Aug. 1863, Thomas Thomson Taylor papers, 1861–1865, Mss 7, OHC; Harley Wayne to W. H. Alden, 8 Nov. 1861, SC 2824 Wayne, Harley, ALPL; Wills, *Army Life of an Illinois Soldier*, 362; "A Fine Gift Worthily Bestowed," *Galena Daily Advertiser*, 20 Nov. 1861; Jackson, *The Colonel's Diary*, 97, 129; Jacob B. Ritner to Emeline, 15 Mar. 1863, in Larimer, *Love and Valor*, 133–34; Taylor to Wife, 26 July 1863, Thomas Thomson Taylor papers, 1861–1865, Mss 7, OHC; Taylor to Wife, 29 July 1863, Thomas Thomson Taylor papers, 1861–1865, Mss 7, OHC; Miller, *Struggle for the Life of the Republic*, 143; Thomas T. Taylor, "Diary," Roll 21, Mic 17 Civil War Collection, OHC; Jacob B. Ritner to Wife, 7 June 1864, in Larimer, *Love and Valor*, 286; Ritner to Wife, 19 Sept. 1864, in Larimer, *Love and Valor*, 361; Luther Cowan Diary, Letters and Diary of Luther H. Cowan, Wis Mss 218S, WHS; Benjamin Grierson to Alice, 4 July 1862, Grierson Box 1, Benjamin Grierson Family Papers, ALPL; DeWitt Clinton Loudon to Hannah, 9 July 1862, DeWitt Clinton Loudon Papers, Mss 610, OHC; Loudon to Hannah, 23 Jan. 1863, DeWitt Clinton Loudon Papers, Mss 610, OHC; Loudon to Hannah, 17 Jan. 1864, DeWitt Clinton Loudon Papers, Mss 610, OHC; Loudon to Hannah, 25 Apr. 1864, DeWitt Clinton Loudon Papers, Mss 610, OHC; Morris, Hartwell, and

NOTES TO PAGES 54–56 243

Kuykendall, *History 31st Regiment Illinois Volunteers*, 19; Warren Gray, "Diary," 1862–1863, SC 531, WHS; Alphonso Barto to Sister, 21 June 1862, SC 2627 Barto, Alphonso, ALPL; Loudon to Hannah, 23 June 1862, DeWitt Clinton Loudon Papers, Mss 610, OHC; Charles Wills to Sister, 7 Mar. 1863, in Wills, *Army Life of an Illinois Soldier*, 160; Luther H. Cowan to Harriet, 7 Mar. 1862, Letters and Diary of Luther H. Cowan, Wis Mss 218S, WHS; Ritner to Wife, 15 June 1863, in Larimer, *Love and Valor*, 187; Wood to Wife, 8 May 1863, Edward Jesup Wood Papers, IHS; Wood to Wife, 2 Aug. 1863, Edward Jesup Wood Papers, IHS.

3. Miller, *Struggle for the Life of the Republic*, 197–98.

4. Wood to Wife, 11 Apr. 1864, Edward Jesup Wood Papers, IHS.

5. Cowan to Harriet, 19 Feb. 1863, Letters and Diary of Luther H. Cowan, Wis Mss 218S, WHS.

6. Luther H. Cowan to Molly, 6 May 1862, Letters and Diary of Luther H. Cowan, Wis Mss 218S, WHS; Cowan to Harriet, 27 Nov. 1862, Letters and Diary of Luther H. Cowan, Wis Mss 218S, WHS; Cowan to Molly, 5 Oct. 1862, Letters and Diary of Luther H. Cowan, Wis Mss 218S, WHS; William VanMeter, "What I Know of the Life of John N. Cromwell, Colonel of the 47th Regiment of Illinois Vol. Infantry," SC 357 Cromwell, John, ALPL; Wills, *Army Life of an Illinois Soldier*, 232.

7. Robert Steele to Father and Mother, 18 Dec. 1862, "Papers, 1827–1891," Wis Mss 113S, WHS.

8. Henry Miller Culbertson to Mother, Brother, and Sister, 5 Aug. 1863, "Civil War Letters," 1861–1864, Wis Mss 216S, WHS.

9. Robert J. Whittleton to Col. Nasmith, 15 Aug. 1863, in Nasmith, Samuel J., "Letters," 1861–1863, Wis Mss 66S, WHS.

10. George Harvey to Wife, 13 Jan. 1862, Captain George Harvey Papers, his.

11. Charles C. Ammack to Brother and Sister, 31 Jan. 1863, Ammack and Howland Family Letters, Wis Mss 123S, WHS; Ammack to Brother and Sister, 21 Mar. 1863, Ammack and Howland Family Letters, Wis Mss 123S, WHS; Henry G. Ankeny to Wife, 31 Jan. 1863, in Cox, *Kiss Josey for Me!*, 125; Henry G. Ankeny to Tina, 20 Feb. 1863, in Cox, *Kiss Josey for Me!*, 131; Ankeny to Wife, 28 Feb. 1863, in Cox, *Kiss Josey for Me!*, 134; Ankeny to Wife, 26 Dec. 1863, in Cox, *Kiss Josey for Me!*, 203; Cowan to Harriet, 4 Jan. 1862, Letters and Diary of Luther H. Cowan, Wis Mss 218S, WHS; Cowan to Harriet, 4 Feb. 1862, Letters and Diary of Luther H. Cowan, Wis Mss 218S, WHS; Barto to Sister, 5 May 1862, SC 2627 Barto, Alphonso, ALPL; Robert B. Latham to Wife, 11 May 1863, SC 895 Latham, R. B., ALPL; Samuel J. Nasmith to Louisa, 19 July 1863, "Letters," 1861–1863, Wis Mss 66S, WHS; Culbertson to Mother, Brother, and Sister, 8 Aug. 1863, "Civil War Letters," 1861–1864, Wis Mss 216S, WHS; Stockton, *War Diary*, 8; Jackson, *The Colonel's Diary*, 132, 138, 144, 172; Harley Wayne to Ellen, 13 July 1861, SC 2824 Wayne, Harley, ALPL; Robert Steele to Wife, 8 Feb. 1863, "Papers, 1827–1891," Wis Mss 113S, WHS; Ritner to Emeline, 24 Jan. 1863, in Larimer, *Love and Valor*, 107; Warren Gray, "Diary," 1862–1863, SC 531, WHS; Cowan to Harriet, 2 Nov. 1862, Letters and Diary of Luther H. Cowan, Wis Mss 218S, WHS; Wills, *Army Life of an Illinois Soldier*, 288.

12. Robert Steele to Father, 28 Jan. 1863, "Papers, 1827–1891," Wis Mss 113S, WHS.

13. Ankeny to Tina, 8 Feb. 1863, in Cox, *Kiss Josey for Me!*, 128.

14. Jackson, *The Colonel's Diary*, 119.

15. Stockton, *War Diary*, 2.

16. Ammack to Brother and Sister, 16 Feb. 1863, Ammack and Howland Family Letters, Wis Mss 123S, WHS.

17. Ammack to Brother and Sister, 16 Feb. 1863, Ammack and Howland Family Letters, Wis Mss 123S, WHS.

18. Wood to Wife, 16 Aug. 1863, Edward Jesup Wood Papers, IHS; Wayne to Ellen, 22 Dec. 1861, SC 2824 Wayne, Harley, ALPL; Jacob Ritner to Emeline, 15 Feb. 1863, in Larimer, *Love and Valor*, 118; Ritner to Emeline, 22 Feb. 1863, in Larimer, *Love and Valor*, 121; Ritner to Emeline," 1 Mar. 1863, in Larimer, *Love and Valor*, 123; Whittleton to Col. Nasmith, 15 Aug. 1863, in Nasmith, Samuel J., "Letters," 1861–1863, Wis Mss 66S, WHS; Wayne to Ellen, 18 Oct. 1861, SC 2824 Wayne, Harley, ALPL; Wayne to Ellen, 23 Sept. 1861, SC 2824 Wayne, Harley, ALPL.

NOTES TO PAGES 56–62

19. Cowan to Harriet, 1 Feb. 1862, Letters and Diary of Luther H. Cowan, Wis Mss 218S, WHS.

20. Loudon to Hannah, 1 Jan. 1863, DeWitt Clinton Loudon Papers, Mss 610, OHC.

21. Loudon to Hannah, 11 Apr. 1864, DeWitt Clinton Loudon Papers, Mss 610, OHC.

22. Z. Payson Shumway to Hattie, 17 Sept. 1863, SC 1388 Shumway, Z. Payson, ALPL; Henry A. Kircher to Mother, 30 Jan. 1863, in Hess, *A German in the Yankee Fatherland*, 62; Cowan to Harriet, 1 Mar. 1862, Letters and Diary of Luther H. Cowan, Wis Mss 218S, WHS; Cowan to Harriet, 23 Mar. 1862, Letters and Diary of Luther H. Cowan, Wis Mss 218S, WHS; Thomas T. Taylor, "Diary," Roll 21, Mic 17 Civil War Collection, OHC; Wood to Wife, 13 May 1864, Edward Jesup Wood Papers, IHS.

23. James Balfour to William Balfour, 4 Apr. 1862, SC 2451 Balfour, James, ALPL.

24. Wills to Sister, 1 Feb. 1863, in Wills, *Army Life of an Illinois Soldier*, 151.

25. Wills to Sister, 15 Feb. 1863, in Wills, *Army Life of an Illinois Soldier*, 156.

26. Wills to Sister, 22 Sept. 1863, in Wills, *Army Life of an Illinois Soldier*, 188.

27. Wills, *Army Life of an Illinois Soldier*, 246, 328, 333; Wills to Sister, 5 Mar. 1863, in Wills, *Army Life of an Illinois Soldier*, 159–60; Wills to Sister, 26 Sept. 1863, in Wills, *Army Life of an Illinois Soldier*, 191; Stockton, *War Diary*, 2, 6, 17.

28. Ankeny to Wife, 28 Nov. 1863, in Cox, *Kiss Josey for Me!*, 194–95.

29. Ankeny to Wife, 28 Nov. 1863, in Cox, *Kiss Josey for Me!*, 194–95.

30. Ankeny to Wife, 28 Nov. 1863, in Cox, *Kiss Josey for Me!*, 195.

31. Ankeny to Wife, 2 Dec. 1863, in Cox, *Kiss Josey for Me!*, 196–97.

32. Ankeny to Wife, 22 Aug. 1864, in Cox, *Kiss Josey for Me!*, 237–38.

33. Vail, *Company K, of the 16th Wisconsin*, 7.

34. Campbell, *The Union Must Stand*, 79.

35. Alexander Ewing to Parents, 18 Mar. 1863, SC 2667 Ewing, Alexander K., ALPL.

36. Force, "Personal Recollections of the Vicksburg Campaign," in in *MOLLUS*, 1:305–6.

37. Force, "Personal Recollections of the Vicksburg Campaign," in *MOLLUS*, 1:305–6.

38. Jacob Ritner to Wife, 26 June 1863, in Larimer, *Love and Valor*, 189.

39. Ritner to Wife, 17 Nov. 1863, in Larimer, *Love and Valor*, 240.

40. Wayne to Ellen, 11 May 1861, SC 2824 Wayne, Harley, ALPL.

41. Crooker, Nourse, and Brown, *Story of the Fifty-Fifth Regiment*, 374.

42. Loudon to Hannah, 23 Jan. 1863, DeWitt Clinton Loudon Papers, Mss 610, OHC; Jackson, *The Colonel's Diary*, 191, 196–97; Luther Cowan Diary, Letters and Diary of Luther H. Cowan, Wis Mss 218S, WHS; Loudon to Hannah, 1 Jan. 1863, DeWitt Clinton Loudon Papers, Mss 610, OHC; Joseph S. Reynolds to Sister, 29 Mar. 1865, Joseph S. Reynolds Papers, #5060-z, Wilson Library, Univ. of North Carolina at Chapel Hill; Owen Stuart to Wife, 17 Jan. 1865, SC 2406 Stuart, Owen, ALPL.

43. Miller, *Struggle for the Life of the Republic*, 198.

44. Miller, *Struggle for the Life of the Republic*, 198.

45. Grierson to Alice, 29 Mar. 1862, Grierson Box 1, Benjamin Grierson Family Papers, ALPL.

46. Grierson, *A Just and Righteous Cause*, 80.

47. Grierson to Alice, 20 Feb. 1862, Grierson Box 1, Benjamin Grierson Family Papers, ALPL; Grierson to Alice, 7 Mar. 1862, Grierson Box 1, Benjamin Grierson Family Papers, ALPL; Grierson to Alice, 25 Mar. 1862, Grierson Box 1, Benjamin Grierson Family Papers, ALPL.

48. Rood, *Story of the Service of Company E*, 130–31.

49. Rood, *Story of the Service of Company E*, 77.

50. Rood, *Story of the Service of Company E*, 86.

51. Rood, *Story of the Service of Company E*, 114.

52. Rood, *Story of the Service of Company E*, 115.

53. Rood, *Story of the Service of Company E*, 151.

54. Rood, *Story of the Service of Company E*, 87, 85–86, 113–14.

55. Rood, *Story of the Service of Company E*, 321–22.

56. Rood, *Story of the Service of Company E*, 321–22.

57. Rood, *Story of the Service of Company E*, 321–22.

NOTES TO PAGES 62–66 245

58. Wills, *Army Life of an Illinois Soldier*, 189.

59. Ritner to Wife, 13 Oct. 1864, in Larimer, *Love and Valor*, 372.

60. Luther H. Cowan to Family, 1 Oct. 1862, Letters and Diary of Luther H. Cowan, Wis Mss 218S, WHS.

61. Cowan to Family, 1 Oct. 1862, Letters and Diary of Luther H. Cowan, Wis Mss 218S, WHS.

62. "Z. Payson Shumway Diary," SC 1388 Shumway, Z. Payson, ALPL.

63. Barto to Sister, 6 Dec. 1861, SC 2627 Barto, Alphonso, ALPL; Cowan to Harriet, 30 Nov. 1862, Letters and Diary of Luther H. Cowan, Wis Mss 218S, WHS; Wills, *Army Life of an Illinois Soldier*, 128; Wills to Sister, 16 Jan. 1863, in Wills, *Army Life of an Illinois Soldier*, 147–48; Wills, *Army Life of an Illinois Soldier*, 207–8, 214, 374–75; Ritner to Wife, 2 Oct. 1864, in Larimer, *Love and Valor*, 367; Ritner to Wife, 30 Nov. 1862, in Larimer, *Love and Valor*, 71; Ritner to Emeline, 8 Feb. 1863, in Larimer, *Love and Valor*, 114; Ritner to Wife, 23 Oct. 1864, in Larimer, *Love and Valor*, 376–77; Wills to Sister, 15 Mar. 1864, in Wills, *Army Life of an Illinois Soldier*, 218; Cowan to Molly, 18 Jan. 1862, Letters and Diary of Luther H. Cowan, Wis Mss 218S, WHS.

64. Luther Cowan to Molly, 28 June 1862, Letters and Diary of Luther H. Cowan, Wis Mss 218S, WHS.

65. Cowan to Molly, 28 June 1862, Letters and Diary of Luther H. Cowan, Wis Mss 218S, WHS.

66. Cowan to Molly, 28 June 1862, Letters and Diary of Luther H. Cowan, Wis Mss 218S, WHS.

67. Culbertson to Mother, Brother, and Sister, 13 Dec. 1862, "Civil War Letters," 1861–1864, Wis Mss 216S, WHS.

68. Ammack to Brother and Sister, 21 Mar. 1863, Ammack Family, Ammack and Howland Family Letters, Wis Mss 123S, WHS.

69. Henry F. Hole to Sister, 19 Aug. 1861, SC 2427 Hole, Henry F., ALPL.

70. Wills, *Army Life of an Illinois Soldier*, 191–92.

5. THE DAILY GRIND

1. Z. Payson Shumway to Hattie, 14 Feb. 1863, SC 1388 Shumway, Z. Payson, ALPL.

2. Charles W. Wills to Sister, 5 Jan. 1864, in Wills, *Army Life of an Illinois Soldier*, 208.

3. Wills to Sister, 5 Mar. 1863, in Wills, *Army Life of an Illinois Soldier*, 158–59.

4. Luther B. Hunt Diary, vol. 1, Vermont Historical Society, James S. McHenry, "Diary," SC 973 McHenry, James S. ALPL; Ephraim Brown to Drusilla, 15 Feb. 1863, Ephraim Brown Papers, Mss 76, OHC; DeWitt Clinton Loudon to Hannah, 24 Apr. 1862, DeWitt Clinton Loudon Papers, Mss 610, OHC; Loudon to Hannah, 14 Oct. 1862, DeWitt Clinton Loudon Papers, Mss 610, OHC; Loudon to Hannah, 11 Apr. 1864, DeWitt Clinton Loudon Papers, Mss 610, OHC; Shumway to Hattie, 3 Oct. 1863, SC 1388 Shumway, Z. Payson, ALPL; Shumway to Hattie, 17 Sept. 1863, SC 1388 Shumway, Z. Payson, ALPL; Shumway to Hattie, 4 Jan. 1863, SC 1388 Shumway, Z. Payson, ALPL; Stockton, *War Diary*, 2, 6; Jackson, *The Colonel's Diary*, 100; Wills, *Army Life of an Illinois Soldier*, 129, 141, 142, 196, 204, 210–12, 215, 219–20, 224, 226; Shumway to Hattie, 2 Mar. 1863, SC 1388 Shumway, Z. Payson, ALPL; Adam W. McLane to Sister, 12 Dec. 1861, Oliver A. Bridgford Papers; Henry Miller Culbertson to Sister, "Civil War Letters," 1861–1864, Wis Mss 216S, WHS.

5. Henry Otis Dwight, "My War Experiences," Henry Otis Dwight Papers (Microform), 1861–1900, Mic 127, OHC.

6. Dwight, "My War Experiences," Henry Otis Dwight Papers (Microform), 1861–1900, Mic 127, OHC.

7. HDwight, "My War Experiences," Henry Otis Dwight Papers (Microform), 1861–1900, Mic 127, OHC.

246 NOTES TO PAGES 66–67

8. Dwight, "My War Experiences, " Henry Otis Dwight Papers (Microform), 1861–1900, Mic 127, OHC; Shumway to Hattie, 9 Jan. 1862, SC 1388 Shumway, Z. Payson, ALPL.

9. Benjamin H. Grierson to Alice, 5 Jan. 1862, Grierson Box 1, Benjamin Grierson Family Papers, ALPL.

10. Ambrose, *From Shiloh to Savannah*, 9, 13, 16; Charles C. Ammack to Brother and Sister, 2 Dec. 1862, Ammack and Howland Family Letters, Wis Mss 123S, WHS; David McKee Claggett, "Diary," SC 2689 Claggett, David McKee, ALPL; Luther Cowan Diary, Letters and Diary of Luther H. Cowan, Wis Mss 218S, WHS; Henry Miller Culbertson to Mother, Brother, and Sister, 21 Nov. 1863, "Civil War Letters," 1861–1864, Wis Mss 216S, WHS; Wardner, "Reminiscences of a Surgeon," in *MOLLUS*, 12:177; Alexander K. Ewing to Parents, 24 Apr. 1863, SC 2667 Ewing, Alexander K., ALPL; Warren Gray, "Diary," 1862–1863, SC 531, WHS; Grierson to Alice, 31 Dec. 1861, Grierson Box 1, Benjamin Grierson Family Papers, ALPL; Grierson to Alice, 13 Jan. 1862, Grierson Box 1, Benjamin Grierson Family Papers, ALPL; Grierson to Alice, 15 Jan. 1862, Grierson Box 1, Benjamin Grierson Family Papers, ALPL; Grierson to Alice, 26 Jan. 1862, Grierson Box 1, Benjamin Grierson Family Papers, ALPL; Grierson to Alice, 24 Mar. 1862, Grierson Box 1, Benjamin Grierson Family Papers, ALPL; Benjamin H. Grierson to Father and John, 31 May 1862, Grierson Box 1, Benjamin Grierson Family Papers, ALPL; Heafford, "The Army of the Tennessee," in *MOLLUS*, 46:311; Henry F. Hole to Sister, 25 Mar. 1862, SC 2427 Hole, Henry F., ALPL; Luther B. Hunt Diary, vol. 1, Vermont Historical Society; Campbell, *The Union Must Stand*, 66–67, 71, 75, 89; Charles Palmetier to Brother & Sister, 25 Nov. 1862, "Civil War Papers," 1861–1865, Wis Mss 53S, WHS; Robert Steele to Wife, 9 Nov. 1862, "Papers, 1827–1891," Wis Mss 113S, WHS; Owen Stuart to Wife, [date unclear, but since it's written from Savannah it must be late December 1864 or early January 1865], SC 2406 Stuart, Owen, ALPL; Harley Wayne to Ellen, 21 June 1861, SC 2824 Wayne, Harley, ALPL; Wayne to Ellen, 2 Aug. 1861, SC 2824 Wayne, Harley, ALPL; John H. White to Relatives One & All, 3 Nov. 1861, SC 2454 White, John H., ALPL; Edward Jesup Wood to Wife, 18 Dec. 1862, Edward Jesup Wood Papers, IHS; Brown to Drusilla, 20 Oct. 1862, Ephraim Brown Papers, Mss 76, OHC; Brown to Drusilla, 11 Dec. 1862, Ephraim Brown Papers, Mss 76, OHC; Rood, *Story of the Service of Company E*, 35, 42, 79, 97, 146, 489; Loudon to Hannah, 13 Mar. 1862, DeWitt Clinton Loudon Papers, Mss 610, OHC; Loudon to Hannah, 24 Apr. 1862, DeWitt Clinton Loudon Papers, Mss 610, OHC; Loudon to Hannah, 23, 27 June 1862, DeWitt Clinton Loudon Papers, Mss 610, OHC; DeWitt Clinton Loudon to Dr. J. W. Gordon, 31 July 1862, DeWitt Clinton Loudon Papers, Mss 610, OHC; Loudon to Hannah, 8 Oct. 1862, DeWitt Clinton Loudon Papers, Mss 610, OHC; Loudon to Hannah, 14 Oct. 1862, DeWitt Clinton Loudon Papers, Mss 610, OHC; Loudon to Hannah, 2 Nov. 1862, DeWitt Clinton Loudon Papers, Mss 610, OHC; Loudon to Hannah, 5 Nov. 1862, DeWitt Clinton Loudon Papers, Mss 610, OHC; Loudon to Hannah, 11 Apr. 1864, DeWitt Clinton Loudon Papers, Mss 610, OHC; Joseph S. Reynolds to Lottie, 20 Jan. 1865, Joseph S. Reynolds Papers, #5060-z, Wilson Library, Univ. of North Carolina at Chapel Hill; Joseph S. Reynolds to Sarah, 28 Jan. 1865, Joseph S. Reynolds Papers, #5060-z, Wilson Library, Univ. of North Carolina at Chapel Hill; "Diary of Z. Payson Shumway," SC 1388 Shumway, Z. Payson, ALPL; Stockton, *War Diary*, 2–4, 13; Thomas Thomson Taylor to Wife, 15 Aug. 1863, Thomas Thomson Taylor papers, 1861–1865, Mss 7, OHC; Wills, *Army Life of an Illinois Soldier*, 170, 189; Howard, *History of the 124th Regiment Illinois Infantry Volunteers*, 159; Dwight, "My War Experiences," Henry Otis Dwight Papers (Microform), 1861–1900, Mic 127, OHC; Jacob B. Ritner to Wife, 20 Sept. 1863, in Larimer, *Love and Valor*, 209; Ritner to Wife, 19 Sept. 1864, in Larimer, *Love and Valor*, 360–61; Grierson to Alice, 19 Dec. 1861, Grierson Box 1, Benjamin Grierson Family Papers, ALPL; Grierson to Alice, 21 Dec. 1861, Grierson Box 1, Benjamin Grierson Family Papers, ALPL; Grierson to Alice, 23 Dec. 1861, Grierson Box 1, Benjamin Grierson Family Papers, ALPL; Grierson to Alice, 28 Dec. 1861, Grierson Box 1, Benjamin Grierson Family Papers, ALPL; Crooker, Nourse, and Brown, *Story of the Fifty-Fifth Regiment*, 71; Brown to Drusilla, 21 Sept. 1862, Ephraim Brown Papers, Mss 76, OHC; Henry A. Kircher, "Diary of Henry Kircher," Engelmann Kircher Family Papers, ALPL; Morton, "A Boy at Shiloh," in *MOLLUS*, 22:53; Luther H. Cowan to Harriet, 12 July 1862, Letters and Diary of Luther H. Cowan, Wis Mss 218S, WHS.

NOTES TO PAGES 68–69   247

11. Grierson, *A Just and Righteous Cause*, 38.

12. Crooker, Nourse, and Brown, *Story of the Fifty-Fifth Regiment*, 27.

13. Grierson, *A Just and Righteous Cause*, 36, 38, 65–66, 68; Grierson to Alice, 4 June 1862, Grierson Box 1, Benjamin Grierson Family Papers, ALPL; Luther B. Hunt Diary, vol. 1, Vermont Historical Society; "Army Correspondence," *Galena Daily Advertiser*, 6 Dec. 1861; W. H. L. Wallace to Major D. F. Hitt, 1861, Hitt Box 1-1/2, Folder 3, Hitt, Daniel Fletcher, ALPL; Wills, *Army Life of an Illinois Soldier*, 192; Dwight, "My War Experiences," Henry Otis Dwight Papers (Microform), 1861–1900, Mic 127, OHC; "Diary of John Stuber," John Stuber, 1896, Vfm 5942, OHC; Rood, *Story of the Service of Company E*, 73–74; Howard, *History of the 124th Regiment Illinois Infantry Volunteers*, 11; Grierson to Alice, 29 Dec. 1861, Grierson Box 1, Benjamin Grierson Family Papers, ALPL; Crooker, Nourse, and Brown, *Story of the Fifty-Fifth Regiment*, 21, 25, 38–39; Lawrence, "Stuart's Brigade at Shiloh," in *MOLLUS*, 53:493; Morris, Hartwell, and Kuykendall, *History 31st Regiment Illinois Volunteers*, 19–20; Grierson to Alice, 18 May 1861, Grierson Box 1, Benjamin Grierson Family Papers, ALPL; Benjamin Franklin Best to Wife, 7 Oct. 1861, SC 2478 Best, Benjamin Franklin, ALPL; Grierson to Alice, 15 Dec. 1861, Grierson Box 1, Benjamin Grierson Family Papers, ALPL; Grierson to Alice, 18 Dec. 1861, Grierson Box 1, Benjamin Grierson Family Papers, ALPL; Loudon to Hannah, 5 Nov. 1862, DeWitt Clinton Loudon Papers, Mss 610, OHC; Campbell, *The Union Must Stand*, 71; Jacob Ritner to Emeline, 2 Dec. 1862, in Larimer, *Love and Valor*, 72.

14. Howard, *History of the 124th Regiment Illinois Infantry Volunteers*, 12.

15. Cowan to Harriet, 16 Feb. 1863, Letters and Diary of Luther H. Cowan, Wis Mss 218S, WHS.

16. Taylor to Wife, 3 Sept. 1863, Thomas Thomson Taylor papers, 1861–1865, Mss 7, OHC; Thomas T. Taylor, "Diary," Roll 21, MIC 17 Civil War Collection, OHC; Wills, *Army Life of an Illinois Soldier*, 142, 159, 226; Henry Giesey Ankeny to Wife, 29 Mar. 1863, in Cox, *Kiss Josey for Me!*, 141; Ritner to Wife, 2 June 1864, in Larimer, *Love and Valor*, 281; Ritner to Wife, 16 Sept. 1864, in Larimer, *Love and Valor*, 357; Ritner to Wife, 25 Dec. 1864, in Larimer, *Love and Valor*, 395–96; Ritner to Wife, 4 Jan. 1865, in Larimer, *Love and Valor*, 402; Ritner to Wife, 8 Jan. 1865, in Larimer, *Love and Valor*, 404; Stockton, *War Diary*, 12–13; George H. Hildt, "Diary of the Siege of Atlanta, May 28—Oct. 7 1864," Typescripts of George H. Hildt letters and diary, 1862–1865, vol. 548, OHC; Jackson, *The Colonel's Diary*, 160; Loudon to Hannah, 2 Apr. 1862, DeWitt Clinton Loudon Papers, Mss 610, OHC; Warren Gray, "Diary," 1862–1863, SC 531, WHS; William E. Strong, "Report of the Inspector General of Seventeenth Army Corps for Jan. 1863," in Letters and Diary of Luther H. Cowan, Wis Mss 218S, WHS; Grierson to Alice, 21 Dec. 1861, Grierson Box 1, Benjamin Grierson Family Papers, ALPL; Wood to Wife, 17 Apr. 1864, Edward Jesup Wood Papers, IHS; Morris, Hartwell, and Kuykendall, *History 31st Regiment Illinois Volunteers*, 81; untitled article in *Warren Independent*, 19 Nov. 1861, in Letters and Diary of Luther H. Cowan, Wis Mss 218S, WHS; Shumway to Hattie, 17 Sept. 1863, SC 1388 Shumway, Z. Payson, ALPL; Ambrose, *From Shiloh to Savannah*, 53; Alphonso Barto to Sister, 21 June 1862, SC 2627 Barto, Alphonso, ALPL; Benjamin Allen to Assistant Adjutant General Kelton, 1 July 1862, "Civil War Letters," 1861–1863, SC 512, WHS; Harlow M. Waller to Slott, 23 Sept. 1862, "Harlow M. & Henrietta Waller Letters, 1861–1869," SC 2952, WHS; "Diary of Lieut. Anthony B. Burton, Commanding 5th Ohio Independent Battery, from May 18, to July 4, 1863, Inclusive," SC 2401 Burton, Anthony B., ALPL; Henry Miller Culbertson to Brother and Sister, 22 Dec. 1861, "Civil War Letters," 1861–1864, Wis Mss 216S, WHS; Wood to Wife, 24 Apr. 1864, Edward Jesup Wood Papers, IHS; Wood to Wife, 27 July 1864, Edward Jesup Wood Papers, IHS; Ritner to Wife, 2 Oct. 1864, in Larimer, *Love and Valor*, 368.

17. Adjutant-General Lorenzo Thomas, "General Orders No. 49," 3 Aug. 1861, in *War of the Rebellion*, ser. 3, 1:382–83.

18. Adjutant-General Lorenzo Thomas, "General Orders No. 47," 25 July 1861, in *War of the Rebellion*, ser. 3, 1:349; Thomas, "General Orders No. 49," 3 Aug. 1861, in *War of the Rebellion*, ser. 3, 1:382–83; Major General Henry W. Halleck to Brig. General C. F. Smith, 26 Nov. 1861, in *War of the Rebellion*, ser. 1, 7:449; Erasmus D. Ward to Mary, 28 Oct. 1862, SC 3110 Ward, Erasmus D., ALPL; Best to Wife, 6 Jan. 1862, SC 2478 Best, Benjamin Franklin, ALPL; Friedrich

248 NOTES TO PAGES 70–73

Martens to Most Dearly Beloved Parents, 3 Feb. 1862, in Kamphoefner and Helbich, *Germans in the Civil War*, 320.

19. James Monroe Ruggles, "Statement in Writing of Lieut. Col. J. M. Ruggles," SC 1308 Ruggles, J. M., ALPL.

20. Ruggles, "Statement in Writing of Lieut. Col. J. M. Ruggles," SC 1308 Ruggles, J. M., ALPL.

21. Ruggles, "Statement in Writing of Lieut. Col. J. M. Ruggles," SC 1308 Ruggles, J. M., ALPL.

22. Ruggles, "Statement in Writing of Lieut. Col. J. M. Ruggles," SC 1308 Ruggles, J. M., ALPL.

23. Ruggles, "Statement in Writing of Lieut. Col. J. M. Ruggles," SC 1308 Ruggles, J. M., ALPL.

24. Howard, *History of the 124th Regiment Illinois Infantry Volunteers*, 63–64.

25. Howard, *History of the 124th Regiment Illinois Infantry Volunteers*, 64.

26. Howard, *History of the 124th Regiment Illinois Infantry Volunteers*, 64.

27. Howard, *History of the 124th Regiment Illinois Infantry Volunteers*, 65.

28. Bledsoe, *Citizen-Officers*, 45–46, 60, 160; Haughton, *Training, Tactics and Leadership*, 86–88.

29. George H. Hildt to Parents, 20 June 1864, Typescripts of George H. Hildt letters and diary, 1862–1865, vol. 548, OHC; Miller, *Struggle for the Life of the Republic*, 51; Sylvester Gridley Beckwith to Dear & beloved wife & children, 6 Apr. 1863, SC 2078 Beckwith, Sylvester Gridley, ALPL; Oliver A. Bridgford to Eliza, 25 Mar. 1852, Oliver A. Bridgford Papers; Hart, *History of the Fortieth Illinois Inf.*, 72–75; Luther H. Cowan to Molly, 12 Aug. 1862, Letters and Diary of Luther H. Cowan, Wis Mss 218S, WHS; Luther H. Cowan to Mollie, 14 Jan. 1863, Letters and Diary of Luther H. Cowan, Wis Mss 218S, WHS; Luther Cowan Diary, Letters and Diary of Luther H. Cowan, Wis Mss 218S, WHS; Luther H. Cowan to Molly and Harriet, 24 July 1862, Letters and Diary of Luther H. Cowan, Wis Mss 218S, WHS; Culbertson to Mother, Brother, and Sister, 27 May 1864, "Civil War Letters," 1861–1864, Wis Mss 216S, WHS; Ewing to Parents, 8 Dec. 1862, SC 2667 Ewing, Alexander K., ALPL; Ewing to Parents, 15 Mar. 1863, SC 2667 Ewing, Alexander K., ALPL; Ewing to Parents, 22 Mar. 1863, SC 2667 Ewing, Alexander K., ALPL; Ewing to Parents, 28 Feb. 1863, SC 2667 Ewing, Alexander K., ALPL; Ewing to Parents, 4 Jan. 1863, SC 2667 Ewing, Alexander K., ALPL; Ewing to Parents, 14 Feb. 1863, SC 2667 Ewing, Alexander K., ALPL; Ewing to Parents, 18 Mar. 1863, SC 2667 Ewing, Alexander K., ALPL; Warren Gray, "Diary," 1862–1863, SC 531, WHS; Heafford, "The Army of the Tennessee," in *MOLLUS*, 46:314–15; Jackson, *The Colonel's Diary*, 91, 101, 103, 109, 112–14, 120, 128, 158; Campbell, *The Union Must Stand*, 68–69, 71, 73–78, 117, 119; Henry A. Kircher to Father, 30 May 1863, in Hess, *A German in the Yankee Fatherland*, 104; Henry A. Kircher, "Diary," Engelmann Kircher Family Papers, ALPL; Loudon to Hannah, 2 Apr. 1862, DeWitt Clinton Loudon Papers, Mss 610, OHC; Loudon to Hannah, 24 Apr. 1862, DeWitt Clinton Loudon Papers, Mss 610, OHC; Loudon to Hannah, 11 Apr. 1864, DeWitt Clinton Loudon Papers, Mss 610, OHC; James S. McHenry, "Diary," SC 973 McHenry, James S., ALPL; John Nilson, "Diary," John Nilson Diary and Papers, HIS; James Kerr Proudfit to Emelie, 30 Sept. 1864, "Correspondence," 1861–1865, Wis Mss 158S, WHS; "Diary of Z. Payson Shumway, SC 1388 Shumway, Z. Payson, ALPL; Shumway to Hattie, 8 Jan. 1863, SC 1388 Shumway, Z. Payson, ALPL; Shumway to Hattie, 14 Feb. 1863, SC 1388 Shumway, Z. Payson, ALPL; Shumway to Hattie, 2 Mar. 1863, SC 1388 Shumway, Z. Payson, ALPL; Shumway to Hattie, 3 Oct. 1863, SC 1388 Shumway, Z. Payson, ALPL; Steele to Wife, 17 Mar. 1863, "Papers, 1827–1891," Wis Mss 113S, WHS; Robert Steele to Father and Mother, 18 Dec. 1862, "Papers, 1827–1891," Wis Mss 113S, WHS; Stuart to Wife, 10 June 1864, SC 2406 Stuart, Owen, ALPL; Stuart to Wife, 26 June 1864, SC 2406 Stuart, Owen, ALPL; Stuart to Wife, 13 June 1864, SC 2406 Stuart, Owen, ALPL; Thomas T. Taylor, "Diary," Roll 21, MIC 17 Civil War Collection, OHC; Wood to Wife, 4 Jan. 1864, Edward Jesup Wood Papers, IHS; Rood, *Story of the Service of Company E*, 187; Ritner to Wife, 23 Oct. 1864, in Larimer, *Love and Valor*, 377; Ritner to Wife, 8 Jan. 1865, in Larimer, *Love and Valor*, 405; Jacob B. Ritner to Emeline, 25 Nov. 1862, in Lar-

NOTES TO PAGES 73–78 249

imer, *Love and Valor*, 67; Dwight, "My War Experiences," Henry Otis Dwight Papers (Microform), 1861–1900, Mic 127, OHC; Stockton, *War Diary*, 2–8, 13, 17, 19; Wills, *Army Life of an Illinois Soldier*, 140–42, 156–58, 161, 163, 166, 169, 172, 177–78, 188, 206, 281, 283, 299, 308, 317, 328, 335; William M. Reid, "Diary," SC 2812 Reid, William M., ALPL; Ewing to Parents, 1 Nov. 1862, SC 2667 Ewing, Alexander K., ALPL; Ewing to Parents, 28 Feb. 1863, SC 2667 Ewing, Alexander K., ALPL; Ewing to Parents, 6 Mar. 1863, SC 2667 Ewing, Alexander K., ALPL; Ewing to Parents, 18 Mar. 1863, SC 2667 Ewing, Alexander K., ALPL; Ewing to Parents, 25 Mar. 1863, SC 2667 Ewing, Alexander K., ALPL; Ewing to Parents, 2 Apr. 1863, SC 2667 Ewing, Alexander K., ALPL; Taylor to Wife, 19 July 1863, Thomas Thomson Taylor papers, 1861–1865.

30. Luther H. Cowan to Family, 4 Jan. 1863, Letters and Diary of Luther H. Cowan, Wis Mss 218S, WHS.

31. Dwight, "My War Experiences," Henry Otis Dwight Papers (Microform), 1861–1900, Mic 127, OHC.

32. Cowan to Family, 27 Apr. 1862, Letters and Diary of Luther H. Cowan, Wis Mss 218S, WHS; Ewing to Parents, 25 Mar. 1863, SC 2667 Ewing, Alexander K., ALPL; Balzar Grebe, "Autobiography and Civil War Diary," SC 2681 Grebe, Balzar, ALPL; Jackson, *The Colonel's Diary*, 146; Loudon to Hannah, 24 May 1862, DeWitt Clinton Loudon Papers, Mss 610, OHC; Shumway to Hattie, 12 June 1863, SC 1388 Shumway, Z. Payson. ALPL; Ritner to Emeline, 23 Nov. 1862, in Larimer, *Love and Valor*, 65–66; Mss 7, OHC; Stockton, *War Diary*, 2–3, 11, 13, 15; Wills, *Army Life of an Illinois Soldier*, 131–32, 151–52, 154–55, 165, 170, 186, 190, 288, 307, 367; William K. Barney to All at Home, May 1863, "Papers," 1845–1874, Wis Mss 123S, WHS.

33. Jackson, *The Colonel's Diary*, 94–95.

34. Jackson, *The Colonel's Diary*, 94–96.

35. Ewing to Parents, 1 Nov. 1862, SC 2667 Ewing, Alexander K., ALPL.

36. Wills, *Army Life of an Illinois Soldier*, 135.

37. Wills, *Army Life of an Illinois Soldier*, 135.

38. Jackson, *The Colonel's Diary*, 96–97.

39. Jackson, *The Colonel's Diary*, 98.

40. Crooker, Nourse, and Brown, *Story of the Fifty-Fifth Regiment*, 155–56.

41. Wills, *Army Life of an Illinois Soldier*, 133–34; "Maj. M. Smith of the 45th," *Galena Daily Advertiser*, 1 Dec. 1862; "The Late Lt. Col. Melancthon Smith, of the Lead Mine Regiment, 45th Illinois," *Galena Daily Advertiser*, 29 Aug. 1863.

42. Wayne to Ellen, 18 Feb. 1862, SC 2824 Wayne, Harley, ALPL.

43. Wayne to Ellen, 18 Feb. 1862, SC 2824 Wayne, Harley, ALPL.

44. Wayne to Ellen, 18 Feb. 1862, SC 2824 Wayne, Harley, ALPL.

45. Dwight, "My War Experiences," Henry Otis Dwight Papers (Microform), 1861–1900, Mic 127, OHC.

46. Best to Wife, 3 Sept. 1861, SC 2478 Best, Benjamin Franklin, ALPL; Wills, *Army Life of an Illinois Soldier*, 134, 137, 329–30; Grierson to Alice, 14 July 1862, Grierson Box 1, Benjamin Grierson Family Papers, ALPL; Luther B. Hunt Diary, vol. 1, Vermont Historical Society; Cowan to Mollie, 21 Nov. 1862, Letters and Diary of Luther H. Cowan, Wis Mss 218S, WHS; Luther Cowan Diary, Letters and Diary of Luther H. Cowan, Wis Mss 218S, WHS; Cowan to Harriet, 15 Nov. 1862, Letters and Diary of Luther H. Cowan, Wis Mss 218S, WHS; Wills to Sister, 31 Mar. 1863, in Wills, *Army Life of an Illinois Soldier*, 168.

47. Stockton, *War Diary*, 3.

48. Stockton, *War Diary*, 19–20.

49. Miller, *Struggle for the Life of the Republic*, 189.

50. Miller, *Struggle for the Life of the Republic*, 189.

51. Force, "Personal Recollections of the Vicksburg Campaign," in *MOLLUS*, 1:300–301.

52. Ritner to Emeline, 27 July 1861, in Larimer, *Love and Valor*, 49–50.

53. Governor Richard Yates, "Lieutenant Colonel's Commission," 31 Oct. 1861, Hitt Box 1-1/2, Folder 3, Hitt, Daniel Fletcher, ALPL; William VanMeter, "What I Know of the Life of John N. Cromwell, Colonel of the 47th Regiment of Illinois Vol. Infantry," SC 357 Cromwell,

250 NOTES TO PAGES 79-83

John, ALPL; B. E. Stevens to Benjamin Allen, 5 Aug. 1862, in Benjamin Allen, "Civil War Letters," 1861–1863, SC 512, WHS; Wood to Wife, 3 Oct. 1863, Edward Jesup Wood Papers, IHS; Adjutant to Col. Benjamin Allen, 14 Aug. 1862, in Benjamin Allen, "Civil War Letters," 1861–1863, SC 512, WHS; Thomas T. Taylor, "Diary," Roll 21, Mic 17 Civil War Collection, OHC; David McKee Claggett, "Diary," SC 2689 Claggett, David McKee, ALPL; Warren Gray, "Diary, 1862–1863," SC 531, WHS; Samuel J. Nasmith to Louisa, 8 Feb. 1863, "Letters," 1861–1863, Wis Mss 66S, WHS; Wayne to Ellen, 22 May 1861, SC 2824 Wayne, Harley, ALPL; Luther B. Hunt Diary, vol. 1, Vermont Historical Society; Rood, *Story of the Service of Company E,* 230; Crooker, Nourse, and Brown, *Story of the Fifty-Fifth Regiment,* 31, 71; "Rowydism," *Galena Daily Advertiser,* 20 Aug. 1861; Wayne to Ellen, 2 Aug. 1861, SC 2824 Wayne, Harley, ALPL; Wayne to Ellen, 13 Aug. 1861, SC 2824 Wayne, Harley, ALPL; Stockton, *War Diary,* 13–14.

54. Wayne to Ellen, 31 May 1861, SC 2824 Wayne, Harley, ALPL.

55. Ewing to Parents, 9 Nov. 1862, SC 2667 Ewing, Alexander K., ALPL.

56. Crooker, Nourse, and Brown, *Story of the Fifty-Fifth Regiment,* 416; Ammack to Brother and Sister, 2 Dec. 1862, Ammack and Howland Family Letters, Wis Mss 123S, WHS; Henry F. Hole to Friends, 25 Aug. 1861, SC 2427 Hole, Henry F., ALPL; Henry A. Kircher to Mother, 10 Mar. 1863, in Hess, *A German in the Yankee Fatherland,* 75.

57. Dwight, "My War Experiences," Henry Otis Dwight Papers (Microform), 1861–1900, Mic 127, OHC.

58. Dwight, "My War Experiences," Henry Otis Dwight Papers (Microform), 1861–1900, Mic 127, OHC.

59. Dwight, "My War Experiences," Henry Otis Dwight Papers (Microform), 1861–1900, Mic 127, OHC.

60. Dwight, "My War Experiences," Henry Otis Dwight Papers (Microform), 1861–1900, Mic 127, OHC.

61. Dwight, "My War Experiences," Henry Otis Dwight Papers (Microform), 1861–1900, Mic 127, OHC.

62. Rood, *Story of the Service of Company E,* 264.

63. Rood, *Story of the Service of Company E,* 264.

64. Rood, *Story of the Service of Company E,* 263–65, 274, 286–87; Higbee, "Personal Recollections of a Line Officer," in *MOLLUS,* 29:314.

65. Grierson, *A Just and Righteous Cause,* 82.

66. Grierson, *A Just and Righteous Cause,* 82.

67. Hart, *History of the Fortieth Illinois Inf.,* 122–23.

68. Hart, *History of the Fortieth Illinois Inf.,* 123–24.

69. Rood, *Story of the Service of Company E,* 262; Hart, *History of the Fortieth Illinois Inf.,* 121–24; "A Letter from a Lead Miner," *Galena Daily Advertiser,* 23 Dec. 1861; "The Lead Mine Regiment," *Galena Daily Advertiser,* 30 Dec. 1861; Hart, *History of the Fortieth Illinois Inf.,* 82.

70. Charles Wills to Sister, 1 Feb. 1863, in Wills, *Army Life of an Illinois Soldier,* 151–52.

71. Wills, *Army Life of an Illinois Soldier,* 163.

72. Campbell, *The Union Must Stand,* 75.

73. Campbell, *The Union Must Stand,* 76.

74. "Diary," John Nilson Diary and Papers, IHS; William A. Green, "Statement in Regard to Private Newton R. Tousley of Co. 'D' 16th Regt Wis Vols," 5 Aug. 1862, in Benjamin Allen "Civil War Letters," 1861–1863, SC 512, WHS; Ankeny to Wife, 22 May 1863, in Cox, *Kiss Josey for Me!,* 153; Bridgford to Eliza, 12 Nov. 1861, Oliver A. Bridgford Papers.

75. Henry Miller Culbertson to Sister, Mother, and Brother, 22 Dec. 1862, "Civil War Letters," 1861–1864, Wis Mss 216S, WHS.

76. Dwight, "My War Experiences," Henry Otis Dwight Papers (Microform), 1861–1900, Mic 127, OHC.

77. Cowan to Harriet, 7 Dec. 1862, Letters and Diary of Luther H. Cowan, WHS; Wood to Wife, 29 May 1864; Edward Jesup Wood Papers, IHS; Ritner to Wife, 16 May 1864, in Larimer, *Love and Valor,* 271; Ritner to Wife, 11 Sept. 1864, in Larimer, *Love and Valor,* 351; Thomas T.

NOTES TO PAGES 83–89   251

Taylor, "Diary," Roll 21, Mic 17 Civil War Collection, OHC; Captain Gray to Col. Benjamin Allen, 24 July 1862, in Benjamin Allen, "Civil War Letters," 1861–1863, SC 512, WHS.

78. Barto to Sister, 26 Aug. 1863, SC 2627 Barto, Alphonso, ALPL.

79. Crooker, Nourse, and Brown, *Story of the Fifty-Fifth Regiment*, 48–49.

80. Hicks, "The Campaign and Capture of Vicksburg," in *MOLLUS*, 31:91.

81. Hicks, "The Campaign and Capture of Vicksburg," in *MOLLUS*, 31:91–92.

82. Grierson to Alice, 6 Apr. 1862, Grierson Box 1, Benjamin Grierson Family Papers, ALPL.

83. Stockton, *War Diary*, 7–8.

84. Jackson, *The Colonel's Diary*, 93, 98–100, 170, 185, 189, 200; Ammack to Brother and Sister, 21 Mar. 1863, Ammack and Howland Family Letters, Wis Mss 123S, WHS; Hart, *History of the Fortieth Illinois Inf.*, 71; Grierson to Alice, 26 Jan. 1862, Grierson Box 1, Benjamin Grierson Family Papers, ALPL; Cowan to Molly, 12 Aug. 1862, Letters and Diary of Luther H. Cowan, WHS; Crooker, Nourse, and Brown, *Story of the Fifty-Fifth Regiment*, 43–44, 47; Brown to Drusilla, 20 Oct. 1862, Ephraim Brown Papers. Mss 76, OHC; Morris, Hartwell, and Kuykendall, *History 31st Regiment Illinois Volunteers*, 80; Crooker, "Episodes and Characters in an Illinois Regiment," in *MOLLUS*, 10:38.

85. Grierson to Alice, 20 Feb. 1862, Grierson Box 1, Benjamin Grierson Family Papers, ALPL.

86. Grierson, *A Just and Righteous Cause*, 73.

87. Stockton, *War Diary*, 12.

88. Stockton, *War Diary*, 12.

89. Hole to Friends, 8 Aug. 1861, SC 2427 Hole, Henry F., ALPL.

90. Dwight, "My War Experiences," Henry Otis Dwight Papers (Microform), 1861–1900, Mic 127, OHC; Grierson to Alice, 26 Jan. 1862, Grierson Box 1, Benjamin Grierson Family Papers, ALPL; Hole to Friends, 25 Aug. 1861, SC 2427 Hole, Henry F., ALPL; Rood, *Story of the Service of Company E*, 376–77.

91. Campbell, *The Union Must Stand*, 130.

92. Campbell, *The Union Must Stand*, 130.

93. Headquarters 4th Division, "General Orders No 70," 12 June 1862, Hitt Box 1-1/2, Folder 3, Hitt, Daniel Fletcher, ALPL; Hart, *History of the Fortieth Illinois Inf.*, 71–72, 76; Ewing to Parents, 29 Mar. 1863, SC 2667 Ewing, Alexander K., ALPL; Cowan to Harriet, 6 May 1863, Letters and Diary of Luther H. Cowan, WHS; Howard, *History of the 124th Regiment Illinois Infantry Volunteers*, 158, 164–67.

94. Ward to Mary, 28 Oct. 1862, SC 3110 Ward, Erasmus D., ALPL.

95. Ward to Mary, 28 Oct. 1862, SC 3110 Ward, Erasmus D., ALPL.

96. Ward to Mary, 28 Oct. 1862, SC 3110 Ward, Erasmus D., ALPL.

97. Ward to Mary, 28 Oct. 1862, SC 3110 Ward, Erasmus D., ALPL.

98. Ward to Mary, 28 Oct. 1862, SC 3110 Ward, Erasmus D., ALPL.

99. Ward to Mary, 28 Oct. 1862, SC 3110 Ward, Erasmus D., ALPL.

100. Ward to Mary, 28 Oct. 1862, SC 3110 Ward, Erasmus D., ALPL.

101. Howard, *History of the 124th Regiment Illinois Infantry Volunteers*, 134–35.

102. Crooker, Nourse, and Brown, *Story of the Fifty-Fifth Regiment*, 353.

103. Crooker, Nourse, and Brown, *Story of the Fifty-Fifth Regiment*, 352–59.

104. Taylor to Wife, 19 Aug. 1863, Thomas Thomson Taylor papers, 1861–1865, Mss 7, OHC.

105. Taylor to Wife, 19 Aug. 1863, Thomas Thomson Taylor papers, 1861–1865, Mss 7, OHC.

106. Taylor to Wife, 19 Aug. 1863, Thomas Thomson Taylor papers, 1861–1865, Mss 7, OHC; Taylor to Wife, 31 Aug. 1863, Thomas Thomson Taylor papers, 1861–1865, Mss 7, OHC.

107. Jackson, *The Colonel's Diary*, 99.

108. Loudon to Hannah, 8 Dec. 1863, DeWitt Clinton Loudon Papers, Mss 610, OHC.

109. Jackson, *The Colonel's Diary*, 191.

110. Jackson, *The Colonel's Diary*, 158.

111. Jackson, *The Colonel's Diary*, 158.

252 NOTES TO PAGES 91–95

6. RED TAPE AND TRIPLICATE FORMS

1. Jacob B. Ritner to Wife, 2 Aug. 1863, in Larimer, *Love and Valor*, 202–3.

2. Edward Jesup Wood to Wife, 17 Apr. 1864, Edward Jesup Wood Papers, Indiana Historical Society.

3. Henry A. Kircher, "Diary of Henry Kircher," Engelmann Kircher Family Papers, ALPL.

4. Howard, *History of the 124th Regiment Illinois Infantry Volunteers*, 12.

5. Henry Otis Dwight, "My War Experiences," Henry Otis Dwight Papers (Microform), 1861–1900, Mic 127, OHC.

6. Miller, *Struggle for the Life of the Republic*, 173.

7. Henry A. Kircher to Father, 6 Oct. 1863, in Hess, *A German in the Yankee Fatherland*, 128.

8. Henry Giesey Ankeny to Wife, 8 Jan. 1864, in Cox, *Kiss Josey for Me!*, 206; Ankeny to Wife, 18 Jan. 1864, in Cox, *Kiss Josey for Me!*, 207; Ankeny to Wife, 22 Jan. 1864, in Cox, *Kiss Josey for Me!*, 208; Grierson, *A Just and Righteous Cause*, 74; Thomas T. Taylor, "Diary," Roll 21, MIC 17 Civil War Collection, OHC.

9. Alphonso Barto to Father, 31 Mar. 1863, in SC 2627 Barto, Alphonso, ALPL.

10. Chief of Ordnance James. W. Ripley, "Circular No. 10—Series of 1863," 16 Mar. 1863, Nathaniel Watson Foster Papers, Mss 585, OHC; Chief of Ordnance James. W. Ripley, "Circular No. 19—Series of 1863," 15 Apr. 1863, Nathaniel Watson Foster Papers, Mss 585, OHC; Chief of Ordnance George D. Ramsay, "Circular No. 42—Series of 1864," 6 Aug. 1864, Nathaniel Watson Foster Papers, Mss 585, OHC; Miller, *Struggle for the Life of the Republic*, 214; Charles C. Ammack to Brother and Sister, 21 Mar. 1863, Ammack and Howland Family Letters. Wis Mss 123S, WHS; Ankeny to Wife, 8 Jan. 1864, in Cox, *Kiss Josey for Me!*, 206; Chief of Ordnance James. W. Ripley, "Circular No. 23—Series of 1863," 1 Aug. 1863, Nathaniel Watson Foster Papers, Mss 585, OHC.

11. "General Orders No. 13," 11 Feb. 1862, Theodore Jones Papers, 1813–1900, Mss 64, OHC.

12. "General Orders No. 13," 11 Feb. 1862, Theodore Jones Papers, 1813–1900, Mss 64, OHC.

13. Chief of Ordnance James. W. Ripley, "Circular No. 42—Series of 1863," 1 Sept. 1863, Nathaniel Watson Foster Papers, Mss 585, OHC.

14. Miller, *Struggle for the Life of the Republic*, 214.

15. Miller, *Struggle for the Life of the Republic*, 214.

16. Thomas T. Taylor, "Diary," Roll 21, MIC 17 Civil War Collection, OHC; John Duer to Lt. Col. Maltby, 3 Sept. 1862, SC 771–45 Smith, John Eugene, ALPL; "Diary," John Nilson Diary and Papers, IHS; Wills, *Army Life of an Illinois Soldier*, 212.

17. "Personal," *Galena Daily Advertiser*, 5 Dec. 1861; J. B. Hawley to Col. Smith, 17 Jan. 1862, SC 771–45 Smith, John Eugene, ALPL; Luther Cowan to Col. Smith, 17 Jan. 1862, SC 771–45 Smith, John Eugene, ALPL; Luther Cowan, "Note," 21 Mar. 1862, SC 771–45 Smith, John Eugene, ALPL; O. A. Bridgford, "Note," 1 Mar. 1862, SC 771–45 Smith, John Eugene, ALPL; "Consolidated Weekly Reports," 12 Oct. 1862, SC 771–45 Smith, John Eugene, ALPL; A. Polsgrove, "Note," no date, SC 771–45 Smith, John Eugene, ALPL; O. A. Bridgford, "Note," no date, SC 771–45 Smith, John Eugene, ALPL; A. Polsgrove, "Requisition," no date, SC 771–45 Smith, John Eugene, ALPL; James Rouse, "Note," no date, SC 771–45 Smith, John Eugene, ALPL; L. Fisk, "Note," no date, SC 771–45 Smith, John Eugene, ALPL; John Eugene Smith to Capt. Dickey, 15 July 1862, SC 771–45 Smith, John Eugene, ALPL; A. Polsgrove, "Members Returned," no date, SC 771–45 Smith, John Eugene, ALPL.

18. Owen Stuart to General Sherman, 24 Dec. 1863, SC 2406 Stuart, Owen, ALPL; Thomas T. Taylor, "Diary," Roll 21, MIC 17 Civil War Collection, OHC; Benjamin H. Grierson, "Report to Maj Genl Sherman," 7 Sept. 1862, Grierson Box 1, Benjamin Grierson Family Papers, ALPL; Benjamin H. Grierson, "Report to Brig Genl Smith," 13 Sept. 1862, Grierson Box 1, Benjamin Grierson Family Papers, ALPL; Col. John M. Oliver to Capt. Dickson, A. A. General 6th Div., 18 Oct. 1862, "Colonel John Hancock Papers, 1862–1889," File 1862 Feb. 14, WHS; Edward Gee Miller, "List of Articles Expended," 31 Mar. 1863, "Civil War Papers, 1861–1906," Wis Mss 62S, WHS; Edward Gee Miller, "Quarterly Return of Ordnance and

Ordnance Stores," 30 Sept. 1863, "Civil War Papers, 1861–1906," Wis Mss 62S, WHS; Edward Gee Miller, "Quarterly Return of Ordnance and Ordnance Stores," 30 June 1863, "Civil War Papers, 1861–1906," Wis Mss 62S, WHS; Edward Gee Miller, "Furlough Authorization," 12 Apr. 1863, "Civil War Papers, 1861–1906," Wis Mss 62S, WHS; Benjamin Grierson to Alice, 11 July 1862, Grierson Box 1, Benjamin Grierson Family Papers, ALPL; Luther H. Cowan to Harriet, 2 Nov. 1862, Letters and Diary of Luther H. Cowan, Wis Mss 218S, WHS; Luther H. Cowan to Mollie, 10 Dec. 1862, Letters and Diary of Luther H. Cowan, Wis Mss 218S, WHS; John E. Smith to Joseph Warren Miller, 16 Aug. 1862, SC 1047 Miller, J. W. ALPL.

19. Alphonso Barto to Sister, 5 May 1862, in SC 2627 Barto, Alphonso, ALPL.

20. Kircher to Father, 6 Oct. 1863, in Hess, *A German in the Yankee Fatherland*, 128.

21. Campbell, *The Union Must Stand*, 116.

22. Jacob B. Ritner to Emeline, 15 Mar. 1863, in Larimer, *Love and Valor*, 134.

23. Thomas T. Taylor, "Diary," Roll 21, MIC 17 Civil War Collection, OHC; James Kerr Proud-fit to Emelie, 30 Sept. 1864, "Correspondence," 1861–1865, Wis Mss 158S, WHS; Henry Miller Culbertson to Mother, Brother, and Sister, 1 June 1863 in "Civil War Letters," 1861–1864, Wis Mss 216S, WHS; Luther B. Hunt Diary, vol. 1, Vermont Historical Society; Oliver A. Bridgford to Eliza, 29 July 1862, Oliver A. Bridgford Papers; Luther Cowan Diary, Letters and Diary of Luther H. Cowan, Wis Mss 218S, WHS; Alexander K. Ewing to Parents, 1 Nov. 1862, SC 2667 Ewing, Alexander K, ALPL; Ewing to Parents, 4 Jan. 1863, SC 2667 Ewing, Alexander K, ALPL; Ewing to Parents, 14 Feb. 1863, SC 2667 Ewing, Alexander K, ALPL; Ewing to Parents, 9 Apr. 1863, SC 2667 Ewing, Alexander K, ALPL; Ewing to Parents, 29 Mar. 1863, SC 2667 Ewing, Alexander K, ALPL; Barto to Sister, 5 May 1862, in SC 2627 Barto, Alphonso, ALPL; Ankeny to Wife, 22 May 1863 [possibly 1864], in Cox, *Kiss Josey for Me!*, 153; Ammack to Brother and Sister, 21 Mar. 1863, Ammack and Howland Family Letters, Wis Mss 123S, WHS; DeWitt Clinton Loudon to Hannah, 29 Apr. 1864, DeWitt Clinton Loudon Papers, MSS 610, OHC; Ewing to Parents, 1–3 Nov. 1862, SC 2667 Ewing, Alexander K, ALPL; Campbell, *The Union Must Stand*, 79, 111, 118–19, 127; Ritner to Emeline, 1 Mar. 1863, in Larimer, *Love and Valor*, 123; Ritner to Emeline, 22 Feb., in Larimer, *Love and Valor*, 120; Ritner to Wife, 26 June 1863, in Larimer, *Love and Valor*, 191; Ritner to Emeline, 4 July 1863, in Larimer, *Love and Valor*, 197; Ritner to Wife, 1 Nov. 1863, in Larimer, *Love and Valor*, 236; Ritner to Wife, 20 Nov. 1863, in Larimer, *Love and Valor*, 243; Ritner to Wife, 24 Aug. 1864, in Larimer, *Love and Valor*, 341; Ritner to Wife, 29 Aug. 1864, in Larimer, *Love and Valor*, 343; Jackson, *The Colonel's Diary*, 128, 159, 188.

24. Luther H. Cowan to Family, 27 Apr. 1862, Letters and Diary of Luther H. Cowan, Wis Mss 218S, WHS.

25. Rood, *Story of the Service of Company E*, 525–26; Bridgford to Eliza, 25 Mar. 1862, in Oliver A. Bridgford Papers; Charles A. Willison to Sister, 1 July 1863, 76th Ohio Volunteer Infantry Correspondence, Vfm 4626, OHC; Ritner to Emeline, 29 Apr. 1763, in Larimer, *Love and Valor*, 161; Joseph S. Reynolds to Sister, 29 Mar. 1865, Joseph S. Reynolds Papers, #5060-z,Wilson Library, Univ. of North Carolina at Chapel Hill.

26. Wood to Wife, 17 Jan. 1864, Edward Jesup Wood Papers, Indiana Historical Society.

27. Wood to Wife, 17 Jan. 1864, Edward Jesup Wood Papers, Indiana Historical Society.

28. Wood to Wife, 17 Jan. 1864, Edward Jesup Wood Papers, Indiana Historical Society.

29. George H. Hildt to Parents, 7 Feb. 1864, Typescripts of George H. Hildt letters and diary, 1862–1865, vol. 548, OHC.

30. Hildt to Parents, 7 Feb. 1864, Typescripts of George H. Hildt letters and diary, 1862–1865, vol. 548, OHC.

31. Hildt to Parents, 26 Feb. 1864,Typescripts of George H. Hildt letters and diary, 1862–1865, vol. 548, OHC.

32. Jackson, *The Colonel's Diary*, 120, 159.

33. Crooker, Nourse, and Brown, *Story of the Fifty-Fifth Regiment*, 380.

34. Crooker, Nourse, and Brown, *Story of the Fifty-Fifth Regiment*, 381–82.

35. Captain George Balch, Ordnance Office, War Department, "Letter to Captain Watson Foster," 15 Feb. 1864, Nathaniel Watson Foster Papers, Mss 585, OHC; Captain George Balch,

Ordnance Office, War Department, "Letter to Captain Watson Foster," 19 Mar. 1864, Nathaniel Watson Foster Papers, Mss 585, OHC; Captain George Balch, Ordnance Office, War Department, "Letter to Captain Watson Foster," 7 June 1864, Nathaniel Watson Foster Papers, Mss 585, OHC; Captain George Balch, Ordnance Office, War Department, "Letter to Captain Watson Foster," 23 Aug. 1864, Nathaniel Watson Foster Papers, Mss 585, OHC; Quartermaster General's Office, "Letter to Capt. W. Foster," 2 Mar. 1865, Nathaniel Watson Foster Papers, Mss 585, OHC; Treasury Department Third Auditor's Office, "Letter to Capt. N. W. Foster," 8 Apr. 1870, Nathaniel Watson Foster Papers, Mss 585, OHC; Daniel Robbins Sylvester, "Quarterly Return," 31 Mar. 1863, "Papers," 1858–1901, Wis Mss 51S, WHS.

36. James W. Judy to Edwin M. Stanton, 14 Apr. 1863, SC 2393 Judy, James W., ALPL; "Special Order No. 211," 4 Aug. 1863, SC 2393 Judy, James W., ALPL; "Special Order No. 118," 5 Aug. 1863, SC 2393 Judy, James W., ALPL; "Resolution," 7 Aug. 1863, SC 2393 Judy, James W., ALPL; R. P. Buckland to Governor Richard Yates, 14 Dec. 1863, SC 2393 Judy, James W., ALPL.

37. Ritner to Wife, 16 May 1864, in Larimer, *Love and Valor,* 272.

38. Ritner to Wife, 20 June 1864, in Larimer, *Love and Valor,* 293–94.

39. Ritner to Wife, 25 July 1864, in Larimer, *Love and Valor,* 316; Ritner to Wife, 20 Nov. 1863, in Larimer, *Love and Valor,* 244.

40. "Oath of Willard Warner," 8 Sept. 1863, Oaths of Army Officers, State Archives Series 4518, OHC.

41. "Oath of William H. Raynor," 5 May 1863, Oaths of Army Officers, State Archives Series 4518, OHC; "Oath of Edward Briggs," 29 Mar. 1865, Oaths of Army Officers, State Archives Series 4518, OHC; "Oath of Wager Swayne," 28 Mar. 1864, Oaths of Army Officers, State Archives Series 4518, OHC; "Oath of Edward F. Noyes," 28 Nov. 1863, Oaths of Army Officers, State Archives Series 4518, OHC; "Oath of Henry T. McDowell," 28 Nov. 1863, Oaths of Army Officers, State Archives Series 4518, OHC; "Oath of William H. Lathrop," 28 Nov. 1863, Oaths of Army Officers, State Archives Series 4518, OHC.

42. Wills, *Army Life of an Illinois Soldier,* 175.

43. Ritner to Wife, 14 Sept. 1864, in Larimer, *Love and Valor,* 355.

44. Ritner to Wife, 14 Sept. 1864, in Larimer, *Love and Valor,* 355.

45. John Nelson Cromwell to Wife, 11 Dec. 1862, SC 357 Cromwell, John Nelson, ALPL; Walter Quintin Gresham to Tillie, 7 May 1863, Walter Quintin Gresham Collection, IHS; William Hyde Clark, A. A. General, "Special Orders No. 37," 9 Aug. 1863, "Civil War Papers, 1861–1906," Wis Mss 62S, WHS; William H. Clark, A. A. General, "Special Orders No. 4," 7 Jan. 1864; "Civil War Papers, 1861–1906," Wis Mss 62S, WHS; "Special Orders No. 36," 17 Feb. 1863, SC 2406 Stuart, Owen, ALPL; George H. Hildt, "Diary of the Siege of Atlanta, May 28—Oct. 7 1864," Typescripts of George H. Hildt letters and diary, 1862–1865, vol. 548, OHC; Benjamin H. Grierson to Alice, 13 Aug. 1862, Grierson Box 1, Benjamin Grierson Family Papers, ALPL; Grierson to Alice, 22 Aug. 1862, Grierson Box 1, Benjamin Grierson Family Papers, ALPL; Loudon to Hannah, 5 Nov. 1862, DeWitt Clinton Loudon Papers, Mss 610, OHC; Howard, *History of the 124th Regiment Illinois Infantry Volunteers,* 147; Loudon to Hannah, 3 Oct. 1862, DeWitt Clinton Loudon Papers, Mss 610, OHC; Loudon to Hannah, 25 Nov. 1862, DeWitt Clinton Loudon Papers, Mss 610, OHC; Loudon to Hannah, 14 Oct. 1862, DeWitt Clinton Loudon Papers, Mss 610, OHC; Loudon to Hannah, 12 Jan. 1863, DeWitt Clinton Loudon Papers, Mss 610, OHC; Loudon to Hannah, 23 Jan. 1863, DeWitt Clinton Loudon Papers, Mss 610, OHC; "General Orders No 40," 18 Apr. 1862, James C. Veatch Papers, IHS; Dwight, "My War Experiences," Henry Otis Dwight Papers (Microform), 1861–1900, Mic 127, OHC; "Special Order No. 68," 8 June 1863, SC 1308 Ruggles, J. M., ALPL; "Charges," SC 1308 Ruggles, J. M., ALPL; Force, "Personal Recollections of the Vicksburg Campaign," in *MOLLUS,* 1:300; Thomas Thomson Taylor to Wife, 18 Sept. 1863, Thomas Thomson Taylor papers, 1861–1865, Mss 7, OHC; Thomas T. Taylor, "Diary," Roll 21, Mic 17 Civil War Collection, OHC; Ritner to Wife, 11 Sept. 1864, in Larimer, *Love and Valor,* 351; Ritner to Wife, 19 Sept. 1864, in Larimer, *Love and Valor,* 359; Wills, *Army Life of an Illinois Soldier,* 140, 173, 175, 212–13, 217–18, 220, 224; Ritner to Wife, 26 Sept. 1864, in Larimer, *Love and Valor,* 362;

NOTES TO PAGES 100–105 255

Jackson, *The Colonel's Diary*, 152, 166, 170, 173.

46. Luther Howard Cowan to Harriet, 12 Sept. 1862, Letters and Diary of Luther H. Cowan, Wis Mss 218S, WHS.

47. Luther Howard Cowan to Molly, 12 Aug. 1862, Letters and Diary of Luther H. Cowan, Wis Mss 218S, WHS; Luther Cowan Diary, Letters and Diary of Luther H. Cowan, Wis Mss 218S, WHS; Cowan to Harriet, 24 Oct. 1862, Letters and Diary of Luther H. Cowan, Wis Mss 218S, WHS; Cowan to Harriet, 2 Nov. 1862, Letters and Diary of Luther H. Cowan, Wis Mss 218S, WHS.

48. Wood to Wife, 9 Aug. 1863, Edward Jesup Wood Papers, IHS.

49. Wood to Wife, 29 May 1864, Edward Jesup Wood Papers, IHS.

50. Wood to Wife, 10 June 1864, Edward Jesup Wood Papers, IHS.

51. Wood to Wife, 4 Jan. 1864, Edward Jesup Wood Papers, IHS; Wood to Wife, 17 Jan. 1864, Edward Jesup Wood Papers, IHS; Wood to Wife, 17 June 1864, Edward Jesup Wood Papers, IHS; Wood to Wife, 1 Jan. 1865, Edward Jesup Wood Papers, HIS; Wood to Wife, 24 Apr. 1864, Edward Jesup Wood Papers, IHS.

52. William M. Reid, "Diary," SC 2812 Reid, William M., ALPL.

7. MORE IMPORTANT THAN GOOD GENERALS

1. Luther Cowan to Family, 26 Oct. 1862, Letters and Diary of Luther H. Cowan, Wis Mss 218S, WHS.

2. Luther Cowan to Family, 26 Oct. 1862, Letters and Diary of Luther H. Cowan, Wis Mss 218S, WHS.

3. Hunt, "The Fort Donelson Campaign," in *MOLLUS*, 13:71.

4. Henry F. Hole to Minerva, 22 Apr. 1862, SC 2427 Hole, Henry F., ALPL.

5. Hole to Minerva, 22 Apr. 1862, SC 2427 Hole, Henry F., ALPL.

6. "Vicksburg Correspondence," *Galena Daily Advertiser*, 12 June 1863; "The 45th In Tennessee—Taking of Fort Henry," *Galena Daily Advertiser*, 13 Feb. 1862; Morton, "A Boy at Shiloh," in *MOLLUS*, 22:53; "Vicksburg Correspondence," *Galena Daily Advertiser*, 10 June 1863; Rood, *Story of the Service of Company E*, 200; DeWitt Loudon to Hannah, 15 Apr. 1862, DeWitt Clinton Loudon Papers, Mss 610, OHC; "Diary of John Stuber," John Stuber, 1896, Vfm 5942, OHC; Campbell, *The Union Must Stand*, 103; Luther H. Cowan to Family, 4 Jan. 1863, Letters and Diary of Luther H. Cowan, Wis Mss 218S, WHS; H. S. Townsend, "Army Correspondence," *Galena Daily Advertiser*, 10 Mar. 1862; Lawrence, "Stuart's Brigade at Shiloh," in *MOLLUS*, 53:492–94; Henry Ankeny to Tina, 22 Dec. 1862, in Cox, *Kiss Josey for Me!*, 112.

7. Miller, *Struggle for the Life of the Republic*, 81.

8. Luther Cowan Diary, Letters and Diary of Luther H. Cowan, Wis Mss 218S, WHS.

9. Henry Kircher to Mother, 17 June 1863, in Hess, *A German in the Yankee Fatherland*, 108.

10. Richard W. Burt to Editor, Newark, Ohio, "North American," 30 May 1863, 76th Ohio Volunteer Infantry Correspondence, Vfm 4626, OHC.

11. Charles C. Ammack to Brother and Sister, 16 Feb. 1863, Ammack and Howland Family Letters, Wis Mss 123S, WHS.

12. Henry A. Kircher, "Diary of Henry Kircher," Engelmann Kircher Family Papers, ALPL.

13. Ammack to Brother and Sister, 2 Dec. 1862, Ammack and Howland Family Letters, Wis Mss 123S, WHS; Campbell, *The Union Must Stand*, 152.

14. Alphonso Barto to Father, 12 Sept. 1864, SC 2627 Barto, Alphonso, ALPL.

15. Barto to Father, 12 Sept. 1864, SC 2627 Barto, Alphonso, ALPL.

16. Alexander Ewing to Parents, 9 Nov. 1862, SC 2667 Ewing, Alexander K., ALPL; Charles Wills to Sister, 15 Feb. 1863, in Wills, *Army Life of an Illinois Soldier*, 155–56.

17. Jacob Ritner to Emeline, 7 Jan. 1863, in Larimer, *Love and Valor*, 99–100.

18. Jacob Ritner to Wife, 20 Nov. 1863, in Larimer, *Love and Valor*, 244.

19. Ritner to Wife, 20 Nov. 1863, in Larimer, *Love and Valor*, 244.

256 NOTES TO PAGES 105–109

20. Ritner to Emeline, 8 Feb. 1863, in Larimer, *Love and Valor,* 115; Ritner to Emeline, 17 Apr. 1863, in Larimer, *Love and Valor,* 154–55; Ritner to Emeline, 23 Nov. 1862, in Larimer, *Love and Valor,* 66.

21. "Diary of Lieut. Anthony B. Burton, Commanding 5th Ohio Independent Battery, from May 18, to July 4, 1863, Inclusive," SC 2401 Burton, Anthony B., ALPL.

22. "Diary of Lieut. Anthony B. Burton, Commanding 5th Ohio Independent Battery, from May 18, to July 4, 1863, Inclusive," SC 2401 Burton, Anthony B., ALPL.

23. Wills to Sister, 28 May 1862, in Wills, *Army Life of an Illinois Soldier,* 94–95.

24. Henry Otis Dwight, "My War Experiences," Henry Otis Dwight Papers (Microform), 1861–1900, Mic 127, OHC.

25. Ewing to Parents, 15 Mar. 1863, SC 2667 Ewing, Alexander K., ALPL.

26. John M. Oliver, "Letter," 1 Sept. 1863, in "Colonel John Hancock Papers, 1862–1889," File 1862 Feb. 14, WHS; William H. W. Cushman, "Farewell Address," 20 Sept. 1862, Hitt Box 1-1/2, Folder 3, Hitt, Daniel Fletcher, ALPL.

27. Michael Griffin, "Captain John Gillispie" in Rood, *Story of the Service of Company E,* 498.

28. Griffin, "Captain John Gillispie" in Rood, *Story of the Service of Company E,* 498.

29. Griffin, "Captain John Gillispie" in Rood, *Story of the Service of Company E,* 498.

30. Griffin, "Captain John Gillispie" in Rood, *Story of the Service of Company E,* 498.

31. Crooker, Nourse, and Brown, *Story of the Fifty-Fifth Regiment,* 193–94.

32. Ritner to Emeline, 7 Jan. 1863, in Larimer, *Love and Valor,* 99–100.

33. Crooker, Nourse, and Brown, *Story of the Fifty-Fifth Regiment,* 223–24.

34. Howard, *History of the 124th Regiment Illinois Infantry Volunteers,* 166–67.

35. Howard, *History of the 124th Regiment Illinois Infantry Volunteers,* 166–67.

36. Henry F. Hole to Sister, 25 Mar. 1862, SC 2427 Hole, Henry F., ALPL; Oliver A. Bridgford to Eliza, 25 Mar. 1862, Oliver A. Bridgford Papers; Edward Jesup Wood to Wife, 14 June 1863, Edward Jesup Wood Papers, HIS; Crooker, Nourse, and Brown, *Story of the Fifty-Fifth Regiment,* 160; Robert J. Whittleton to Col. Nasmith, 15 Aug. 1863, in Nasmith, Samuel J., "Letters," 1861–1863, Wis Mss 66S, WHS.

37. Vail, *Company K, of the 16th Wisconsin,* 6.

38. Vail, *Company K, of the 16th Wisconsin,* 6.

39. Vail, *Company K, of the 16th Wisconsin,* 6.

40. Thomas Thomson Taylor to Wife, 19 Aug. 1863, Thomas Thomson Taylor papers, 1861–1865, Mss 7, OHC.

41. Taylor to Wife, 19 Aug. 1863, Thomas Thomson Taylor papers, 1861–1865, Mss 7, OHC.

42. Taylor to Wife, 19 Aug. 1863, Thomas Thomson Taylor papers, 1861–1865, Mss 7, OHC.

43. Taylor to Wife, 19 Aug. 1863, Thomas Thomson Taylor papers, 1861–1865, Mss 7, OHC.

44. Taylor to Wife, 19 Aug. 1863, Thomas Thomson Taylor papers, 1861–1865, Mss 7, OHC.

45. Wood to Wife, 21 Oct. 1864, Edward Jesup Wood Papers, IHS.

46. Wood to Wife, 21 Oct. 1864, Edward Jesup Wood Papers, IHS.

47. "Diary of Lieut. Anthony B. Burton, Commanding 5th Ohio Independent Battery, from May 18, to July 4, 1863, Inclusive," SC 2401 Burton, Anthony B., ALPL.

48. DeWitt Clinton Loudon to Hannah, 3 Oct. 1862, Mss 610, DeWitt Clinton Loudon Papers, OHC.

49. Ephraim Brown to Drusilla, 15 Feb. 1863, Ephraim Brown Papers, Mss 76, OHC; Officers of 31st Indiana to Lt. Col. John Osborn, 13 Mar. 1862, Charles M. Smith Documents and Papers, HIS; Jackson, *The Colonel's Diary,* 120.

50. "Account of Lt. J. B. Johnson," in Crooker, Nourse, and Brown, *Story of the Fifty-Fifth Regiment,* 144.

51. "Account of Lt. J. B. Johnson," in Crooker, Nourse, and Brown, *Story of the Fifty-Fifth Regiment,* 144–45.

52. "Account of Lt. J. B. Johnson," in Crooker, Nourse, and Brown, *Story of the Fifty-Fifth Regiment,* 145.

53. "Account of Lt. J. B. Johnson," in Crooker, Nourse, and Brown, *Story of the Fifty-Fifth Regiment,* 145.

NOTES TO PAGES 110–115 257

54. "Account of Lt. J. B. Johnson," in Crooker, Nourse, and Brown, *Story of the Fifty-Fifth Regiment*, 145.

55. "Account of Lt. J. B. Johnson," in Crooker, Nourse, and Brown, *Story of the Fifty-Fifth Regiment*, 145.

56. Crooker, Nourse, and Brown, *Story of the Fifty-Fifth Regiment*, 170–71.

57. David Stuart to Governor Richard Yates, 23 Nov. 1862, in Crooker, Nourse, and Brown, *Story of the Fifty-Fifth Regiment*, 174–75.

58. Stuart to Governor Richard Yates, 23 Nov. 1862, in Crooker, Nourse, and Brown, *Story of the Fifty-Fifth Regiment*, 174–75.

59. Officers of the 55th Illinois to Governor Richard Yates, 21 Nov. 1862, in Crooker, Nourse, and Brown, *Story of the Fifty-Fifth Regiment*, 171–72; Crooker, Nourse, and Brown, *Story of the Fifty-Fifth Regiment*, 170–71, 173, 184–85; Stuart to Governor Richard Yates, 23 Nov. 1862, in Crooker, Nourse, and Brown, *Story of the Fifty-Fifth Regiment*, 173.

60. Crooker, Nourse, and Brown, *Story of the Fifty-Fifth Regiment*, 176.

61. "Charges and Specifications," in Crooker, Nourse, and Brown, *Story of the Fifty-Fifth Regiment*, 264.

62. "Charges and Specifications," in Crooker, Nourse, and Brown, *Story of the Fifty-Fifth Regiment*, 265.

63. Crooker, Nourse, and Brown, in Crooker, Nourse, and Brown, *Story of the Fifty-Fifth Regiment*, 263.

64. Ritner to Wife, 12 Oct. 1863, in Larimer, *Love and Valor*, 220.

65. Ritner to Wife, 17 Nov. 1863, in Larimer, *Love and Valor*, 240.

66. Ritner to Wife, 31 Jan. 1865, in Larimer, *Love and Valor*, 417–18.

67. Ritner to Wife, 12 Oct. 1863, in Larimer, *Love and Valor*, 221.

68. "Diary of Lieut. Anthony B. Burton, Commanding 5th Ohio Independent Battery, from May 18, to July 4, 1863, Inclusive," SC 2401 Burton, Anthony B., ALPL.

69. Joseph R. Vail to Mrs. Cromwell, 15 July 1863, SC 357 Cromwell, John, ALPL; Rood, *Story of the Service of Company E*, 74–75, 290–91, 410–11; Diary of John A. Griffin, Griffin Box 1, Folder 2 BV, Griffin, John Alexander. ALPL; Rood, *Story of the Service of Company E*, 410–11.

8. FOR THE CAUSE

1. Miller, *Struggle for the Life of the Republic*, 45, 79–80.

2. Adair, *Historical Sketch of the Forty-Fifth Illinois Regiment*, 15; Morris, Hartwell, and Kuykendall, *History 31st Regiment Illinois Volunteers*, 53–54; Vail, *Company K, of the 16th Wisconsin*, 7; "Correspondence," *Peoria Daily Transcript*, 28 Aug. 1861, SC 357 Cromwell, John Nelson, ALPL; Edward Gee Miller, "Athenaean Volunteers," 9 May 1862, "Civil War Papers, 1861–1906," Wis Mss 62S, WHS; Miller, *Struggle for the Life of the Republic*, 4; Ambrose, *From Shiloh to Savannah*, 5–7, 90; "War! War!! War!!!," *Galena Daily Advertiser*, 24 July 1861; "Galena Greys Attention!," in *Galena Daily Advertiser*, 30 Apr. 1861; Harlow M. Waller to Slott, 23 Sept. 1862, "Harlow M. & Henrietta Waller Letters, 1861–1869," SC 2952, WHS; Walter Quintin Gresham to Tillie, 7 May 1863, Walter Quintin Gresham Collection, IHS.

3. Henry Otis Dwight, "My War Experiences," Henry Otis Dwight Papers (Microform), 1861–1900, Mic 127, OHC.

4. Dwight, "My War Experiences," Henry Otis Dwight Papers (Microform), 1861–1900, Mic 127, OHC.

5. Dwight, "My War Experiences," Henry Otis Dwight Papers (Microform), 1861–1900, Mic 127, OHC.

6. Hart, *History of the Fortieth Illinois Inf.*, 16.

7. Hart, *History of the Fortieth Illinois Inf.*, 17.

8. Hart, *History of the Fortieth Illinois Inf.*, 105.

9. Crooker, Nourse, and Brown, *Story of the Fifty-Fifth Regiment*, 271.

10. Crooker, Nourse, and Brown, *Story of the Fifty-Fifth Regiment*, 187.

258 NOTES TO PAGES 116–120

11. Crooker, Nourse, and Brown, *Story of the Fifty-Fifth Regiment,* 219.

12. Crooker, Nourse, and Brown, *Story of the Fifty-Fifth Regiment,* 220.

13. Friedrich Martens to Dear Ones, 15 June 1861, in Kamphoefner and Helbich, *Germans in the Civil War,* 317.

14. Martens to Dear Ones, 15 June 1861, in Kamphoefner and Helbich, *Germans in the Civil War,* 317.

15. Martens to Dear Ones, 24 Aug. 1861, in Kamphoefner and Helbich, *Germans in the Civil War,* 317.

16. Martens to Dear Ones, 24 Aug. 1861, in Kamphoefner and Helbich, *Germans in the Civil War,* 319.

17. Martens to Dear Ones, 24 Aug. 1861, in Kamphoefner and Helbich, *Germans in the Civil War,* 319.

18. Martens to Dear Ones, 24 Aug. 1861, in Kamphoefner and Helbich, *Germans in the Civil War,* 319.

19. Campbell, *The Union Must Stand,* 2–3.

20. John Quincy Adams Campbell to the *Ripley Bee,* 19 Jan. 1863, in Grimsley and Miller, *The Union Must Stand,* 218.

21. Campbell, *The Union Must Stand,* 78.

22. Luther H. Cowan to Family, 26 Oct. 1862, Letters and Diary of Luther H. Cowan, Wis Mss 218S, WHS.

23. Luther H. Cowan to Editor of *Warren Independent,* 23 Nov. 1862, Letters and Diary of Luther H. Cowan, Wis Mss 218S, WHS.

24. Cowan to Editor of *Warren Independent,* 23 Nov. 1862, Letters and Diary of Luther H. Cowan, Wis Mss 218S, WHS.

25. Luther H. Cowan to Kingsley Olds, 25 Feb. 1863, Letters and Diary of Luther H. Cowan, Wis Mss 218S, WHS.

26. Cowan to Kingsley Olds, 25 Feb. 1863, Letters and Diary of Luther H. Cowan, Wis Mss 218S, WHS.

27. Cowan to Kingsley Olds, 25 Feb. 1863, Letters and Diary of Luther H. Cowan, Wis Mss 218S, WHS.

28. Cowan to Kingsley Olds, 25 Feb. 1863, Letters and Diary of Luther H. Cowan, Wis Mss 218S, WHS.

29. Cowan to Kingsley Olds, 25 Feb. 1863, Letters and Diary of Luther H. Cowan, Wis Mss 218S, WHS.

30. Luther H. Cowan to M. P. Rindlaub, 21 Apr. 1863, Letters and Diary of Luther H. Cowan, Wis Mss 218S, WHS.

31. Balzar Grebe, "Autobiography and Civil War Diary," SC 2681 Grebe, Balzar, ALPL.

32. Grebe, "Autobiography and Civil War Diary," SC 2681 Grebe, Balzar, ALPL.

33. Grierson, *A Just and Righteous Cause,* 69.

34. Oliver A. Bridgford to Eliza, 22 Feb. 1862, Oliver A. Bridgford Papers, Private collection.

35. Bridgford to Eliza, 22 Feb. 1862, Oliver A. Bridgford Papers, Private collection.

36. Bridgford to Eliza, 22 Feb. 1862, Oliver A. Bridgford Papers, Private collection.

37. Alphonso Barto to Father, 27 May 1862, SC 2627 Barto, Alphonso, ALPL.

38. Barto to Father, 27 May 1862, SC 2627 Barto, Alphonso, ALPL.

39. Barto to Father, 12 Sept. 1864, SC 2627 Barto, Alphonso, ALPL.

40. Hezekiah Cole Clock to Alonzo, 15 Feb. 1863, SC 3098 Clock, Hezekiah Cole, ALPL.

41. Clock to Alonzo, 15 Feb. 1863, SC 3098 Clock, Hezekiah Cole, ALPL.

42. Clock to Alonzo, 15 Feb. 1863, SC 3098 Clock, Hezekiah Cole, ALPL.

43. Alexander K. Ewing to Parents, 9 Nov. 1862, SC 2667 Ewing, Alexander K., ALPL.

44. Ewing to Parents, 9 Nov. 1862, SC 2667 Ewing, Alexander K., ALPL.

45. Ewing to Parents, 28 Feb. 1863, SC 2667 Ewing, Alexander K., ALPL.

46. Ewing to Parents, 28 Feb. 1863, SC 2667 Ewing, Alexander K., ALPL.

47. Henry A. Kircher, "Diary of Henry Kircher," Engelmann Kircher Family Papers, ALPL.

48. Henry Kircher to Mother, 17 June 1863, in Hess, *A German in the Yankee Fatherland,* 107–8.

NOTES TO PAGES 120–126 259

49. Henry Adolph Kircher to Mother, 18 Nov. 1863, in Hess, *A German in the Yankee Fatherland*, 141.

50. James Kerr Proudfit to Emelie, 30 Sept. 1864, "Correspondence." 1861–1865, Wis Mss 158S, WHS.

51. Proudfit to Emelie, 30 Sept. 1864, "Correspondence," 1861–1865, Wis Mss 158S, WHS.

52. Arndt, "Reminiscences of an Artillery Officer," in *MOLLUS*, 50:293.

53. Arndt, "Reminiscences of an Artillery Officer," in *MOLLUS*, 50:293.

54. Harley Wayne to W. H. Alden, 8 Nov. 1861, SC 2824 Wayne, Harley, ALPL.

55. Harley Wayne to Ellen, 29 Dec. 1861, SC 2824 Wayne, Harley, ALPL.

56. Wayne to Ellen, 29 Dec. 1861, SC 2824 Wayne, Harley, ALPL.

57. Stockton, *War Diary*, 1.

58. Stockton, *War Diary*, 1.

59. Stockton, *War Diary*, 5.

60. Wills, *Army Life of an Illinois Soldier*, 32.

61. Wills, *Army Life of an Illinois Soldier*, 121.

62. Wills, *Army Life of an Illinois Soldier*, 121.

63. Wills, *Army Life of an Illinois Soldier*, 152.

64. Wills, *Army Life of an Illinois Soldier*, 255.

65. Benjamin Franklin Best to Wife, 7 Oct. 1861, SC 2478 Best, Benjamin Franklin, ALPL.

66. Best to Wife, 7 Oct. 1861, SC 2478 Best, Benjamin Franklin, ALPL.

67. Best to Wife, 7 Oct. 1861, SC 2478 Best, Benjamin Franklin, ALPL.

68. Best to Wife, 7 Oct. 1861, SC 2478 Best, Benjamin Franklin, ALPL.

69. Henry Giesey Ankeny to Wife, 15 July 1862, in Cox, *Kiss Josey for Me!*, 73.

70. Ankeny to Wife, 6 Nov. 1862, in Cox, *Kiss Josey for Me!*, 100.

71. Ankeny to Wife, 31 Aug. 1861, in Cox, *Kiss Josey for Me!*, 23.

72. Ankeny to Wife, 10 Dec. 1862, in Cox, *Kiss Josey for Me!*, 110.

73. Ankeny to Wife, 16 Mar. 1863, in Cox, *Kiss Josey for Me!*, 136.

74. Ankeny to Wife, 26 May 1863, in Cox, *Kiss Josey for Me!*, 157.

75. Ankeny to Wife, 4 Oct. 1863, in Cox, *Kiss Josey for Me!*, 183.

76. Ankeny to Tina, 18 June 1864, in Cox, *Kiss Josey for Me!*, 222.

77. Ankeny to Wife, 10 Dec. 1862, in Cox, *Kiss Josey for Me!*, 110.

78. Benjamin Henry Grierson to Alice, 13 May 1861, Grierson Box 1, Benjamin Grierson Family Papers, ALPL.

79. Grierson to Alice, 14 June 1861, Grierson Box 1, Benjamin Grierson Family Papers, ALPL.

80. Grierson to Alice, 14 June 1861, Grierson Box 1, Benjamin Grierson Family Papers, ALPL.

81. Grierson to Alice, 3 July 1861, Grierson Box 1, Benjamin Grierson Family Papers, ALPL.

82. Benjamin Henry Grierson to Alice & Charlie, 17 July 1861, Grierson Box 1, Benjamin Grierson Family Papers, ALPL.

83. Thomas Thomson Taylor to Wife, 19 Aug. 1863, MSS 7, Thomas Thomson Taylor papers, 1861–1865, OHC.

84. Taylor to Wife, 19 Aug. 1863, MSS 7, Thomas Thomson Taylor papers, 1861–1865, OHC.

85. Taylor to Wife, 19 Aug. 1863, MSS 7, Thomas Thomson Taylor papers, 1861–1865, OHC.

86. Taylor to Wife, 19 Aug. 1863, MSS 7, Thomas Thomson Taylor papers, 1861–1865, OHC.

87. DeWitt Clinton Loudon to Hannah, 6 Mar. 1862, MSS 610, DeWitt Clinton Loudon Papers, OHC.

88. Loudon to Hannah, 23 Mar. 1862, MSS 610, DeWitt Clinton Loudon Papers, OHC.

89. Loudon to Hannah, 3 May 1862, MSS 610, DeWitt Clinton Loudon Papers, OHC.

90. DeWitt Clinton Loudon to Fanny and Betty, no date, MSS 610, DeWitt Clinton Loudon Papers, OHC.

91. Loudon to Fanny and Betty, no date, MSS 610, DeWitt Clinton Loudon Papers, OHC.

92. Jacob B. Ritner to Emeline, 15 Mar. 1863, in Larimer, *Love and Valor*, 133.

93. Jacob B. Ritner to Wife, 7 July 1864, in Larimer, *Love and Valor*, 304–5.

94. Ritner to Wife, 15 June 1863, in Larimer, *Love and Valor*, 185; Ritner to Emeline, 16 May 1861, in Larimer, *Love and Valor*, 20; Jacob B. Ritner to Thomas E. Bereman, 19 May 1861, in

260   NOTES TO PAGES 127–131

Larimer, *Love and Valor*, 22; Ritner to Emeline, 3 Jan. 1863, *Love and Valor*, 95; Jacob B. Ritner to Samuel E. Bereman, 16 Mar. 1863, in Larimer, *Love and Valor*, 138; Ritner to Emeline, 7 Jan. 1863, in Larimer, *Love and Valor*, 98; Ritner to Wife, 22 Jan. 1865, in Larimer, *Love and Valor*, 415.

95. Jacob B. Ritner to Nellie, 11 July 1864 in Larimer, *Love and Valor*, 306–7.

96. Ritner to Wife, 31 July 1864, in Larimer, *Love and Valor*, 326.

97. Ritner to Wife, 31 July 1864, in Larimer, *Love and Valor*, 326.

98. Ritner to Wife, 31 July 1864, in Larimer, *Love and Valor*, 326.

99. Ritner to Wife, 5 Feb. 1865, in Larimer, *Love and Valor*, 421–22.

100. Edward Jesup Wood to Wife, 9 Aug. 1864, in Edward Jesup Wood Papers, IHS.

101. William T. Burnett to Sister, 17 May 1862, SC 359 Crum Family, ALPL.

9. SUFFERING

1. Strayer and Baumgartner, *Echoes of Battle: The Atlanta Campaign*, 141.

2. Rood, *Story of the Service of Company E*, 312, 404; Michael Griffin, "Captain John Gillispie" in Rood, *Story of the Service of Company E*, 497, 499; William VanMeter, "What I Know of the Life of John N. Cromwell, Colonel of the 47th Regiment of Illinois Vol. Infantry," SC 357 Cromwell, John Nelson, ALPL; John Nelson Cromwell to Wife, 11 Dec. 1862, SC 357 Cromwell, John Nelson, ALPL; "The Late Col. Cromwell," 13 Dec. 1865, *Plainfield Union*, SC 357 Cromwell, John Nelson, ALPL; William VanMeter, "A Condensed History of the 47th Regiment of Illinois Vol. Infantry, " SC 357 Cromwell, John Nelson, ALPL; Wills, *Army Life of an Illinois Soldier*, 206; William M. Reid, "Diary," SC 2812 Reid, William M., ALPL; William H. VanMeter, "A Condensed History of the 47th Regiment of Illinois Vol. Infantry, " SC 357 Cromwell, John Nelson, ALPL; Z. Payson Shumway to Hattie, 2 July 1863, SC 1388 Shumway, Z. Payson, ALPL; Brigadier General James Cooper, "Special Order No. 21," 9 Jan. 1863, Theodore Jones Papers, 1813–1900, Mss 64, OHC; Day, "The Fifteenth Iowa at Shiloh," in *MOLLUS*, 56:184–85.

3. Searle, "Personal Reminiscences of Shiloh," in *MOLLUS*, 55:335.

4. Searle, "Personal Reminiscences of Shiloh," in *MOLLUS*, 55:336.

5. Henry Otis Dwight, "My War Experiences," Henry Otis Dwight Papers (Microform), 1861–1900, Mic 127, OHC.

6. Luther H. Cowan to Harriet, 16 Feb. 1863, Letters and Diary of Luther H. Cowan, Wis Mss 218S, WHS.

7. Luther B. Hunt Diary, vol. 1, Vermont Historical Society; Crummer, *With Grant at Fort Donelson, Shiloh, and Vicksburg*, 38; Troy Moore to Alice, 13 June 1863, SC 2757 Moore, Troy, ALPL; Campbell, *The Union Must Stand*, 83; Benjamin H. Grierson to Alice, 10 Aug. 1862, Grierson Box 1, Benjamin Grierson Family Papers, ALPL; Jackson, *The Colonel's Diary*, 129, 138; Grierson to Alice, 3 Mar. 1862, Grierson Box 1, Benjamin Grierson Family Papers, ALPL; Grierson to Alice, 11 Jan. 1862, Grierson Box 1, Benjamin Grierson Family Papers, ALPL; Thomas T. Taylor, "Diary," Roll 21, Mic 17 Civil War Collection, OHC; William Reid, "Diary," SC 2812 Reid, William M., ALPL; Robert J. Whittleton to Col. Nasmith, 10 Aug. 1863, Nasmith, Samuel J., "Letters," 1861–1863, Wis Mss 66S, WHS; Robert Steele to Wife, 14 Feb. 1863, "Papers, 1827–1891," Wis Mss 113S, WHS; Charles Palmetier to Brother & Sister, 25 Nov. 1862, Demarest, Burnett, "Civil War Papers," 1861–1865, Wis Mss 53S, WHS; Charles Palmetier to Brother, 1 Aug. 1863, Demarest, Burnett, "Civil War Papers," 1861–1865, Wis Mss 53S, WHS; Ambrose, *From Shiloh to Savannah*, 15; Howard, *History of the 124th Regiment Illinois Infantry Volunteers*, 17–18, 71; Henry Ankeny to Wife, 16 Jan. 1863, in Cox, *Kiss Josey for Me!*, 118–19; Henry Ankeny to Tina, 23 Jan. 1863,in Cox, *Kiss Josey for Me!*, 120; James Balfour to Louisa, 26 Mar. 1862, SC 2451 Balfour, James, ALPL; Alphonso Barto to Sister," 27 Apr. 1862, SC 2627 Barto, Alphonso, ALPL; Sylvester Beckwith to Wife, 25 Mar. 1863, SC 2078 Beckwith, Sylvester Gridley, ALPL; Hart, *History of the Fortieth Illinois Inf.*, 119; Oliver A. Bridgford to Eliza, 1 Dec. 1861, Oliver A. Bridgford Papers; Bridgford to Eliza, 5 Feb. 1862, Oliver A. Bridgford Papers; Oliver A. Bridgford, "Letter to Eliza," 22 Feb. 1862, Oliver A. Bridgford Papers; Ankeny to Tina, 18 Jan. 1863, in Cox, *Kiss Josey for Me!*, 119; Bridgford to

Eliza, 9 Mar. 1862, Oliver A. Bridgford Papers; David M. Claggett, "Diary," SC 2689 Claggett, David McKee, ALPL; Luther H. Cowan to Family, 26 Oct. 1862, Letters and Diary of Luther H. Cowan, Wis Mss 218S, WHS; Warren Gray, "Diary, 1862–1863," SC 531, WHS; Alexander Ewing to Parents, 25 Mar. 1863, SC 2667 Ewing, Alexander K., ALPL; Luther H. Cowan to Family, 27 Apr. 1862, Letters and Diary of Luther H. Cowan, Wis Mss 218S, WHS; DeWitt Clinton Loudon to Hannah, 28 Apr. 1862, DeWitt Clinton Loudon Papers, Mss 610, OHC; Thomas Thomson Taylor to Wife, 11 Aug. 1863, Thomas Thomson Taylor papers, 1861–1865, Mss 7, OHC; Wills, *Army Life of an Illinois Soldier,* 296, 306; Jacob Ritner to Wife, 1 Feb. 1863, in Larimer, *Love and Valor,* 109–10; Jacob Ritner to Emeline, 8 Feb. 1863, in Larimer, *Love and Valor,* 113; Ritner to Emeline, 29 Apr. 1863, in Larimer, *Love and Valor,* 161; Ritner to Wife, 16 May 1864, in Larimer, *Love and Valor,* 271; Jacob B. Ritner to Wife, 31 Jan. 1865, in Larimer, *Love and Valor,* 417; Shumway to Hattie, 2 July 1863, SC 1388 Shumway, Z. Payson, ALPL; Crooker, Nourse, and Brown, *Story of the Fifty-Fifth Regiment,* 275; Taylor to Wife, 19 Aug. 1863, Thomas Thomson Taylor papers, 1861–1865, Mss 7, OHC; Taylor to Wife, 11 Sept. 1863, Thomas Thomson Taylor papers, 1861–1865, Mss 7, OHC; Joseph Dwight Tredway, "J. Dwight Tredway Memoir," 24 Sept. 1911, High Box 4, Folder 13, High, James L. Family Papers, ALPL; Head Quarters District of West Tennessee, "Special Orders," 17 Aug. 1862, Hitt Box 1-1/2, Folder 3, Hitt, Daniel Fletcher, ALPL; Luther H. Cowan to Harriet, 17–19 Mar. 1863, Letters and Diary of Luther H. Cowan, Wis Mss 218S, WHS; Edward Jesup Wood to Wife, 26 Feb. 1863, Edward Jesup Wood Papers, IHS; Wood to Wife, 2 Apr. 1863, Edward Jesup Wood Papers, IHS; Wood to Wife, 10 Apr. 1863, Edward Jesup Wood Papers, IHS; Wood to Wife, 21 Apr. 1863, Edward Jesup Wood Papers, IHS; Wood to Wife, 17 Apr. 1864, Edward Jesup Wood Papers, IHS; Wood to Wife, 29 May 1864, Edward Jesup Wood Papers, IHS; Loudon to Hannah, 15 Apr. 1862, DeWitt Clinton Loudon Papers, Mss 610, OHC; Loudon to Hannah, 24 Apr. 1862, DeWitt Clinton Loudon Papers, Mss 610, OHC; Loudon to Hannah, 11 May 1862, DeWitt Clinton Loudon Papers, Mss 610, OHC; Loudon to Hannah, 24 May 1862, DeWitt Clinton Loudon Papers, Mss 610, OHC; Loudon to Hannah, 8 Dec. 1863, DeWitt Clinton Loudon Papers, Mss 610, OHC; Loudon to Hannah, 3 Apr. 1864, DeWitt Clinton Loudon Papers, Mss 610, OHC; Loudon to Hannah, 11 Apr. 1864, DeWitt Clinton Loudon Papers, Mss 610, OHC; Loudon to Hannah, 23 June 1862, DeWitt Clinton Loudon Papers, Mss 610, OHC; Loudon to Hannah, 8 June 1864, DeWitt Clinton Loudon Papers, Mss 610, OHC; Loudon to Hannah, 13 Dec. 1863, DeWitt Clinton Loudon Papers, Mss 610, OHC; Henry A. Kircher, "Diary of Henry Kircher," Engelmann Kircher Family Papers, ALPL.

8. Jackson, *The Colonel's Diary,* 138–39.

9. Ritner to Wife, 16 Sept. 1864, in Larimer, *Love and Valor,* 359.

10. Bridgford to Eliza, 25 Mar. 1862, Oliver A. Bridgford Papers.

11. Gray, "Diary, 1862–1863," SC 531, WHS.

12. Ephraim Brown to Drusilla, 20 Jan. 1863, Ephraim Brown Papers, Mss 76, OHC.

13. James Leeper to Mary, 28 Mar. 1863, James Leeper Papers, IHS; Balfour to Louisa, 26 Mar. 1862, SC 2451 Balfour, James, ALPL; Joseph S. Reynolds to Charles, 12 July 1864, Joseph S. Reynolds Papers, #5060-z, Southern Historical Collection, Wilson Library, Univ. of North Carolina at Chapel Hill; Wills, *Army Life of an Illinois Soldier,* 201, 208, 210, 235–36; Henry A. Kircher, "Diary of Henry Kircher," Engelmann Kircher Family Papers, ALPL.

14. Ritner to Wife, 2 July 1864, in Larimer, *Love and Valor,* 298.

15. Ritner to Wife, 7 July 1864, in Larimer, *Love and Valor,* 302.

16. Ritner to Wife, 20 June 1864, in Larimer, *Love and Valor,* 292; Ritner to Wife, 2 July 1864, in Larimer, *Love and Valor,* 299–300.

17. Ritner to Wife, 7 July 1864, in Larimer, *Love and Valor,* 302.

18. Jacob Ritner to Nellie, 11 July 1864, in Larimer, *Love and Valor,* 306.

19. Compton, "Some Incidents Not Recorded in the Rebellion Records," in *MOLLUS,* 31:251–52.

20. Compton, "Some Incidents Not Recorded in the Rebellion Records," in *MOLLUS,* 31:252.

21. Compton, "Some Incidents Not Recorded in the Rebellion Records," in *MOLLUS,* 31:253.

22. Compton, "Some Incidents Not Recorded in the Rebellion Records," in *MOLLUS,* 31:253.

23. Compton, "Some Incidents Not Recorded in the Rebellion Records," in *MOLLUS,* 31:253.

262 NOTES TO PAGES 133–134

24. Compton, "Some Incidents Not Recorded in the Rebellion Records," in *MOLLUS*, 31:253.

25. Compton, "Some Incidents Not Recorded in the Rebellion Records," in *MOLLUS*, 31:253.

26. Compton, "Some Incidents Not Recorded in the Rebellion Records," in *MOLLUS*, 31:253.

27. Compton, "Some Incidents Not Recorded in the Rebellion Records," in *MOLLUS*, 31:254.

28. Compton, "Some Incidents Not Recorded in the Rebellion Records," in *MOLLUS*, 31:254.

29. "Report of Operations of 30th O.V.I. in Campaign from May 21st up to and Including the Occupation of Atlanta," 9 Sept. 1864, Typescripts of George H. Hildt letters and diary, 1862–1865, vol. 548, OHC; George H. Hildt, "Diary of the Siege of Atlanta, May 28–Oct. 7 1864," Typescripts of George H. Hildt letters and diary, 1862–1865, vol. 548, OHC; George H. Hildt to Parents, 28 June 1864, Typescripts of George H. Hildt letters and diary, 1862–1865, vol. 548, OHC; John E. Smith, "The Killed and Wounded of the Forty-Fifth," *Galena Daily Advertiser*, 13 Mar. 1862; "Lieut. Joseph Warren Miller," *Galena Daily Advertiser*, 16 Apr. 1862; "Casualties to the 45th," *Galena Daily Advertiser,* 16 Apr. 1862; Killed and Wounded at Pittsburg Landing: 45th Illinois Regiment," *Galena Daily Advertiser*, 19 Apr. 1862; "The Wounded," *Galena Daily Advertiser*, 28 Apr. 1862; "Lieut. J. W. Miller," *Galena Daily Advertiser*, 25 July 1862; William VanMeter, "A Condensed History of the 47th Regiment of Illinois Vol. Infantry," SC 357 Cromwell, John Nelson, ALPL; Howard, *History of the 124th Regiment Illinois Infantry Volunteers*, 79, 98–99; Nesbitt Baugher to Father, 9 Apr. 1862, Letters and Diary of Luther H. Cowan, Wis Mss 218S, WHS; Sylvester Gridley Beckwith to Wife, 21 May 1863, SC 2078 Beckwith, Sylvester Gridley, ALPL; Rood, *Story of the Service of Company E*, 525; Bridgford to Eliza, 25 Mar. 1862, Oliver A. Bridgford Papers; Hart, *History of the Fortieth Illinois Inf.*, 34, 88–89, 91–92, 95, 110–11, 158; Benjamin Grierson to Alice, 7 Sept. 1862, Grierson Box 1, Benjamin Grierson Family Papers, ALPL; Benjamin Grierson to Alice, 13 Sept. 1862, Grierson Box 1, Benjamin Grierson Family Papers, ALPL; Wood to Wife, 6 Dec. 1862, Edward Jesup Wood Papers, IHS; Wills, *Army Life of an Illinois Soldier*, 271, 298; Owen Stuart to Wife, 10 June 1864, SC 2406 Stuart, Owen, ALPL; Jackson, *The Colonel's Diary*, 153, 177; "Special Orders No. 39," 19 Dec. 1863, SC 2406 Stuart, Owen, ALPL; "Special Order No. 79," 17 Aug. 1864, SC 2406 Stuart, Owen, ALPL; Stuart to Wife, 4 Oct. 1864, SC 2406 Stuart, Owen, ALPL; "Capt. Rouse," *Galena Daily Advertiser*, 3 Sept. 1863; Shumway to Hattie, 8 Apr. 1862, SC 1388 Shumway, Z. Payson, ALPL; James Balfour to William Balfour, 4 Apr. 1862, SC 2451 Balfour, James, ALPL; Bridgford to Eliza, 22 Feb. 1862, Oliver A. Bridgford Papers; Strayer and Baumgartner, *Echoes of Battle: The Atlanta Campaign*, 162–63; Miller, *Struggle for the Life of the Republic*, 160; Arndt, "Reminiscences of an Artillery Officer," in *MOLLUS*, 50:286–89; Crooker, Nourse, and Brown, *Story of the Fifty-Fifth Regiment*, 327–28; "Lieut. Col. Maltby," *Galena Daily Advertiser*, 19 Feb. 1862; "Lieut. Colonel Maltby," *Galena Daily Advertiser*, 5 Mar. 1862; W. F. C., "Army Correspondence," *Galena Daily Advertiser*, 10 Mar. 1862; "Lieut. Col. Maltby," *Galena Daily Advertiser*, 19 Mar. 1862; "Lieut. Col. Maltby," *Galena Daily Advertiser*, 21 Apr. 1862; "Lieut. Col. Maltby," *Galena Daily Advertiser*, 28 Apr. 1862; "Col. Maltby," *Galena Daily Advertiser*, 29 Apr. 1862; "The New Regiment—Its Officers," *Galena Daily Advertiser*, 25 July 1861; Benjamin Franklin Best, "Diary," SC 2478 Best, Benjamin Franklin, ALPL; Stockton, *War Diary*, 15; Miller, *Struggle for the Life of the Republic*, 158; Leeper to Mary, 23 May 1863, James Leeper Papers, IHS; Campbell, *The Union Must Stand*, 138; Ritner to Wife, 29 Nov. 1863, in Larimer, *Love and Valor*, 256–57; Ritner to Wife, 1 Dec. 1863, in Larimer, *Love and Valor*, 258–61; Hickenlooper, "The Battle of Shiloh Part I.—Personal Experiences in the Battle," in *MOLLUS*, 5: 421, 429, 437–38.

30. Bridgford to Eliza, 9 Apr. 1862, Oliver A. Bridgford Papers.

31. Bridgford to Eliza, 20 Apr. 1862, Oliver A. Bridgford Papers.

32. Bridgford to Eliza, 20 Apr. 1862, Oliver A. Bridgford Papers.

33. Bridgford to Eliza, 20 Apr. 1862, Oliver A. Bridgford Papers.

34. Bridgford to Eliza, 20 Apr. 1862, Oliver A. Bridgford Papers.

35. Bridgford to Eliza, 7 July 1862, Oliver A. Bridgford Papers; Bridgford to Eliza, 20 July 1862, Oliver A. Bridgford Papers; Bridgford to Eliza, 27 July 1862, Oliver A. Bridgford Papers; Bridgford to Eliza, 29 July 1862, Oliver A. Bridgford Papers; O. A. Bridgford to Col. Smith,

15 Sept. 1862, SC 771–45 Smith, John Eugene, ALPL; "Army Correspondence," *Galena Daily Advertiser*, 6 Aug. 1862.

36. Vail, *Company K, of the 16th Wisconsin*, 4–5.

37. Henry A. Kircher, "Diary of Henry Kircher," Engelmann Kircher Family Papers, ALPL.

38. Kircher, *A German in the Yankee Fatherland*, 144–50; Charles Stierlin to Joseph Kircher, 7 Dec. 1863, in Hess, *A German in the Yankee Fatherland*, 151–52.

39. William H. Van Meter, "A Condensed History of the 47th Regiment of Illinois Vol. Infantry," SC 357 Cromwell, John Nelson. ALPL; "Diary," John Nilson Diary and Papers, IHS; Rood, *Story of the Service of Company E*, 374, 376; Rood, *Story of the Service of Company E*, 324, 333, 345–46, 502–3.

40. Harley Wayne to Ellen, 23 Sept. 1861, SC 2824 Wayne, Harley, ALPL.

41. Crooker, Nourse, and Brown, *Story of the Fifty-Fifth Regiment, 1861–1865*, 121.

42. "Casualties to the 45th," *Galena Daily Advertiser*, 16 Apr. 1862; "Lieut. N. Baugher," *Galena Daily Advertiser*, 16 Apr. 1862; "Wounded at Pittsburg," *Galena Daily Advertiser*, 19 Apr. 1862; "Lieut. N. Baugher," *Warren Independent*, 22 Apr. 1862; "The Wounded," *Galena Daily Advertiser*, 28 Apr. 1862; "Lieut. N. Baugher," *Galena Daily Advertiser*, 29 Apr. 1862; "Lieut. N. Baugher," *Warren Independent*, 29 Apr. 1862; "From Lieut. Baugher," *Warren Independent*, 6 May 1862; "Lieut. Baugher," *Galena Daily Advertiser*, 8 May 1862; "Death of Lieut. N. Baugher," *Galena Daily Advertiser*, 17 May 1862; "Letter of Acknowledgment," *Galena Daily Advertiser*, 24 May 1862; "Death of Lieut. Baugher," *Galena Daily Advertiser*, 6 June 1862; Baugher to Father, 9 Apr. 1862, Letters and Diary of Luther H. Cowan, Wis Mss 218S, WHS; E. J. Hart, *History of the Fortieth Illinois Inf.*, 30; "Death of Capt. T. D. Connor," *Galena Daily Advertiser*, 16 Apr. 1862; "Casualties to the 45th," *Galena Daily Advertiser*, 16 Apr. 1862; "Death of Lieut. Geo. Moore," *Galena Daily Advertiser*, 16 Apr. 1862; Morton, "A Boy at Shiloh," in *MOLLUS*, 22:63.

43. "The Death of Col. Cromwell," *Peoria Daily Transcript*, 22 June 1863, SC 357 Cromwell, John Nelson, ALPL; "The Death of Col. Cromwell," *Peoria Daily Transcript*, 31 July 1863, SC 357 Cromwell, John Nelson, ALPL; "The Late Col. Cromwell," 13 Dec. 1865, *Plainfield Union*, SC 357 Cromwell, John Nelson, ALPL; William H. Van Meter, "A Condensed History of the 47th Regiment of Illinois Vol. Infantry," SC 357 Cromwell, John Nelson, ALPL; Joseph R. Vail to Mrs. Cromwell, 15 July 1863, SC 357 Cromwell, John Nelson, ALPL; "Col. Cromwell," *Peoria Daily Transcript*, 23 June 1863, SC 357 Cromwell, John Nelson, ALPL; Joseph R. Vail to Mrs. Cromwell, 15 July 1863, SC 357 Cromwell, John Nelson, ALPL.

44. Beckwith to Wife, 12 Mar. 1863, SC 2078 Beckwith, Sylvester Gridley, ALPL.

45. Sylvester G. Beckwith to Wife, 17 Mar. 1863, SC 2078 Beckwith, Sylvester Gridley, ALPL.

46. Beckwith to Wife, 25 Mar. 1863, SC 2078 Beckwith, Sylvester Gridley, ALPL.

47. Beckwith to Wife, 21 May 1863, SC 2078 Beckwith, Sylvester Gridley, ALPL.

48. Beckwith to Wife, 21 May 1863, SC 2078 Beckwith, Sylvester Gridley, ALPL.

49. Beckwith to Wife, 22 June 1863, SC 2078 Beckwith, Sylvester Gridley, ALPL.

50. Beckwith to Wife, 14 June 1863, SC 2078 Beckwith, Sylvester Gridley, ALPL; "Death of Lieut. Beckwith," *Hawkeye Flag*, 10 July 1863, SC 2078 Beckwith, Sylvester Gridley, ALPL.

51. Luther H. Cowan to Harriet, 13 Jan. 1862, Letters and Diary of Luther H. Cowan, Wis Mss 218S, WHS.

52. Luther H. Cowan to Family, 27 Apr. 1862, Letters and Diary of Luther H. Cowan, Wis Mss 218S, WHS.

53. Kingsley E. Olds to Kingsley Olds [son to father of same name], 25 May 1863, Letters and Diary of Luther H. Cowan, Wis Mss 218S, WHS.

54. Daniel W. Cowan to Harriet, 25 May 1863, Letters and Diary of Luther H. Cowan, Wis Mss 218S, WHS; "Death of Maj. L. H. Cowen (from the Warren Independent)," *Galena Daily Advertiser*, 16 June 1863; Crummer, *With Grant at Fort Donelson, Shiloh, and Vicksburg*, 112; Luther H. Cowan to Harriet, 23 Mar. 1862, Letters and Diary of Luther H. Cowan, Wis Mss 218S, WHS; Luther H. Cowan to Harriet, 7 Mar. 1862, Letters and Diary of Luther H. Cowan, Wis Mss 218S, WHS.

55. Howard, *History of the 124th Regiment Illinois Infantry Volunteers*, 115; Miller, *Struggle for the Life of the Republic*, 80; "Brave Deeds of Noble Men," *Galena Daily Advertiser*, 3 July 1863;

264 NOTES TO PAGES 139–144

"The Late Lt. Col. Melancthon Smith, of the Lead Mine Regiment, 45th Illinois," *Galena Daily Advertiser,* 29 Aug. 1863; R. W. Burt to Editor, *North American,* 30 May 1863, Vfm 4626, 76th Ohio Volunteer Infantry Correspondence, OHC.

56. George H. Hildt Diary, Typescripts of George H. Hildt letters and diary, 1862–1865, vol. 548, OHC.

57. "Report of Operations of 30th O.V.I. in Campaign from May 21st up to and Including the Occupation of Atlanta," 9 Sept. 1864, Typescripts of George H. Hildt letters and diary, 1862–1865, vol. 548, OHC; Hildt to Parents, 28 June 1864, Typescripts of George H. Hildt letters and diary, 1862–1865, vol. 548, OHC.

58. Loudon to Hannah, 3 Oct. 1862, Mss 610, DeWitt Clinton Loudon Papers, OHC.

59. Loudon to Hannah, 3 Oct. 1862, Mss 610, DeWitt Clinton Loudon Papers, OHC.

60. Townsend P. Heaton to Jack, 11 Oct. 1862, Vfm 1302, Townsend P. Heaton Papers, 1862–1863, OHC.

61. Crooker, Nourse, and Brown, *Story of the Fifty-Fifth Regiment,* 150, 213; George Elliott to Emily J. Dean, 8 Aug. 1863, in Zachariah Dean Papers, HIS.

62. Joe P. Stevens, "Civil War Murder: The Strange and Tragic Story of Lt. Col. Reuben Loomis of Du Quoin," *Duquoin Evening Call,* 24 Sept. 2013, http://www.duquoin.com/article /20130924/news/701223865/.

63. Illinois in the Civil War, accessed 20 May 2016, http://civilwar.illinoisgenweb.org/.

64. Friedrich Martens to Dear Ones, 24 Sept. 1862, in Kamphoefner and Helbich, *Germans in the Civil War,* 322.

65. Robert Steele to Father and Mother, 18 Dec. 1862, "Papers, 1827–1891," Wis Mss 113S, WHS.

66. Charles Palmetier to Brother and Sister, 14 Apr. 1863, Palmetier, Charles, "Civil War Letters," 1861–1864, Wis Mss 168S, WHS.

67. Ritner to Wife, 1 Nov. 1863, in Larimer, *Love and Valor,* 235.

68. Ritner to Wife, 1 Nov. 1863, in Larimer, *Love and Valor,* 237.

69. Ritner to Wife, 1 Nov. 1863, in Larimer, *Love and Valor,* 237.

70. Dwight, "My War Experiences," Henry Otis Dwight Papers (Microform), 1861–1900, Mic 127, OHC; Henry Giesey Ankeny to Wife, 15 Dec. 1863, in Cox, *Kiss Josey for Me!,* 199; Ankeny to Wife, 20 Dec. 1863, in Cox, *Kiss Josey for Me!,* 201.

71. Loudon to Hannah, 3 May 1862, Mss 610, DeWitt Clinton Loudon Papers, OHC.

72. Loudon to Hannah, 25 May 1862, DeWitt Clinton Loudon Papers, Mss 610, OHC.

73. Loudon to Hannah, 25 May 1862, DeWitt Clinton Loudon Papers, Mss 610, OHC.

74. Loudon to Hannah, 29 Nov. 1862, DeWitt Clinton Loudon Papers, Mss 610, OHC.

75. Loudon to Hannah, 29 Nov. 1862, DeWitt Clinton Loudon Papers, Mss 610, OHC.

10. A DAWNING DAY OF LIBERTY

1. Stockton, *War Diary,* 10.

2. Joseph S. Reynolds to Brother Willie, 26 July 1862, in Joseph S. Reynolds Papers #5060-z, Southern Historical Collection, Wilson Library, Univ. of North Carolina at Chapel Hill.

3. James W. Kays to Friends, 22 Oct. 1862, in SC 3042 Kays Family, ALPL.

4. Harlow M. Waller to Sister, 31 May 1863, in "Harlow M. & Henrietta Waller Letters, 1861–1869," SC 2952, WHS.

5. Henry Miller Culbertson to Sister, 3 Mar. 1864, in Culbertson, Henry Miller, "Civil War Letters," 1861–1864, Wis Mss 216S, WHS.

6. Oliver A. Bridgford to Eliza, 7 July 1862, in Oliver A. Bridgford Papers; Thomas T. Taylor, "Diary," Roll 21, MIC 17 Civil War Collection, OHC; Albert J. Rockwell to Mrs. Anna Rockwell, 23 July 1863, "Civil War Letters," 1827–1864, Wis Mss 92S, WHS; Edward Gee Miller, "Captain Edward Gee Miller of the 20th Wisconsin: His War, 1861–1865," edited by W. J. Lemke, Washington County Historical Society: Fayetteville, AR, 1960, in "Civil War Papers,

NOTES TO PAGES 144–150 265

1861–1906," Wis Mss 62S, WHS; Miller, *Struggle for the Life of the Republic*, 66; Rood, *Story of the Service of Company E*, 187–88.

7. "Army Correspondence," *Galena Daily Advertiser*, 6 Aug. 1862.

8. Henry F. Hole to Sister Mine, 13 Oct. 1862, SC 2427 Hole, Henry F., ALPL.

9. Crooker, "Episodes and Characters in an Illinois Regiment," in *MOLLUS*, 10:47–48; Robert B. Latham to Wife, 22 Jan. 1863, in SC 895 Latham, R. B. ALPL; Henry J. Traber to Sister, 2 May 1863, in Traber, Henry J., Civil War Letters, 1862–1865, Wis Mss 49S, WHS.

10. Luther H. Cowan to Harriet, 7 Feb. 1862, in Letters and Diary of Luther H. Cowan, Wis Mss 218S, WHS.

11. Luther Cowan Diary, 23 Feb. 1863, in Letters and Diary of Luther H. Cowan, Wis Mss 218S, WHS.

12. Luther H. Cowan to Kingsley Olds, 25 Feb. 1863, in Letters and Diary of Luther H. Cowan, Wis Mss 218S, WHS.

13. Luther H. Cowan to M. P. Rindlaub, 21 Apr. 1863, in Letters and Diary of Luther H. Cowan, Wis Mss 218S, WHS.

14. Luther H. Cowan to Josephine & Harriet, 3 Aug. 1862, in Letters and Diary of Luther H. Cowan, Wis Mss 218S, WHS; Luther H. Cowan to Family, 26 Aug. 1862, in Letters and Diary of Luther H. Cowan, Wis Mss 218S, WHS; Cowan to Harriet, 27 Nov. 1862, in Letters and Diary of Luther H. Cowan, Wis Mss 218S, WHS; Cowan to Kingsley Olds, 25 Feb. 1863, in Letters and Diary of Luther H. Cowan, Wis Mss 218S, WHS.

15. Jasper A. Maltby, "Letter from Col. Maltby," *Galena Daily Advertiser*, 22 Aug. 1862.

16. Maltby, "Letter from Col. Maltby," *Galena Daily Advertiser*, 22 Aug. 1862.

17. Alexander K. Ewing to Uncle, Aunt, and Cousins, 9 Jan. 1863, in SC 2667 Ewing, Alexander K., ALPL.

18. Ewing to Uncle, Aunt, and Cousins, 9 Jan. 1863, in SC 2667 Ewing, Alexander K., ALPL.

19. Alexander K. Ewing to Parents, 28 Feb. 1863, in SC 2667 Ewing, Alexander K., ALPL.

20. Ewing to Parents, 25 Mar. 1863, in SC 2667 Ewing, Alexander K., ALPL.

21. "Diary of Z. Payson Shumway," in SC 1388 Shumway, Z. Payson, ALPL.

22. Friedrich Martens to Most Dearly Beloved Parents, 3 Dec. 1862, in Kamphoefner and Helbich, *Germans in the Civil War*, 322.

23. Friedrich Martens to Dear Ones, 19 Sept. 1863, in Kamphoefner and Helbich, *Germans in the Civil War*, 323.

24. Ambrose, *From Shiloh to Savannah*, 64.

25. "Diary of Z. Payson Shumway," in SC 1388 Shumway, Z. Payson, ALPL.

26. Henry Giesey Ankeny to Wife, 26 May 1862, in Cox, *Kiss Josey for Me!*, 67–68.

27. Henry Giesey Ankeny to Tina, 17 Aug. 1862, in Cox, *Kiss Josey for Me!*, 79.

28. Ankeny to Tina, 17 Aug. 1862, in Cox, *Kiss Josey for Me!*, 78.

29. Ankeny to Tina, 8 June 1862, in Cox, *Kiss Josey for Me!*, 163.

30. Ankeny to Wife, 15 July 1862, in Cox, *Kiss Josey for Me!*, 73.

31. Jacob B. Ritner to Emeline, 2 Dec. 1862, in Larimer, *Love and Valor*, 73–74.

32. Ritner to Emeline, 2 Dec. 1862, in Larimer, *Love and Valor*, 74.

33. Ritner to Emeline, 2 Dec. 1862, in Larimer, *Love and Valor*, 74.

34. Ritner to Emeline, 19 Dec. 1862, in Larimer, *Love and Valor*, 79; Ritner to Emeline, 2 Dec. 1862, in Larimer, *Love and Valor*, 73; Ritner to Emeline, 30 Mar. 1863, and Ritner to Emeline, 17 Apr. 1863, in Larimer, *Love and Valor*, 142 and 155.

35. Ritner and Ritner, *Love and Valor*, 87.

36. Ritner to Emeline, 17 Nov. 1863, in Larimer, *Love and Valor*, 240–41.

37. Ritner to Emeline, 17 Apr. 1863, in Larimer, *Love and Valor*, 154.

38. Ritner to Emeline, 17 Apr. 1863, in Larimer, *Love and Valor*, 154.

39. Ritner to Emeline, 17 Apr. 1863, in Larimer, *Love and Valor*, 154.

40. Ritner to Emeline, 22 Apr. 1863, in Larimer, *Love and Valor*, 157.

41. Ritner to Emeline, 29 Apr. 1863, in Larimer, *Love and Valor*, 159.

42. Ritner to Emeline, 29 Apr. 1863, in Larimer, *Love and Valor*, 159.

266 NOTES TO PAGES 150–157

43. Ritner to Emeline, 29 Apr. 1863, in Larimer, *Love and Valor*, 160.

44. Jacob B. Ritner to Wife, 22 Jan. 1865, in Larimer, *Love and Valor*, 413.

45. Ritner to Wife, 22 Jan. 1865, in Larimer, *Love and Valor*, 413.

46. Ritner to Wife, 22 Jan. 1865, in Larimer, *Love and Valor*, 413.

47. Ritner to Wife, 22 Jan. 1865, in Larimer, *Love and Valor*, 413.

48. Ritner to Wife, 14 Mar. 1865, in Larimer, *Love and Valor*, 431.

49. Ritner to Wife, 14 Mar. 1865, in Larimer, *Love and Valor*, 431.

50. Jacob B. Ritner, "Letter Fragment Written Sometime after the Burning of Columbia SC," 1865, in Larimer, *Love and Valor*, 426.

51. Jacob B. Ritner, "Letter Fragment Written Sometime after the Burning of Columbia SC," 1865, in Larimer, *Love and Valor*, 426.

52. Ritner to Emeline, 4 Apr. 1863, in Larimer, *Love and Valor*, 147; Ritner to Emeline, 12 Apr. 1863, in Larimer, *Love and Valor*, 151; Ritner to Emeline, 17 Apr. 1863, in Larimer, *Love and Valor*, 154; Ritner to Emeline, 22 Apr. 1863, in Larimer, *Love and Valor*, 157; Jacob B. Ritner, "Letter Fragment Written Sometime after the Burning of Columbia SC," 1865, in Larimer, *Love and Valor*, 426.

53. Campbell, *The Union Must Stand*, 39.

54. Campbell, *The Union Must Stand*, 91.

55. Campbell, *The Union Must Stand*, 61.

56. Campbell, *The Union Must Stand*, 61.

57. Campbell to *Ripley Bee*, 19 Jan. 1863, in Grimsley and Miller, *The Union Must Stand*, 217.

58. Campbell to *Ripley Bee*, 19 Jan. 1863, in Grimsley and Miller, *The Union Must Stand*, 217.

59. Campbell, *The Union Must Stand*, 50.

60. Campbell to *Ripley* Bee, 9 July 1862, in Grimsley and Miller, *The Union Must Stand*, 207.

61. Campbell to *Ripley Bee*, 4 Dec. 1862, in Grimsley and Miller, *The Union Must Stand*, 213–14.

62. Campbell to *Ripley Bee*, 19 Jan. 1863, in Grimsley and Miller, *The Union Must Stand*, 217.

63. Campbell to *Ripley Bee*, 19 Jan. 1863, in Grimsley and Miller, *The Union Must Stand*, 218.

64. Benjamin Henry Grierson to Alice, 6 Nov. 1861, in Grierson Box 1, Benjamin Grierson Family Papers, ALPL.

65. Grierson, *A Just and Righteous Cause*, 56.

66. Grierson to Alice, 6 July 1862, in Grierson Box 1, Benjamin Grierson Family Papers, ALPL.

67. Grierson, *A Just and Righteous Cause*, 22, 31–33, 61; Grierson to Alice, 11 July 1862, in Grierson Box 1, Benjamin Grierson Family Papers, ALPL.

68. Jackson, *The Colonel's Diary*, 27.

69. Jackson, *The Colonel's Diary*, 260.

70. Jackson, *The Colonel's Diary*, 55.

71. Jackson, *The Colonel's Diary*, 90.

72. Jackson, *The Colonel's Diary*, 164–65.

73. Jackson, *The Colonel's Diary*, 175.

74. Jackson, *The Colonel's Diary*, 193.

75. Jackson, *The Colonel's Diary*, 193.

76. Jackson, *The Colonel's Diary*, 193.

77. Jackson, *The Colonel's Diary*, 193.

78. DeWitt Clinton Loudon to Hannah, 9 July 1862, MSS 610, DeWitt Clinton Loudon Papers, OHC.

79. Loudon to Hannah, 9 July 1862, MSS 610, DeWitt Clinton Loudon Papers, OHC.

80. Loudon to Hannah, 9 July 1862, MSS 610, DeWitt Clinton Loudon Papers, OHC.

81. DeWitt Clinton Loudon to Dr. J. W. Gordon, 31 July 1862, MSS 610, DeWitt Clinton Loudon Papers, OHC.

82. Loudon to Hannah, 28 Oct. 1862, MSS 610, DeWitt Clinton Loudon Papers, OHC.

83. Loudon to Hannah, 1 Jan. 1863, MSS 610, DeWitt Clinton Loudon Papers, OHC.

84. Loudon to Hannah, 1 Jan. 1863, MSS 610, DeWitt Clinton Loudon Papers, OHC.

85. Loudon to Hannah, 1 Jan. 1863, MSS 610, DeWitt Clinton Loudon Papers, OHC.

NOTES TO PAGES 157–166 267

86. Loudon to Hannah, 1 Jan. 1863, MSS 610, DeWitt Clinton Loudon Papers, OHC.

87. Alphonso Barto to Father, 9 Feb. 1863, SC 2627 Barto, Alphonso, ALPL.

88. Barto to Father, 7 July 1863, SC 2627 Barto, Alphonso, ALPL.

89. Barto to Father, 7 July 1863, SC 2627 Barto, Alphonso, ALPL.

90. Barto to Father, 7 July 1863, SC 2627 Barto, Alphonso, ALPL.

91. Barto to Father, 7 July 1863, SC 2627 Barto, Alphonso, ALPL.

92. Wills, *Army Life of an Illinois Soldier*, 17.

93. Wills, *Army Life of an Illinois Soldier*, 83.

94. Wills, *Army Life of an Illinois Soldier*, 122–23.

95. Wills, *Army Life of an Illinois Soldier*, 123.

96. Wills, *Army Life of an Illinois Soldier*, 123.

97. Wills, *Army Life of an Illinois Soldier*, 125–26.

98. Wills, *Army Life of an Illinois Soldier*, 127.

99. Wills, *Army Life of an Illinois Soldier*, 141.

100. Charles W. Wills to Sister, 21 Nov. 1862, in Wills, *Army Life of an Illinois Soldier*, 142.

101. Charles W. Wills to Sister, 16 Jan. 1863, in Wills, *Army Life of an Illinois Soldier*, 148.

102. Wills, *Army Life of an Illinois Soldier*, 150–51.

103. Wills, *Army Life of an Illinois Soldier*, 166–67.

104. Charles W. Wills to Sister, 29 May 1863, in Wills, *Army Life of an Illinois Soldier*, 176–77.

105. Charles W. Wills to Sister, 26 June 1863, in Wills, *Army Life of an Illinois Soldier*, 183–84.

106. Wills, *Army Life of an Illinois Soldier*, 185.

107. Wills, *Army Life of an Illinois Soldier*, 195–96.

108. Wills, *Army Life of an Illinois Soldier*, 246.

109. Wills, *Army Life of an Illinois Soldier*, 312.

110. Wills, *Army Life of an Illinois Soldier*, 320.

111. Wills, *Army Life of an Illinois Soldier*, 330.

112. Wills, *Army Life of an Illinois Soldier*, 332.

113. Wills, *Army Life of an Illinois Soldier*, 350.

114. Henry A. Kircher to Mother, 19 Jan. 1863, in Hess, *A German in the Yankee Fatherland*, 57.

115. Kircher to Mother, 19 Jan. 1863, in Hess, *A German in the Yankee Fatherland*, 57.

116. Kircher to Mother, 19 Jan. 1863, in Hess, *A German in the Yankee Fatherland*, 57.

117. Henry A. Kircher, "Diary of Henry Kircher," Engelmann Kircher Family Papers, ALPL.

118. Kircher to Mother, 2 Mar. 1863, in Hess, *A German in the Yankee Fatherland*, 74.

119. Henry A. Kircher to Father, 19 Apr. 1863, in Hess, *A German in the Yankee Fatherland*, 91–92.

120. Kircher to Father, 19 Apr. 1863, in Hess, *A German in the Yankee Fatherland*, 92.

121. Kircher to Father, 19 Apr. 1863, in Hess, *A German in the Yankee Fatherland*, 92.

122. Kircher to Father, 19 Apr. 1863, in Hess, *A German in the Yankee Fatherland*, 92.

123. Kircher to Father, 19 Apr. 1863, in Hess, *A German in the Yankee Fatherland*, 92.

124. Kircher to Mother, 22 Apr. 1863, in Hess, *A German in the Yankee Fatherland*, 94.

125. Kircher to Mother, 22 Apr. 1863, in Hess, *A German in the Yankee Fatherland*, 95.

126. Henry A. Kircher, "Diary of Henry Kircher," Engelmann Kircher Family Papers, ALPL.

127. Henry A. Kircher, "Diary of Henry Kircher," Engelmann Kircher Family Papers, ALPL.

128. Warren Gray, "Diary, 1862–1863," SC 531, WHS; Horace Wardner, "Reminiscences of a Surgeon," in *MOLLUS*, 12:183; Loudon to Hannah, 5 Nov. 1862, MSS 610, DeWitt Clinton Loudon Papers, OHC; Loudon to Hannah, 1 Jan. 1863, MSS 610, DeWitt Clinton Loudon Papers, OHC; "Diary," John Nilson Diary and Papers, IHS; Campbell, *The Union Must Stand*, 126; Ephraim Brown to Drusilla, 25 Jan. 1863, Mss 76, Ephraim Brown Papers, OHC; Townsend P. Heaton to Jack, 11 Feb. 1863, Townsend P. Heaton Papers, 1862–1863, Vfm 1302, OHC; Bennet Grigsby to Wife & Children, 18 May 1863, Bennet Grigsby Civil War Letters, IHS; Waller to Sister, 31 May 1863, in "Harlow M. & Henrietta Waller Letters, 1861–1869," SC 2952, WHS; Robert Steele to Wife, 3 Mar. 1863, "Papers, 1827–1891," Wis Mss 113S, WHS; Steele to Wife, 12 June 1863, in "Papers, 1827–1891," Wis Mss 113S, WHS; Brown to Drusilla, 19 Dec. 1862, Mss 76, Ephraim Brown Papers, OHC; Stockton, *War Diary*, 14.

268   NOTES TO PAGES 167–169

11. THE VERY LIFE OF THE COUNTRY

1. Castel, *Tom Taylor's Civil War*, 6; Walter Quintin Gresham Collection Guide, Indiana Historical Society, http://www.indianahistory.org/; Crooker, Nourse, and Brown, *Story of the Fifty-Fifth Regiment*, 19; James M. Bull, "Memorial of Captain Edward Gee Miller," 8 July 1906, "Civil War Papers, 1861–1906," Wis Mss 62S, WHS; Rood, *Story of the Service of Company E*, 501; Henry F. Hole, "When I Saw Mr. Lincoln!," 12 Feb. 1925, SC 2427 Hole, Henry F., ALPL; "Brig. Gen. Maltby," *Galena Daily Advertiser*, 3 Sept. 1863; Edward Gee Miller, "Speech at Joint Debate of Republican and Democratic Clubs," 20 Oct. 1860, "Civil War Papers, 1861–1906," Wis Mss 62S, WHS; Friedrich Martens to Most dearly Beloved Parents, 24 Sept. 1858, in Kamphoefner and Helbich, *Germans in the Civil War*, 316; Ritner to Wife, 8 June 1864, in Larimer, *Love and Valor*, 291; "Democratic Meeting: Attack on a Union Soldier," *Galena Daily Advertiser*, 21 Feb. 1863; Henry Giesey Ankeny to Wife, 28 Feb. 1863, in Cox, *Kiss Josey for Me!*, 134; William K. Barney to All at Home, May 1863, "Papers," 1845–1874, Wis Mss 123S, WHS; Henry A. Kircher to Mother, 7 Feb. 1863, in Hess, *A German in the Yankee Fatherland*, 66; Henry A. Kircher, "Diary of Henry Kircher," Engelmann Kircher Family Papers, ALPL; Kircher to Mother, 29 Sept. 1863, in Hess, *A German in the Yankee Fatherland*, 127

2. Crooker, Nourse, and Brown, *Story of the Fifty-Fifth Regiment*, 219–20.

3. Edward Jesup Wood to Wife, 2 July 1863, Edward Jesup Wood Papers, IHS.

4. Wood to Wife, 2 Aug. 1863, Edward Jesup Wood Papers, IHS.

5. Jacob B. Ritner to Wife, 9 Sept. 1864, in Larimer, *Love and Valor*, 350.

6. Ritner to Wife, 19 Sept. 1864, in Larimer, *Love and Valor*, 361.

7. DeWitt Clinton Loudon to Hannah, 8 Oct. 1862, DeWitt Clinton Loudon Papers, Mss 610, OHC; Alexander K. Ewing to Parents, 22 Mar. 1863, SC 2667 Ewing, Alexander K., ALPL; Kircher to Mother, 24 Mar. 1863, in Hess, *A German in the Yankee Fatherland*, 85; "Letter from the 45th," *Galena Daily Advertiser*, 17 Mar. 1863; Henry Miller Culbertson to Mother, Brother, and Sister," 5 Aug. 1863, "Civil War Letters," 1861–1864, Wis Mss 216S, WHS; Ritner to Wife, 17 Nov. 1863, in Larimer, *Love and Valor*, 240; Ritner to Wife, 24 Aug. 1864, in Larimer, *Love and Valor*, 341; Ritner to Wife, 11 Sept. 1864, in Larimer, *Love and Valor*, 351; Ritner to Wife, 14 Sept. 1864, in Larimer, *Love and Valor*, 355; Ritner to Wife, 13 Oct. 1864, in Larimer, *Love and Valor*, 372; Wood to Wife, 9 Nov. 1863, Edward Jesup Wood Papers, IHS; Charles Wills to Sister, 20 Mar. 1864, in Wills, *Army Life of an Illinois Soldier*, 220–21; Wood to Wife, 10 June 1864, Edward Jesup Wood Papers, IHS.

8. Z. Payson Shumway to Hattie, 2 Mar. 1863, SC 1388 Shumway, Z. Payson. ALPL; Robert J. Whittleton to Col. Nasmith, 15 Aug. 1863, in Nasmith, Samuel J., "Letters," 1861–1863, Wis Mss 66S, WHS; Charles Stanton to Mr. Day, 5 Feb. 1863, SC 2379 Joshua Day Family, ALPL; Ambrose, *From Shiloh to Savannah*, 113; Friedrich Martens to Dear Ones, 24 Sept. 1862, in Kamphoefner and Helbich, *Germans in the Civil War*, 322; Friedrich Martens to Most Dearly Beloved Parents, 3 Feb. 1862, in Kamphoefner and Helbich, *Germans in the Civil War*, 320; Miller, *The Struggle for the Life of the Republic*, 134; Robert Steele to Father and Mother, 5 Jan. 1863, "Papers, 1827–1891," Wis Mss 113S, WHS; Robert Steele to Father, 18 Apr. 1863, "Papers, 1827–1891," Wis Mss 113S, WHS; Ritner to Wife, 24 Aug. 1864, in Larimer, *Love and Valor*, 341; Wills, *Army Life of an Illinois Soldier*, 203, 343; Loudon to Hannah, 19 Oct. 1862, DeWitt Clinton Loudon Papers, Mss 610, OHC; "Our Company at Galena," *Warren Independent*, 17 Sept. 1861; "Lead-Mine Regiment," *Galena Daily Advertiser*, 21 Dec. 1861; "From the Forty-Fifth," *Galena Daily Advertiser*, 29 Sept. 1863; "Presentation of the Old Colors of the 45th," *Galena Daily Advertiser*, 1 Oct. 1863; "A Card of Thanks," *Galena Daily Advertiser*, 6 Oct. 1863; Charles Palmetier to Brother, 22 Mar. 1863, "Civil War Letters," 1861–1864, Wis Mss 168S, WHS.

9. Erasmus D. Ward to Sister, 12 Apr. 1862, SC 3110 Ward, Erasmus D., ALPL.

10. Alphonso Barto to Father, 9 Feb. 1863, SC 2627 Barto, Alphonso, ALPL.

11. Barto to Father, 9 Feb. 1863, SC 2627 Barto, Alphonso, ALPL.

12. Barto to Father, 9 Feb. 1863, SC 2627 Barto, Alphonso, ALPL.

13. Bennet Grigsby to Wife & Children, 18 May 1863, Bennet Grigsby Civil War Letters, IHS.

14. Henry F. Hole to Minerva, 25 Jan. 1862, SC 2427 Hole, Henry F., ALPL.

NOTES TO PAGES 170–176 269

15. Hole to Minerva, 25 Jan. 1862, SC 2427 Hole, Henry F., ALPL.

16. Hole to Minerva, 25 Jan. 1862, SC 2427 Hole, Henry F., ALPL.

17. Henry F. Hole to Sister Mine, 13 Oct. 1862, SC 2427 Hole, Henry F., ALPL.

18. Hole to Sister Mine, 13 Oct. 1862, SC 2427 Hole, Henry F., ALPL.

19. Loudon to Hannah, 9 July 1862, DeWitt Clinton Loudon Papers, Mss 610, OHC.

20. Loudon to Hannah, 9 July 1862, DeWitt Clinton Loudon Papers, Mss 610, OHC.

21. Loudon to Hannah, 9 July 1862, DeWitt Clinton Loudon Papers, Mss 610, OHC.

22. Loudon to Hannah, 9 July 1862, DeWitt Clinton Loudon Papers, Mss 610, OHC.

23. Loudon to Hannah, 9 July 1862, DeWitt Clinton Loudon Papers, Mss 610, OHC.

24. DeWitt Clinton Loudon to Dr. J. W. Gordon, 31 July 1862, DeWitt Clinton Loudon Papers, Mss 610, OHC.

25. Loudon to Dr. J. W. Gordon, 31 July 1862, DeWitt Clinton Loudon Papers, Mss 610, OHC.

26. Loudon to Dr. J. W. Gordon, 31 July 1862, DeWitt Clinton Loudon Papers, Mss 610, OHC.

27. Loudon to Dr. J. W. Gordon, 31 July 1862, DeWitt Clinton Loudon Papers, Mss 610, OHC.

28. Loudon to Dr. J. W. Gordon, 31 July 1862, DeWitt Clinton Loudon Papers, Mss 610, OHC.

29. Loudon to Dr. J. W. Gordon, 31 July 1862, DeWitt Clinton Loudon Papers, Mss 610, OHC.

30. Loudon to Dr. J. W. Gordon, 31 July 1862, DeWitt Clinton Loudon Papers, Mss 610, OHC.

31. Loudon to Hannah, 1 Jan. 1863, DeWitt Clinton Loudon Papers, Mss 610, OHC.

32. Loudon to Hannah, 1 Jan. 1863, DeWitt Clinton Loudon Papers, Mss 610, OHC.

33. Loudon to Hannah, 1 Jan. 1863, DeWitt Clinton Loudon Papers, Mss 610, OHC.

34. Loudon to Hannah, 1 Jan. 1863, DeWitt Clinton Loudon Papers, Mss 610, OHC.

35. Loudon to Hannah, 1 Jan. 1863, DeWitt Clinton Loudon Papers, Mss 610, OHC.

36. Loudon to Hannah, 23 Jan. 1863, DeWitt Clinton Loudon Papers, Mss 610, OHC.

37. Loudon to Hannah, 23 Jan. 1863, DeWitt Clinton Loudon Papers, Mss 610, OHC.

38. Loudon to Hannah, 23 Jan. 1863, DeWitt Clinton Loudon Papers, Mss 610, OHC.

39. Wills, *Army Life of an Illinois Soldier,* 145–46.

40. Wills to Sister, 7 Feb. 1863, in Wills, *Army Life of an Illinois Soldier,* 153–54.

41. Wills to Sister, 7 Feb. 1863, in Wills, *Army Life of an Illinois Soldier,* 154.

42. Wills, *Army Life of an Illinois Soldier,* 160.

43. Wills, *Army Life of an Illinois Soldier,* 160.

44. Wills to Sister, 15 Mar. 1863, in Wills, *Army Life of an Illinois Soldier,* 163.

45. Wills, *Army Life of an Illinois Soldier,* 151–54.

46. Ewing to Parents, 9 Nov. 1862, SC 2667 Ewing, Alexander K., ALPL.

47. Ewing to Parents, 6 Feb. 1863, SC 2667 Ewing, Alexander K., ALPL.

48. Ewing to Parents, 6 Feb. 1863, SC 2667 Ewing, Alexander K., ALPL.

49. Ewing to Parents, 2 Apr. 1863, SC 2667 Ewing, Alexander K., ALPL.

50. Alexander K. Ewing to Uncle, 7 Feb. 1863, SC 2667 Ewing, Alexander K., ALPL; Ewing to Parents, 18 Mar. 1863, SC 2667 Ewing, Alexander K., ALPL

51. Robert B. Latham to Wife, 22 Jan. 1863, SC 895 Latham, R. B., ALPL.

52. Latham to Wife, 22 Jan. 1863, SC 895 Latham, R. B., ALPL.

53. Latham to Wife, 22 Jan. 1863, SC 895 Latham, R. B., ALPL.

54. Latham to Wife, 11 May 1863, SC 895 Latham, R. B., ALPL.

55. Kircher to Mother, 17 Dec. 1862, in Hess, *A German in the Yankee Fatherland,* 35.

56. Henry A. Kircher to Father, 26 Jan. 1863, in Hess, *A German in the Yankee Fatherland,* 61.

57. Kircher to Father, 26 Jan. 1863, in Hess, *A German in the Yankee Fatherland,* 61.

58. Kircher to Father, 26 Jan. 1863, in Hess, *A German in the Yankee Fatherland,* 61.

59. Kircher to Mother, 7 Feb. 1863, in Hess, *A German in the Yankee Fatherland,* 66.

60. Kircher to Mother, 7 Apr. 1863, in Hess, *A German in the Yankee Fatherland,* 86.

61. Kircher to Mother, 19 Jan. 1863, in Hess, *A German in the Yankee Fatherland,* 57; Kircher to Father, 26 Jan. 1863, in Hess, *A German in the Yankee Fatherland,* 60; Kircher to Mother, 17 Feb. 1863, in Hess, *A German in the Yankee Fatherland,* 69.

62. Luther H. Cowan to Family, 26 Oct. 1862, Letters and Diary of Luther H. Cowan, Wis Mss 218S, WHS.

63. Cowan to Family, 26 Oct. 1862, Letters and Diary of Luther H. Cowan, Wis Mss 218S, WHS.

270 NOTES TO PAGES 176–180

64. Luther H. Cowan to Mollie, 18 Nov. 1862, Letters and Diary of Luther H. Cowan, Wis Mss 218S, WHS.

65. Luther H. Cowan to the Editor, *Warren Independent,* 23 Nov. 1862, Letters and Diary of Luther H. Cowan, Wis Mss 218S, WHS.

66. Cowan to the Editor, *Warren Independent,* 23 Nov. 1862, Letters and Diary of Luther H. Cowan, Wis Mss 218S, WHS.

67. Luther H. Cowan to Harriet, 27 Nov. 1862, Letters and Diary of Luther H. Cowan, Wis Mss 218S, WHS; Cowan to Mollie, 14 Jan. 1863, Letters and Diary of Luther H. Cowan, Wis Mss 218S, WHS; Cowan to Harriet, 19 Feb. 1863, Letters and Diary of Luther H. Cowan, Wis Mss 218S, WHS; Cowan to Mollie, 27 Mar. 1863, Letters and Diary of Luther H. Cowan, Wis Mss 218S, WHS.

68. Ambrose, *From Shiloh to Savannah,* 97.

69. Ambrose, *From Shiloh to Savannah,* 97.

70. Ambrose, *From Shiloh to Savannah,* 98.

71. Ambrose, *From Shiloh to Savannah,* 98.

72. Ambrose, *From Shiloh to Savannah,* 98–99.

73. Ambrose, *From Shiloh to Savannah,* 99.

74. John E. Smith, "The Killed and Wounded of the Forty-Fifth," *Galena Daily Advertiser,* 13 Mar. 1862; Campbell, *The Union Must Stand,* 16, 18–21, 25, 29, 43, 46, 51, 52; Thomas Thomson Taylor to Wife, 7 Sept. 1863, Thomas Thomson Taylor papers, 1861–1865, Mss 7, OHC; Zachariah Dean to Emily, 30 Apr. 1863, Zachariah Dean Papers, IHS; Wills to Sister, 9 Mar. 1863, in Wills, *Army Life of an Illinois Soldier,* 161; George H. Hildt to Parents, 19 June 1863, Typescripts of George H. Hildt letters and diary, 1862–1865, vol. 548, OHC.

75. Crooker, Nourse, and Brown, *Story of the Fifty-Fifth Regiment,* 219–20.

76. Crooker, Nourse, and Brown, *Story of the Fifty-Fifth Regiment,* 219–20.

77. Crooker, Nourse, and Brown, *Story of the Fifty-Fifth Regiment,* 219–20.

78. Crooker, Nourse, and Brown, *Story of the Fifty-Fifth Regiment,* 219–20.

79. Miller, *The Struggle for the Life of the Republic,* 169.

80. Wills to Sister, 10 June 1864, in Wills, *Army Life of an Illinois Soldier,* 257–58.

81. Ritner to Wife, 29 Aug. 1864, in Larimer, *Love and Valor,* 344.

82. Wills, *Army Life of an Illinois Soldier,* 296.

83. Ritner to Wife, 25 July 1864, in Larimer, *Love and Valor,* 317.

84. Ritner to Wife, 19 Sept. 1864, in Larimer, *Love and Valor,* 361.

85. Ritner to Wife, 19 Sept. 1864, in Larimer, *Love and Valor,* 361.

86. Ritner to Wife, 13 Oct. 1864, in Larimer, *Love and Valor,* 373.

87. "How The 45th Regiment Votes," *Galena Daily Gazette,* 12 Oct. 1864; "Vote Of The 45th Regiment," *Galena Daily Gazette,* 25 Oct. 1864; Wood to Wife, 10 Sept. 1864, Edward Jesup Wood Papers, IHS; Ritner to Wife, 26 Sept. 1864, in Larimer, *Love and Valor,* 364; Ritner to Wife, 2 Oct. 1864, in Larimer, *Love and Valor,* 369.

88. Thomas T. Taylor, "Diary," Roll 21, MIC 17 Civil War Collection, OHC.

89. Thomas T. Taylor, "Diary," Roll 21, MIC 17 Civil War Collection, OHC.

90. Thomas T. Taylor, "Diary," Roll 21, MIC 17 Civil War Collection, OHC.

91. Thomas Thomson Taylor to Sir, 24 Aug. 1864, Thomas Thomson Taylor papers, 1861–1865, Mss 7, OHC.

92. Thomas T. Taylor, "Diary," Roll 21, MIC 17 Civil War Collection, OHC.

93. Jackson, *The Colonel's Diary,* 156.

94. Jackson, *The Colonel's Diary,* 159.

95. Ritner to Wife, 7 Nov. 1864, in Larimer, *Love and Valor,* 383–84.

96. Ritner to Wife, 7 Nov. 1864, in Larimer, *Love and Valor,* 383–84.

97. Crooker, Nourse, and Brown, *Story of the Fifty-Fifth Regiment,* 386.

98. Jackson, *The Colonel's Diary,* 190; "General Election. 1864: Co. 'K' of 12th Wisconsin Regiment of Infantry," 8 Nov. 1864, Sylvester, Daniel Robbins, "Papers," 1858–1901, Wis Mss 51S, WHS.

99. George B. Carter to Bill, 31 Jan. 1863, "Civil War Letters, 1861–1864," Wis Mss 140S, WHS.

100. Taylor to Wife, 31 Aug. 1863, Thomas Thomson Taylor papers, 1861–1865, Mss 7, OHC.

101. Taylor to Wife, 31 Aug. 1863, Thomas Thomson Taylor papers, 1861–1865, Mss 7, OHC.

102. Taylor to Wife, 7 Sept. 1863, Thomas Thomson Taylor papers, 1861–1865, Mss 7, OHC.

103. Taylor to Wife, 7 Sept. 1863, Thomas Thomson Taylor papers, 1861–1865, Mss 7, OHC.

104. Taylor to Wife, 7 Sept. 1863, Thomas Thomson Taylor papers, 1861–1865, Mss 7, OHC.

105. Wills, *Army Life of an Illinois Soldier*, 192; Hildt to Parents, 30 Oct. 1863, Typescripts of George H. Hildt letters and diary, 1862–1865, vol. 548, OHC.

106. Benjamin H. Grierson to Father, 21 May 1862, Grierson Box 1, Benjamin Grierson Family Papers, ALPL.

107. Grierson to Father, 21 May 1862, Grierson Box 1, Benjamin Grierson Family Papers, ALPL.

108. Ritner to Wife, 18 Oct. 1863, in Larimer, *Love and Valor*, 225.

109. Ewing to Parents, 15 Mar. 1863, SC 2667 Ewing, Alexander K., ALPL.

110. Grierson, *A Just and Righteous Cause*, 85; Wills, *Army Life of an Illinois Soldier*, 145; Henry Giesey Ankeny to Tina, 14 Oct. 1863, in Cox, *Kiss Josey for Me!*, 186; Ritner to Wife, 12 Oct. 1863, in Larimer, *Love and Valor*, 222.

111. Loudon to Hannah, 14 Oct. 1862, DeWitt Clinton Loudon Papers, Mss 610, OHC.

112. Loudon to Hannah, 14 Oct. 1862, DeWitt Clinton Loudon Papers, Mss 610, OHC.

113. Loudon to Hannah, 28 Oct. 1862, DeWitt Clinton Loudon Papers, Mss 610, OHC.

114. Loudon to Hannah, 28 Oct. 1862, DeWitt Clinton Loudon Papers, Mss 610, OHC.

115. Loudon to Hannah, 25 Apr. 1864, DeWitt Clinton Loudon Papers, Mss 610, OHC.

116. Loudon to Hannah, 9 July 1862, DeWitt Clinton Loudon Papers, Mss 610, OHC; Loudon to Hannah, 8 Dec. 1863, DeWitt Clinton Loudon Papers, Mss 610, OHC; Loudon to Hannah, 11 Apr. 1864, DeWitt Clinton Loudon Papers, Mss 610, OHC.

12. THAT CLASS OF GENERALS WHO THINK THAT WAR MEANS FIGHTING

1. Henry A. Kircher to Father, 2 Aug. 1862, in Hess, *A German in the Yankee Fatherland*, 14–15; Jackson, *The Colonel's Diary*, 116, 160–61; Edward Jesup Wood to Wife, 12 Nov. 1863, Edward Jesup Wood Papers, IHS; Wills, *Army Life of an Illinois Soldier*, 312; Hickenlooper, "The Battle of Shiloh Part I.—Personal Experiences in the Battle," in *MOLLUS*, 5:411, 422; "Diary of Lieut. Anthony B. Burton, Commanding 5th Ohio Independent Battery, from May 18, to July 4, 1863, Inclusive," SC 2401 Burton, Anthony B., ALPL; Wills, *Army Life of an Illinois Soldier*, 145, 153; Henry F. Hole to Sister, 25 Mar. 1862, SC 2427 Hole, Henry F., ALPL; DeWitt Clinton Loudon to Hannah, 2 Apr. 1862, DeWitt Clinton Loudon Papers, Mss 610, OHC; Harley Wayne to W. H. Alden, 8 Nov. 1861, SC 2824 Wayne, Harley, ALPL; Benjamin H. Grierson to Alice, 19 June 1862, Grierson Box 1, Benjamin Grierson Family Papers, ALPL; Wood to Wife, 24 May 1864, Edward Jesup Wood Papers, IHS.

2. Wills, *Army Life of an Illinois Soldier*, 180–81.

3. Wills, *Army Life of an Illinois Soldier*, 183.

4. Wills, *Army Life of an Illinois Soldier*, 183.

5. Wills, *Army Life of an Illinois Soldier*, 174–75, 180–83, 187, 198.

6. Miller, *Struggle for the Life of the Republic*, 89.

7. "Diary of Lieut. Anthony B. Burton, Commanding 5th Ohio Independent Battery, from May 18, to July 4, 1863, Inclusive," SC 2401 Burton, Anthony B., ALPL.

8. Wills, *Army Life of an Illinois Soldier*, 187.

9. Wills, *Army Life of an Illinois Soldier*, 187.

10. Ambrose, *From Shiloh to Savannah*, 51–52; Robert Steele to Washington, no date [probably circa January 1862], "Papers, 1827–1891," Wis Mss 113S, WHS; "Cairo Correspondence," *Galena Daily Advertiser*, 23 Jan. 1861.

272 NOTES TO PAGES 186–192

11. John Hancock to Henry, 13 Apr. 1862, "Colonel John Hancock Papers, 1862–1889," File 1862 Feb. 14, WHS.

12. Henry F. Hole to Minerva, 22 Apr. 1862, SC 2427 Hole, Henry F., ALPL.

13. Hole to Minerva, 22 Apr. 1862, SC 2427 Hole, Henry F., ALPL.

14. Ambrose, *From Shiloh to Savannah*, 40.

15. Luther H. Cowan to the Editor, Warren Independent, 6 Oct. 1862, Letters and Diary of Luther H. Cowan, Wis Mss 218S, WHS.

16. Luther H. Cowan to Mollie, 10 Dec. 1862, Letters and Diary of Luther H. Cowan, Wis Mss 218S, WHS.

17. Wills, *Army Life of an Illinois Soldier*, 144.

18. Henry Otis Dwight, "My War Experiences," Henry Otis Dwight Papers (Microform), 1861–1900, Mic 127, OHC.

19. Luther H. Cowan to Harriet, 30 Nov. 1862, Letters and Diary of Luther H. Cowan, Wis Mss 218S, WHS.

20. Loudon to Hannah, 1 Jan. 1863, DeWitt Clinton Loudon Papers, Mss 610, OHC.

21. James Kerr Proudfit to Sister, 20 Jan. 1863, "Correspondence, 1861–1865," Wis Mss 158S, WHS.

22. Proudfit to Sister, 20 Jan. 1863, "Correspondence, 1861–1865," Wis Mss 158S, WHS.

23. Wills, *Army Life of an Illinois Soldier*, 175.

24. Henry A. Kircher to Mother, 26 May 1863, in Hess, *A German in the Yankee Fatherland*, 102.

25. Kirchner to Mother, 17 June 1863, in Hess, *A German in the Yankee Fatherland*, 107.

26. Richard W. Burt to Editor, *North American*, 10 June 1863, 76th Ohio Volunteer Infantry Correspondence, Vfm 4626, OHC.

27. Burt to Editor, *North American*, 21 June 1863, 76th Ohio Volunteer Infantry Correspondence, Vfm 4626, OHC.

28. Wood to Wife, 21 June 1863, Edward Jesup Wood Papers, IHS.

29. Henry Miller Culbertson to Mother, Brother, and Sister, 1 June 1863, "Civil War Letters," 1861–1864, Wis Mss 216S, WHS.

30. Culbertson to Mother, Brother, and Sister, 8 Aug. 1863, "Civil War Letters," 1861–1864, Wis Mss 216S, WHS.

31. Jacob B. Ritner to Wife, 29 Nov. 1863, in Larimer, *Love and Valor*, 257.

32. Wills, *Army Life of an Illinois Soldier*, 203.

33. George B. Carter to Bill, 24 July 1863, "Civil War Letters," 1861–1864, Wis Mss 140S, WHS.

34. Wood to Wife, 13 May 1864, Edward Jesup Wood Papers, IHS.

35. Wood to Wife, 24 May 1864, Edward Jesup Wood Papers, IHS.

36. Grierson, *A Just and Righteous Cause*, 74.

37. Grierson, *A Just and Righteous Cause*, 74.

38. Wills, *Army Life of an Illinois Soldier*, 314.

39. Jackson, *The Colonel's Diary*, 169.

40. "Diary," John Nilson Diary and Papers, IHS.

41. Crooker, Nourse, and Brown, *Story of the Fifty-Fifth Regiment*, 77.

42. Kircher to Mother, 3 Jan. 1863, in Hess, *A German in the Yankee Fatherland*, 48.

43. Kircher to Mother, 3 Jan. 1863, in Hess, *A German in the Yankee Fatherland*, 48.

44. Robert Steele to Wife, 4 Jan. 1863, "Papers, 1827–1891," Wis Mss 113S, WHS.

45. Robert Steele to Father and Mother, 5 Jan. 1863, "Papers, 1827–1891," Wis Mss 113S, WHS.

46. Henry Giesey Ankeny to Wife, 31 Dec. 1862, in Cox, *Kiss Josey for Me!*, 116.

47. Henry Giesey Ankeny to Tina, 8 Feb. 1863, in Cox, *Kiss Josey for Me!*, 128.

48. Kircher to Mother, 24 May 1863, in Hess, *A German in the Yankee Fatherland*, 100.

49. George H. Hildt to Parents, 28 Apr. 1863, Typescripts of George H. Hildt letters and diary, 1862–1865, vol. 548, OHC.

50. Campbell, *The Union Must Stand*, 138.

51. Ankeny to Wife, 1 Nov. 1863, in Cox, *Kiss Josey for Me!*, 190.

52. Loudon to Hannah, 28 Dec. 1863, DeWitt Clinton Loudon Papers, Mss 610, OHC.

NOTES TO PAGES 192–197 273

53. Loudon to Hannah, 3 Apr. 1864, DeWitt Clinton Loudon Papers, Mss 610, OHC.

54. Loudon to Hannah, 3 Apr. 1864, DeWitt Clinton Loudon Papers, Mss 610, OHC.

55. Loudon to Hannah, 2 Apr. 1862, DeWitt Clinton Loudon Papers, Mss 610, OHC; Loudon to Hannah, 15 Apr. 1862, DeWitt Clinton Loudon Papers, Mss 610, OHC; Loudon to Hannah, 9 July 1862, DeWitt Clinton Loudon Papers, Mss 610, OHC; Wills, *Army Life of an Illinois Soldier*, 207.

56. Ritner to Wife, 7 June 1864, in Larimer, *Love and Valor*, 285–86.

57. Owen Stuart to Wife, 10 June 1864, SC 2406 Stuart, Owen, ALPL.

58. Stuart to Wife, 25 June 1864, SC 2406 Stuart, Owen, ALPL.

59. Wood to Wife, 10 July 1864, Edward Jesup Wood Papers, IHS.

60. Wills, *Army Life of an Illinois Soldier*, 260.

61. Wills, *Army Life of an Illinois Soldier*, 256.

62. Wills, *Army Life of an Illinois Soldier*, 291–92.

63. Jackson, *The Colonel's Diary*, 151.

64. Alphonso Barto to Father, 25 Sept. 1864, SC 2627 Barto, Alphonso, ALPL.

65. Stuart to Wife, 10 June 1864, SC 2406 Stuart, Owen, ALPL; Miller, *Struggle for the Life of the Republic*, 161–62; Wills, *Army Life of an Illinois Soldier*, 239, 258 299.

66. Wills, *Army Life of an Illinois Soldier*, 307.

67. Wills, *Army Life of an Illinois Soldier*, 337.

68. Ritner to Wife, 25 Dec. 1864, in Larimer, *Love and Valor*, 398.

69. Ritner to Wife, 12 Jan. 1865, in Larimer, *Love and Valor*, 408.

70. Stuart to Wife, 16 Jan. 1865, SC 2406 Stuart, Owen, ALPL.

71. Wills, *Army Life of an Illinois Soldier*, 374, 339.

72. Worthington, *Brief History of the 46th Ohio Volunteers*, 18.

73. Worthington, *Brief History of the 46th Ohio Volunteers*, 18.

74. Worthington, *Brief History of the 46th Ohio Volunteers*, 23.

75. Worthington, *Report of the Flank March to Join on McClernand's Right*, 20.

76. Worthington, *Brief History of the 46th Ohio Volunteers*, 7, 10, 11, 13, 14, 16, 17, 18, 19, 21; Worthington, *Report of the Flank March to Join on McClernand's Right*, 18, 21.

77. Crooker, Nourse, and Brown, *Story of the Fifty-Fifth Regiment*, 142.

78. Dwight, "My War Experiences," Henry Otis Dwight Papers (Microform), 1861–1900, Mic 127, OHC.

79. Dwight, "My War Experiences," Henry Otis Dwight Papers (Microform), 1861–1900, Mic 127, OHC.

80. Dwight, "My War Experiences," Henry Otis Dwight Papers (Microform), 1861–1900, Mic 127, OHC.

81. John Quincy Adams Campbell to the *Ripley Bee*, 12 Mar. 1863, in Grimsley and Miller, *The Union Must Stand*, 219.

82. Alphonso Barto to Father, Sister, Mother, & Brother, 24 July 1864, SC 2627 Barto, Alphonso, ALPL.

83. Wood to Wife, 27 July 1864, Edward Jesup Wood Papers, IHS.

84. Wood to Wife, 27 July 1864, Edward Jesup Wood Papers, IHS.

85. Ritner to Wife, 22 July 1864, in Larimer, *Love and Valor*, 313.

86. Ritner to Wife, 2 June 1864, in Larimer, *Love and Valor*, 279.

87. Dwight, "My War Experiences," Henry Otis Dwight Papers (Microform), 1861–1900, Mic 127, OHC.

88. Dwight, "My War Experiences," Henry Otis Dwight Papers (Microform), 1861–1900, Mic 127, OHC.

89. Charles W. Wills, "Diary," in Strayer and Baumgartner, *Echoes of Battle: The Atlanta Campaign*, 129; Miller, *Struggle for the Life of the Republic*, 191; Luther H. Cowan to Kingsley Olds, 25 Feb. 1863, Letters and Diary of Luther H. Cowan, Wis Mss 218S, WHS.

90. Ritner to Wife, 29 July 1864, in Larimer, *Love and Valor*, 322.

91. Wills, *Army Life of an Illinois Soldier*, 289.

274   NOTES TO PAGES 197–205

92. Wood to Wife, 17 Dec. 1864, Edward Jesup Wood Papers, IHS.

93. Ritner to Wife, 22 Jan. 1865, in Larimer, *Love and Valor,* 415.

94. Jacob Ritner to Wife, 25 Dec. 1864, in Larimer, *Love and Valor,* 395.

95. Wood to Wife, 17 Apr. 1864, Edward Jesup Wood Papers, IHS.

96. Thomas Thomson Taylor to Wife, 15 July 1863, Thomas Thomson Taylor papers, 1861–1865, Mss 7, OHC.

97. Thomas T. Taylor, "Diary," Roll 21, Mic 17 Civil War Collection, OHC.

98. Thomas T. Taylor, "Diary," Roll 21, Mic 17 Civil War Collection, OHC.

99. Thomas T. Taylor, "Diary," Roll 21, Mic 17 Civil War Collection, OHC.

100. Henry A. Kircher, "Diary of Henry Kircher," Engelmann Kircher Family Papers, ALPL.

101. Kircher to Mother, 26 Sept. 1863, in Hess, *A German in the Yankee Fatherland,* 125.

102. Henry A. Kircher, "Diary of Henry Kircher," Engelmann Kircher Family Papers, ALPL.

103. Ritner to Wife, 8 Jan. 1865, in Larimer, *Love and Valor,* 404.

104. Kircher to Father, 12 Sept. 1863, in Hess, *A German in the Yankee Fatherland,* 121; Jacob B. Ritner to Emeline, 26 Sept. 1863, in Larimer, *Love and Valor,* 212; Wills, *Army Life of an Illinois Soldier,* 309–10.

105. Wills, *Army Life of an Illinois Soldier,* 212.

106. Wills, *Army Life of an Illinois Soldier,* 338–39.

107. Wills, *Army Life of an Illinois Soldier,* 220, 231–32, 235, 248.

108. "Diary of Lieut. Anthony B. Burton, Commanding 5th Ohio Independent Battery, from May 18, to July 4, 1863, Inclusive," SC 2401 Burton, Anthony B., ALPL.

109. Z. Payson Shumway to Hattie, 3 Oct. 1863, SC 1388 Shumway, Z. Payson, ALPL.

110. Shumway to Hattie, 3 Oct. 1863, SC 1388 Shumway, Z. Payson, ALPL.

111. Wills, *Army Life of an Illinois Soldier,* 194.

112. Dwight, "My War Experiences," Henry Otis Dwight Papers (Microform), 1861–1900, Mic 127, OHC.

113. Dwight, "My War Experiences," Henry Otis Dwight Papers (Microform), 1861–1900, Mic 127, OHC.

114. Jackson, *The Colonel's Diary,* 131–32.

115. Hole to Sister, 4 Aug. 1861, SC 2427 Hole, Henry F., ALPL.

116. Hole to Sister, 25 Mar. 1862, SC 2427 Hole, Henry F., ALPL.

117. Harley Wayne to Ellen, 4 Apr. 1862, SC 2824 Wayne, Harley, ALPL.

118. Alexander K. Ewing to Parents, 1 Nov. 1862, SC 2667 Ewing, Alexander K., ALPL.

119. Wills, *Army Life of an Illinois Soldier,* 144.

120. Charles W. Wills to Sister, 22 Jan. 1863, in Wills, *Army Life of an Illinois Soldier,* 149.

121. Wills, *Army Life of an Illinois Soldier,* 144.

122. Kircher to Mother, 22 Sept. 1863, in Hess, *A German in the Yankee Fatherland,* 122.

123. Charles H. Floyd to Mrs. Turner, 13 Sept. 1862, SC 504 Floyd, Charles H., ALPL.

124. Strayer and Baumgartner, *Echoes of Battle: The Struggle for Chattanooga,* 279.

125. Wood to Wife, 2 Dec. 1863, Edward Jesup Wood Papers, IHS.

126. Campbell to the *Ripley Bee,* 21 Nov. 1863, in Grimsley and Miller, *The Union Must Stand,* 222.

127. George H. Hildt, "Diary of the Siege of Atlanta, May 28—Oct. 7 1864," Typescripts of George H. Hildt letters and diary, 1862–1865, vol. 548, OHC.

128. Jackson, *The Colonel's Diary,* 150.

129. Wills, *Army Life of an Illinois Soldier,* 373.

130. Wayne to Ellen, 20 Oct. 1861, SC 2824 Wayne, Harley, ALPL.

131. Luther Cowan to Harriet, 2 Nov. 1862, Letters and Diary of Luther H. Cowan, Wis Mss 218S, WHS.

132. Kircher to Mother, 10 Mar. 1863, in Hess, *A German in the Yankee Fatherland,* 76.

133. Kircher to Mother, 10 Mar. 1863, in Hess, *A German in the Yankee Fatherland,* 76.

134. Grierson, *A Just and Righteous Cause,* 92.

NOTES TO PAGES 205–208   275

135. Wayne to Ellen, 18 Oct. 1861, SC 2824 Wayne, Harley, ALPL; Grierson to Alice, 25 Aug. 1862, Grierson Box 1, Benjamin Grierson Family Papers, ALPL; Loudon to Hannah, 8 Oct. 1862, DeWitt Clinton Loudon Papers, Mss 610, OHC; Wood to Wife, 3 Oct. 1863, Edward Jesup Wood Papers, IHS; Thomas T. Taylor, "Diary," Roll 21, Mic 17 Civil War Collection, OHC; Taylor to Wife, 15 July 1863, Thomas Thomson Taylor papers, 1861–1865, Mss 7, OHC.

13. NOTHING BUT VICTORY

1. Adam W. McLane to Sister, 26 Jan. 1865, Oliver A. Bridgford Papers.

2. Benjamin Franklin Best to Wife, 2 Feb. 1862, SC 2478 Best, Benjamin Franklin, ALPL; Benjamin Grierson to Alice, 26 Feb. 1862, Grierson Box 1, Benjamin Grierson Family Papers, ALPL; James Balfour to Wife, [no date, circa February or March 1862?], SC 2451 Balfour, James, ALPL; Oliver A. Bridgford to Eliza, 9 Mar. 1862, Oliver A. Bridgford Papers; Bridgford to Eliza, 25 Mar. 1862, Oliver A. Bridgford Papers; Bridgford to Eliza, 9 Apr. 1862, Oliver A. Bridgford Papers; William T. Burnett to Sister, 17 May 1862, SC 359 Crum Family, ALPL; Jacob B. Ritner to Emeline, 20 Mar. 1863, in Larimer, *Love and Valor*, 140; Henry Giesey Ankeny to Wife, 23 Jan. 1864, in Cox, *Kiss Josey for Me!*, 209; George H. Hildt to Parents, 7 Feb. 1864, Typescripts of George H. Hildt letters and diary, 1862–1865, vol. 548, OHC; Henry Giesey Ankeny to Tina, 16 Apr. 1864, in Cox, *Kiss Josey for Me!*, 215; Jacob B. Ritner to Wife, 7 June 1864, in Larimer, *Love and Valor*, 287–88; Ritner to Wife, 20 June 1864, in Larimer, *Love and Valor*, 293; Ritner to Wife, 2 July 1864, in Larimer, *Love and Valor*, 300; Ritner to Wife, 25 July 1864, in Larimer, *Love and Valor*, 316; Hildt to Parents, 26 Feb. 1864, Typescripts of George H. Hildt letters and diary, 1862–1865, vol. 548, OHC; Ritner to Emeline, 22 Dec. 1862, in Larimer, *Love and Valor*, 82.

3. Ankeny to Wife, 6 Dec. 1863, in Cox, *Kiss Josey for Me!*, 184.

4. Ankeny to Wife, 6 Jan. 1863, in Cox, *Kiss Josey for Me!*, 116–17; Ankeny to Wife, 4 Oct. 1863, in Cox, *Kiss Josey for Me!*, 182–83; Ankeny to Wife, 29 Apr. 1864, in Cox, *Kiss Josey for Me!*, 216; Ankeny to Wife, 6 May 1864, in Cox, *Kiss Josey for Me!*, 217; Owen Stuart to Wife [no date, circa late December 1864 or early January 1865], SC 2406 Stuart, Owen, ALPL; Edward Jesup Wood to Wife, 10 June 1864, Edward Jesup Wood Papers, IHS; Ephraim Brown to Drusilla, 21 Dec. 1862, Ephraim Brown Papers, Mss 76, OHC; Wood to Wife, 10 Dec. 1863, Edward Jesup Wood Papers, IHS; Bridgford to Eliza, 7 July 1862, Oliver A. Bridgford Papers; Henry A. Kircher to Mother, 26 Sept. 1863, in Hess, *A German in the Yankee Fatherland*, 124–25; Ankeny to Wife, 1 Oct. 1864, in Cox, *Kiss Josey for Me!*, 244; Wills, *Army Life of an Illinois Soldier*, 133, 163, 246, 256, 267, 313, 316, 337, 357, 363; Hildt to Parents, 30 Oct. 1863 Typescripts of George H. Hildt letters and diary, 1862–1865, vol. 548, OHC; Hildt to Parents, 22 Sept. 1864, Typescripts of George H. Hildt letters and diary, 1862–1865, vol. 548, OHC; Hildt to Parents, 28 Apr. 1863, Typescripts of George H. Hildt letters and diary, 1862–1865, vol. 548, OHC; Joseph S. Reynolds to Sarah, 28 Jan. 1865, Joseph S. Reynolds Papers, #5060-z, Wilson Library, Univ. of North Carolina at Chapel Hill; Ritner to Emeline, 19 Dec. 1862, in Larimer, *Love and Valor*, 79; Ritner to Emeline, 29 Apr. 1863, in Larimer, *Love and Valor*, 160; Ritner to Emeline, 7 May 1863, in Larimer, *Love and Valor*, 165; Rood, *Story of the Service of Company E*, 353; DeWitt Clinton Loudon to Hannah, 23 Jan. 1863, DeWitt Clinton Loudon Papers, Mss 610, OHC; Hildt to Parents, 2 Jan. 1864, Typescripts of George H. Hildt letters and diary, 1862–1865, vol. 548, OHC; Ankeny to Wife, 2 May 1864, in Cox, *Kiss Josey for Me!*, 216–17; Loudon to Hannah, 25 Nov. 1862, DeWitt Clinton Loudon Papers, Mss 610, OHC; Alexander K. Ewing to Parents, 23 Jan. 1863, SC 2667 Ewing, Alexander K., ALPL; Stuart to Wife, 8 Nov. 1864, SC 2406 Stuart, Owen, ALPL; Ritner to Wife, 8 Jan. 1865, in Larimer, *Love and Valor*, 404.

5. Alexander K. Ewing to Uncle, 7 Feb. 1863, SC 2667 Ewing, Alexander K., ALPL.

6. Ewing to Uncle, 7 Feb. 1863, SC 2667 Ewing, Alexander K., ALPL.

7. Ewing to Uncle, 7 Feb. 1863, SC 2667 Ewing, Alexander K., ALPL.

276 NOTES TO PAGES 208–211

8. Ewing to Uncle, 7 Feb. 1863, SC 2667 Ewing, Alexander K., ALPL.

9. Ewing to Uncle, 7 Feb. 1863, SC 2667 Ewing, Alexander K., ALPL.

10. Luther Cowan to Harriet, 4 Feb. 1862, Wis Mss 218S, WHS.

11. Ankeny to Wife, 4 Jan. 1863, in Cox, *Kiss Josey for Me!*, 39.

12. Charles C. Ammack to Brother and Sister, 21 Mar. 1863, Ammack and Howland Family Letters, Wis Mss 123S, WHS.

13. James Kerr Proudfit to Emilie, 31 Jan. 1865, "Correspondence," 1861–1865, Wis Mss 158S, WHS.

14. Wills, *Army Life of an Illinois Soldier*, 150, 156, 161, 198, 200, 238, 247, 280, 305, 314, 344, 352; Z. Payson Shumway to Hattie, 16 Nov. 1862, SC 1388 Shumway, Z. Payson, ALPL; Shumway to Hattie, 8 Jan. 1863, SC 1388 Shumway, Z. Payson, ALPL; Ritner to Emeline, 1 Jan. 1863, in Larimer, *Love and Valor*, 92; Ritner to Emeline, 7 Jan. 1863, in Larimer, *Love and Valor*, 100; Ritner to Wife, 8 June 1864, in Larimer, *Love and Valor*, 291; Bridgford to Eliza, 1 Dec. 1861, Oliver A. Bridgford Papers; Bridgford to Eliza, 22 Feb. 1862, Oliver A. Bridgford Papers; Bridgford to Eliza, 25 Mar. 1862, Oliver A. Bridgford Papers; Robert Steele to Washington, 3 Dec. 1862, "Papers, 1827–1891," Wis Mss 113S, WHS; Charles W. Wills to Sister, 20 Oct. 1864, in Wills, *Army Life of an Illinois Soldier*, 314.

15. Kircher to Mother, 3 Jan. 1863, in Hess, *A German in the Yankee Fatherland*, 52.

16. Kircher to Mother, 30 Jan. 1863, in Hess, *A German in the Yankee Fatherland*, 63.

17. Jenney, "Personal Recollections of Vicksburg," in *MOLLUS*, 12:256.

18. Luther H. Cowan to Family, 26 Oct. 1862, Letters and Diary of Luther H. Cowan, Wis Mss 218S, WHS.

19. Rood, *Story of the Service of Company E*, 210; Bridgford to Eliza, 9 Mar. 1862, Oliver A. Bridgford Papers.

20. Kircher to Mother, 28 Nov. 1862, in Hess, *A German in the Yankee Fatherland*, 28–29.

21. Kircher to Mother," 28 Nov. 1862, in Hess, *A German in the Yankee Fatherland*, 28–29.

22. Kircher to Mother, 2 Mar. 1863, in Hess, *A German in the Yankee Fatherland*, 73.

23. Collins German to English Dictionary, https://www.collinsdictionary.com/us/dictionary/german-english.

24. Shumway to Hattie, 18 July 1863, SC 1388 Shumway, Z. Payson, ALPL; Ewing to Parents, 6 Feb. 1863, SC 2667 Ewing, Alexander K., ALPL; Wills, *Army Life of an Illinois Soldier*, 189.

25. Charles Wills to Sister, 11 Dec. 1863, in Wills, *Army Life of an Illinois Soldier*, 205.

26. Wills to Sister, 11 Dec. 1863, in Wills, *Army Life of an Illinois Soldier*, 205.

27. Luther Cowan to Molly, 25 Jan. 1862, Letters and Diary of Luther H. Cowan, Wis Mss 218S, WHS.

28. Henry F. Hole to Friends, 25 Aug. 1861, SC 2427 Hole, Henry F., ALPL.

29. Friedrich Martens to Most Dearly Beloved Parents, 3 Feb. 1862, in Kamphoefner and Helbich, *Germans in the Civil War*, 320.

30. Bridgford to Eliza, 25 Mar. 1862, Oliver A. Bridgford Papers.

31. Loudon to Hannah, 2 Apr. 1862, DeWitt Clinton Loudon Papers, Mss 610, OHC.

32. Loudon to Hannah," 24 Apr. 1862, DeWitt Clinton Loudon Papers, Mss 610, OHC.

33. Luther H. Cowan to Molly, 6 May 1862, Letters and Diary of Luther H. Cowan, Wis Mss 218S, WHS.

34. Loudon to Hannah, 24 May 1862, DeWitt Clinton Loudon Papers, Mss 610, OHC.

35. Luther H. Cowan to Harriet, 27 May 1862, Letters and Diary of Luther H. Cowan, Wis Mss 218S, WHS.

36. Bridgford to Eliza, 21 Feb. 1862, Oliver A. Bridgford Papers; Henry F. Hole to Sister, 25 Mar. 1862, SC 2427 Hole, Henry F., ALPL; Luther H. Cowan to Dear Ones, 30 Mar. 1862, Letters and Diary of Luther H. Cowan, Wis Mss 218S, WHS.

37. Loudon to Hannah, 9 July 1862, DeWitt Clinton Loudon Papers, Mss 610, OHC.

38. Cowan to Molly, 5 Oct. 1862, Letters and Diary of Luther H. Cowan, Wis Mss 218S, WHS.

39. Cowan to Molly, 5 Oct. 1862, Letters and Diary of Luther H. Cowan, Wis Mss 218S, WHS.

NOTES TO PAGES 211–216 277

40. Henry Otis Dwight, "My War Experiences," Henry Otis Dwight Papers (Microform), 1861–1900, Mic 127, OHC.

41. Kircher to Mother, 24 Nov. 1862, in Hess, *A German in the Yankee Fatherland*, 27.

42. Wills, *Army Life of an Illinois Soldier*, 132.

43. Loudon to Hannah, 3 Oct. 1862, DeWitt Clinton Loudon Papers, Mss 610, OHC; Loudon to Hannah," 29 Nov. 1862, DeWitt Clinton Loudon Papers, Mss 610, OHC; Loudon to Hannah, 14 Oct. 1862, DeWitt Clinton Loudon Papers, Mss 610, OHC.

44. Wills, *Army Life of an Illinois Soldier*, 145–46.

45. Ankeny to Wife, 6 Jan. 1863, in Cox, *Kiss Josey for Me!*, 117.

46. Ankeny to Wife, 6 Jan. 1863, in Cox, *Kiss Josey for Me!*, 117.

47. Robert Steele to Wife, 31 Jan. 1863, "Papers, 1827–1891," Wis Mss 113S, WHS.

48. Steele to Wife, 31 Jan. 1863, "Papers, 1827–1891," Wis Mss 113S, WHS.

49. Wills, *Army Life of an Illinois Soldier*, 157.

50. Perry, "The Entering Wedge," in *MOLLUS*, 24:361.

51. Ankeny to Wife, 15 Feb. 1863, in Cox, *Kiss Josey for Me!*, 130; Warren Gray, "Diary," 1862–1863, SC 531, WHS; Wills, *Army Life of an Illinois Soldier*, 159

52. Ritner to Emeline, 8 Feb. 1863, in Larimer, *Love and Valor*, 114.

53. Jacob Ritner to Emeline, 20 Mar. 1863, in Larimer, *Love and Valor*, 139.

54. Ritner to Emeline, 4 Apr. 1863, in Larimer, *Love and Valor*, 147.

55. Ritner to Emeline, 10 Mar. 1863, in Larimer, *Love and Valor*, 127; Ritner to Emeline, 20 Mar. 1863, in Larimer, *Love and Valor*, 139; Ritner to Emeline, 30 Mar. 1863, in Larimer, *Love and Valor*, 143.

56. Ankeny to Wife, 20 Dec. 1862, in Cox, *Kiss Josey for Me!*, 111.

57. George B. Carter to Bill, 16 May 1863, "Civil War Letters," 1861–1864, Wis Mss 140S, WHS.

58. Ritner to Emeline, 24 Jan. 1863, in Larimer, *Love and Valor*, 106.

59. Ritner to Wife, 15 June 1863, in Larimer, *Love and Valor*, 186.

60. Campbell, *The Union Must Stand*, 105; Ritner to Wife, 26 June 1863, in Larimer, *Love and Valor*, 190.

61. Thomas Thomson Taylor to Wife, 15 July 1863, Thomas Thomson Taylor papers, 1861–1865, Mss 7, OHC.

62. Taylor to Wife, 10 Sept. 1863, Thomas Thomson Taylor papers, 1861–1865, Mss 7, OHC.

63. Wood to Wife, 16 Oct. 1863, Edward Jesup Wood Papers, IHS.

64. Ankeny to Wife, 19 Nov. 1863, in Cox, *Kiss Josey for Me!*, 192.

65. Ritner to Wife, 17 Nov. 1863, in Larimer, *Love and Valor*, 239–40.

66. Ritner to Wife, 17 Nov. 1863, in Larimer, *Love and Valor*, 239–40.

67. Campbell to the *Ripley Bee*, 21 Nov. 1863, in Grimsley and Miller, *The Union Must Stand*, 222.

68. Ritner to Wife, 17 Nov. 1863, in Larimer, *Love and Valor*, 240.

69. Troy Moore to Alice, 22 Oct. 1863, SC 2757 Moore, Troy, ALPL.

70. Wills to Sister, 15 Mar. 1864, in Wills, *Army Life of an Illinois Soldier*, 218.

71. Loudon to Hannah, 25 Apr. 1864, DeWitt Clinton Loudon Papers, Mss 610, OHC.

72. Wills, *Army Life of an Illinois Soldier*, 227.

73. Loudon to Hannah, 11 Apr. 1864, DeWitt Clinton Loudon Papers, Mss 610, OHC; Loudon to Hannah, 25 Apr. 1864, DeWitt Clinton Loudon Papers, Mss 610, OHC.

74. Ritner to Wife, 16 May 1864, in Larimer, *Love and Valor*, 270.

75. Wills, *Army Life of an Illinois Soldier*, 244.

76. Alphonso Barto to Sister, 29 May 1864, SC 2627 Barto, Alphonso, ALPL.

77. Ritner to Wife, 2 June 1864, in Larimer, *Love and Valor*, 280.

78. Stuart to Wife, 13 June 1864, SC 2406 Stuart, Owen, ALPL.

79. Wills, *Army Life of an Illinois Soldier*, 276.

278 NOTES TO PAGES 216–223

80. Ritner to Wife, 31 July 1864, in Larimer, *Love and Valor*, 327.

81. Wills, *Army Life of an Illinois Soldier*, 289.

82. Wills, *Army Life of an Illinois Soldier*, 298.

83. Ritner to Wife, 16 May 1864, in Larimer, *Love and Valor*, 271; Wills, *Army Life of an Illinois Soldier*, 235, 237, 260, 287; Ritner to Wife, 29 July 1864, in Larimer, *Love and Valor*, 322; Wood to Wife, 27 July 1864, Edward Jesup Wood Papers, IHS.

84. Wills, *Army Life of an Illinois Soldier*, 305.

85. Jackson, *The Colonel's Diary*, 158.

86. Wills to Sister, 21 Oct. 1864, in Wills, *Army Life of an Illinois Soldier*, 315.

87. Wood to Wife, 21 Oct. 1864, Edward Jesup Wood Papers, IHS.

88. Crooker, Nourse, and Brown, *The Story of the Fifty-Fifth Regiment*, 382.

89. Wills, *Army Life of an Illinois Soldier*, 318.

90. Joseph S. Reynolds to Charles, 10 Nov. 1864, Joseph S. Reynolds Papers, #5060-z, Wilson Library, Univ. of North Carolina at Chapel Hill.

91. Wood to Wife, 9 Nov. 1864, Edward Jesup Wood Papers, IHS.

92. Wood to Wife, 9 Nov. 1864, Edward Jesup Wood Papers, IHS.

93. Wood to Wife, 9 Nov. 1864, Edward Jesup Wood Papers, IHS.

94. Ritner to Wife, 7 Nov. 1864, in Larimer, *Love and Valor*, 382.

95. Wills, *Army Life of an Illinois Soldier*, 322.

96. Wills, *Army Life of an Illinois Soldier*, 325.

97. Wills, *Army Life of an Illinois Soldier*, 335.

98. Ritner to Wife, 22 Jan. 1865, in Larimer, *Love and Valor*, 415.

99. Stuart to Wife, 16 Jan. 1865, SC 2406 Stuart, Owen, ALPL.

100. Stuart to Wife, 28 Jan. 1865, SC 2406 Stuart, Owen, ALPL.

101. Jackson, *The Colonel's Diary*, 175–76.

102. Rood, *Story of the Service of Company E*, 421–22.

103. Wills, *Army Life of an Illinois Soldier*, 337–38.

104. Wills, *Army Life of an Illinois Soldier*, 344.

105. Jackson, *The Colonel's Diary*, 196.

106. Ritner to Wife, 14 Mar. 1865, in Larimer, *Love and Valor*, 429.

107. Laurens W. Wolcott to Father, 2 Apr. 1865, SC 2485 Wolcott, Laurens W., ALPL.

108. Wills to Sister, 15 Apr. 1865, in Wills, *Army Life of an Illinois Soldier*, 370–71.

109. Wills to Sister, 15 Apr. 1865, in Wills, *Army Life of an Illinois Soldier*, 370–71.

110. Charles H. Floyd to Mrs. Turner, 13 Sept. 1862, SC 504 Floyd, Charles H., ALPL.

111. Wills, *Army Life of an Illinois Soldier*, 144.

112. Jacob Ritner to Wife, 20 Nov. 1863, in Larimer, *Love and Valor*, 243–44.

113. Ritner to Wife, 20 Nov. 1863, in Larimer, *Love and Valor*, 243–44.

114. Wills, *Army Life of an Illinois Soldier*, 378–79.

115. Harlow M. Waller to Sister, 31 May 1863, "Harlow M. & Henrietta Waller Letters, 1861–1869," SC 2952, WHS; Jackson, *The Colonel's Diary*, 215; Wills, *Army Life of an Illinois Soldier*, 134.

116. Wills, *Army Life of an Illinois Soldier*, 370.

CONCLUSION

1. Owen Stuart to Wife, 8 Apr. 1865, SC 2406 Stuart, Owen, ALPL.

2. Stuart to Wife, 8 Apr. 1865, SC 2406 Stuart, Owen, ALPL.

3. Wills, *Army Life of an Illinois Soldier*, 369.

4. Jackson, *The Colonel's Diary*, 206.

5. Jackson, *The Colonel's Diary*, 207.

6. Wills, *Army Life of an Illinois Soldier*, 383.

Bibliography

UNPUBLISHED PRIMARY SOURCES

Abraham Lincoln Presidential Library, Springfield, IL.
Indiana Historical Society, Indianapolis, IN.
The Ohio History Connection, Columbus, OH.
Oliver A. Bridgford Papers, private collection.
Vermont Historical Society, Barre, VT.
Wilson Library at University of North Carolina at Chapel Hill.
Wisconsin Historical Society, Madison, WI.

PUBLISHED PRIMARY SOURCES

Adair, John M. *Historical Sketch of the Forty-Fifth Illinois Regiment, with a Complete List of the Officers and Privates and an Individual Record of Each Man in the Regiment.* Lanark, IL: Carroll County Gazette Print, 1869.

Ambrose, Daniel Leib. *From Shiloh to Savannah: The Seventh Illinois Infantry in the Civil War.* 1868. Reprint, DeKalb: Northern Illinois Univ. Press, 2003.

Andrews, Christopher Columbus. *Hints to Company Officers on Their Military Duties.* New York: D. Van Nostrand, 1863.

Ankeny, Henry Giesey. *Kiss Josey for Me!* Edited by Florence Marie Ankeny Cox. Santa Ana, CA: Friis-Pioneer Press, 1974.

Arndt, Albert F. R. "Reminiscences of an Artillery Officer." In *Papers of the Military Order of the Loyal Legion of the United States,* vol. 50. Wilmington, NC: Broadfoot, 1993.

Barr, Gene. *A Civil War Captain and His Lady: Love, Courtship, and Combat from Fort Donelson through the Vicksburg Campaign.* El Dorado Hills, CA: Savas Beatie, 2016.

Belknap, William W. *History of the Fifteenth Regiment, Iowa Veteran Volunteer Infantry.* Keokuk, IA: Ogden and Son, 1887.

Bering, John A., and Thomas Montgomery. *History of the Forty-Eighth Ohio Vet. Vol. Inf.* Hillsboro, OH: Highland News Office, 1880.

Brinkerhoff, Henry F. *History of the Thirtieth Regiment Ohio Volunteer Infantry.* Columbus, OH: James W. Osgood, 1863.

Brobst, John. *Well, Mary: Civil War Letters of a Wisconsin Volunteer.* Edited by Margaret B. Roth. Wausau, WI: Marathon Press, 1960.

Brown, Alonzo L. *History of the Fourth Regiment of Minnesota Infantry Volunteers during the Great Rebellion, 1861–1865.* St. Paul, MN: Pioneer Press, 1892.

280 BIBLIOGRAPHY

Camm, William, and Fritz Haskell. "Diary of Colonel William Camm, 1861 to 1865." *Journal of the Illinois State Historical Society (1908–1984)* 18, no. 4 (1926): 793–969. http://www.jstor.org/stable/40187132.

Campbell, John Quincy Adams. *The Union Must Stand: The Civil War Diary of John Quincy Adams Campbell, Fifth Iowa Volunteer Infantry.* Edited by Mark Grimsley and Todd D. Miller. Knoxville: Univ. of Tennessee Press, 2000.

Chamberlin, William H. "The Skirmish Line in the Atlanta Campaign." In *Papers of the Military Order of the Loyal Legion of the United States,* vol. 3. Wilmington, NC: Broadfoot, 1991.

Chetlain, Augustus L. *Recollections of Seventy Years.* Galena, IL: Gazette, 1899.

Civil War Index. http://www.civilwarindex.com/army.html.

Cluett, William W. *History of the 57th Regiment Illinois Volunteer Infantry.* Princeton, IL: T. P. Streeter, 1886.

Compton, James. "The Second Division of the 16th Army Corps, in the Atlanta Campaign." In *Papers of the Military Order of the Loyal Legion of the United States,* vol. 30. Wilmington, NC: Broadfoot, 1992.

———. "Some Incidents Not Recorded in the Rebellion Records." In *Papers of the Military Order of the Loyal Legion of the United States,* vol. 31. Wilmington, NC: Broadfoot, 1992.

Connelly, T. W. *History of the Seventieth Ohio Regiment.* Cincinnati, OH: Peak Bros., 1902.

Crooker, Lucien B. "Episodes and Characters in an Illinois Regiment." In *Papers of the Military Order of the Loyal Legion of the United States,* vol. 10. Wilmington, NC: Broadfoot, 1992.

Crooker, Lucien B., Henry Stedman Nourse, and John G. Brown. *The Story of the Fifty-Fifth Regiment Illinois Volunteer Infantry in the Civil War, 1861–1865.* Clinton, MA: W. J. Coulter, 1887.

Crummer, Wilbur F. *With Grant at Fort Donelson, Shiloh, and Vicksburg, and an Appreciation of General U. S. Grant.* Oak Park, IL: E. C. Crummer, 1915.

Dawes, Ephraim C. "My First Day Under Fire at Shiloh." In *Papers of the Military Order of the Loyal Legion of the United States,* vol. 4. Wilmington, NC: Broadfoot, 1991.

Day, James G. "The Fifteenth Iowa at Shiloh." In *Papers of the Military Order of the Loyal Legion of the United States,* vol. 56. Wilmington, NC: Broadfoot, 1994.

Duke, John K. *History of the Fifty-Third Regiment Ohio Volunteer Infantry during the War of the Rebellion.* Portsmouth, OH: Blade Printing, 1900.

Dunbar, Aaron, and Harvey M. Trimble. *History of the Ninety-Third Regiment Illinois Volunteer Infantry.* Chicago: Blakely Printing, 1898.

Strayer, Larry M., and Richard A. Baumgartner, eds. *Echoes of Battle: The Atlanta Campaign.* Huntington, WV: Blue Acorn Press, 2004.

———, eds. *Echoes of Battle: The Struggle for Chattanooga.* Huntington, WV: Blue Acorn Press, 1996.

Force, Manning F. "Personal Recollections of the Vicksburg Campaign." In *Papers of the Military Order of the Loyal Legion of the United States,* vol. 1. Wilmington, NC: Broadfoot, 1991.

Fowler, James A., and Miles M. Miller. *History of the Thirtieth Iowa Infantry Volunteers.* Mediapolis, IA: Merrill, 1908.

Fulfer, Richard J. *A History of the Trials and Hardships of the Twenty-Fourth Indiana Volunteer Infantry.* Indianapolis: Indianapolis Printing, 1913.

Grierson, Benjamin H. *A Just and Righteous Cause: Benjamin H. Grierson's Civil War Memoir.* Edited by Bruce J. Dinges and Shirley A. Leckie. Carbondale: Southern Illinois Univ. Press, 2008.

Hart, E. J. *History of the Fortieth Illinois Inf., (Volunteers.).* Cincinnati, OH: H. S. Bosworth, 1864.

Heafford, George H. "The Army of the Tennessee." In *Papers of the Military Order of the Loyal Legion of the United States,* vol. 46. Wilmington, NC: Broadfoot, 1993.

Hickenlooper, Andrew. "The Battle of Shiloh Part I.—Personal Experiences in the Battle." In *Papers of the Military Order of the Loyal Legion of the United States,* vol. 5. Wilmington, NC: Broadfoot, 1992.

Hicks, Henry G. "The Campaign and Capture of Vicksburg." In *Papers of the Military Order of the Loyal Legion of the United States,* vol. 31. Wilmington, NC: Broadfoot, 1992.

BIBLIOGRAPHY 281

———. "Fort Donelson." In *Papers of the Military Order of the Loyal Legion of the United States*, vol. 29. Wilmington, NC: Broadfoot, 1992.

Higbee, Chester G. "Personal Recollections of a Line Officer." In *Papers of the Military Order of the Loyal Legion of the United States*, vol. 29. Wilmington, NC: Broadfoot, 1992.

History of the 37th Regiment, O.V.V.I. Furnished by Comrades at the Ninth Reunion Held at St. Marys, Ohio, Tuesday and Wednesday September 10 and 11, 1889. Toledo, OH: Montgomery and Vrooman, 1890.

Howard, Richard L. *History of the 124th Regiment Illinois Infantry Volunteers, Otherwise Known as the "Hundred and Two Dozen," from August, 1862, to August, 1865*. Springfield, IL: H. W. Rokker, 1880.

Hubert, Charles F. *History of the Fiftieth Regiment Illinois Volunteer Infantry in the War of the Union*. Kansas City, MO: Western Veteran, 1894.

Hunt, George. "The Fort Donelson Campaign." In *Papers of the Military Order of the Loyal Legion of the United States*, vol. 13. Wilmington, NC: Broadfoot, 1992.

Illinois in the Civil War. http://civilwar.illinoisgenweb.org/.

Indiana Archives and Records Administration. https://secure.in.gov/apps/iara/search/.

Iowa, Adjutant General Office. *Roster and Record of Iowa Soldiers in the War of the Rebellion, Together with Historical Sketches of Volunteer Organizations, 1861–1866*. 6 vols. Des Moines, IA: E. H. English, State Printer, E. D. Chassell, State Binder, 1908–11. http://iagenweb.org/civilwar/books/logan.htm.

Jackson, Oscar Lawrence. *The Colonel's Diary: Journals Kept before and during the Civil War by the Late Colonel Oscar L. Jackson of New Castle, Pennsylvania, Sometime Commander of the 63rd Regiment O.V.I.* Edited by David P. Jackson. Sharon, PA: n.p., 1922.

Jenney, William L. B. "Personal Recollections of Vicksburg." In *Papers of the Military Order of the Loyal Legion of the United States*, vol. 12. Wilmington, NC: Broadfoot, 1992.

Kamphoefner, Walter D., and Wolfgang Helbich, eds. *Germans in the Civil War: The Letters They Wrote Home*. Translated by Susan Carter Vogel. Chapel Hill: Univ. of North Carolina Press, 2006.

Kimbell, Charles B. *History of Battery "A" First Illinois Light Artillery Volunteers*. Chicago: Cushing Printing, 1899.

Kircher, Henry A. *A German in the Yankee Fatherland: The Civil War Letters of Henry A. Kircher*. Edited by Earl J. Hess. Kent, OH: Kent State Univ. Press, 1983.

Lawrence, Elijah J. "Stuart's Brigade at Shiloh." In *Papers of the Military Order of the Loyal Legion of the United States*, vol. 53. Wilmington, NC: Broadfoot, 1993.

Miller, Charles Dana. *The Struggle for the Life of the Republic: A Civil War Narrative by Brevet Major Charles Dana Miller, 76th Ohio Volunteer Infantry*. Edited by Stewart Bennett and Barbara Tillery. Kent, OH: Kent State Univ. Press, 2004.

Morris, William S., Lorenzo D. Hartwell, and Joseph B. Kuykendall. *History 31st Regiment Illinois Volunteers Organized by John A. Logan*. 1902. Reprint, Carbondale: Southern Illinois Univ. Press, 1998.

Morrison, Marion. *A History of the Ninth Regiment Illinois Volunteer Infantry*. Monmouth, IL: John S. Clark, 1864.

Morton, Charles. "A Boy at Shiloh." In *Papers of the Military Order of the Loyal Legion of the United States*, vol. 22. Wilmington, NC: Broadfoot, 1992.

———. "Opening of the Battle of Shiloh." In *Papers of the Military Order of the Loyal Legion of the United States*, vol. 45. Wilmington, NC: Broadfoot, 1993.

Perry, Oran. "The Entering Wedge." In *Papers of the Military Order of the Loyal Legion of the United States*, vol. 24. Wilmington, NC: Broadfoot, 1992.

Reminiscences of the Civil War from Diaries of Members of the 103d Illinois Volunteer Infantry. Edited by committee. Chicago: J. F. Leaming, 1904.

Ritner, Jacob B., and Emeline Ritner. *Love and Valor: The Intimate Civil War Letters between Captain Jacob and Emeline Ritner*. Edited by Charles F. Larimer. Western Springs, IL: Sigourney Press, 2000.

282 BIBLIOGRAPHY

Rood, Hosea W. *Story of the Service of Company E, and the Twelfth Wisconsin Regiment, Veteran Volunteer Infantry, in the War of the Rebellion.* Milwaukee, WI: Swain and Tate, 1893.

Saunier, Joseph A., ed. *A History of the Forty-Seventh Regiment Ohio Veteran Volunteer Infantry.* Hillsboro, OH: Lyle Printing, 1903.

Searle, Charles P. "Personal Reminiscences of Shiloh." In *Papers of the Military Order of the Loyal Legion of the United States,* vol. 55. Wilmington, NC: Broadfoot, 1994.

Stevenson, Thomas M. *History of the 78th Regiment O.V.V.I.* Zanesville, OH: Hugh Dunne, 1865.

Stillwell, Leander. "In the Ranks at Shiloh." In *Papers of the Military Order of the Loyal Legion of the United States,* vol. 15. Wilmington, NC: Broadfoot, 1992.

Stockton, Joseph. *War Diary (1862–5) of Brevet Brigadier General Joseph Stockton.* Chicago: John T. Stockton, 1910.

Strong, William E. "The Campaign against Vicksburg." In *Papers of the Military Order of the Loyal Legion of the United States,* vol. 11. Wilmington, NC: Broadfoot, 1992.

Tuthill, Richard S. "An Artilleryman's Recollections of the Battle of Atlanta." In *Papers of the Military Order of the Loyal Legion of the United States,* vol. 10. Wilmington, NC: Broadfoot, 1992.

United States War Department. *The War of the Rebellion: Official Records of the Union and Confederate Armies.* 128 vols. Washington, DC: Government Printing Office, 1881–1901.

Vail, David Franklin. *Company K, of the 16th Wisconsin, at the Battle of Shiloh Recollections of Lieut. D. F. Vail.* N.p.: n.p., 1897.

Wallace, Isabel. *Life and Letters of W. H. L. Wallace.* Chicago: R. R. Donnelly and Sons, 1909.

Wardner, Horace. "Reminiscences of a Surgeon." In *Papers of the Military Order of the Loyal Legion of the United States,* vol. 12. Wilmington, NC: Broadfoot, 1992.

Williams, Thomas J. "The Battle of Champion's Hill." In *Papers of the Military Order of the Loyal Legion of the United States,* vol. 5. Wilmington, NC: Broadfoot, 1992.

———. *An Historical Sketch of the 56th Ohio Volunteer Infantry.* Columbus, OH: Lawrence Press, 1899.

Wills, Charles W. *Army Life of an Illinois Soldier.* Washington, DC: Globe Printing, 1906.

Wisconsin, Adjutant General's Office. *Roster of Wisconsin Volunteers, War of the Rebellion, 1861–1865.* 2 vols. Madison, WI: Democrat Print, 1886. http://www.wisconsinhistory.org/Content.aspx?dsNav=N:4294963828-4294963805&dsRecordDetails=R:CS4267.

Worthington, Thomas. *Brief History of the 46th Ohio Volunteers.* N.p.: printed by the author, 1878.

———. *Report of the Flank March to Join on McClernand's Right, at 9 A.M., and Operations of the 46th Reg't Ohio Vols., 1st Brigade, 5th Division, on the Extreme Union Right, at Shiloh, April 6, 1862.* Washington, DC: n.p., 1880.

Wright, Henry H. *A History of the Sixth Iowa Infantry.* Iowa City: State Historical Society of Iowa, 1923.

SECONDARY SOURCES

Barton, Michael. *Goodmen: The Character of Civil War Soldiers.* University Park: Pennsylvania State Univ. Press, 1981.

Bledsoe, Andrew S. *Citizen-Officers: The Union and Confederate Volunteer Junior Officer Corps in the American Civil War.* Baton Rouge: Louisiana State Univ. Press, 2015.

The British Controversialist, and Literary Magazine. London: Houlston and Sons, 1879.

Castel, Albert. *Tom Taylor's Civil War.* Lawrence: Univ. Press of Kansas, 2000.

Collins German to English Dictionary. https://www.collinsdictionary.com/us/dictionary/german-english.

Daniel, Larry J. *Soldiers in the Army of Tennessee: A Portrait of Life in a Confederate Army.* Chapel Hill: Univ. of North Carolina Press, 1991.

Davis, William C. *Lincoln's Men: How President Lincoln Became Father to an Army and a Nation.* New York: Free Press, 1999.

Frank, Joseph Allan, and George A. Reaves. *"Seeing the Elephant": Raw Recruits at the Battle of Shiloh*. Urbana: Univ. of Illinois Press, 1989.

Gallagher, Gary W. *The Union War*. Cambridge, MA: Harvard Univ. Press, 2011.

Glatthaar, Joseph T. *Soldiering in the Army of Northern Virginia*. Chapel Hill: Univ. of North Carolina Press, 2011.

Grimsley, Mark. *The Hard Hand of War: Union Military Policy toward Southern Civilians, 1861–65*. Cambridge: Cambridge Univ. Press, 1995.

Haughton, Andrew. *Training, Tactics and Leadership in the Confederate Army of Tennessee: Seeds of Failure*. Portland, OR: Frank Cass, 2000.

Hess, Earl J. *The Union Soldier in Battle: Enduring the Ordeal of Combat*. Lawrence: Univ. Press of Kansas, 1997.

Linderman, Gerald F. *Embattled Courage: The Experience of Combat in the American Civil War*. New York: Free Press, 1987.

Manning, Chandra. *What This Cruel War Was Over: Soldiers, Slavery, and the Civil War*. New York: Knopf, 2007.

McEnany, Brian R. *For Brotherhood & Duty: The Civil War History of the West Point Class of 1862*. Lexington: Univ. Press of Kentucky, 2015.

McKee, Christopher. *A Gentlemanly and Honorable Profession: The Creation of the U.S. Naval Officer Corps, 1794–1815*. Annapolis, MD: Naval Institute Press, 1991.

McMurry, Richard M. "Civil War Leaders." In *Leadership during the Civil War*, edited by Roman J. Heleniak and Lawrence L. Hewitt. Shippensburg, PA: White Mane, 1992.

McPherson, James M. *For Cause and Comrades: Why Men Fought in the Civil War*. New York: Oxford Univ. Press, 1997.

Power, J. Tracy. *Lee's Miserables: Life in the Army of Northern Virginia from the Wilderness to Appomattox*. Chapel Hill: Univ. of North Carolina Press, 1998.

Robertson, James I., Jr. *Soldiers Blue and Gray*. Columbia: Univ. of South Carolina Press, 1988.

Skelton, William B. *An American Profession of Arms: The Army Officer Corps, 1784–1861*. Lawrence: Univ. Press of Kansas, 1992.

Solonick, Justin S. *Engineering Victory: The Union Siege of Vicksburg*. Carbondale: Southern Illinois Univ. Press, 2015.

Teters, Kristopher A. *Practical Liberators: Union Officers in the Western Theater during the Civil War*. Chapel Hill: Univ. of North Carolina Press, 2018.

Wiley, Bell Irvin. *The Life of Billy Yank: The Common Soldier of the Union*. Baton Rouge: Louisiana State Univ. Press, 1952.

———. *The Life of Johnny Reb: The Common Soldier of the Confederacy*. Indianapolis, IN: Bobbs-Merrill, 1943.

Williams, T. Harry. *Hayes of the Twenty-Third: The Civil War Volunteer Officer*. Lincoln: Univ. of Nebraska Press, 1965.

Woodworth, Steven. E. *Nothing but Victory: The Army of the Tennessee, 1861–1865*. New York: Knopf, 2005.

———. *While God Is Marching On: The Religious World of Civil War Soldiers*. Lawrence: Univ. Press of Kansas, 2001.

NEWSPAPERS

Galena (IL) Daily Advertiser
Galena (IL) Daily Gazette
Hawkeye Flag (Winterset, IA)
North American (Newark, OH)
Peoria (IL) Daily Transcript
Plainfield (NJ) Union
Warren (OH) Independent

Index

1st Michigan Light Artillery, 15–16, 121
3rd Illinois Cavalry, 70
4th Iowa, 12, 48, 57–58, 208; reenlistment in, 92
5th Iowa, 84, 104, 151
5th Ohio Light Artillery Battery, 105
6th Illinois Cavalry, 60–61, 68, 118; discipline in, 80–81; murder in, 139–40
6th Iowa, 119
7th Illinois Cavalry, 105
8th Iowa, 130
8th Kentucky (Confederate army), 76
9th Illinois Cavalry, 83
12th Illinois, 103
12th Missouri, 120, 135, 163
12th Wisconsin, 10, 53, 61–62, 121; discipline in, 80–81; leadership of, 106; morale of, 218–19
13th US Infantry, 209
14th Illinois, 27, 86, 113, 118
15th Corps (Union army), 198–200, 215
15th Illinois, 28, 59, 121
16th Corps (Union army), 200
16th Wisconsin, 55, 107, 134
17th Corps (Union army), 200–202, 215
17th Missouri, 16
20th Ohio, 66, 76, 114, 187, 211; at Vicksburg, 201
23rd Iowa, 136
23rd Wisconsin, 55
25th Indiana, 190
25th Iowa, 17, 25, 27, 78, 125, 148; bookkeeping in, 99; drinking in, 105; politics in, 213; voting in, 180
30th Ohio, 93, 96, 138–39, 203
31st Illinois, 68–69
31st Indiana, 55
32nd Illinois, 44
33rd Wisconsin, 180
37th Ohio, 88, 108
39th Ohio, 129
40th Illinois, 115; discipline in, 81

42nd Ohio, 83
45th Illinois, 68, 137–38, 144, 211
46th Indiana, 106
46th Ohio, 194
47th Ohio, 32, 88, 124; casualties in, 136; voting in, 181
48th Indiana, 12, 23, 69, 100; bookkeeping in, 96; in the Savannah Campaign, 217
50th Illinois, 220
52nd Illinois, 10, 119, 132–33
55th Illinois, 9, 68, 75, 115–16, 118; bookkeeping in, 97; discipline in, 79, 83, 87–88; leadership of, 106–7, 109–11; politics in, 168, 177–78
63rd Illinois, 21
63rd Ohio, 201, 218; voting in, 180
64th Illinois, 217
69th Indiana, 212
70th Ohio, 97, 140, 211, 215; casualties in, 139; Sherman and, 192
72nd Illinois, 122
76th Ohio, 54, 58, 60, 103, 138, 188
93rd Illinois, 84
103rd Illinois, 57, 158–60, 199, 216; at Vicksburg, 185
106th Illinois, 29, 55
114th Illinois, 98
114th Ohio, 131
124th Illinois, 45, 68–71; casualties in, 138; discipline in, 87

abatis (fortification), 198. *See also* fortifications
abolitionism, 117, 144, 146, 148–49, 151–55, 157, 162, 165–66. *See also* emancipation
African Americans: discrimination against, 88; officers' views of, 4, 64, 77, 117, 145–50, 152–56, 159–66; politics and, 167; as prisoners of war, 130; racism against, 4, 117, 130, 143–46, 149, 158–66; rights of, 223; support for the Union, 152–55; in the Union army, 5, 75, 144–45, 147–49, 153, 160–66, 197; violence against, 74–75, 88, 158

INDEX   285

agriculture, 34, 150

Alabama, 212, 214–15; skirmishes in, 17–19

alcohol. *See* drinking

Alexandria, Virginia, 222

Allen, Benjamin, 107–8

Ambrose, Daniel L., 147

American Civil War: debates about, 32; emancipation and, 144–46, 149, 156–58, 165–66; end of, 203–4, 219, 222–23; health in, 54–56; historic relics from, 38; historiography of, 1–4; letters from, 20–36; marriages during, 27–28; officers in, 1, 3–5, 8, 9, 12; officers' views of, 22, 26, 50, 114–28, 206–12, 214–18, 220; photography and, 38–39; politics of, 174–79, 182–83; in popular culture, 32; records of, 101; skirmishing in, 17–18; slavery and, 116–17, 125, 143, 145–47, 154–56, 165, 207; tactics in, 66–68; violence in, 16–17; volunteers in, 114

Ammack, Charles C., 47–48, 56, 63, 104, 208

amputations, 134. *See also* wounds

Anderson, Robert, 114

Andersonville, Georgia, 59

animals: in ancient Egypt, 156; military treatment of, 133

Ankeny, Henry G., 12, 20, 48–49, 55, 57–58, 82, 123–24, 208; on emancipation, 147–48; furloughs and, 92; on Sherman, 191–92; views of the Civil War, 207, 212–14

Ankeny, Jessie, 20, 48–49

Ankeny, Tina, 20, 48–49, 57–58, 123–24, 147

Arkansas, 162

Arkansas Post, Battle of, 103

Arlington, Virginia, 222

Army of the Cumberland, 72, 200, 203–4, 214

Army of the Potomac, 3, 72, 104, 178, 207, 214–15; Army of the Tennessee officers on, 220; generals of, 202–3, 205; Grant and, 189–90

Army of the Tennessee: in the Atlanta Campaign, 192–93, 201–2, 216; bookkeeping in, 91–99, 101; in the Carolinas Campaign, 218–19; casualties in, 54–55, 57–58, 129–30, 135–42; chaplains in, 44–45; at Chattanooga, 203; combat success of, 12; daily routine in, 66, 89–90; desertion from, 82–83; discipline in, 61, 64–65, 72, 78–89; elections in, 178–82; examination boards for officers, 69–72; experiences of officers, 21, 29, 40; generals of, 184–85, 195–202, 204; Grant and, 3–4, 185–90, 195, 205; health in, 54–57, 65–66, 129–32, 139, 141–42; historiography of, 1, 3–4; leadership in, 102–13; morale of officers, 206–7, 209–21; motivations of, 128; movements of, 59, 208–9, 220, 222; officers of, 4–5, 8, 53, 63–64, 118, 122, 221, 223–24; photography in, 38–39; politics in, 127, 167–78, 182–83; prisoners of, 75–78; regiments in, 6–7; religion in, 20, 41–52, 118, 194; reputation of, 215, 221; role in Union victory, 207, 219, 221, 223–24; in the Savannah

Campaign, 217–18; Sherman and, 190–95, 197; soldiers in, 4, 62–64; supplies of, 74; training of, 66–68, 70, 89; at Vicksburg, 188–89; volunteers in, 114, 116. *See also* Union army

Arndt, Albert, 15–16, 121

Arnold, Benedict, 32

arson, 80

Athens, Alabama, 18

Atlanta, 1, 193, 207, 223; capture of, 216

Atlanta, Battle of, 196

Atlanta Campaign, 6, 36, 50, 100, 119, 122, 124, 133; bookkeeping during, 92; casualties of, 58, 129, 138–39; combat during, 62, 104, 201–2; discipline during, 87–88; expectations of, 207; health during, 55–56, 130–31; morale during, 215–16; Sherman and, 138, 192–93, 215–16

Balfour, James, 13, 57

Balfour, Louisa, 13

Banbury, Jabez, 86

Barney, Sam, 37

Barney, William K., 32, 37, 73

Barto, Alphonso, 10, 36, 83, 93, 95; on McPherson, 196; political views of, 104, 169; on Sherman, 193; on slavery, 157–58; views of the Civil War, 119, 216

bathing, 53

Baugher, Nesbit, 96, 136

Beaufort, South Carolina, 38, 43, 150, 154, 194

Beauregard, P. G. T., 218

Beckwith, Sylvester Gridley, 46–47, 136–37

Bennett, Thomas W., 212

Bereman, Alvah, 27

Bereman, Eleanor, 33–34, 51

Bereman, Samuel, 33

Best, Benjamin Franklin, 123

Best, Mary, 123

Bible, 37, 41–43, 47, 51, 82, 151–52

Bickerdyke, Mary Ann, 134

Big Black River, 137

Big Black River Bridge, Battle of, 47, 137

Blair, Francis P., Jr., 107, 198

Bledsoe, Andrew F., 2, 4

Bolivar, Tennessee, 86

bookkeeping, 91–99, 101

books, 37–38, 87

Boothe, James, 115

Boston, 32–33

bounties, 84–85

Bragg, Braxton, 189

Bridgford, Eliza, 44, 134, 210

Bridgford, Oliver, 44, 119, 131, 134, 210

Bringhurst, Thomas, 106

Brown, Ephraim, 41

Brown, John, 119

Bryant, George E., 61–62; disciplinary policy of, 80–81

286 INDEX

Buell, Don Carlos, 186
Bull Run, First Battle of, 115
Bull Run, Second Battle of, 203
Burnett, William, 128
Burnsville, Mississippi, 195
Burt, Richard W., 188–89
Burton, Anthony B., 105, 109, 113, 186, 200
Butler, Benjamin, 205
Byrkit, Barnet, 96
Byron, Lord, 23

Cairo, Illinois, 60, 118
Cam, William, 86–87
camp (military), 54, 65–66
Campbell, John Quincy Adams, 14, 44, 46, 50, 58;
    on the Army of the Tennessee, 215; arrest of,
    86; on bookkeeping, 95; on discipline, 82, 86;
    on leadership, 104; on Sherman, 192; on slav-
    ery, 116–17, 151–52, 155; views of generals, 103
Campbell, Rufus, 57–58
Canada, 180
captains, 54, 93; administrative duties of, 95. See
    also officers
card games, 46, 63, 112. See also gambling
Carolinas Campaign, 193–94, 196, 207–8, 218–19
Carter, Bill, 213
Carter, George B., 180–81, 189–90, 213
Cass County, Georgia, 180
Cass County, Indiana, 175
cats, 156
cavalry, 21–22, 70, 136, 158, 187; skirmishing and,
    17–18
Cavanaugh, Thomas, 60, 118
chaplains, 44, 81. See also ministers, in the Army
    of the Tennessee
Charleston, 218
Chase, Daniel, 209
Chattanooga, Tennessee, 17, 86, 97, 131–32, 140, 200
Chattanooga Campaign, 6, 50, 120, 189, 203,
    214–15, 220, 223
Chicago, 118, 178–79, 193
Chicago Times, 174
Chickasaw Bayou, Battle of, 16, 74, 106, 178, 211–12
Chickasaw Bayou expedition, 190–91, 195
children, of officers, 29–32, 38–39, 46–47. See also
    family
Christianity, 33; in the Army of the Tennessee, 5,
    41–52; emancipation and, 156. See also religion
Christmas, 30, 67, 217
churches, 144; regimental, 45
church services, 44–45, 81, 86–87
civilians, 64, 75; officers' views of, 77
civil rights movement, 223
Civil War. See American Civil War
clarity, as skill for officers, 109
class consciousness, 64, 151
Clock, Alonzo, 119

Clock, Hezekiah, 119–20
clothing, 53, 59, 68–69, 91, 93–94, 96, 173; theft
    of, 84
Coe, Lauren, 86–87
colonels, administrative duties of, 94. See also
    officers
Colton, James, 57
Columbia, South Carolina, 151
Columbus, Kentucky, 77
combat: casualties in, 135; injuries from, 133–34;
    leadership in, 15, 113; officers in, 12–19; records
    of, 94, 101
companies, in the Union army, 54, 56; administra-
    tion of, 94–95, 101; drilling of, 66–67
Compton, James, 132–33
Confederacy (American Civil War), 167, 180;
    defeat of, 207, 218–19; guerrilla forces of, 27,
    72, 74, 77, 132; officers' relatives in, 32; officers'
    views of, 50, 114, 120–21, 123–28, 172, 207–8,
    212, 214; prisoners of, 59, 129–30, 132, 136; rac-
    ism of, 130; slavery and, 116–17, 143–46, 151–53,
    155–57, 159; soldiers' views of, 178; support for,
    115, 119, 170, 174–75
Confederate army: at Atlanta, 138, 202; defeat of,
    222–23; examination boards for officers, 69–72;
    guerrilla forces, 27, 72, 74, 77, 132; leadership in,
    105; mail and, 36–37; officers in, 3, 105; officers'
    views of, 215–16, 219; prisoners from, 75–78,
    179; pursuit of, 97; surrender of, 203–4, 219
Confederate Army of Tennessee: examination
    boards for officers, 72; officers in, 3
Connecticut, 32
conscription, 114, 167–68
Constantinople, 115
Convers, James, 57
Copperheads (political faction), 115; elections and,
    180–82; Emancipation Proclamation and, 151;
    officers' views of, 149, 154, 167–69, 173–77, 193,
    206, 212–14, 219–20
Corinth, Battle of, 154, 185–86, 211
Corinth, Mississippi, 119, 140, 177, 189, 195
Corinth Campaign, 13, 109, 210–11
cotton, 75, 86, 147–48, 150, 159
courage, 102–4, 108, 112
courts-martial, 99–101, 111, 113, 195
Cowan, George, 30–31, 38
Cowan, Harriet, 30–31, 56, 137, 208
Cowan, Josephine, 38
Cowan, Luther Howard, 13–14, 30–32, 35, 38, 54,
    56, 73, 131; on the army, 102; on bookkeeping,
    95–96; court-martial duty, 100; death of,
    137–38; at Fort Donelson, 16; on Grant, 186–87,
    204; on leadership, 103; political views of, 176;
    views of the Civil War, 117–18, 208–11, 214;
    views of soldiers, 62–63, 68
Cowan, Mary "Molly," 14, 30–31, 38, 102, 187
Crane, Baron, 112

INDEX 287

cricket (sport), 61
Cromwell, John Nelson, 22, 136
Cromwell, Oliver, 172
Crooker, Lucien B., 111, 115, 195
Crutchfield House (Chattanooga), 131–32
Culbertson, Henry Miller, 55, 63, 144, 189; on
theft, 82

Dalton, Georgia, 162
Damascus, 171
David (biblical figure), 51
Davis, Jefferson, 76, 170, 175
Dean, Emily, 22, 47
Dean, Zachariah, 22, 47
Decatur, Alabama, 18–19
Decatur, Stephen, 120
Delaware, 33
Delaware, Ohio, 115
democracy, 119. See also freedom, Union motivations and; liberty
Democratic Party, 146, 148, 153, 167, 169–70,
174–82, 193, 213
desertion, 82–83, 97
discipline, 65, 72, 78–90, 104, 106, 200; of officers, 85–88, 194–95
dishes, 84
Douglas, Stephen A., 153
draft. See conscription
Drake, Milly, 163
dress parades, 68, 86
drill, 66–68, 70, 113. See also training
drinking, 46, 63, 84–85, 104–5
drums, 66
ducks, 18
dueling, 78
Dwight, Henry Otis, 32–33, 66, 73, 76, 130, 197;
on discipline, 79–80; enlistment of, 114–15; on
Grant, 187; on McPherson, 195–96; on payment,
92; soldiers' views of, 106; on theft, 82–83; at
Vicksburg, 200; views of the Civil War, 211
Dwight, Susie, 33

Eddyville, Kentucky, 76
education, 30–31, 126–27, 150
egalitarianism, 4, 105
Egypt, 156
elections, 104, 153, 167–68, 178–83. See also politics
elitism, 64, 107, 113
emancipation, 4–5; Christianity and, 156; Civil
War and, 144–46, 149, 156–58, 165–66; support
for, 143–63. See also abolitionism; Emancipation
Proclamation; slavery
Emancipation Proclamation, 50, 117, 144–47,
151–53, 156–57, 160, 166, 176; Army of the
Tennessee and, 223
Enrollment Act, 167–68
equipment, records of, 93–94, 97–99

Eucharist, 44
Europe, 16, 116, 119, 209; officers from, 108
Evans, Zebulon P., 60
Ewing, Alexander K., 58–59, 106, 202; on disci-
pline, 79; on emancipation, 146; political views
of, 174, 181; as provost guard, 74; views of the
Civil War, 120, 207–8
examination boards, 69–72

faith, 223. See also religion
family: of officers, 5, 21–26, 29–40, 122–27; of
soldiers, 20–21
farming. See agriculture
Fayetteville, North Carolina, 219
Field, Henry, 45
Fiske, Leander, 138
Florida, 32, 212, 222
Floyd, Charles, 202, 220
food, 53, 87, 131, 135. See also supplies
foraging, 9, 72–73, 82, 154
Force, Manning F., 15, 33, 59, 78, 83; arrest of, 201
forms: regulation of, 93; supplies of, 92. See also
bookkeeping
Fort Donelson, Battle of, 6, 13, 16, 38, 75, 103,
119, 223
Fort Henry, 208, 223
fortifications, 9–10, 220
Fort Stedman, 220
Fort Sumter, 114
Foster, Nathaniel Watson, 93, 97–98
France, 119, 162, 172
freedmen, 150. See also slaves: liberation of
freedom, Union motivations and, 3. See also liberty
Freeman, Caroline, 33
Freeman, Henry C., 200
Freeman, James, 33
Frémont, John Charles, 153, 179, 202
French Revolution, 172
Fry, John C., 201
Fuller, John Wallace, 201–2
Fulton County Ledger, 177–78
furloughs, 21, 23, 27, 29, 33, 80, 123, 138; reenlist-
ment and, 12, 92

Gallagher, Gary W., 3–4
gambling, 78, 85, 105. See also card games
Garfield, James A., 83
generals: historiography of, 1; officers' views of, 5,
184–205, 208–9, 219; reputation of, 102
Georgia, 32, 57, 212, 214, 216–18; military voting
in, 180
German Americans, 57, 116, 118, 199
Germantown, Tennessee, 139
Germany, 16, 116
Gillispie, John, 106
God, officers' trust in, 41–48, 51, 118, 194. See also
Providence, officers' trust in

288 INDEX

Goldsboro, North Carolina, 190
Grand Review, of the Union army, 196, 222–23
Grant, Julia, 185–86
Grant, Ulysses S.: Army of the Tennessee and, 3–4, 185–90, 195, 205; disciplinary policy of, 80; horses and, 185; officers and, 172, 184–90, 192–96, 201–2, 204; at Petersburg, 222; reputation of, 220; at Shiloh, 186; staff of, 74; tactics of, 204–5; at Vicksburg, 6, 188–89, 200–201, 215–16
Gray, Warren, 16, 131, 211
Grebe, Balthazar, 118
Grebe, Christina, 118
Greenville, Mississippi, 149
Grenada, Mississippi, 187, 201
Grierson, Alice, 24–25, 124, 153
Grierson, Benjamin Henry, 17–18, 21–22, 24–25, 60–61; disciplinary policy of, 80–81, 85; on drilling, 67; political views of, 181; on Sherman, 190; on slavery, 153; on tactics, 205; training of, 67–68; views of the Civil War, 124
Griffin, Michael, 106
Grigsby, Bennet, 169
guard duty, 61–62, 65–66, 70, 133, 136, 200–201, 211; for officers, 72–75, 78, 150. See also provost guard
guerillas, 27, 72, 74, 77, 132

Hall, Cyrus, 87
Halleck, Henry W., 1, 69, 153, 189, 194–96
Hancock, John, 186
handwriting, 135
Harrow, William, 199–200
Harvey, George, 55
Haughton, Andrew, 2–3
Hazen, William B., 198–200
health, 34, 54–57, 65–66, 103, 129–35, 139, 141–42
Heaton, Townsend P., 139
heaven, 47–49, 52, 193
Hedges, Daniel, 177–78
Helena, Arkansas, 74, 207
Hemans, Felicia, 124–25
Herod, Thomas, 139–40
Hess, Earl J., 3–4
Hicks, Stephen G., 81, 115
Hildt, George H., 96–97, 138–39, 203
Hodges, Theodore W., 136
Hole, Henry F., 21, 63, 103; on emancipation, 144; on gambling, 85; political views of, 169–70; views of the Civil War, 210; views of generals, 186, 202
Hole, Minerva, 21, 144, 169, 186, 202
Holly Springs, Mississippi, 187, 201
home, officers' views of, 20–21, 40
Hood, John Bell, 97, 216–19
Hooker, Joseph, 203
horses, 74, 83, 132, 139, 163; Grant and, 185

hospitals, 131–32, 137; escape from, 134–35
Howard, Oliver O., 197–98
Howard, Richard, 45, 70–71; on bookkeeping, 92; on leadership, 107
Hunt, George, 103
hymns, 41

ideology: Civil War and, 2–4; of officers, 7. See also politics
Illinois, 88, 138, 160, 174–78; elections in, 181; soldiers from, 211
Independence Day, 115, 207
Indiana, 27, 174; recruitment in, 12
inspections, in the Union army, 68, 71
inspectors, in the Union army, 93–94
intelligence, 150, 155
Iowa, 26–27, 126, 132, 134–35; elections in, 181; recruitment in, 11; regiments from, 84
Irish Americans, 57

Jackson, Andrew, 120
Jackson, Mississippi, 136
Jackson, Oscar Lawrence, 11–12, 18–19, 21, 43, 55–56, 74–75, 89, 131; in the Atlanta Campaign, 201–2; in the Carolinas Campaign, 218–19; on the Confederate army, 216–17; on the end of the Civil War, 222; on fortifications, 220; on Sherman, 190, 193; on slavery, 153–55; supervision of voting, 180; views of generals, 203
Jackson, Tennessee, 65
Jesus Christ, 45, 51
Jim Crow, 223
Job, Book of, 47
Johnson, Andrew, 104, 140
Johnson, John B., 109–10
Johnston, Joseph E., 138, 189, 193, 203–4, 214–15, 219, 222
Jones, Theodore, 93
Judy, James W., 98

Kansas, 61
Kays, James W., 144
Kennesaw Mountain, Battle of, 138–39
Kentucky, 124
Keokuk, Iowa, 137
King, Henry, 88
Kinney, Lucien S., 132–33
Kircher, Henry Adolph, 35, 37, 57, 163–65, 208–9; on bookkeeping, 91, 95; on Grant, 188; on leadership, 103–4; political views of, 175–76; on Sherman, 191; views of the Civil War, 120, 211; views of generals, 199, 203–5, 208–9; wounding of, 135

Lake Providence, Louisiana, 74
Latham, Robert B., 29, 55; political views of, 175
Lauman, Jacob G., 200

INDEX 289

law enforcement, 75
leadership: in combat, 15, 113; of Grant, 187; of officers, 102–13; officers' views of, 5; of Sherman, 195
Lee, Robert E., 203, 207, 215, 218–19, 222
letters: to newspapers, 177–78; of officers, 21–36, 54, 89, 130–31, 140; of soldiers, 20–21, 53
"Lexington, The" (poem), 141
liberty: as motivation, 3, 49–50, 114, 119–20, 123–25, 208, 223; slavery and, 116, 147, 150–52, 165, 223. *See also* emancipation; freedom, Union motivations and
Lightburn, Joseph A.J., 199
Limestone Creek, 18
Lincoln, Abraham, 88, 167–68; administration of, 120; Emancipation Proclamation and, 50, 144–46, 151, 156; officers' views of, 146, 151, 153, 156, 161, 163–64, 170, 178–79; reelection of, 104, 178–80
Linderman, Gerald F., 2, 4
"Little Egypt" (region), 181
Lofland, John, 141
Logan, John A., 92, 193, 196–97, 199, 201, 215
Lookout Mountain, 50, 132
Loomis, Reuben, 139
Loudon, Betty, 125
Loudon, DeWitt Clinton, 13, 43, 49, 89, 109, 139–41; on emancipation, 155–57; on Grant, 187–88; marriage of, 24, 37; political views of, 170–73, 182; on Sherman, 192; at Shiloh, 210; views of the Civil War, 125, 211, 215
Loudon, Fanny, 125
Loudon, Hannah, 13, 43, 89, 125, 140–41, 155–56, 172, 182, 211; marriage of, 24, 37
Louisiana, 74, 165, 212–13, 220
love, 51
Luminary (steamboat), 74
Luther, Charles, 138
Lyon, Nathaniel, 121

Macon, Georgia, 218
mail, 35–38, 74. *See also* letters; packages
malaria, 87
Malmborg, Oscar, 68, 106–7, 109–11
Maltby, Jasper A., 103, 145
management, officers and, 1, 8
"Marching through Georgia" (song), 217
March to the Sea. *See* Savannah Campaign
marriage: during the Civil War, 27–28; of officers, 5, 21–29, 36, 39
Martens, Friedrich, 16–17, 140; on slavery, 116–17, 147; views of the Civil War, 47, 116–17, 210
Matthew, Gospel of, 42–43, 51
McArthur, John, 103
McClellan, George B., 3, 104, 170, 178–79, 194, 202
McElroy, Charles H., 76, 83

McFerran, John W., 109, 139
McLane, Adam W., 207
McLane, Eliza, 207
McPherson, James (historian), 3–4
McPherson, James B. (general), 131, 193, 195–96
Meade, George G., 203, 207
Measure for Measure (Shakespeare), 199
Medon, Tennessee, 94
Meigs, Montgomery Cunningham, 194
Memphis, 74–75, 89, 160, 213
Mexican War, 67–68, 80, 174
Miller, Charles Dana, 15, 54, 59–60, 77–79, 103, 114; on bookkeeping, 92, 94; on Grant, 185; political views of, 178
Miller, Edward Gee, 11
Milliken's Bend, Battle of, 165, 188
mines (weapons), 138
ministers, in the Army of the Tennessee, 45, 47. *See also* chaplains
Missionary Ridge, Battle of, 135
Mississippi, 152, 212
Mississippi River, 185–86
Missouri, 26–27; regiments from, 84
monarchy, 119
money, 34–35. *See also* payment
Moore, Alice, 42
Moore, Troy, 42, 44
morale: of officers, 206–7, 209–21; of soldiers, 214–15, 217–19
morality: emancipation and, 146–47, 156–57; officers' views of, 4–7, 46, 78–79, 104–5, 108, 112
Morray, James B., 80–81
Morton, Oliver, 12
mosquitoes, 73
mules, 78, 147–48, 163
murder, 139–40
muskets, 93
mustering, 92
muster rolls, 91–92, 101
mutiny, 81

Napoleon Bonaparte, 47, 172
Nashville, 11, 89, 97, 192
Native Americans, racism against, 159
Newland, Abraham, 45
New Orleans, Battle of, 75
newspapers, 114–17, 119, 151–52, 167, 174, 176–78
New York City, 114
Nield, Wright L., 58–59
Nilson, John, 190
North Carolina, 219
Northerners, 151, 154
notaries, 99
Nourse, Henry Stedman, 59; views of the Civil War, 115
Noyes, Edward, 129

290 INDEX

Oberlin, Ohio, 162
officers: administrative duties of, 91–99, 101; capture of, 129–30, 132, 136, 141; careers of, 118; casualties among, 129, 135–42; children of, 29–32, 38–39, 46–47; civilians and, 77; combat experiences of, 12–19; in the Confederate army, 3, 105; conflicts among, 112; courts-martial and, 99–101; daily routines of, 66, 73, 89–90; definition of, 6–8; discipline and, 78–90, 194–95; discipline of, 85–88, 194–95; duties of, 9–12, 19, 53–54, 65, 72–75, 121–22; elections and, 178–82; examination boards for, 69–72; family and, 5, 21–26, 29–40, 122–27; generals and, 5, 184–205, 208–9, 219; guard duty of, 72–75, 78, 150; health of, 130–35, 139, 141–42; health policies of, 54–57; historiography of, 1–3; leadership of, 102–13; letters of, 21–36, 54, 89, 130–31, 140; mail and, 35–37; marriages of, 5, 21–29, 36, 39; morale of, 206–7, 209–21; moral values of, 4–7, 46, 78–79, 104–5, 108, 112; motivations of, 114–28; murder of, 139–40; photography and, 38–39; political views of, 5, 7, 167–77, 182–83; prisoners and, 75–78; qualifications of, 2–3; racism among, 4, 143–46, 158–66; recruitment and, 10–12, 19; religion of, 41–52, 118, 194; resignation of, 93, 96, 98, 213; role in Union victory, 223–24; soldiers and, 53–61, 63–64, 105–8; soldiers' views of, 53, 60–61, 68, 70–71, 81, 98, 109–10, 113; speeches of, 115; statistics on, 8; thefts by, 82–83; training of, 66–68, 70; views of the Civil War, 22, 26, 50, 114–28, 206–12, 214–18, 220; views of Grant, 185–90, 193–94, 204; views of Sherman, 190–95; views of slavery, 4–5, 50, 116–17, 122, 143–66, 171 223; views of soldiers, 62–63, 77–79, 204
Oglesby, Richard J., 178, 185
Ohio, 125, 154; elections in, 180–82; laws of, 99
Ohio River, 124
Ohio Wesleyan University, 115
Oliver, Robert, 97
onions, 195–96
Osterhaus, Peter J., 199–200
Owens (captain), 132–33
Oxford, Mississippi, 201

packages, 37–38. See also letters; mail
Paducah, Kentucky, 76, 83, 190
patriotism, 118, 212, 223; Wiley on, 2
Pattison, Rufus P., 87
payment, 53–54, 91–92, 98, 101; as motivation, 118, 128
Peck, George W., 80
Petersburg, Virginia, 220, 222
photography, 38–39, 135–36
picket lines, 72, 89
pigs, 71, 132–33
Pioneer Corps, 216

Pittsburg Landing, Tennessee, 13, 49, 61, 125, 169, 202, 210
poetry, 24–25, 67, 71, 124–25
politics: American Civil War and, 174–79, 182–83; of officers, 5, 7, 167–83; of soldiers, 177–82
Pope, John, 202–3
Potomac River, 190, 222–23. See also Army of the Potomac
Pratt, Julius A., 138
Pratt, Norman, 138
prayer, 43–44
Prentiss, Benjamin, 67
Presbyterianism, 44
Price, Sterling, 186–87, 204
prisoners of war, 50–51, 59, 75–77, 81, 129–30, 132, 136, 141; exchanges of, 76
prostitution, 78, 88–89
Proudfit, Emelie, 121, 208
Proudfit, James Kerr, 10, 121, 188, 208
Providence, officers' trust in, 4, 41–44, 47, 49, 52, 171. See also God, officers' trust in
provost guard, 74–75. See also guard duty
Pulaski, Tennessee, 132
Putnam, Holden, 84

Quinby, Isaac F., 201

race, officers' views of, 4, 64, 77, 117, 145–50, 152–56, 159–66. See also African Americans; slavery; white supremacy
racism, 149; of the Confederacy, 130; in the Union army, 117; among Union officers, 4, 143–46, 158–66
railroads, 65, 72, 75, 200. See also trains
rape, 78, 88–89, 158
Rapidan River, 215
rations, 86–87. See also food
reconstruction, 223
recruitment, for the Union army, 10–12, 19
reenlistment, 11–12, 19, 92
regiments, training of, 67–68, 70
Reid, William, 101
religion, 20, 41–52, 118, 194. See also faith; Providence, officers' trust in
Republican Party, 153, 178–81
reviews (military), 68–69
Reynolds, Charles, 217
Reynolds, Joseph S., 144, 217
Reynolds, Willie, 144
Richmond, Virginia, 218–20
Ringgold, Georgia, 135
Ritner, Emeline, 33, 50–51, 59, 95, 98–99, 126, 140, 218; children of, 30, 149; marriage of, 25–27, 39, 98–99
Ritner, Henry, 33, 148–49
Ritner, Jacob B., 33, 36, 38, 50–51, 73, 98–99, 140; on bookkeeping, 91, 95, 98–99; children of,

30, 149; court-martial duty, 99; on discipline, 78; on the draft, 168; on emancipation, 148–51, 155; on Grant, 189; on Howard, 197–98; on leadership, 104–5, 107, 112; marriage of, 25–27, 39, 98–99; on McPherson, 196; on military hospitals, 131–32; political views of, 179–81; on Sherman, 192–94; views of the Civil War, 59, 125–27, 207, 212–16, 218, 220; views of generals, 199; views of soldiers, 62

Ritner, Judson, 33

Ritner, Lulie, 30, 127

Ritner, Nellie, 30, 126–27

Ritner, Tommy, 30, 38

Robertson, James I., Jr., 3–4

Robinson Crusoe (novel), 100

Roman Empire, 156

Rome, Georgia, 97, 133

Rood, Hosea, 62

Rosecrans, William S., 187, 200, 202–4, 214

Ruggles, James Monroe, 70

Russia, 47

sanitation, 56

Saul of Tarsus, 171

Savannah, Georgia, 100, 121, 194, 217–18, 223

Savannah Campaign, 6, 32, 154, 163, 190, 193–94, 196, 217–18

Schiller, Friedrich, 16–17

Schleich, Casper, 106–7

scouting, 10

Searle, Charles, 130

Selkirk, Alexander, 100

sexuality: in officers' letters, 27; Victorian views of, 89

Seymour, Horatio, 168

Shakespeare, William, 199

Shaw, Francis H., 87–88, 97

Sherman, William T., 60, 121, 197; at Atlanta, 138, 192–93, 215–16; in the Carolinas Campaign, 218–19; at Chickasaw Bayou, 191, 195, 211; on officers, 1; officers and, 184–86, 190–96; role in negotiations, 203–4, 222; supplies of, 97; tactics of, 217

Shiloh, Battle of, 6, 13, 38, 169, 178, 207, 210; casualties at, 28, 96, 122, 136; Grant at, 186; Sherman at, 192, 194–95; wounds at, 134

shoes, 53, 59. *See also* clothing

Shumway, Hattie Pray, 27–28, 36, 49, 65

Shumway, Z. Payson, 27–28, 36, 43–45, 49, 56, 65; on slavery, 146–47; views of generals, 200; views of soldiers, 63

Siber, Edward, 88, 108

Siegel, Franz, 204

skirmishing, 17–19

slaveholders, 3

slavery: Civil War and, 116–17, 125, 143, 145–47, 154–56, 165, 207; end of, 223–24; influence

of, 151; officers' views of, 4–5, 50, 116–17, 122, 143–66, 171, 223; politics and, 167, 183. *See also* emancipation

slaves: escape of, 145–47, 150, 153, 157, 163, 166; liberation of, 143–45, 147, 154; Southerners' views of, 150–51; support for the Union, 152–55; violence against, 158

sleds, 30

Sloan, Thomas J., 70–71, 107

Smith, Adam (lieutenant), 86–87

Smith, John Allison, 181

Smith, John E., 134, 198

Smith, Melancthon, 138

Snack Creek Gap, 216

social media, 39

soldiers: African Americans as, 160–66, 197; in the Army of the Tennessee, 4, 62–64; combat experiences of, 14–16; conditions for, 173; discipline of, 78–90, 100; duties of, 9, 72; experiences of, 206; family and, 20–21; health of, 54–57, 131; historiography of, 1–3; knowledge of war, 208–9; letters of, 20–21, 53; morale of, 214–15, 217–19; murder of, 75; officers and, 53–61, 63–64, 105–8; officers' views of, 62–63, 77–79, 204; politics of, 177–82; records of, 91–92, 95–96; reenlistment of, 11–12, 19; religious practices of, 44–45; thefts by, 82–84; thefts from, 84; training of, 66–68, 89, 149; views of generals, 195–97, 199–200; views of officers, 53, 60–61, 68, 70–71, 81, 98, 109–10, 113; voting rights of, 182

South Carolina, 89, 127; emancipation in, 150

Southerners, 116–17, 121–22; in Illinois, 181; officers' views of, 154, 170–71; views of slaves, 150–51

Southey, Robert, 23

Springfield, Illinois, 118

spying, 10, 75

Stanton, Edwin, 194

"Star-Spangled Banner, The" (song), 165

steamboats, 58, 72, 74, 76, 85, 150, 185–86, 208

Steele, Frederick, 107, 149–50, 199

Steele, Rhoda, 42, 46

Steele, Robert, 29, 42, 46–47, 54–55, 140; on Sherman, 191; views of the Civil War, 212

Steele, Wesley, 29

St. Louis, Missouri, 199

Stockton, Joseph, 56, 76–77, 84–85, 122, 143

Stuart, David, 43, 68, 107, 110, 118; disciplinary policy of, 83–84

Stuart, Margaret, 218

Stuart, Owen, 193–94, 216, 218, 222

Sullivan, Jeremiah C., 174

Sumner, Charles, 169

supplies, 74, 97, 216. *See also* food; weapons

Swedish Americans, 68

swords, 54, 60, 75, 86–87, 110, 136, 139

292 INDEX

tactics, 66–69, 71, 204–5, 217
Tallahatchie River, 58, 74
Taylor, Margaret, 28–29, 124–25
Taylor, Thomas Thomson, 28–29, 32, 88; on leadership, 108; political views of, 179–81; views of the Civil War, 124–25, 214; views of generals, 198–99
Tennessee, 75, 187, 211, 218
Tennessee River, 18, 186, 208, 215. *See also* Army of the Tennessee
Texas, 222
theft, 82–84
theology, 49. *See also* religion
Thomas, George H., 203–4, 217–18
Thomas, Lorenzo, 165, 196–97
Thompson, S.C., 159
Thurston, George Lee, 38
Thurston, Willie, 38
Trader, George, 57
training, 66–68, 70, 89, 149. *See also* drill
trains, 80, 97. *See also* railroads
turkey buzzards, 200
"Two Homes, The" (Hemans), 124–25

Union (American Civil War): African American support for, 152–55; officers' views of, 49–50, 114–28, 170, 172–73, 182–83, 208, 211–13, 223. *See also* United States
Union army: African Americans in, 5, 75, 144–45, 147–49, 153, 160–66, 197; conscription and, 168; discipline in, 78; examination boards for officers, 69–72; generals of, 202; health in, 56; inspections in, 68, 71; inspectors in, 93–94; mail and, 36–37; motivations of, 2–3, 5; officers in, 3, 9–11; officers' views of, 211; payment of, 92; recruitment of, 10–12, 19; slavery and, 143, 145, 153; soldiers in, 9; Southerners' views of, 117; supply lines of, 216; victory of, 219, 223–24; volunteers in, 68–69, 78, 114–16; voting in, 167–68, 179–81; war effort of, 47. *See also* Army of the Tennessee
United States: elections in, 178–83; emancipation in, 156–57; officers from, 108; officers' views of, 116, 119–20, 126, 128; politics of, 167, 176–77; racism in, 143–44, 155; soldiers' views of, 178. *See also* Union (American Civil War)
Updyke, Lyman, 47–48, 56
US Christian Commission, 131
US Congress, 69, 88, 169–70
US Constitution, 114, 117, 119, 179
US Sanitary Commission, 131

Vail, David F., 58, 107–8, 134–35
Vallandigham, Clement L., 144, 171, 180–81, 214
Van Buren, John, 152
Vicksburg, Mississippi, 136, 144, 176, 204, 213–15; supply lines to, 74

Vicksburg, Siege of, 6, 111, 122–23, 165, 185, 188–89, 220, 223; casualties at, 33, 59, 118, 138; Grant and, 6, 188–89; leadership at, 15, 109, 200; morale during, 214; supplies for, 74
Vicksburg Campaign, 6, 103–4, 187, 191–92, 200, 213–16; casualties of, 136–38; Grant and, 188, 200–201, 215–16; morale during, 206, 213–14
Virginia, 190, 212, 220, 222
volunteers, in the Union army, 68–69, 114–16; contrast with regular army, 78
Von Wangelin, Aurelius, 103

Waller, Harlow, 144, 220
Walnut Hills, 191
war: ambition and, 108; experience of, 206, 219; foraging in, 82; perils of, 141–42; religion and, 41–44, 47–48, 50–52
Ward, Erasmus D., 86–87, 169
Ward, Mary, 86–87
War Department, 87, 91, 93, 97–98, 101
War of 1812, 174
Washington, DC, 87, 167, 194, 196, 215, 222
water, 56
Waterford, Mississippi, 74
Wayne, Ellen, 28, 39, 55, 121–22, 135–36
Wayne, Harley, 28, 39, 55, 59, 75, 121–22; death of, 135–36; on McClellan, 202; on tactics, 204; views of morality, 79
weapons, 60–61, 67, 71, 216; of prisoners, 75; records of, 96. *See also* muskets; swords
weather, 37, 56, 65, 67, 73, 132, 172–73, 218
West Point, 67, 186
White, Chilton, 32
white supremacy, 223. *See also* racism; slavery
Whittleton, Robert, 55
Wiley, Bell, 1–4
Williams, George, 108
Wills, Charles W., 65, 158–63, 209–10; court-martial duty, 99; on desertion, 82; on the end of the war, 222–23; political views of, 173–74, 178–79; as provost guard, 74–75; on Sherman, 192–94, 204; soldiers and, 11, 57, 62, 64, 105; views of the Civil War, 122, 211–12, 215–17, 219–21; views of generals, 199–200, 202–4
Wilson, Henry, 169
Wilson's Creek, Battle of, 121
Wisconsin, regiments from, 61
Wisconsin, University of, 11
Wolcott, Laurens W., 219
Wolf, George, 58
women: officers' views of, 26, 89; violence against, 78, 88, 158
Wood, Edward Jesup, 12, 54, 56, 69, 108, 198, 214; on bookkeeping, 96; court-martial duty, 100–101; on the draft, 168; family of, 22–23, 32, 38; on Grant, 189–90; on Howard, 197; on McPherson, 196; religion of, 42, 49; in the Sa-